# Azure Data Factory Cookbook

## Second Edition

Build ETL, Hybrid ETL, and ELT pipelines using ADF, Synapse Analytics, Fabric and Databricks

**Dmitry Foshin**

**Tonya Chernyshova**

**Dmitry Anoshin**

**Xenia Ireton**

BIRMINGHAM—MUMBAI

# Azure Data Factory Cookbook
## Second Edition

**Senior Publishing Product Manager:** Gebin George

**Acquisition Editor – Peer Reviews:** Tejas Mhasvekar

**Project Editor:** Janice Gonsalves

**Content Development Editors:** Soham Amburle, Elliot Dallow

**Copy Editor:** Safis Editing

**Technical Editor:** Anjitha Murali

**Proofreader:** Safis Editing

**Indexer:** Tejal Daruwale Soni

**Presentation Designer:** Ajay Patule

**Developer Relations Marketing Executive:** Vignesh Raju

First published: December 2020

Second edition: February 2024

Production reference: 2010324

Published by Packt Publishing Ltd.

Grosvenor House

11 St Paul's Square

Birmingham

B3 1RB, UK.

ISBN 978-1-80324-659-8

www.packt.com

# Contributors

## About the authors

**Dmitry Foshin** is a lead data engineer with 12+ years of experience in IT and Big Data. He focuses on delivering business insights through adept data engineering, analytics, and visualization. He excels in leading and executing full-stack big data analytics solutions, from ETL processes to data warehouses, utilizing Azure cloud technologies and modern BI tools. Along with being a co-author of the *Azure Data Factory Cookbook*, Dmitry has also launched successful data analytics projects for FMCG corporations across Europe.

*I would like to express my heartfelt gratitude to my wife, Mariia, my parents, my brother, Ilya, and all my family and friends who supported me and provided encouragement throughout the journey of producing this book. Your unwavering support has been invaluable, and I am deeply grateful for your presence in my life.*

**Tonya Chernyshova** is an experienced Data Engineer with over 10 years in the field, including time at Amazon. Specializing in Data Modeling, Automation, Cloud Computing (AWS and Azure), and Data Visualization, she has a strong track record of delivering scalable, maintainable data products. Her expertise drives data-driven insights and business growth, showcasing her proficiency in leveraging cloud technologies to enhance data capabilities.

**Dmitry Anoshin** is a data engineering leader with 15 years of experience working in business intelligence, data warehousing, data integration, big data, cloud, and machine learning space across North America and Europe.

He leads data engineering initiatives on a petabyte-scale data platform that was built using cloud and big data technologies to support machine learning experiments, data science models, business intelligence reporting, and data exchange with internal and external partners. He is also responsible for handling privacy compliance and security-critical datasets.

Besides that work, he teaches a cloud computing course at the University of Victoria, Canada, wherein he mentors high-school students in the CS faculty, and he also teaches people how to land data jobs at Surfalytics.com. In addition, he is an author of analytics books and a speaker at data-related conferences and user groups.

*I want to thank my beautiful wife, Lana, and my kids, Vasily, Anna, and Michael, who give me the energy to work, grow, and contribute to the data industry.*

**Xenia Ireton** is a Senior Software Engineer at Microsoft. She has extensive knowledge in building distributed services, data pipelines and data warehouses.

# About the reviewers

**Deepak Goyal** is a certified Azure Cloud Solution Architect, and he posseses over fifteen years of expertise in Designing, Developing and Managing Enterprise Cloud solutions. He is also a Big Data Certified professional and a passionate Cloud advocate.

**Saikat Dutta** is an Azure Data Engineer with over 13 years of experience. He has worked extensively with Microsoft Data products, from SQL Server 2000 to ADF, Synapse Pipelines, and MS Fabric. His career is shaped by various employers. The highlights of his career have been adaptability and a commitment to staying at the forefront of technology.

This is his first book review, wherein he has tried to provide practical insights into Microsoft Data products and tried to help the book become more than a cookbook. He has also contributed to a popular Data Newsletter and blog to share knowledge in the tech community.

Excited about the book's impact, I look forward to continuing my journey in the evolving field of Data Engineering.

*I express gratitude to my family for their unwavering support during the review process. Balancing work and family, especially with a younger kid, wouldn't have been possible without their cooperation.*

## Join our community on Discord

Join our community's Discord space for discussions with the authors and other readers:

https://discord.gg/U229qmBmT3

# Table of Contents

## Chapter 3: Setting Up Synapse Analytics                          79

## Chapter 7: Extending Azure Data Factory with Logic Apps and Azure Functions                                  239

# Preface

**Azure Data Factory (ADF)** is a modern data integration tool available on Microsoft Azure. This *Azure Data Cookbook, Second Edition* helps you get up and running by showing you how to create and execute your first job in ADF. You'll learn how to branch and chain activities, create custom activities, and schedule pipelines. This book will help you discover the benefits of cloud data warehousing, Azure Synapse Analytics, Azure Data Lake Storage Gen2, and Databricks, which are frequently used for Big Data Analytics. Through practical recipes, you'll learn how to actively engage with analytical tools from Azure Data Services and leverage your on-premises infrastructure with cloud-native tools to get relevant business insights.

As you advance, you'll be able to integrate the most commonly used Azure services into ADF and understand how Azure services can be useful in designing ETL pipelines. The book will take you through the common errors that you may encounter while working with ADF and guide you in using the Azure portal to monitor pipelines. You'll also understand error messages and resolve problems in connectors and data flows with the debugging capabilities of ADF.

Additionally, there is also a focus on the latest cutting-edge technology in Microsoft Fabric. You'll explore how this technology enhances its capabilities for data integration and orchestration.

By the end of this book, you'll be able to use ADF as the main ETL and orchestration tool for your data warehouse and data platform projects.

## Who this book is for

This book is for ETL developers, data warehouse and ETL architects, software professionals, and anyone who wants to learn about the common and not-so-common challenges that are faced while developing traditional and hybrid ETL solutions using Microsoft's ADF, Synapse Analytics, and Fabric. You'll also find this book useful if you are looking for recipes to improve or enhance your existing ETL pipelines. Basic knowledge of data warehousing is expected.

# What this book covers

*Chapter 1, Getting Started with ADF*, will provide a general introduction to the Azure data platform. In this chapter, you will learn about the ADF interface and options as well as common use cases. You will perform hands-on exercises in order to find ADF in the Azure portal and create your first ADF job.

*Chapter 2, Orchestration and Control Flow*, will introduce you to the building blocks of data processing in ADF. The chapter contains hands-on exercises that show you how to set up linked services and datasets for your data sources, use various types of activities, design data-processing workflows, and create triggers for data transfers.

*Chapter 3, Setting Up Synapse Analytics*, covers key features and benefits of cloud data warehousing and Azure Synapse Analytics. You will learn how to connect and configure Azure Synapse Analytics, load data, build transformation processes, and operate data flows.

*Chapter 4, Working with Data Lake and Spark Pools*, will cover the main features of the Azure Data Lake Storage Gen2. It is a multimodal cloud storage solution that is frequently used for big data analytics. We will load and manage the datasets that we will use for analytics in the next chapter.

*Chapter 5, Working with Big Data and Databricks*, will actively engage with analytical tools from Azure's data services. You will learn how to build data models in Delta Lake using Azure Databricks and mapping data flows. Also, this recipe will show you how to set up HDInsights clusters and how to work with delta tables.

*Chapter 6, Data Migration – Azure Data Factory and Other Cloud Services*, will walk though several illustrative examples on migrating data from Amazon Web Services and Google Cloud providers. In addition, you will learn how to use ADF's custom activities to work with providers who are not supported by Microsoft's built-in connectors.

*Chapter 7, Extending Azure Data Factory with Logic Apps and Azure Functions*, will show you how to harness the power of serverless execution by integrating some of the most commonly used **Azure services**: Azure Logic Apps and Azure Functions. These recipes will help you understand how Azure services can be useful in designing **Extract, Transform, Load** (ETL) pipelines.

*Chapter 8, Microsoft Fabric and Power BI, Azure ML, and Cognitive Services*, will teach you how to build an ADF pipeline that operates on a pre-built Azure ML model. You will also create and run an ADF pipeline that leverages Azure AI for text data analysis. In the last three recipes, you'll familiarize yourself with the primary components of Microsoft Fabric Data Factory.

*Chapter 9, Managing Deployment Processes with Azure DevOps*, will delve into setting up CI and CD for data analytics solutions in ADF using Azure DevOps. Throughout the process, we will also demonstrate how to use Visual Studio Code to facilitate the deployment of changes to ADF.

*Chapter 10, Monitoring and Troubleshooting Data Pipelines*, will introduce tools to help you manage and monitor your ADF pipelines. You will learn where and how to find more information about what went wrong when a pipeline failed, how to debug a failed run, how to set up alerts that notify you when there is a problem, and how to identify problems with your integration runtimes.

*Chapter 11, Working with Azure Data Explorer*, will help you to set up a data ingestion pipeline from ADF to Azure Data Explorer: it includes a step-by-step guide to ingesting JSON data from Azure Storage and will teach you how to transform data in Azure Data Explorer with ADF activities.

*Chapter 12, The Best Practices of Working with ADF*, will guide you through essential considerations, strategies, and practical recipes that will elevate your ADF projects to new heights of efficiency, security, and scalability.

# To get the most out of this book

Basic knowledge of data warehousing is expected. You'll need an Azure subscription to follow all the recipes given in the book. If you're using a paid subscription, make sure to pause or delete the services after you are done using them, to avoid high usage costs.

| Software/Hardware covered in the book | OS Requirements |
|---|---|
| Azure subscription (`portal.azure.com`) | Windows, macOS, or Linux |
| SQL Server Management Studio | Windows |
| Azure Data Studio | Windows, macOS, or Linux |
| Power BI or Microsoft Fabric subscription account | Windows, macOS, or Linux |

If you are using the digital version of this book, we advise you to type the code yourself or access the code via the GitHub repository (link available in the next section). Doing so will help you avoid any potential errors related to the copying and pasting of code.

# Download the example code files

You can download the example code files for this book from GitHub at `https://github.com/PacktPublishing/Azure-Data-Factory-Cookbook-Second-Edition`. In case there's an update to the code, it will be updated on the existing GitHub repository.

We also have other code bundles from our rich catalog of books and videos available at `https://github.com/PacktPublishing/`. Check them out!

# Download the color images

We also provide a PDF file that has color images of the screenshots/diagrams used in this book. You can download it here: `https://packt.link/gbp/9781803246598`.

# Conventions used

There are a number of text conventions used throughout this book.

`CodeInText`: Indicates code words in text, database table names, folder names, filenames, file extensions, pathnames, dummy URLs, user input, and Twitter handles. For example: "Mount the downloaded `WebStorm-10*.dmg` disk image file as another disk in your system."

A block of code is set as follows:

```
[default]
exten => s,1,Dial(Zap/1|30)
exten => s,2,Voicemail(u100)
exten => s,102,Voicemail(b100)
exten => i,1,Voicemail(s0)
```

When we wish to draw your attention to a particular part of a code block, the relevant lines or items are set in bold:

```
[default]
exten => s,1,Dial(Zap/1|30)
exten => s,2,Voicemail(u100)
exten => s,102,Voicemail(b100)
exten => i,1,Voicemail(s0)
```

Any command-line input or output is written as follows:

```
# cp /usr/src/asterisk-addons/configs/cdr_mysql.conf.sample
    /etc/asterisk/cdr_mysql.conf
```

**Bold**: Indicates a new term, an important word, or words that you see on the screen. For instance, words in menus or dialog boxes also appear in the text like this. For example: "Select **System info** from the **Administration** panel."

Warnings or important notes appear like this.

 Tips and tricks appear like this.

# Get in touch

Feedback from our readers is always welcome.

**General feedback**: Email feedback@packtpub.com, and mention the book's title in the subject of your message. If you have questions about any aspect of this book, please email us at questions@packtpub.com.

**Errata**: Although we have taken every care to ensure the accuracy of our content, mistakes do happen. If you have found a mistake in this book we would be grateful if you would report this to us. Please visit, http://www.packtpub.com/submit-errata, selecting your book, clicking on the Errata Submission Form link, and entering the details.

**Piracy**: If you come across any illegal copies of our works in any form on the Internet, we would be grateful if you would provide us with the location address or website name. Please contact us at copyright@packtpub.com with a link to the material.

**If you are interested in becoming an author**: If there is a topic that you have expertise in and you are interested in either writing or contributing to a book, please visit http://authors.packtpub.com.

# Share your thoughts

Once you've read *Azure Data Factory Cookbook*, we'd love to hear your thoughts! Scan the QR code below to go straight to the Amazon review page for this book and share your feedback.

https://packt.link/r/1803246596

Your review is important to us and the tech community and will help us make sure we're delivering excellent quality content.

# Download a free PDF copy of this book

Thanks for purchasing this book!

Do you like to read on the go but are unable to carry your print books everywhere?

Is your eBook purchase not compatible with the device of your choice?

Don't worry, now with every Packt book you get a DRM-free PDF version of that book at no cost.

Read anywhere, any place, on any device. Search, copy, and paste code from your favorite technical books directly into your application.

The perks don't stop there, you can get exclusive access to discounts, newsletters, and great free content in your inbox daily

Follow these simple steps to get the benefits:

1.  Scan the QR code or visit the link below

https://packt.link/free-ebook/9781803246598

2.  Submit your proof of purchase
3.  That's it! We'll send your free PDF and other benefits to your email directly

# 1

# Getting Started with ADF

Microsoft Azure is a public cloud vendor. It offers different services for modern organizations. The Azure cloud has several key components, such as compute, storage, databases, and networks. They serve as building blocks for any organization that wants to reap the benefits of cloud computing. There are many benefits to using the cloud, including utilities, metrics, elasticity, and security. Many organizations across the world already benefit from cloud deployment and have fully moved to the Azure cloud. They deploy business applications and run their business on the cloud. As a result, their data is stored in cloud storage and cloud applications.

Microsoft Azure offers a cloud analytics stack that helps us to build modern analytics solutions, extract data from on-premises and the cloud, and use data for decision-making progress, searching patterns in data, and deploying machine learning applications.

In this chapter, we will meet Azure data platform services and the main cloud data integration service – **Azure Data Factory** (**ADF**). We will log in to Azure and navigate to the Data Factory service in order to create the first data pipeline and run the copy activity. Then, we will do the same exercise but will use different methods of data factory management and control by using Python, PowerShell, and the Copy Data tool.

If you don't have an Azure account, we will cover how you can get a free Azure account.

In this chapter, we will cover the following recipes:

- Introduction to the Azure data platform
- Creating and executing our first job in ADF
- Creating an ADF pipeline using the Copy Data tool
- Creating an ADF pipeline using Python

- Creating a data factory using PowerShell
- Using templates to create ADF pipelines
- Creating an Azure Data Factory using Azure Bicep

# Introduction to the Azure data platform

The Azure data platform provides us with a number of data services for databases, data storage, and analytics. In *Table 1.1*, you can find a list of services and their purpose:

| Service Name | Definition |
|---|---|
| Azure Synapse Analytics | A limitless analytics service with unmatched time to insight (formerly SQL Data Warehouse) |
| Power BI | A business intelligence solution for building reports and dashboards and data visualization |
| Azure Stream Analytics | Real-time analytics on fast-moving streams of data from applications and devices |
| ADF | Hybrid data integration at an enterprise scale made easy |
| Azure Databricks | Apache Spark-based analytics platform optimized for the Microsoft Azure cloud services platform |
| Azure Cognitive Services | Cloud-based services with REST **application programming interfaces (APIs)** and client library **software development kits (SDKs)**, available to help developers build cognitive intelligence into applications without having direct **artificial intelligence (AI)** or data science skills or knowledge |
| Azure Event Hubs | Big data streaming platform and event ingestion service |
| Azure Data Lake Storage | Set of capabilities dedicated to big data analytics, built on Azure Blob storage |
| Azure HDInsight | Provisions cloud Hadoop, Spark, R Server, HBase, and Storm clusters |
| Azure Cosmos DB | Fast NoSQL database with open APIs for any scale |
| Azure SQL Database | Managed, intelligent SQL in the cloud |

*Figure 1.1: Azure data platform services*

Using Azure data platform services can help you build a modern analytics solution that is secure and scalable. The following diagram shows an example of a typical modern cloud analytics architecture:

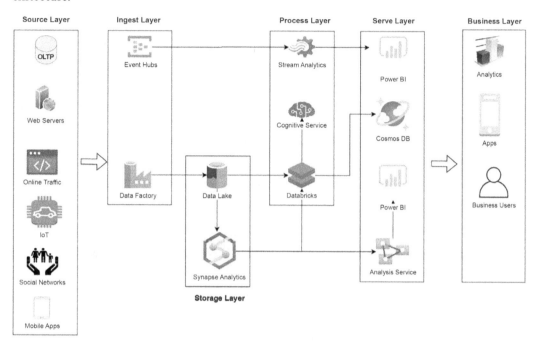

*Figure 1.2: Modern analytics solution architecture*

You can find most of the Azure data platform services here. ADF is a core service for data movement and transformation.

Let's learn more about the reference architecture in *Figure 1.1*. It starts with source systems. We can collect data from files, databases, APIs, IoT, and so on. Then, we can use Event Hubs for streaming data and ADF for batch operations. ADF will push data into Azure Data Lake as a staging area, and then we can prepare data for analytics and reporting in Azure Synapse Analytics. Moreover, we can use Databricks for big data processing and machine learning models. Power BI is the ultimate data visualization service. Finally, we can push data into Azure Cosmos DB if we want to use data in business applications.

# Getting ready

In this recipe, we will create a free Azure account, log in to the Azure portal, and locate ADF services. If you have an Azure account already, you can skip the creation of the account and log straight in to the portal.

# How to do it...

Open `https://azure.microsoft.com/free/`, then take the following steps:

1.  Click **Start Free**.

2.  You can sign into your existing Microsoft account or create a new one. Let's create one as an example.

3.  Enter an email address in the format someone@example.com and click **Next**.

4.  Enter a password of your choice.

5.  Verify your email by entering the code and click **Next**.

6.  Fill in the information for your profile (**Country**, **Name**, and so on). It will also require your credit card information.

7.  After you have finished the account creation, it will bring you to the Microsoft Azure portal, as shown in the following screenshot:

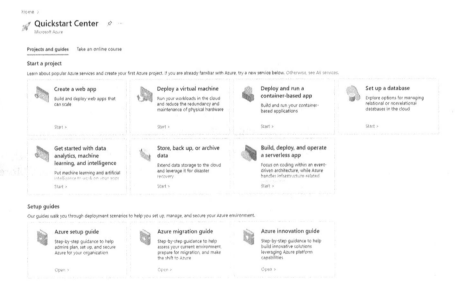

*Figure 1.3: Azure portal*

8.  Now, we can explore the Azure portal and find Azure data services. Let's find Azure Synapse Analytics. In the search bar, enter `Azure Synapse Analytics` and choose **Azure Synapse Analytics**. It will open the Synapse control panel, as shown in the following screenshot:

*Figure 1.4: Azure Synapse Analytics menu*

Here, we can launch a new instance of a **Synapse Analytics** workspace. Or you can find the **Data Factories** menu and launch a new **Data Factory** by using the Azure portal:

*Figure 1.5: Azure Data factories menu*

In the next recipe, we will create a new data factory.

Before doing anything with ADF, though, let's review what we have covered about an Azure account and the difference between **Synapse Analytics** and **Data Factories**.

## How it works...

Now that we have created a free Azure account, it gives us the following benefits:

- 12 months of free access to popular products
- $250 worth of credit
- 25+ always-free products

The Azure account we created is free and you won't be charged unless you choose to upgrade.

Moreover, we discovered the Azure data platform products, which we will use over the course of the book. The Azure portal has a friendly UI where we can easily locate, launch, pause, or terminate the service. Aside from the UI, Azure offers us other ways of communicating with Azure services, using the **Command-line Interface (CLI)**, APIs, SDKs, and so on.

Using the Microsoft Azure portal, you can choose the **Analytics** category and it will show you all the analytics services, as shown in the following screenshot:

*Figure 1.6: Azure analytics services*

Both **Azure Synapse Analytics (ASA)** and ADF have overlap. ASA workspaces are an integrated analytics service that combines big data and data warehousing. It allows you to perform data integration, data warehousing, and big data analytics using a single service. Moreover, it allows you to do a wide range of data integration options, including **SQL Server Integration Services (SSIS)**, ADF, or Spark transformations.

So, when to use what? If you need a simple and cost-effective way to move and transform data from various sources to various destinations, ADF is a good choice. However, if you need a more comprehensive analytics solution that can handle both big data and data warehousing, ASA is the way to go. In other words, standalone ADF is good for the orchestration of your data pipelines and workloads in general. But if you are willing to leverage Synapse Data Warehouse or big data solutions, you should consider using ADF as a part of ASA workspaces. Both have similar interfaces and functionality.

In this chapter, we will be using a standalone ADF.

# Creating and executing our first job in ADF

ADF allows us to create workflows for transforming and orchestrating data movement. You may think of ADF as an **Extract, Transform, Load (ETL)** tool for the Azure cloud and the Azure data platform. ADF is **Software as a Service (SaaS)**. This means that we don't need to deploy any hardware or software. We pay for what we use. Often, ADF is referred to as code-free ETL as a service or managed service. The key operations of ADF are listed here:

- **Ingest:** Allows us to collect data and load it into Azure data platform storage or any other target location. ADF has 90+ data connectors.
- **Control flow:** Allows us to design code-free extracting and loading workflows.
- **Data flow:** Allows us to design code-free data transformations.
- **Schedule:** Allows us to schedule ETL jobs.
- **Monitor:** Allows us to monitor ETL jobs.

We have learned about the key operations of ADF. Next, we should try them.

## Getting ready

In this recipe, we will continue from the previous recipe, where we found ASA in the Azure console. We will create a data factory using a straightforward method – through the ADF **User Interface (UI)** via the Azure portal UI. It is important to have the correct permissions to create a new data factory. In our example, we are using a super admin, so we should be good to go.

*During the exercise, we will create a new resource group. It is a collection of resources that share the same life cycle, permissions, and policies.*

## How to do it...

Let's get back to our data factory:

1.  If you have closed the **Data Factory** console, you should open it again. Search for Data factories and click *Enter*.

2.  Click **Create data factory**, or **Add** if you are on the **Data factories** screen, and it will open the project details, where we will choose a subscription (in our case, **Free Trial**).

3.  We haven't created a resource group yet. Click **Create new** and type the name ADFCookbook. Choose **East US** for **Region**, give the name as ADFcookbookJob-<YOUR NAME> (in my case, ADFcookbookJob-Dmitry), and leave the version as **V2**. Then, click **Next: Git Configuration**.

4.  We can use GitHub or Azure DevOps. We won't configure anything yet so we will select **Configure Git later**. Then, click **Next: Networking**.

5.  We have an option to increase the security of our pipelines **using Managed Virtual Network** and **Private endpoint**. For this recipe, we will use the default settings. Click **Next**.

6.  Optionally, you can specify tags. Then, click **Next: Review + Create**. ADF will validate your settings and will allow you to click **Create**.

7.  Azure will deploy the data factory. We can choose our data factory and click **Launch Studio**. This will open the ADF UI home page, where we can find lots of useful tutorials and webinars under **Help/Information** in the top-right corner.

8.  From the left panel, choose the **New Pipeline** icon, as shown in the following screenshot, and it will open a window where we will start the creation of the pipeline. Choose **New pipeline** and it will open the **pipeline1** window, where we must provide the following information: input, output, and compute. Add the name **ADF-cookbook-pipeline1** and click **Validate All**:

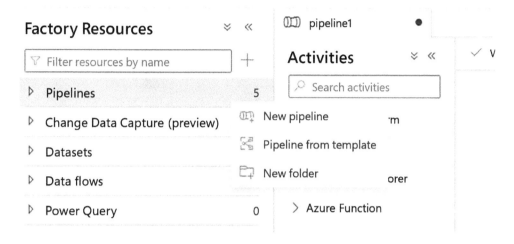

*Figure 1.7 : ADF resources*

9.  When executing *Step 8*, you will find out that you can't save the pipeline without the activity. For our new data pipeline, we will do a simple *copy data* activity. We will copy the file from one blob folder to another. In this chapter, we won't spend time on spinning resources such as databases, Synapse, or Databricks. Later in this book, you will learn about using ADF with other data platform services. In order to copy data from Blob storage, we should create an Azure storage account and a Blob container.

10. Let's create the Azure storage account. Go to **All Services | Storage | Storage Accounts**.

11. Click **+ Add**.

12. Use our **Free Trial** subscription. For the resource group, we will use **ADFCookbook**. Give a name for the storage account, such as adfcookbookstoragev2, then click **Review and Create**. The name should be unique to you.

13. Click **Go to Resource** and select **Containers** on the left sidebar:

*Figure 1.8 : Azure storage account UI*

14. Click **+ Container** and enter the name adfcookbook.

15. Now, we want to upload a data file into the SalesOrders.txt file. You can get this file from the book's GitHub account at https://github.com/PacktPublishing/Azure-Data-Factory-Cookbook-Second-Edition/Chapter01/. Go to the **adfcookbook** container and click **Upload**. We will specify the folder name as input. We just uploaded the file to the cloud! You can find it with the /container/folder/file - adfcookbook/input/SalesOrders.txt path.

16. Next, we can go back to ADF. In order to finish the pipeline, we should add an input dataset and create a new linked service.

17. In the ADF studio, click the **Manage** icon from the left sidebar. This will open the linked services. Click **+ New** and choose **Azure Blob Storage**, then click **Continue**.

18. We can optionally change the name or leave it as the default, but we have to specify the subscription in **From Azure Subscription** and choose the **Azure Subscriptions** and **Storage account name** that we just created.

19. Click **Test Connection** and, if all is good, click **Create**.

20. Next, we will add a dataset. Go to our pipeline and click **New dataset**, as shown in the following screenshot:

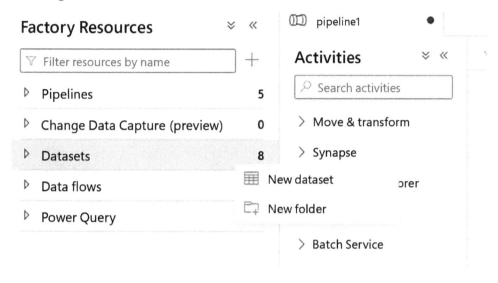

*Figure 1.9: ADF resources*

21. Choose **Azure Blob Storage** and click **Continue**. Choose the **Binary** format type for our text file and click **Continue**.

22. Now, we can specify the **AzureBlobStorage1** linked services and we will specify the path to the adfcookbook/input/SalesOrders.txt file and click **Create**.

23. We can give the name of the dataset in **Properties**. Type in SalesOrdersDataset and click **Validate all**. We shouldn't encounter any issues with data.

24. We should add one more dataset as the output for our job. Let's create a new dataset with the name SalesOrdersDatasetOutput and path adfcookbook/output/SalesOrders.txt.

25. Now, we can go back to our data pipeline. We couldn't save it when we created it without a proper activity. Now, we have all that we need in order to finish the pipeline. Add the new pipeline and give it the name ADF-cookbook-pipeline1. Then, from the activity list, expand **Move & transform** and drag and drop the **Copy Data** step to the canvas.

26. We have to specify the parameters of the step – the source and sink information. Click the **Source** tab and choose our dataset, **SalesOrdersDataset**.

27. Click the **Sink** tab and choose **SalesOrdersDatasetOutput**. This will be our output folder.

28. Now, we can publish two datasets and one pipeline. Click **Publish All**.

29. Then, we can trigger our pipeline manually. Click **Add trigger**, as shown in the following screenshot:

*Figure 1.10 : ADF canvas with the Copy Data activity*

30. Select **Trigger Now**. It will launch our job.

31. We can click on **Monitor** from the left sidebar and find the pipeline runs. In the case of failure, we can pick up the logs here and find the root cause. In our case, the ADF-cookbook-pipeline1 pipeline succeeds. In order to see the outcome, we should go to **Azure Storage** and open our container. You can find the additional Output folder and a file named SalesOrders.txt there.

We have just created our first job using the UI. Let's learn more about ADF.

## How it works...

Using the ADF UI, we created a new pipeline – an ETL job. We specified input and output datasets and used Azure Blob storage as a linked service. The linked service itself is a kind of connection string. ADF is using the linked service in order to connect external resources. On the other hand, we have datasets. They represent the data structure for the data stores. We performed the simple activity of copying data from one folder to another. After the job ran, we reviewed the **Monitor** section with the job run logs.

# There's more...

An ADF pipeline is a set of JSON config files. You can also view the JSON for each pipeline, dataset, and so on in the portal by clicking the three dots in the top-right corner. We are using the UI to create the configuration file and run the job. You can review the JSON config file by clicking on **Download support files** to download a JSON file, as shown in the following figure:

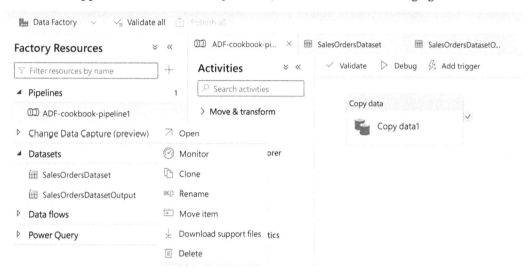

*Figure 1.11 : Downloading the pipeline config files*

This will save the archive file. Extract it and you will find a folder with the following subfolders:

- `Dataset`
- `LinkedService`
- `Pipeline`

Each folder has a corresponding JSON config file.

# See also

You can find more information about ADF in this Microsoft video, *Introduction to Azure Data Factory*: https://azure.microsoft.com/en-us/resources/videos/detailed-introduction-to-azure-data-factory/.

# Creating an ADF pipeline using the Copy Data tool

We just reviewed how to create the ADF job using the UI. However, we can also use the **Copy Data tool (CDT)**. The CDT allows us to load data into Azure storage faster. We don't need to set up linked services, pipelines, and datasets as we did in the previous recipe. In other words, depending on your activity, you can use the ADF UI or the CDT. Usually, we will use the CDT for simple load operations, when we have lots of data files and we would like to ingest them into Data Lake as fast as possible.

## Getting ready

In this recipe, we will use the CDT in order to do the same task of copying data from one folder to another.

## How to do it...

We already created the ADF job with the UI. Let's review the CDT:

1.  In the previous recipe, we created the Azure Blob storage instance and container. We will use the same file and the same container. However, we have to delete the file from the output location.

2.  Go to **Azure Storage Accounts**, choose **adfcookbookstorage**, and click **Containers**. Choose **adfcookbook**. Go to the **Output** folder and delete the SalesOrders.txt file.

3.  Now, we can go back to the **Data Factory Studio**. On the home page, we can see the tile for **Ingest**. Click on it. It will open with the CDT wizard.

4.  Click **Built-in copy task**. Choose **Run once now**. Click **Next**.

5.  We should choose the data source – **AzureBlobStorage1** – and specify the folder and file. You can browse the blob storage and you will find the filename. The path should look like adfcookbook/input/SalesOrders.txt. Mark **Binary copy**. When we choose the binary option, the file will be treated as binary and won't enforce the schema. This is a great option to just copy the file as is. Click **Next**.

6.  Next, we will choose the destination. Choose **AzureBlobStorage2** and click **Next**. Enter the adfcookbook/output output path and click **Next** until you reach the end.

7.  Give it the task name CDT-copy-job and Click **Next**. As a result, you should get a similar output as I have, as you can see in the following screenshot:

*Figure 1.12: CDT UI*

8.  If we go to the storage account, we will find that CDT copied data into the **Output** folder.

We have created a copy job using CDT.

## How it works...

CDT basically created the data pipeline for us. If you go to **ADF author**, you will find a new job and new datasets.

## There's more...

You can learn more about the CDT at the Microsoft documentation page: https://docs.microsoft.com/en-us/azure/data-factory/copy-data-tool.

# Creating an ADF pipeline using Python

We can use PowerShell, .NET, and Python for ADF deployment and data integration automation. Here is an extract from the Microsoft documentation:

> *"Azure Automation delivers a cloud-based automation and configuration service that provides consistent management across your Azure and non-Azure environments. It consists of process automation, update management, and configuration features. Azure Automation provides complete control during deployment, operations, and decommissioning of workloads and resources."*

In this recipe, we want to cover the Python scenario because Python is one of the most popular languages for analytics and data engineering. We will use Jupyter Notebook with example code.

You can use Jupyter notebooks or Visual Code notebooks.

## Getting ready

For this exercise, we will use Python in order to create a data pipeline and copy our file from one folder to another. We need to use the azure-mgmt-datafactory and azure-mgmt-resource Python packages as well as some other libraries that we will cover in the example.

## How to do it...

We will create an ADF pipeline using Python. We will start with some preparatory steps:

1.  We will start with the deletion of our file in the output directory. Go to **Azure Storage Accounts**, choose **adfcookbookstorage**, and click **Containers**. Choose **adfcookbook**. Go to the **Output** folder and delete the SalesOrders.txt file.

2.  We will install the Azure management resources Python package by running this command from the CLI. In my example, I used Terminal on macOS:

    ```
    pip install azure-mgmt-resource
    ```

3.  Next, we will install the ADF Python package by running this command from the CLI:

    ```
    pip install azure-mgmt-datafactory
    ```

4.  Also, I installed these packages to run code from Jupyter:

    ```
    pip install msrestazure
    ```

```
pip install azure.mgmt.datafactory
pip install azure.identity
```

When we finish installing the Python packages, we should use these packages in order to create the data pipeline, datasets, and linked service, as well as to run the code. Python gives us flexibility and we could embed this into our analytics application or Spark/Databricks.

The code itself is quite big and you can find the code in the Git repo for this chapter, ADF_Python_Run.ipynb.

5.  In order to control Azure resources from the Python code, we have to register the app with Azure Active Directory and assign a contributor role to this app in **Identity and Access Management (IAM)** under our subscription. We have to get tenant_id, client_id, and client_secret. You can learn more about this process at the Microsoft official documentation: https://learn.microsoft.com/en-us/azure/active-directory/develop/howto-create-service-principal-portal. We will provide brief steps.

6.  Go to Azure Active Directory and click **App registrations**. Click **+ New registration**. Enter the name ADFcookbookapp and click **Register**. From the app properties, you have to copy **Application (client) ID** and **Directory (tenant) ID**.

7.  Still in **ADFcookbookapp**, go to **Certificates & secrets** on the left sidebar. Click **+ New client secret** and add new client secret. Copy the value.

8.  Next, we should give permissions to our app. Go to the subscriptions. Choose **Free Trial**. Click on **IAM**. Click on **Add role assignments**. Select the **Contributor** role under **Privileged administrator roles** and click **Next**. Assign access to a user, group, or service principal. Finally, search for our app, ADFcookbookapp, and click **Save**. As a result, we just granted access to the app and we can use these credentials in our Python code. If you don't give permission, you will get the following error message: **AuthorizationFailed**.

9.  Open ADF_Python_Run.ipynb and make sure that you have all the libraries in place by executing the first code block. You can open the file in Jupyter Notebook:

```
from azure.identity import ClientSecretCredential
from azure.mgmt.resource import ResourceManagementClient
from azure.mgmt.datafactory import DataFactoryManagementClient
from azure.mgmt.datafactory.models import *
from datetime import datetime, timedelta
import time
```

10. You should run this piece without any problems. If you encounter an issue, it means you are missing the Python package. Make sure that you have installed all of the packages. Run *section 2* in the notebook. You can find the notebook in the GitHub repository with the book files.

11. In section 3, *Authenticate Azure*, you have to enter the user_name, subscription_id, tenant_id, client_id, and client_secret values. The resource group and data factory name we can leave as is. Then, run *section 4, Created Data Factory*.

12. The Python code will also interact with the Azure storage account, and we should provide the storage account name and key. For this chapter, we are using the adfcookbookstorage storage account and you can find the key under the **Access keys** section of this storage account menu. Copy the key value and paste it into *section 5, Created a Linked Service*, and run it.

13. In *sections 6* and *7*, we are creating input and output datasets. You can run the code as is. In *section 8*, we will create the data pipeline and specify the CopyActivity activity.

14. Finally, we will run the pipeline at section 9, *Create a pipeline run*.

15. In section 10, *Monitor a pipeline run*, we will check the output of the run. We should get the following:

```
Pipeline run status: Succeeded
```

We just created an ADF job with Python. Let's add more details.

## How it works...

We used Azure Python packages in order to control Azure resources. We registered an app in order to authenticate the Python code and granted contributor permissions. Using Jupyter Notebook, we ran the code step by step and created a data factory, as well as executed the copy command.

## There's more...

We used notebooks in order to demonstrate the sequence of steps and their output. We can also create a Python file and run it.

## See also

There are lots of useful resources available online about the use of Python for ADF. Here are a few of them:

- Serverless Python in ADF: https://medium.com/asos-techblog/serverless-python-in-azure-data-factory-42f841e06dc3

- ADF libraries for Python: https://docs.microsoft.com/en-us/python/api/overview/azure/datafactory?view=azure-python
- Tutorial: *Run Python scripts through ADF using Azure Batch*: https://docs.microsoft.com/en-us/azure/batch/tutorial-run-python-batch-azure-data-factory
- Python Quick Starts: https://learn.microsoft.com/en-us/azure/developer/python/quickstarts-data-solutions

# Creating a data factory using PowerShell

Often, we don't have access to the UI and we want to create infrastructure as code. It is easily maintainable and deployable and allows us to track versions and have code commit and change requests. In this recipe, we will use PowerShell to create a data factory. If you have never used PowerShell before, you can find information about how to get PowerShell and install it onto your machine at the end of this recipe.

## Getting ready

For this exercise, we will use PowerShell to create a data pipeline and copy our file from one folder to another.

## How to do it...

Let's create an ADF job using PowerShell:

1. In the case of macOS, we can run the following command to install PowerShell:

```
brew install powershell/tap/powershell
```

2. Check that it is working:

```
pwsh
```

Optionally, we can download PowerShell for our OS from https://github.com/PowerShell/PowerShell/.

3. Next, we have to install the Azure module. Run the following command:

```
Install-Module -Name Az -AllowClobber
```

4. Next, we should connect to the Azure account by running this command:

```
Connect-AzAccount
```

It will ask us to open the `https://microsoft.com/devicelogin` page and enter the code for authentication, and will tell us something like this:

```
Account                    SubscriptionName
TenantId                              Environment
-------                    ----------------
- --------                            ----------
datalearn4all@gmail.com Free Trial    1c204124 -0ceb-41de-b366-
1983c14c1628 AzureCloud
```

5.  Run the command in order to check the Azure subscription:

```
Get-AzSubscription
```

6.  Now, we can create a data factory. As usual, we should specify the resource group:

```
$resourceGroupName = "ADFCookbook"
```

Then, run the code that will create or update the existing resource group:

```
$ResGrp = New-AzResourceGroup $resourceGroupName -location 'East US'
```

You can choose your region, then specify the ADF name:

```
$dataFactoryName = "ADFCookbook-PowerShell"
```

Now, we can run the command that will create a data factory under our resource group:

```
$DataFactory = Set-AzDataFactoryV2 -ResourceGroupName $ResGrp.
ResourceGroupName
    -Location $ResGrp.Location -Name $dataFactoryName
```

As a result, PowerShell will create a new data factory for us.

7.  The next steps would be the same as we did in Python – creating a linked service, datasets, and pipeline. In the case of PowerShell, we should use JSON config files where we would specify the parameters.

We used PowerShell to create an ADF job. Let's add more details.

## How it works...

We used PowerShell to connect to Azure and control Azure resources. We created a new data factory using the PowerShell command. In the same way, we can create datasets, data flows, linked services, and pipelines using JSON files for configuration, and then execute the command with PowerShell. For example, we can define a JSON file for the input dataset using the following code block:

```
{
    "name": "InputDataset",
    "properties": {
        "linkedServiceName": {
            "referenceName": "AzureStorageLinkedService",
            "type": "LinkedServiceReference"
        },
        "annotations": [],
        "type": "Binary",
        "typeProperties": {
            "location": {
                "type": "AzureBlobStorageLocation",
                "fileName": "emp.txt",
                "folderPath": "input",
                "container": "adftutorial"
            }
        }
    }
}
```

Save it as `input.json` and then execute the following PowerShell command:

```
Set-AzDataFactoryV2Dataset -DataFactoryName $DataFactory.DataFactoryName
    -ResourceGroupName $ResGrp.ResourceGroupName -Name "InputDataset"
    -DefinitionFile ".\Input.json"
```

This command will create a dataset for our data factory.

## There's more...

You can learn about the use of PowerShell with ADF by reviewing the available samples from Microsoft at https://docs.microsoft.com/en-us/azure/data-factory/samples-powershell.

## See also

You can refer to the following links to get more information about the use of PowerShell:

- You can find information about installing Azure PowerShell on Windows here: https://docs.microsoft.com/en-us/powershell/azure/get-started-azureps
- If you have macOS, you can use this doc: https://docs.microsoft.com/en-us/powershell/scripting/install/installing-powershell-core-on-macos?view=powershell-7

# Using templates to create ADF pipelines

Modern organizations are operating in a fast-paced environment. It is important to deliver insights faster and have shorter analytics iterations. Moreover, Azure found that many organizations have similar use cases for their modern cloud analytics deployments. As a result, Azure built a number of predefined templates. For example, if you have data in Amazon S3 and you want to copy it into Azure Data Lake, you can find a specific template for this operation; or say you want to move an on-premises Oracle data warehouse to the Azure Synapse Analytics data warehouse – you are covered with ADF templates.

## Getting ready

ADF provides us with templates in order to accelerate data engineering development. In this recipe, we will review the common templates and see how to use them.

## How to do it...

We will find and review an existing template using Data Factories:

1. In the Azure portal, choose **Data Factories**.
2. Open our existing data factory, **ADFcookbookJob1-Dmitry**.
3. Click **Author and Monitor** and it will open the ADF portal.

4.  From the home page, click on **Create pipeline from template**. It will open the page to the list of templates.

5.  Let's open **Slow Changing Dimension Type 2**. This is one of the most popular techniques for building a data warehouse and dimensional modeling. From the description page, we can review the documentation, examples, and user input. For this example, we have **Delimited Text** as input and the **Azure SQL** database as output. If you would like to proceed and use this template, you have to fill in the user input and click **Use this template**. It will import this template into ADF and you can review the steps in detail as well as modify them.

    Let's review one more template.

6.  Let's choose the **DistinctRows** template. For the user input, let's choose the existing **AzureBlobStorage1** and click **Use this template**.

7.  It will import the pipeline, datasets, and data flows, as shown in the following screenshot:

*Figure 1.13 : ADF data flow activity*

8.  We should review the datasets and update the information about the file path for the input dataset and output location. We won't run this job.

9. You can also review the data flow's **DistinctRows** feature, where you can see all the logic, as shown in the following screenshot:

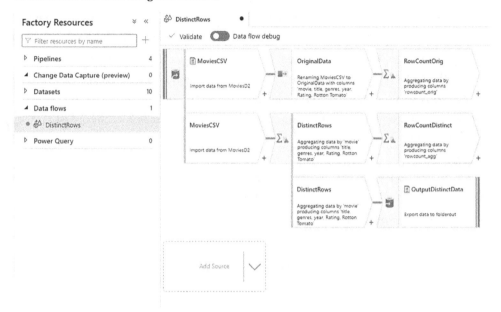

*Figure 1.14: ADF data flow*

You can review other templates and see many examples of ADF design.

## How it works...

We learned that ADF is a set of JSON files with configuration. As a result, it is relatively easy to create new components and share them as a template. We can deploy each template right to ADF or we can download the template bundle and modify the JSON file. These templates help us learn best practices and avoid reinventing the wheel.

## See also

There are useful materials about the use of templates available online:

- You can learn more about ADF templates at the Microsoft blog: `https://azure.microsoft.com/en-us/blog/get-started-quickly-using-templates-in-azure-data-factory/`

- You can learn more about SCD 2 templates in this blog post: `https://mssqldude.wordpress.com/2019/04/15/adf-slowly-changing-dimension-type-2-with-mapping-data-flows-complete/`

- You can learn more about the DistinctRows data flow in this blog post: `https://mssqldude.wordpress.com/2019/09/18/adf-data-flows-distinct-rows/`

# Creating an Azure Data Factory using Azure Bicep

Azure Bicep is a domain-specific language that offers a more readable and maintainable approach to creating and managing Azure resources. It simplifies the process of creating, deploying, and managing ADF resources, reducing the complexity and tediousness of managing raw JSON files. In this recipe, we will create an Azure Data Factory using Azure Bicep and the Visual Studio Code Azure Bicep extension. The Azure Bicep extension for Visual Studio Code provides syntax highlighting, code snippets, and IntelliSense to make working with Azure Bicep files more efficient.

## Getting ready

Before diving into the creation of an Azure Data Factory using Azure Bicep and Visual Studio Code, ensure that you have the necessary prerequisites in place:

- An active Azure subscription
- Visual Studio Code installed on your local machine
- Azure CLI installed on your local machine
- Azure Bicep CLI extension installed on your local machine
- Azure Bicep extension for Visual Studio Code installed

If you don't have the Azure Bicep extension installed, you can check the Microsoft official documentation on how to add a plug-in for Visual Studio Code, at https://learn.microsoft.com/en-us/azure/azure-resource-manager/bicep/visual-studio-code.

## How to do it...

This section will demonstrate how to create an Azure Data Factory using Azure Bicep and Visual Studio Code:

1. Create a new folder named `ADF_Bicep` on your local machine.
2. Open Visual Studio Code and open the `ADF_Bicep` folder as a workspace.
3. Create a new file called `main.bicep` inside the `bicep` folder, and add the following code:

```
param resourceGroupName string = 'AFDCookBookRG'
param dataFactoryName string = 'BicepADF'
param location string = 'centralus'

resource dataFactory
  'Microsoft.DataFactory/factories@2018-06-01' = {
    name: dataFactoryName
```

```
    location: location
  }
output dataFactoryId string = dataFactory.id
```

4.  Open the integrated terminal in Visual Studio Code by selecting **Terminal > New Terminal** from the menu.

5.  In the terminal, use az `login` to log in to the Azure portal.

6.  Create a new resource group using az group `create --name AFDCookBookRG --location` `"Central US"`.

7.  Finally, we can execute Bicep code to create the desired resource. Run the following command:

```
az deployment group create --name ADFDeploymentGroup --resource-
group AFDCookBookRG --template-file main.bicep
```

This command will create the Azure resource for us – a Data Factory instance with the name BicepADF.

## How it works...

Azure Bicep, when used with the Visual Studio Code extension, offers a more streamlined development experience. The extension provides features like syntax highlighting, code snippets, and IntelliSense to simplify the creation and management of Azure resources. The Azure Bicep code is compiled into **Azure Resource Manager** (ARM) templates, which are then used by the Azure CLI to create or modify Azure resources, such as Azure Data Factory.

When you execute a Bicep script using the Azure CLI or PowerShell, several things happen behind the scenes to orchestrate the deployment of your Azure resources:

1.  The Bicep CLI first compiles your .`bicep` file into an ARM template in JSON format. Bicep is essentially a friendlier syntax on top of ARM JSON templates. ARM templates are the underlying platform used by Azure to manage resources.

2.  Azure then validates the resulting ARM template. This includes checking for syntactic errors, ensuring resource types are valid, and verifying that required properties are included. If there are any issues with the template, Azure will return an error message at this stage.

3.  Your Azure session must be authenticated to deploy resources. If you're not already authenticated (for example, if you haven't run az `login`), Azure will prompt you to authenticate.

4. Azure checks whether your user account has the necessary permissions to create or modify the resources described in the template. If you don't have the necessary permissions, Azure will return an authorization error.

5. Assuming the template is valid and you have the necessary permissions, Azure then begins the deployment process. It creates or modifies resources as described in the template, in the order specified by the dependencies between resources. If any issues arise during this process (like a resource quota being exceeded), Azure will stop the deployment and return an error.

6. Throughout the process, Azure provides feedback on the status of the deployment. This includes a summary of changes made once the deployment is complete.

The deployment is idempotent, meaning that if you deploy the same Bicep file multiple times to the same environment, the result after the second and subsequent deployments will be the same as after the first deployment. Azure will only make changes if the template differs from the current state of resources.

## There's more...

We used a simple example of the deployment of Data Factory. However, in the real world, you should deploy 100% of your infrastructure as a code. In our case, you may completely deploy our simple pipeline and create datasets and linked services using Azure Bicep code: `https://learn.microsoft.com/en-us/azure/templates/microsoft.datafactory/factories`.

## See also

To learn more about Azure Bicep, Visual Studio Code, and their extensions, check out the following resources:

- Azure Bicep documentation: `https://docs.microsoft.com/en-us/azure/azure-resource-manager/bicep/overview`
- Azure Bicep extension for Visual Studio Code: `https://marketplace.visualstudio.com/items?itemName=ms-azuretools.vscode-bicep`
- Visual Studio Code: `https://code.visualstudio.com/`
- Azure CLI documentation: `https://docs.microsoft.com/en-us/cli/azure/install-azure-cli`

# Join our community on Discord

Join our community's Discord space for discussions with the authors and other readers:

`https://discord.gg/U229qmBmT3`

# 2

# Orchestration and Control Flow

Azure Data Factory is an excellent tool for designing and orchestrating your **Extract, Transform, Load (ETL)** processes. In this chapter, we introduce several fundamental data factory concepts and guide you through the creation and scheduling of increasingly complex data-driven workflows. All the work in this chapter is done using the Microsoft data factory online portal. You'll learn how to create and configure **linked services** and datasets, take advantage of built-in expressions and functions, and, most importantly, learn how and when to use the most popular **Data Factory** activities.

This chapter covers the following topics:

- Using parameters and built-in functions
- Using the Metadata and Stored Procedure activities
- Using the ForEach and Filter activities
- Chaining and branching activities within a pipeline
- Using the Lookup, Web, and Execute Pipeline activities
- Creating event-based pipeline triggers

# Technical requirements

NOTE

To make fully understanding the recipes easier, we make naming suggestions for the accounts, pipelines, and so on throughout the chapter. Many services, such as Azure Storage and SQL Server, require that the names you assign are unique. Follow your own preferred naming conventions, making appropriate substitutions as you follow the recipes. For the Azure resource naming rules, refer to the documentation at https://learn.microsoft.com/en-us/azure/azure-resource-manager/management/resource-name-rules.

In addition to Azure Data Factory, we shall be using three other Azure services: **Logic Apps**, **Blob Storage**, and **Azure SQL Database**. You will need to have Azure Blob Storage and Azure SQL Database accounts set up to follow the recipes. The following steps describe the necessary preparation:

- Create an Azure Blob Storage account and name it adforchestrationstorage. When creating the storage account, select the same region (that is, East US) as you selected when you created the Data Factory instance. This will reduce our costs when moving data.

- Create a container named data within this storage account, and upload two CSV files to the folder: airlines.csv and countries.csv (the files can be found on GitHub: https://github.com/PacktPublishing/Azure-Data-Factory-Cookbook/tree/master/data).

- Create an Azure SQL Database instance and name it AzureSQLDatabase. When you create the Azure SQL Database instance, you will have the option of creating a server on which the SQL database will be hosted. Create that server and take note of the credentials you entered. You will need these credentials later when you log in to your database.

Choose the basic configuration for your SQL server to save on costs. Once your instance is up and running, configure the **Networking** settings for the SQL server as highlighted in *Figure 2.1*. Go to the **Networking** page under the **Security** menu, then under **Firewall rules**, create a rule to allow your IP to access the database. Under **Exceptions**, make sure that you check the **Allow Azure services and resources to access this database** option.

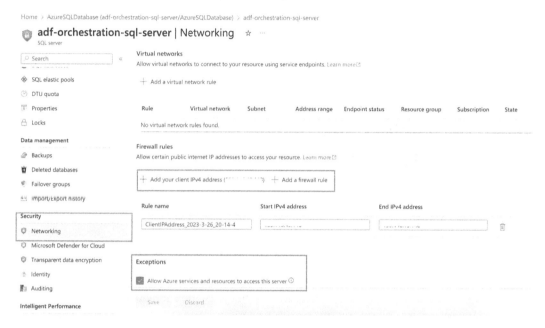

*Figure 2.1: Firewall configuration*

Download the following SQL scripts from GitHub at `https://github.com/PacktPublishing/Azure-Data-Factory-Cookbook/tree/master/Chapter02/sql-scripts`:

- `CreateAirlineTable.sql` and `CreateCountryTable.sql`: These scripts will add two tables, `Country` and `Airline`, which are used in several recipes, including the first one.

- `CreateMetadataTable.sql`: This will create the `FileMetadata` table and a stored procedure to insert data into that table. This table is necessary for the *Using Metadata and Stored Procedure activities* and *Filtering your data and looping through your files* recipes.

- `CreateActivityLogsTable.sql`: This will create the `PipelineLog` table and a stored procedure to insert data into that table. This table is necessary for the *Chaining and branching activities within your pipeline* recipe.

- `CreateEmailRecipients.sql`: This script will create the `EmailRecipients` table and populate it with a record. This table is used in the *Using the Lookup, Web, and Execute Pipeline activities* recipe. You will need to edit it to enter email recipient information.

To create tables from the downloaded files, open your Azure SQL Database instance, go to the Query editor page, then paste the SQL scripts from the downloaded files and run them one by one.

Now that we're all set up, let's move on to the first recipe.

# Using parameters and built-in functions

In this recipe, we shall demonstrate the power and versatility of ADF by performing a common task: importing data from several files (blobs) from a storage container into tables in Azure SQL Database. We shall create a pipeline, define datasets, and use a Copy activity to tie all the pieces together and transfer the data. We shall also see how easy it is to back up data with a quick modification to the pipeline.

## Getting ready

In this recipe, we shall be using most of the services that were mentioned in the *Technical requirements* section of this chapter. Make sure that you have access to Azure SQL Database (with the AzureSQLDatabase instance we created) and the Azure storage account with the necessary `.csv` files already uploaded.

## How to do it...

First, open your Azure Data Factory instance in the Azure portal and go to the **Author and Monitor** interface. Here, we shall define the datasets for input files and database tables, along with the linked services (for Azure Blob Storage and Azure SQL Database):

1.  Start by creating linked services for the Azure storage account and AzureSQLDatabase.

2.  Create the linked service for the `adforchestrationstorage` storage account:

    a.  In the **Manage** tab, select **Linked Services** and click on the **New** button. On the **New linked service** blade, select **Azure Blob Storage**:

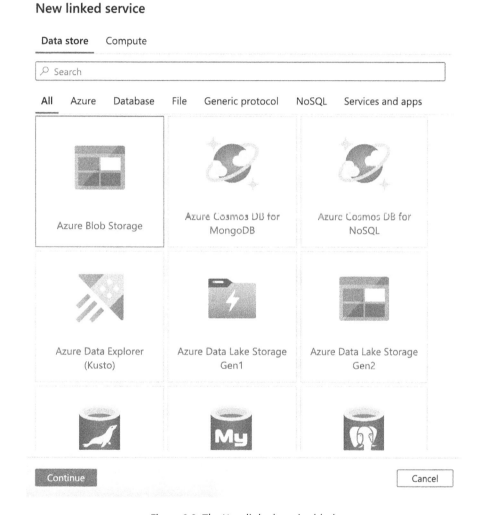

*Figure 2.2: The New linked service blade*

b.  On the next screen, configure the linked service connection properties as shown
    in the following screenshot. Name your linked service according to your naming
    convention (in our example, we named it `OrchestrationAzureBlobStorage1`).

---

### New linked service

🖼 Azure Blob Storage   Learn more ◰

**Name** *

```
OrchestrationAzureBlobStorage1
```

**Description**

```

```

**Connect via integration runtime** * ⓘ

```
AutoResolveIntegrationRuntime                                          ⌄
```

**Authentication type**

```
Account key                                                           ⌄
```

( **Connection string**    Azure Key Vault )

**Account selection method** ⓘ

● From Azure subscription     ◯ Enter manually

**Azure subscription** ⓘ

```
Azure subscription 1 (1176c393-e348-4cdf-95b8-090923b3908e)           ⌄
```

**Storage account name** *

```
adforchestrationstorage                                         ⌄   ↻
```

**Additional connection properties**

---

                                                             ✓ Connection successful

[ Create ]   [ Back ]                                        ⌀ Test connection   [ Cancel ]

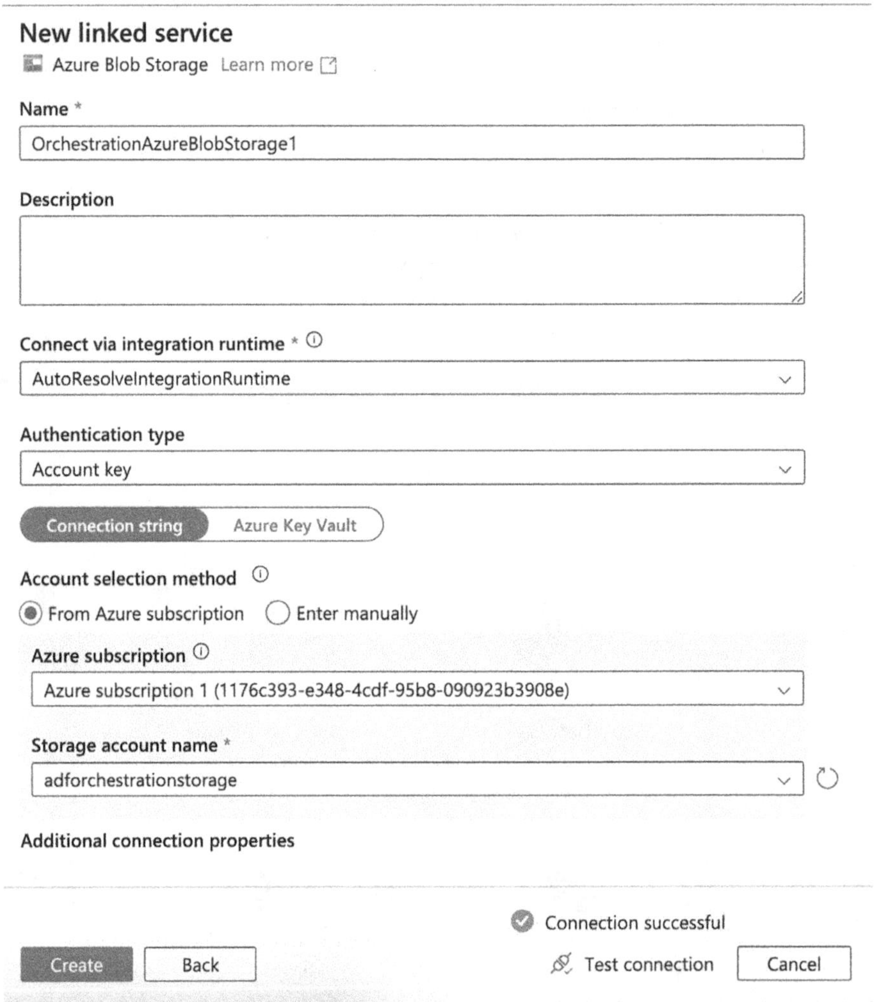

*Figure 2.3: Connection configurations for Azure Blob Storage*

Select the appropriate subscription and enter the name of your storage account (where you store the .csv files):

- For **Integration Runtime**, select **AutoResolveIntegrationRuntime**.
- For **Authentication method**, select **Account Key**.

NOTE

In this recipe, we are using Account Key authentication to access our storage account, primarily for the sake of simplicity. However, in your work environment, it is recommended to authenticate using Managed Identity, taking advantage of the Azure Active Directory service. This is more secure and allows you to avoid using credentials in your code. You can review the references for more information about using Managed Identity with Azure Data Factory in the *See also* section of this recipe.

c. Click the **Test Connection** button at the bottom and verify that you can connect to the storage account.

d. Finally, click on the **Create** button and wait for the linked service to be created.

3.  Create the second linked service for `AzureSQLDatabase`:

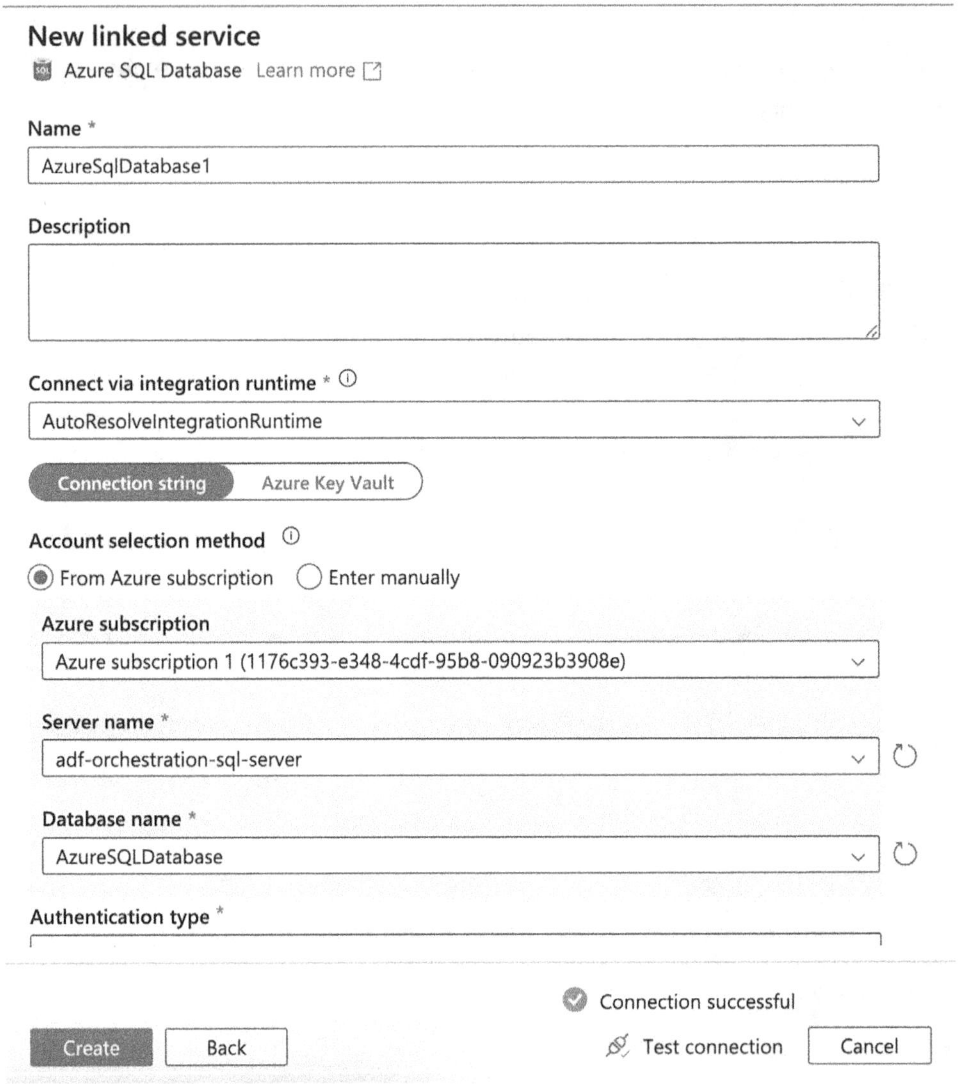

## New linked service

Azure SQL Database   Learn more 

**Name** *

> AzureSqlDatabase1

**Description**

> 

**Connect via integration runtime** * ⓘ

> AutoResolveIntegrationRuntime                                    ⌄

( **Connection string**    Azure Key Vault )

**Account selection method** ⓘ

⦿ From Azure subscription    ◯ Enter manually

**Azure subscription**

> Azure subscription 1 (1176c393-e348-4cdf-95b8-090923b3908e)    ⌄

**Server name** *

> adf-orchestration-sql-server                                 ⌄   ↻

**Database name** *

> AzureSQLDatabase                                             ⌄   ↻

**Authentication type** *

> 

                                                    ✅ Connection successful

[ Create ]   [ Back ]                          🖉 Test connection   [ Cancel ]

*Figure 2.4: Connection properties for Azure SQL Database*

a.  In the **Manage** tab, create a new linked service, but this time select **Azure SQL** from the choices in the **New linked service** blade. You can enter Azure SQL into the search field to find it easily.

b.   Select the subscription information and the SQL server name (the dropdown will present you with choices). Once you have selected the SQL server name, you can select your database (AzureSQLDatabase) from the dropdown in the **Database Name** section.

c.   Select **SQL Authentication** for **Authentication Type**. Enter the username and password for your database.

d.   Make sure to test the connection. If the connection fails, ensure that you have configured the access correctly in **Firewall and Network Settings**. Once you have successfully tested the connection, click on **Create** to save your linked service.

Now, we shall create two datasets, one for each linked service.

4.   In the **Author** tab, define the dataset for Azure Storage as shown in the following screenshot:

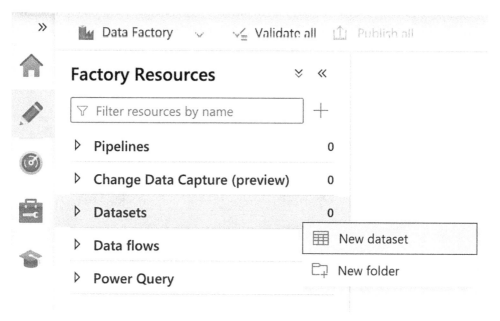

*Figure 2.5: Create a new dataset*

a.   Go to **Datasets** and click on **New dataset**. Select **Azure Blob Storage** from the choices and click **Continue**.

b.   In the **Select Format** blade, select **Delimited Text** and hit **Continue**.

c.  Call your new dataset CsvData and select **OrchestrationAzureBlobStorage** in the **Linked Service** dropdown.

d.  With the help of the **folder** button, navigate to your Azure folder and select any file from there to specify the file path:

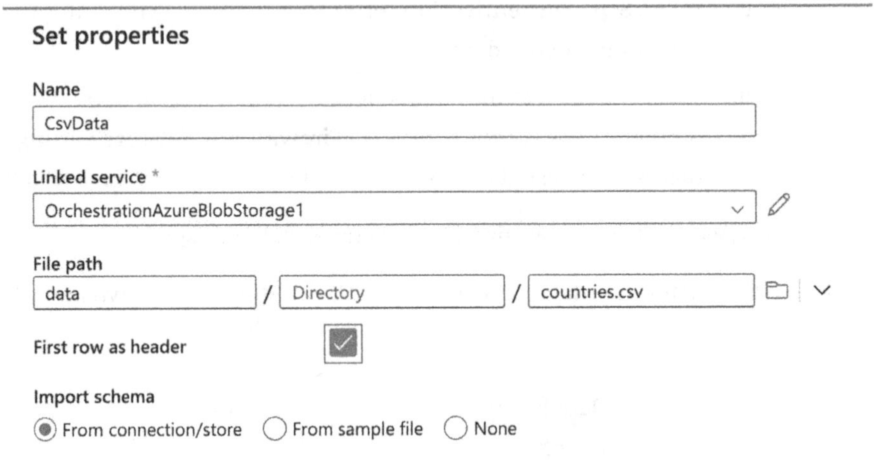

### Set properties

Name

CsvData

Linked service *

OrchestrationAzureBlobStorage1

File path

| data | / | Directory | / | countries.csv |

First row as header ☑

Import schema
◉ From connection/store    ◯ From sample file    ◯ None

*Figure 2.6: Dataset properties*

e.  Check the **First Row as Header** checkbox and click on **Ok**.

5.  In the same **Author** tab, create a dataset for the Azure SQL table:

a.  Go to **Datasets** and click on **New dataset**.

b.  Select **Azure SQL Database** from the choices in the **New Dataset** blade.

c.  Name your dataset AzureSQLTables.

d.  In the **Linked Service** dropdown, select **AzureSQLDatabase1**. For the table name, select **Country** from the dropdown.

e.  Click on **Create**.

6.  Parameterize the AzureSQLTables dataset:

a.  In the **Parameters** tab, enter the name of your new parameter, tableName:

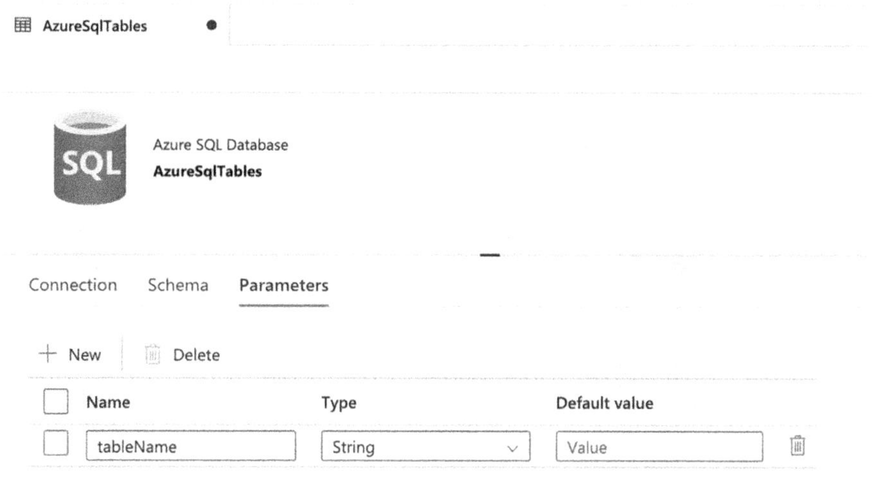

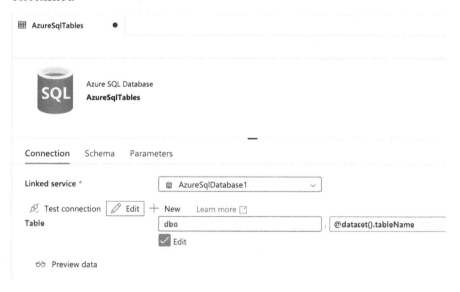

*Figure 2.7: Parameterizing the dataset*

b.  Next, in the **Connection** tab, click on the **Edit** checkbox and enter dbo as the schema and @dataset().tableName in the table text field, as shown in the following screenshot:

*Figure 2.8: Specifying a value for the dataset parameter*

7.  In the same way, parameterize and add dynamic content in the **Connection** tab for the
    CsvData dataset:

    a.  Select your dataset, open the **Parameters** tab, and create a parameter named
        filename.

    b.  In the **Connections** tab, in the **File Path** section, click inside the **File** text box, then
        click on the **Add Dynamic Content** link. This will bring up the **Dynamic Content**
        interface. In that interface, find the **Parameters** section and click on filename.
        This will generate the correct code to refer to the dataset's filename parameter
        in the dynamic content text box:

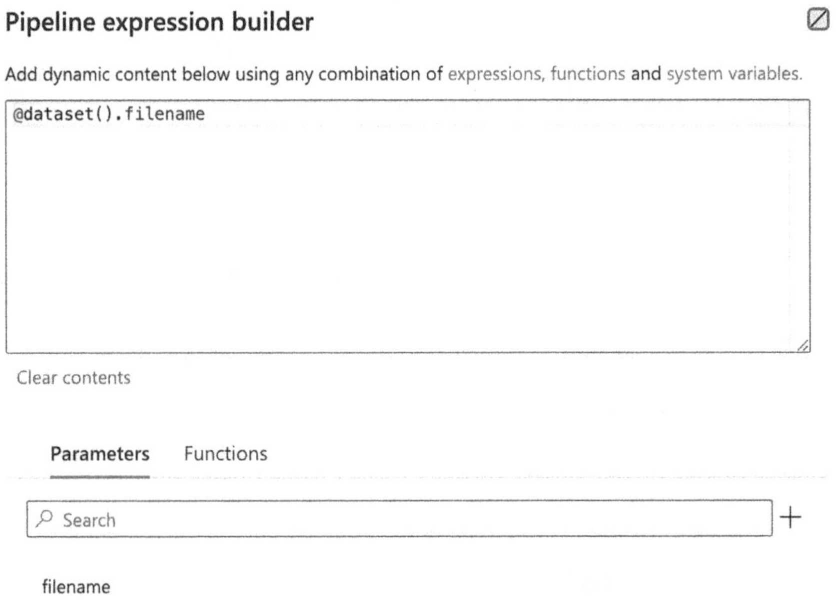

### Pipeline expression builder                                                      ▣

Add dynamic content below using any combination of expressions, functions and system variables.

```
@dataset().filename
```

Clear contents

**Parameters**    Functions

🔍 Search                                                                            +

filename

*Figure 2.9: Dynamic content interface*

Click on the **Finish** button to finalize your choice.

Verify that you can see both datasets on the **Datasets** tab:

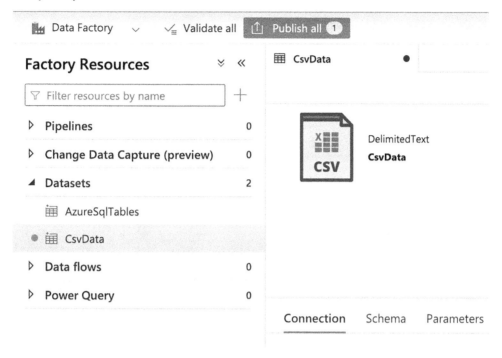

*Figure 2.10: Datasets resource in the Author tab of Data Factory*

8.  We are now ready to design the pipeline.

    In the **Author** tab, create a new pipeline. Change its name to pl_orchestration_recipe_1.

9.  From the **Move and Transform** menu in the **Activities** pane (on the left), drag a **Copy** activity onto the canvas:

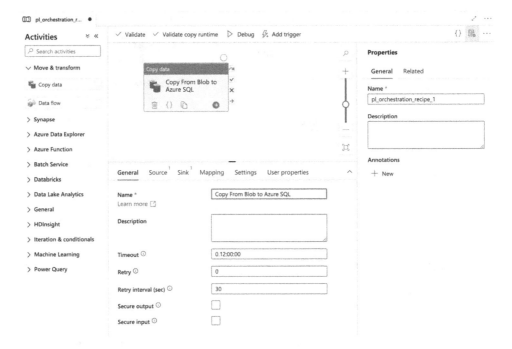

*Figure 2.11: Pipeline canvas with a Copy activity*

- On the bottom of the canvas, you will see some tabs: **General**, **Source**, **Sink**, and so on. Configure your **Copy** activity.

- In the **General** tab, you can configure the name for your activity. Call it **Copy From Blob to Azure SQL**.

- In the **Source** tab, select the CsvData dataset and specify countries.csv in the filename textbox.

- In the **Sink** tab, select the AzureSQLTables dataset and specify Country in the **tableName** text field.

10. We are ready to run the pipeline in **Debug** mode:

NOTE

You will learn more about using the debug capabilities of Azure Data Factory in *Chapter 9, Managing Deployment Processes with Azure DevOps*. In this recipe, we introduce you to the **Output** pane, which will help you understand the design and function of this pipeline.

a. Click the **Debug** button in the top panel. This will run your pipeline.

b. Put your cursor anywhere on the pipeline canvas. You will see the report with the status of the activities in the bottom panel in the **Output** tab. Hover your cursor over the row representing the activity to see the **inputs** and **outputs** buttons. We shall make use of these in later chapters.

*Figure 2.12: Debug output*

After your pipeline has run, you should see that the dbo.Country table in your Azure SQL database has been populated with the countries data:

*Figure 2.13: Contents of the Country table in Azure SQL Database*

We have copied the contents of the `Countries.csv` file into the database. In the next steps, we shall demonstrate how parameterizing the datasets gives us the flexibility to define which file we want to copy and which SQL table we want as the destination without redesigning the pipeline.

11. Edit the pipeline: click on the **Copy from Blob To Azure SQL** activity to select it, and specify `airlines.csv` for the filename in the **Source** tab and `Airline` for the table name in the **Sink** tab. Run your pipeline again (in **Debug** mode), and you should see that the second table is populated with the data – using the same pipeline!

12. Now, let's say we want to back up the contents of the tables in an Azure SQL database before overwriting them with data from `.csv` files. We can easily enhance the existing pipeline to accomplish this.

13. Drag another instance of the **Copy** activity from the **Activities** pane, name it `Backup Copy Activity`, and configure it in the following way:

    a. For the source, select `AzureSQLDatabase` for the linked service, and add `Airline` in the text box for the table name.

    b. In **Sink**, specify `CsvData` as the linked service, and enter the following formula into the `filename` textbox: `@concat('Airlines-', utcnow(), '.backup' )`.

    c. Connect **Backup Copy Activity** to the **Copy from Blob to AzureSQL** copy activity:

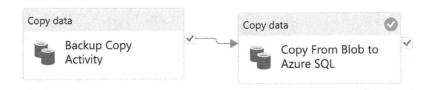

*Figure 2.14: Adding backup functionality to the pipeline*

14. Run the pipeline in debug mode. After the run is complete, you should see the backup file in your storage account.

15. We have created two linked services and two datasets, and we have a functioning pipeline. Click on the **Publish All** button at the top to save your work.

Let's look at how this works!

# How it works...

In this recipe, we became familiar with all the major components of an Azure Data Factory pipeline: linked services, datasets, and activities:

- Linked services represent configured connections between your Data Factory instance and the service that you want to use.

- Datasets are more granular: they represent the specific view of the data that your activities will use as input and output.

- Activities represent the actions that are performed on the data. Many activities require you to specify where the data is extracted from and where it is loaded to. The ADF terms for these entities are source and sink.

Every pipeline that you design will have those components.

In *step 1* and *step 2*, we created the linked services to connect to Azure Blob Storage and Azure SQL Database. Then, in *step 3* and *step 4*, we created datasets that connected to those linked services and referred to specific files or tables. We created parameters that represented the data we referred to in *step 5* and *step 6*, and this allowed us to change which files we wanted to load into tables without creating additional pipelines. In the remaining steps, we worked with instances of the Copy activity, specifying the inputs and outputs (sources and sinks) for the data.

# There's more...

We used a built-in function for generating UTC timestamps in *step 12*. Data Factory provides many convenient built-in functions and expressions, as well as system variables, for your use. To see them, click on **Backup SQL Data activity** in your pipeline and go to the **Source** tab below it. Put your cursor inside the **tableName** text field.

You will see an **Add dynamic content** link appear underneath. Click on it, and you will see the **Add dynamic content** blade:

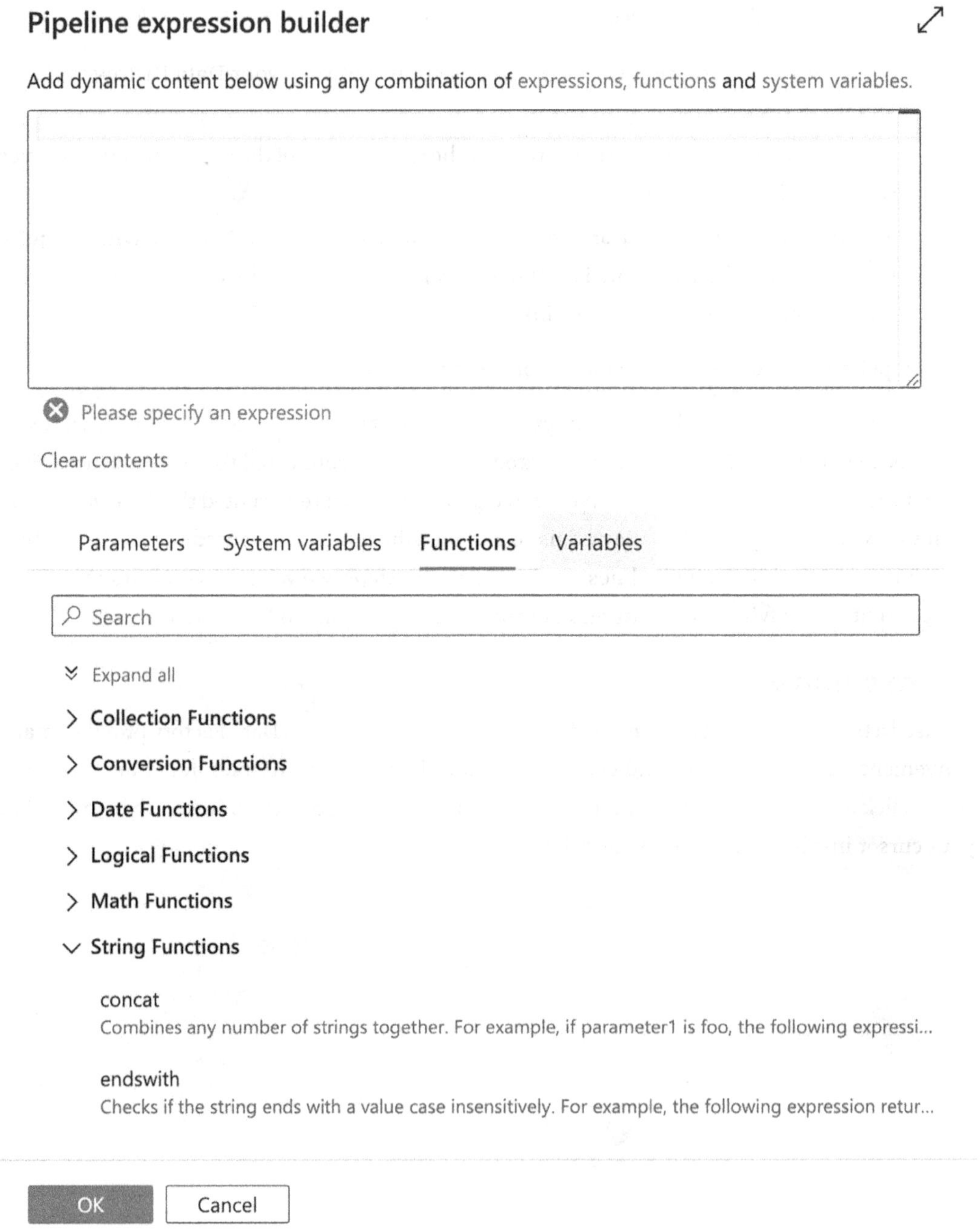

## Pipeline expression builder                                                              ↗

Add dynamic content below using any combination of expressions, functions **and** system variables.

❌  Please specify an expression

Clear contents

| Parameters | System variables | **Functions** | Variables |

🔍 Search

⌄ Expand all

> **Collection Functions**

> **Conversion Functions**

> **Date Functions**

> **Logical Functions**

> **Math Functions**

⌄ **String Functions**

concat
Combines any number of strings together. For example, if parameter1 is foo, the following expressi...

endswith
Checks if the string ends with a value case insensitively. For example, the following expression retur...

OK          Cancel

*Figure 2.15: Data Factory functions and system variables*

This blade lists many useful functions and system variables to explore. We will use some of them in later recipes.

## See also

Microsoft keeps extensive documentation on Data Factory. For a more detailed explanation of the concepts used in this recipe, refer to the following pages:

- Linked services in Azure Data Factory: `https://learn.microsoft.com/en-us/azure/data-factory/concepts-linked-services?tabs=data-factory`

- Pipelines and activities in Azure Data Factory: `https://learn.microsoft.com/en-us/azure/data-factory/concepts-pipelines-activities?tabs=data-factory`

- Setting up and using Managed Identity with Azure Data Factory: `https://learn.microsoft.com/en-us/azure/data-factory/data-factory-service-identity`

# Using the Metadata and Stored Procedure activities

In this recipe, we shall create a pipeline that fetches some metadata from an Azure storage container and stores it in an Azure SQL database table. You will work with two frequently used activities, the **Metadata** activity and the **Stored Procedure** activity.

## Getting ready

- In the first recipe, we created two datasets and two linked services. We shall be using the `AzureSqlDatabase` and `OrchestrationAzureBlobStorage` linked services in this recipe as well, so if you did not create them before, please go through the necessary steps in the previous recipe.

- We shall be using `AzureSQLDatabase`. If you haven't done so already, create the `FileMetadata` table and the stored procedure to insert the data as described in the *Technical requirements* section of this chapter.

## How to do it...

1. Create a new pipeline in the **Author** tab, and call it `pl_orchestration_recipe_2`.

2. Create a new dataset named `CsvDataFolder`, pointing to the Azure Storage container (`adforchestrationstorage`) we specified in the *Technical requirements* section. Use the delimited text file format. This time, do not specify the filename; leave it pointing to the data container itself. Use the same linked service for Azure Blob Storage as we used in the previous recipe.

3.  From the **Activities** pane on the left, find the **Get Metadata** activity (under the **General** tab) and drag it onto the pipeline canvas. Using the configuration tabs at the bottom, configure it in the following way:

    a.  In the **General** tab, rename this **Metadata** activity `CsvDataFolder Metadata`.

    b.  In the **Source** tab, pick the `CsvDataFolder` dataset. In the same tab, under **Field list**, use the **New** button to add two fields, and select **Item Name** and **Last Modified** as the values for those fields:

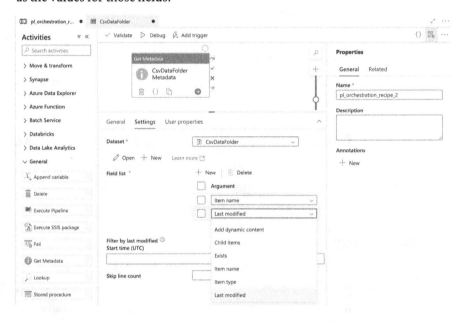

*Figure 2.16: Get Metadata activity configuration*

4.  In the **Activities** pane, find the **Stored Procedure** activity (on the **General** tab) and drag it onto the canvas. In the pipeline canvas, connect the **CsvDataFolder** Metadata activity to the **Stored Procedure** activity.

5.  Configure the **Stored Procedure** activity in the following way:

    a.  In the **General** tab, change the activity name to `Insert Metadata`.

    b.  In the **Settings** tab, specify the linked service (`AzureSqlDatabase`) and the name of the stored procedure: `[dbo].[InsertFileMetadata]`.

    c.  In the same **Settings** tab, click on **Import Parameters** to display the text fields to specify the parameters for the Stored Procedure activity. Use the following values:

        •   **FileName:** `@activity('CsvDataFolder Metadata').output.itemName`

- **ModifiedAt:** `@convertFromUtc(activity('CsvDataFolder Metadata'). output.lastModified, 'Pacific Standard Time')`
- **UpdatedAt:** `@convertFromUtc(utcnow(), 'Pacific Standard Time'):`

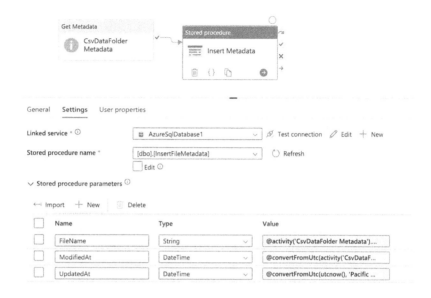

*Figure 2.17: Stored Procedure activity configuration*

6. Run your pipeline in **Debug** mode. After the run is done, go to **AzureSqlDatabase** and verify that the **FileMetadata** table is populated with one record: the last-modified date of the folder where we keep the `.csv` files.

7. Do not forget to publish your pipeline in order to save your changes.

## How it works...

In this simple recipe, we introduced two new activities. In *step 2*, we have used the Metadata activity, with the dataset representing a folder in our container. In this step, we were only interested in the item name and the last-modified date of the folder. In *step 3*, we added a Stored Procedure activity, which allows us to directly invoke a stored procedure in the remote database. In order to configure the Stored Procedure activity, we needed to obtain the parameters (`itemName`, `lastModified`, and `UpdatedAt`). The formulas used in *step 5* (such as `@activity('CsvDataFolder Metadata').output.itemName`) define which activity the value is coming from (the `CsvDataFolder Metadata` activity) and which parts of the output are required (`output.itemName`). We have used the built-in `convertFromUtc` conversion function in order to present the time in a specific time zone (Pacific Standard Time, in our case).

# There's more...

In this recipe, we only specified the `itemName` and `lastModified` fields as the metadata outputs. However, the Metadata activity supports many more options. Here is the list of currently supported options from the Data Factory documentation at https://learn.microsoft.com/en-us/azure/data-factory/control-flow-get-metadata-activity#capabilities:

## Metadata options

You can specify the following metadata types in the Get Metadata activity field list to retrieve the corresponding information:

| Metadata type | Description |
| --- | --- |
| itemName | Name of the file or folder. |
| itemType | Type of the file or folder. Returned value is `File` or `Folder`. |
| size | Size of the file, in bytes. Applicable only to files. |
| created | Created datetime of the file or folder. |
| lastModified | Last modified datetime of the file or folder. |
| childItems | List of subfolders and files in the given folder. Applicable only to folders. Returned value is a list of the name and type of each child item. |
| contentMD5 | MD5 of the file. Applicable only to files. |
| structure | Data structure of the file or relational database table. Returned value is a list of column names and column types. |
| columnCount | Number of columns in the file or relational table. |
| exists | Whether a file, folder, or table exists. Note that if `exists` is specified in the Get Metadata field list, the activity won't fail even if the file, folder, or table doesn't exist. Instead, `exists: false` is returned in the output. |

*Figure 2.18: Metadata activity options*

The Metadata type options that are available to you will depend on the dataset: for example, the `contentMD5` option is only available for files, while `childItems` is only available for folders.

# Using the ForEach and Filter activities

In this recipe, we introduce you to the **Filter** and **ForEach** activities. We shall enhance the pipeline from the previous recipe to not just examine the data in the Azure Storage container, but filter it based on the file type and then record the last-modified date for every .csv file in the folder.

## Getting ready

The preparation steps are the same as for the previous recipe. We shall be reusing the pipeline from the *Using Metadata and Stored Procedure activities* recipe, so if you did not go through the steps then, do so now.

## How to do it...

1. Clone the pipeline from the previous recipe and rename it pl_orchestration_recipe_3.

2. Delete the **Stored Procedure** activity.

3. Select the Metadata activity and configure it in the following way:

    a. In the **Dataset** tab, verify that CsvDataFolder is selected as the dataset.

    b. Verify that the **Item Name** and **Last Modified** fields are added as arguments. Add one more field, **Child Items**.

4. Now, select the Filter activity from the **Activities** pane on the left (find it in the **Iteration and Conditionals** section) and drop it into the pipeline canvas to the right of the Metadata activity.

5. Connect the Metadata activity to the Filter activity.

6. Configure the Filter activity as follows:

    a. In the **General** tab, change the name to FilterOnCsv.

    b. In the **Settings** tab, fill in the values as follows:

    - **Items:** @activity('CsvDataFolder Metadata').output.childItems

    - **Condition:** @endswith(item().name, '.csv')

7. Run this pipeline in **Debug** mode:

*Figure 2.19: Pipeline status overview in Debug mode*

After the pipeline is finished running, hover over the row representing the **Get Metadata** activity run in the **Output** pane and examine the activity's output. You should see that the **Get Metadata** activity fetched the metadata for all the files in the folder, as follows:

## Output

```
[ ]  Copy to clipboard
```

```
{
    "itemName": "data",
    "lastModified": "2023-03-29T14:47:27Z",
    "childItems": [
        {
            "name": "Airlines-2023-04-11T19:21:59.4183732Z.backup",
            "type": "File"
        },
        {
            "name": "airlines.csv",
            "type": "File"
        },
        {
            "name": "countries.csv",
            "type": "File"
        }
    ],
    "effectiveIntegrationRuntime": "AutoResolveIntegrationRuntime (East US)",
    "executionDuration": 0,
    "durationInQueue": {
        "integrationRuntimeQueue": 0
    },
    "billingReference": {
        "activityType": "PipelineActivity",
        "billableDuration": [
            {
                "meterType": "AzureIR",
                "duration": 0.016666666666666666,
                "unit": "Hours"
            }
        ]
    }
}
```

*Figure 2.20: Get Metadata activity output*

Do the same for the **FilterOnCSV** activity and verify that the outputs were filtered to only the csv files.

8.  From the **Activities** pane, add an instance of the **ForEach** activity (find it in the **Iteration and Conditionals** section) on the canvas, connect it to the **FilterOnCsv** activity, and configure it in the following way:

    a.  In the **Settings** tab, enter the following value in the **Items** textbox: @ activity('FilterOnCSV').output.Value.

    b.  Within the **ForEach** activity square, click on the pencil image (meaning **Edit**). This will open another canvas. We shall configure the actions for the **ForEach** activity within this canvas.

9.  Add an instance of the **Get Metadata Activity** onto the **ForEach Activity** canvas, and configure it as follows:

    a.  In the **General** tab, change the name to ForEach Metadata.

    b.  In the **Dataset** tab, specify CsvData (the parameterized dataset we created in the *Using parameters and built-in functions* recipe) as the dataset for this activity. If you do not have this dataset, please refer to the *Using parameters and built-in functions* recipe to see how to create a parameterized dataset.

    c.  For the filename parameter, enter @item().name.

d.  In the same **Dataset** tab, in the **Field list** section, add two arguments: **Item name** and **Last modified**, as shown in the following screenshot:

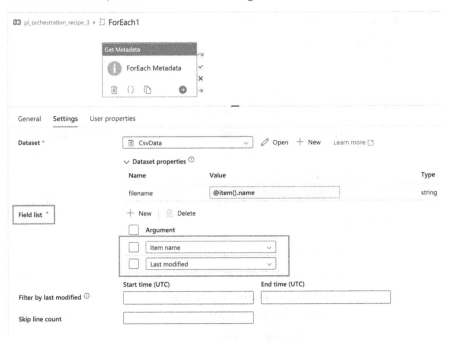

*Figure 2.21: Adding arguments in the Field list section*

10. Add an instance of **Stored Procedure Activity** onto the **ForEach Activity** canvas. Connect **ForEach Metadata** to **Stored Procedure Activity** and configure **Stored Procedure Activity** as follows:

a.  In the **Settings** tab at the bottom, select **AzureSQLDatabase** as the linked service and `[dbo][InsertFileMetadata]` as the stored procedure name.

b.  Click on **Import** under **Stored procedure parameters** and enter the following values:

- **FileName:** `@{item().name}`
- **ModifiedAt:** `@convertFromUtc(activity('ForEach Metadata').output.lastModified,'Pacific Standard Time')`

- **UpdatedAt**: `@convertFromUtc(utcnow(), 'Pacific Standard Time')` (you can use your own time zone here, as well):

*Figure 2.22: Stored Procedure activity configuration*

Run your whole pipeline in **Debug** mode. When it is finished, you should see two additional rows in your **FileMetadata** table (in Azure SQL Database) showing the last-modified date for `airlines.csv` and `countries.csv`.

11. Publish your pipeline to save the changes.

# How it works...

In this recipe, we used the Metadata activity again and took advantage of the `childItems` option to retrieve information about the folder. After this, we filtered the output to restrict processing to CSV files only with the help of the Filter activity.

Next, we needed to select only the CSV files from the folder for further processing. For this, we added a Filter activity. Using `@activity('Get Metadata').output.childItems`, we specified that the Filter activity's input is the metadata of all the files inside the folder. We configured the Filter activity's condition to only keep files whose name ends with `csv` (the built-in `endswith` function gave us a convenient way to do this).

Finally, in order to process each file separately, we used the ForEach activity, which we used in *step 6*. ForEach is what is called a *compound* activity, because it contains a group of activities that are performed on each of the items in a loop. We configured the Filter activity to take as input the filtered file list (the output of the Filter activity), and in *steps 7* and *8*, we designed the sequence of actions that we want to have performed on each of the files. We used a second instance of the Metadata activity for this sub-pipeline and configured it to retrieve information about a particular file. To accomplish this, we configured it with the parameterized `CsvData` dataset and specified the filename. In order to refer to the file, we used the built-in formula `@item` (which provides a reference to the current file in the `ForEach` loop) and indicated that we need the `name` property of that object.

The configuration of the Stored Procedure activity is similar to the previous step. In order to provide the filename for the Stored Procedure parameters, we again referred to the provided *current object* reference, `@item`. We could also have used `@activity('ForEach Metadata').output.itemName`, as we did in the previous recipe.

# Chaining and branching activities within a pipeline

In this recipe, we shall build a pipeline that will extract the data from the CSV files in Azure Blob Storage, load this data into the Azure SQL table, and record a log message with the status of this job. The status message will depend on whether the extract and load succeeded or failed.

## Getting ready

We shall be using all the Azure services that are mentioned in the *Technical requirements* section at the beginning of the chapter. We shall be using the `PipelineLog` table and the `InsertLogRecord` stored procedure. If you have not created the table and the stored procedure in your Azure SQL database yet, please do so now.

## How to do it...

1.  In this recipe, we shall reuse portions of the pipeline from the *Using parameters and built-in functions* recipe. If you completed that recipe, just create a clone of that pipeline and name it `pl_orchestration_recipe_4`. If you did not, go through *steps 1-10* of that recipe and create a parameterized pipeline.

2.  Observe that each activity by default has a little green check mark on the right. This denotes that the activity runs on a successful outcome of the previous activity. However, sometimes activities fail. We want to add an action to take place on the failure of the **Copy from Blob to Azure SQL** activity. To denote a failure, each activity has a red cross on the right.

*Figure 2.23: Possible activity outcomes*

3. From the **Activities** pane on the left, drag two Stored Procedure activities onto the canvas. Connect one of them to the green check mark of the **Copy From Blob to Azure SQL** activity and another one to the red cross.

4. First, configure the **Stored Procedure** activity that is connected to the green cross in the following way:

    a. In the **General** tab, rename it On Success.

    b. In the **Settings** tab, specify AzureSQLTables as the linked service and [dbo]. [InsertPipelineLog] as the Stored Procedure name. Click on **Test Connection** to verify that you can connect to the Azure SQL database.

    c. Click on the **Import Parameters** button and fill in the values as follows:

        • **PipelineID:** @pipeline().Pipeline
        • **RunID:** @pipeline().RunId
        • **Status:** Success
        • **UpdatedAt:** @utcnow()

NOTE

You can also use the *Add dynamic content* functionality to fill in the values. For each one, put your cursor into the field and then click on the little *blue Add dynamic content* link that appears underneath the field. You will see a blade that gives you a selection of system variables, functions, and activity outputs to choose from.

5.  Now, select the stored procedure that is connected to the red cross in the **Copy Data** activity. Configure it in a similar way to the previous step, but give it the name `On Failure`, and for the **Status** parameter, enter `Failure`:

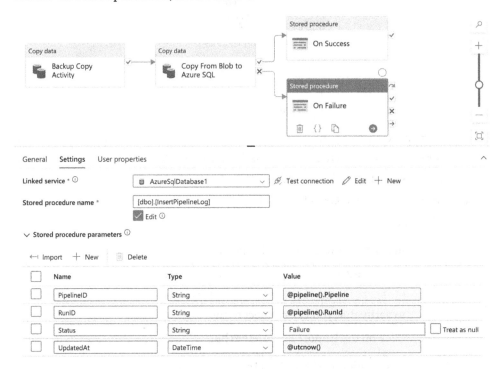

*Figure 2.24: A full pipeline with On Success and On Failure branches*

6.  It is time to test the pipeline. Run it in Debug mode and verify that, when your pipeline succeeds, you have a corresponding entry in the **PipelineLog** table.

7.  Now, in order to see the branching in action, let's imitate the failure of our pipeline. Edit your **Copy From Blob To Azure SQL** activity: in the **Sink** tab below the canvas, put any string into the **tableName** textbox.

8. Run your pipeline in debug mode. You will see that now the **Copy From Blob To Azure SQL** activity failed, and the **On Failure** stored procedure was invoked. Verify that the **PipelineLog** table in the Azure SQL database has a new record:

```
1    SELECT TOP (1000) * FROM [dbo].[PipelineLog]
```

Results     Messages

| PipelineID | RunID | Status | UpdatedAt |
|---|---|---|---|
| pl_orchestration_recipe_4 | e2a8bf7f-a41a-427a-859d-daa767dfb30e | Success | 2023-04-11T20:22:16.5130000 |
| pl_orchestration_recipe_4 | 3270d37c-db31-4e33-9190-4f94670ae468 | Failure | 2023-04-11T20:23:39.7470000 |

*Figure 2.25: Entries in PipelineLog after successful and failed pipeline runs*

9. Publish your changes to save them.

# There's more...

ADF offers another option for branching out on a condition during pipeline execution: the If Condition activity. This activity is another example of a compound activity (like the ForEach activity in the previous recipe): it contains two activity subgroups and a condition. Only one of the activity subgroups is executed, based on whether the condition is true or false.

The use case for the If Condition activity is different than the approach we illustrated in this recipe. While the recipe branches out on the outcome (success or failure) of the previous activity, you design the condition in the If Condition activity to branch out on the inputs from the previous activity. For example, let's suppose that we want to retrieve metadata about a file, and perform one stored procedure if the file is a CSV and another stored procedure if the file is of a different type.

Here is how we would configure an `If Condition` activity to accomplish this:

*Figure 2.26: Configuring the If Condition activity*

The full formula used in the **Expression** field is: `@not(endswith(activity('CsvDataFolder Metadata').output.itemName, 'csv'))`.

# Using the Lookup, Web, and Execute Pipeline activities

In this recipe, we shall implement error-handling logic for our pipeline similar to the previous recipe, but with a more sophisticated design: we shall isolate the error-handling flow in its own pipeline. Our main **parent** pipeline will then call the **child** pipeline. This recipe also introduces three very useful activities to the user: **Lookup**, **Web**, and **Execute Pipeline**. The recipe will illustrate how to retrieve information from an Azure SQL table and how to invoke other Azure services from the pipeline.

## Getting ready

We shall be using all the Azure services mentioned in the *Technical requirements* section at the beginning of the chapter. In addition, this recipe requires a table to store the email addresses of the status email recipients. Please refer to the *Technical requirements* section for the table creation scripts and instructions.

We shall be building a pipeline that sends an email in the case of failure. There is no activity in ADF capable of sending emails, so we shall be using the Azure Logic Apps service. Follow these steps to create an instance of this service:

1.  In the Azure portal, look for **Logic Apps** in the Azure services. Then, use the **Add** button to create a new logic app.

2.  Name your logic app `ADF-Email-Logic-App` and fill in the **Subscription**, **Resource Group**, and **Region information** fields.

3.  It's better to choose **Consumption** plan type as we're not going to run this logic app regularly. Click on **Create** and wait until your logic app is deployed. Then, click on **Go to Resource**.

4.  In the Logic App Designer, select the **When a HTTP request is received** trigger:

*Figure 2.27: HTTP trigger*

5.  In the displayed tile, click on **Use sample payload to generate schema**, and use the following code block:

```
{
"subject": "<subject of the email message>",
"messageBody": "<body of the email message >",
"emailAddress": "<email-address>"
}
```

Enter the code in the box as shown in the following figure:

*Figure 2.28: Configuring a logic app – The capture message body*

6.  Click on the + **Next Step** button and choose the email service that you want to use to send the notification emails. For the purposes of this tutorial, we shall use Gmail.

NOTE

Even though we use Gmail for the purposes of this tutorial, you can also send emails using Office 365 Outlook or Outlook.com. In the *See also* section of this recipe, we include a link to a tutorial on how to send emails using those providers.

7. Select **Gmail** from the list of services and **Send Email** from **Actions**. Log in with your account credentials:

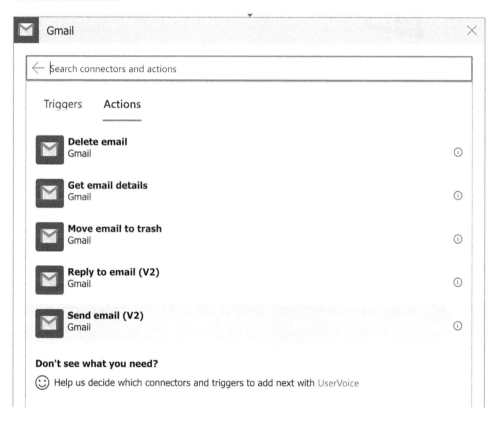

*Figure 2.29: Configuring a logic app – Specifying an email service*

8.  From the **Add new parameter** dropdown, check the **Subject** and **Body** checkboxes:

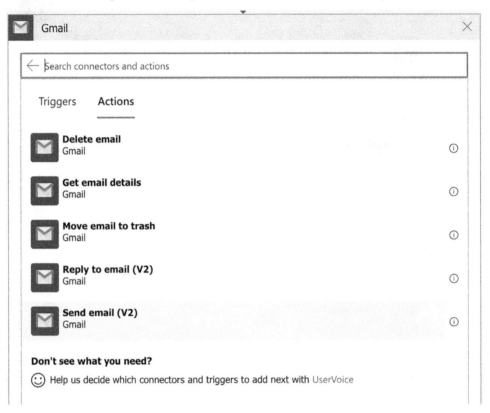

*Figure 2.30: Configuring a logic app – specifying the Body, Subject, and Recipient fields*

9.  Place your cursor inside the **To** text field and enter `@{triggerBody()['emailAddress']}`.

10. In a similar way, enter `@{triggerBody()['subject']}` in the **Subject** text field.

11. Finally, in the **Body** text box, enter `@{triggerBody()['messageBody']}`. You should end up with something similar to the following screenshot:

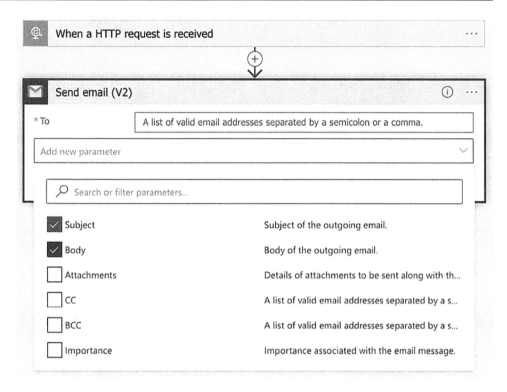

*Figure 2.31: Configuring a logic app – Specifying the To, Subject, and Body values*

12. Save your logic app. In the first tile, you should see that **HTTP POST URL** was populated. This is the URL we'll use to invoke this logic app from the Data Factory pipeline.

## How to do it...

First, we shall create the child pipeline to retrieve the email addresses of the email recipients and send the status email:

1.  Create a new pipeline and name it `pl_orchestration_recipe_5_child`.

2.  From the **Activities** pane, select a **Lookup** activity and add it to the pipeline canvas. Configure it in the following way:

    a.  In the **General** tab, change the activity name to **Get Email Recipients**.

    b.  In the **Settings** tab, select **AzureSQLTables** as the value for **Source dataset**, and specify **EmailRecipients** for **tableName**.

c.   Also, in the **Settings** tab, select the **Use Query** radio button and enter `SELECT *` `FROM [dbo].[EmailRecipient]` into the text box. Make sure to uncheck the `First` `row only` checkbox at the bottom. Your **Settings** tab should look similar to the following figure:

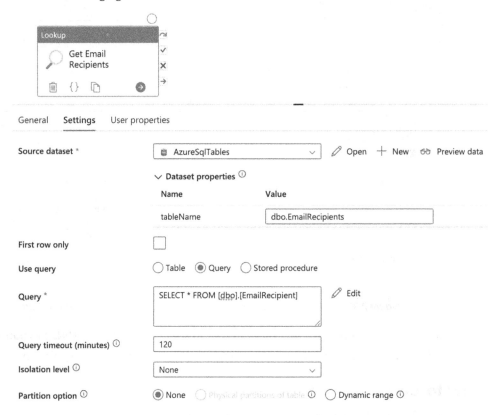

*Figure 2.32: The Get Email Recipients activity settings*

3.   Next, add a **ForEach** activity to the canvas, connect it to **Get Email Recipients** activity and configure it in the following way:

In the **Settings** tab, enter `@activity('Get Email Recipients').output.value` into the **Items** textbox.

4.   Click on the pencil icon within the **ForEach** activity. This will open a new canvas. Add a Web activity onto this canvas.

We shall now configure the Web activity. First, go to the **General** tab, and rename it Send Email. Then, in the URL text field, paste the URL for the logic app (which you created in the *Getting ready* section):

- In the **Method** textbox, select **POST**.

- In the **Headers** section, click on the **New** button to add a header. Enter **Content-Type** into the **Name** text box and application/json into the **Value** textbox.

- In the **Body text** box, enter the following text (be sure to copy the quotes accurately):

```
@json(concat('{"emailAddress": "', item().emailAddress,
'", "subject": "ADF Pipeline Failure", "messageBody": "ADF
Pipeline Failed"}'))
```

Your **Settings** tab should look similar to *Figure 2.33*:

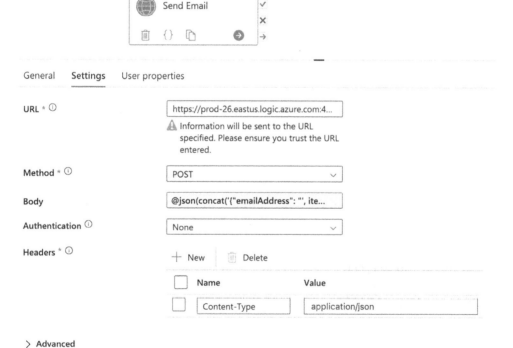

*Figure 2.33: The Send Email activity settings*

5.   Run this pipeline in **Debug** mode and verify that it works. You should have some test email addresses in the EmailRecipients table in order to test your pipeline. You can also verify that the email was sent out by going to the **ADF-Email-LogicApp** UI in the Azure portal and examining the run in the **Overview** pane:

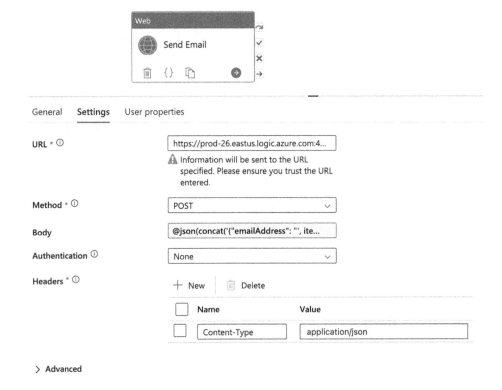

*Figure 2.34: Logic Apps portal view*

6.   We are ready to design the parent pipeline, which will invoke the child pipeline we just tested. For this, clone the pipeline we designed in the *Chaining and branching activities within your pipeline* recipe. Rename your clone pl_orchestration_recipe_5_parent.

7.   In this pipeline, delete the **On Failure** Stored Procedure activity, and instead add an **Execute Pipeline** activity to the canvas. Connect it to the red cross in the **Copy From Blob to Azure SQL** activity.

8.   Configure the **Execute Pipeline** activity as follows:

  •   In the **General** tab, change the name to Send Email On Failure.

  •   In the **Settings** tab, specify the name of the invoked pipeline as pl_orchestration_recipe_5_child.

9. The parent pipeline should already be configured with the incorrect table name in the **Copy** activity sink (we deliberately misconfigured it in order to test the **On Failure** flow). Verify that this is still the case and run the pipeline in **Debug** mode:

*Figure 2.35: Parent pipeline after modifying the On Failure activity*

10. Verify that the email was sent to the recipients.

11. Publish your changes to save them.

## How it works...

In this recipe, we introduced the concept of parent and child pipelines and used the pipeline hierarchy to incorporate the error-handling functionality. This technique offers several benefits:

- It allows us to reuse existing pipelines.
- It makes it easier to design/debug parts of the pipeline separately.
- Finally, it allows users to design pipelines that contain more than 40 activities (Microsoft limits the number of activities per pipeline).

To craft the child pipeline, we started by adding a Lookup activity to retrieve a list of email recipients from the database table. This is a very common use for the Lookup activity: fetching a dataset for subsequent processing. In the configuration, we specified a query for the dataset retrieval: `SELECT * from [dbo].[EmailRecipient]`. We can also use a more sophisticated query to filter the email recipients, or we can retrieve all the data by selecting the **Table** radio button. The ability to specify a query gives users a lot of choice and flexibility in filtering a dataset or using field projections with very little effort.

The list of email recipients was processed by the ForEach activity. We encountered the ForEach activity in the previous recipe. However, inside the ForEach activity, we introduced a new kind of activity: the Web activity, which we configured to invoke a simple logic app. This illustrates the power of the Web activity: it enables the user to invoke external REST APIs without leaving the Data Factory pipeline.

## There's more...

There is another ADF activity that offers the user an option to integrate external APIs into a pipeline: the **Webhook** activity. It has a lot of similarities to the Web activity, with two major differences:

- The Webhook activity always passes an implicit `callBackUri` property to the external service, along with the other parameters you specify in the request body. It expects to receive a response from the invoked web application. If the response is not received within the configurable timeout period, the Webhook activity fails. The Web activity does not have a `callBackUri` property, and, while it does have a timeout period, it is not configurable and is limited to 1 minute.

  This feature of the Webhook activity can be used to control the execution flow of the pipeline – for example, to wait for user input into a web form before proceeding with further steps.

- The Web activity allows users to pass linked services and datasets. This can be used for data movement to a remote endpoint. The Webhook activity does not offer this capability.

## See also

- For more information about the Webhook activity, refer to the Microsoft documentation: `https://learn.microsoft.com/en-us/azure/data-factory/control-flow-webhook-activity`

- If you want to learn how to configure a logic app to send emails using providers other than Gmail, follow this tutorial: `https://learn.microsoft.com/en-us/azure/logic-apps/tutorial-process-email-attachments-workflow`

# Creating event-based pipeline triggers

Often, it is convenient to run a data movement pipeline in response to an event. One of the most common scenarios is triggering a pipeline run in response to the addition or deletion of blobs in a monitored storage account. Azure Data Factory supports this functionality.

In this recipe, we shall create an **event-based trigger** that will invoke a pipeline whenever new backup files are added to a monitored folder. The pipeline will move backup files to another folder.

## Getting ready

- To demonstrate the trigger in action, we shall use the pipeline from the *Using parameters and built-in functions* recipe. If you did not follow the recipe, do so now.

- We shall be creating a pipeline that is similar to the pipeline in the *Using the ForEach and Filter activities* recipe. If you did not follow that recipe, do so now.

- In the storage account (see the *Technical requirements* section), create another container called backups.

- Following *steps 1 to 3* of the *Using the Copy activity with parameterized datasets* recipe, create a new dataset and point it to the backups container. Call it Backups.

- Register Event.Grid Provider with your subscription:

  a.  Go to the portal and look for **Subscription**. Click on your subscription name.

  b.  In the **Subscription** blade, look for **Resource Providers**.

  c.  Find **Microsoft.EventGrid** in the list and hit the **Register** button. Wait until the button turns green (an indication that the registration succeeded).

## How to do it...

First, we create the pipeline that will be triggered when a new blob is created:

1.  Clone the pipeline from the *Using the ForEach and Filter activities* recipe. Rename the clone pl_orchestration_recipe_7_trigger.

2.  Rename the **FilterOnCSV** activity Filter for Backup. In the **Settings** tab, change **Condition** to @endswith(item().name, '.backup'):

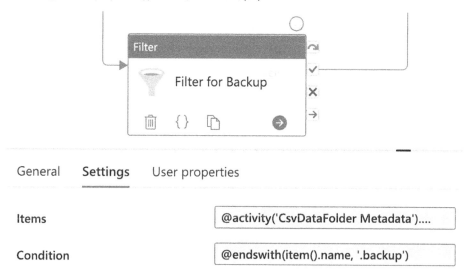

*Figure 2.36: Configuring the Filter for Backup activity*

3.   In the **ForEach** activity, change the **Items** value to `@activity('Filter For Backup').`
     `output.Value` in the **Settings** tab:

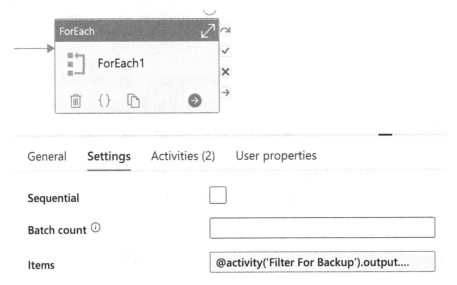

*Figure 2.37: Updating the ForEach activity*

4.   In the **ForEach** activity canvas, remove the **Metadata** and **Stored Procedure** activities.
     Add a **Copy** activity to the **ForEach** canvas and configure it the following way:

     - **Name:** `Copy from Data to Backup`
     - **Source Dataset:** `CsvData` (the parameterized dataset created in the first recipe)
     - **Filename:** `@item().name`
     - **Sink Dataset:** The `Backups` dataset

5.   In the same **ForEach** canvas, add a **Delete** activity. Leave the default name (`Delete1`).
     Configure it in the following way.

     In the **Source** tab, specify **Source Dataset** as `CsvData`. In the **Filename** field, enter `@item().`
     `name`.

In the **Logging Settings** tab, uncheck the **Enable Logging** checkbox.

NOTE

In this tutorial, we do not need to keep track of the files we deleted. However, in a production environment, you will want to evaluate your requirements very carefully: it might be necessary to set up a logging store and enable logging for your Delete activity.

6. Connect the **Copy from Data to Backup** activity to the **Delete1** activity:

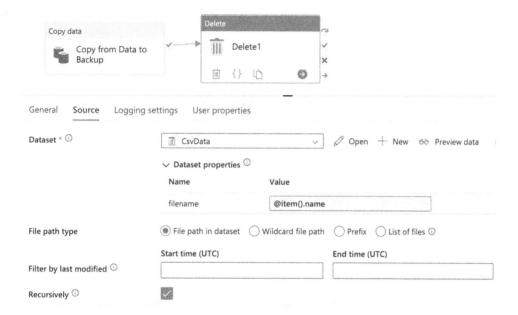

*Figure 2.38: The ForEach activity canvas and configurations for the Delete activity*

7.   Configure the event trigger. In the **Manage** tab, select **Triggers** and click on the **New** button to create a new trigger. In the **New trigger** blade, configure it as shown in *Figure 2.39*. Make sure to select the **Started** radio button in the **Status** section:

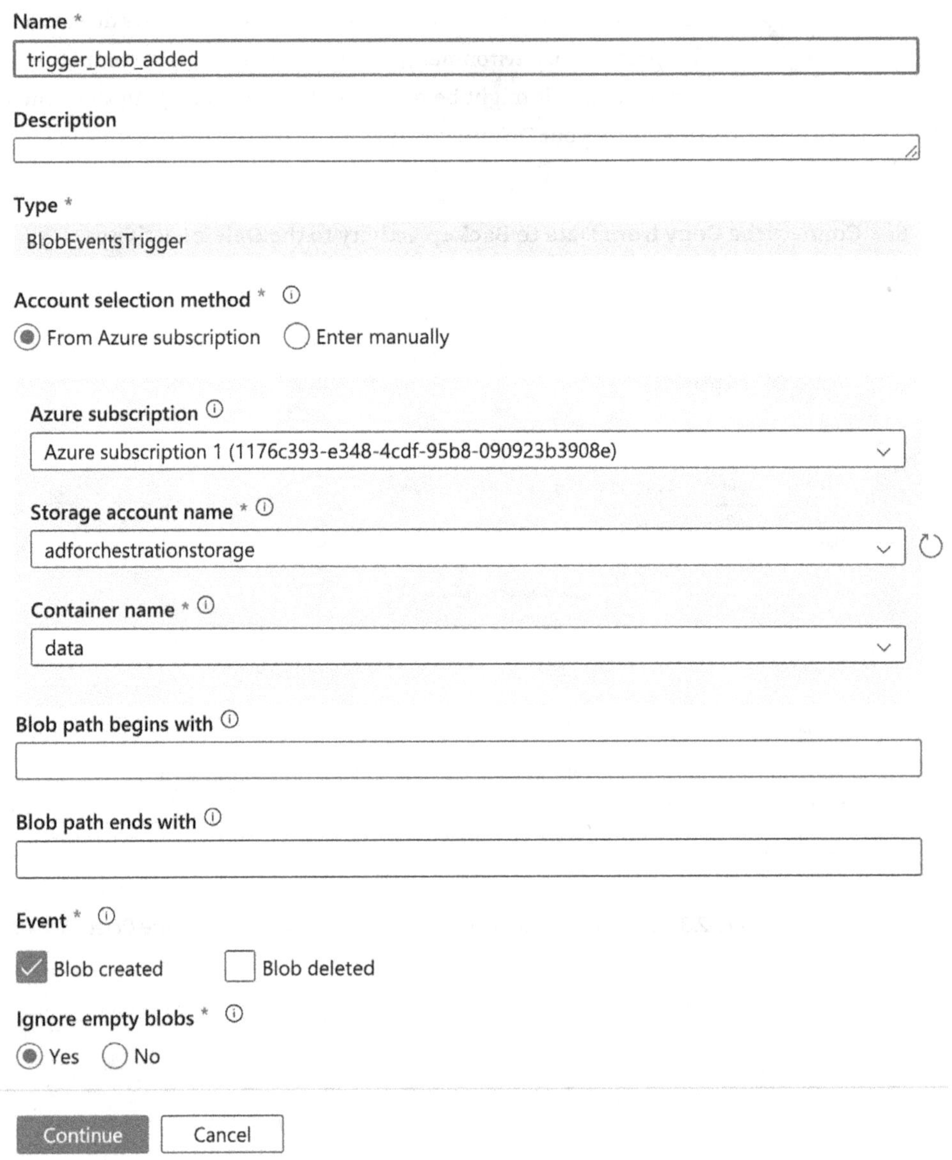

Name *

> trigger_blob_added

Description

Type *

> BlobEventsTrigger

Account selection method * ⓘ

( ● ) From Azure subscription     ( ) Enter manually

Azure subscription ⓘ

> Azure subscription 1 (1176c393-e348-4cdf-95b8-090923b3908e)                    ⌄

Storage account name * ⓘ

> adforchestrationstorage                                                        ⌄   ↻

Container name * ⓘ

> data                                                                           ⌄

Blob path begins with ⓘ

Blob path ends with ⓘ

Event * ⓘ

[✓] Blob created        [ ] Blob deleted

Ignore empty blobs * ⓘ

( ● ) Yes   ( ) No

[ Continue ]   [ Cancel ]

*Figure 2.39: Trigger configuration*

After you select **Continue**, you will see the **Data Preview** blade. Click **OK** to finish creating the trigger.

We have created a pipeline and a trigger, but we did not assign the trigger to the pipeline. Let's do so now.

8. In the **Author** tab, select the pipeline we created in *step 1* (pl_orchestration_recipe_7). Click the **Add Trigger** button and select the **New/Edit** option.

   In the **Add trigger** blade, select the newly created **trigger_blob_added** trigger. Review the configurations in the **Edit trigger** and **Data preview** blades, and hit **OK** to assign the trigger to the pipeline:

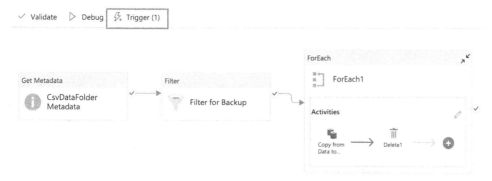

*Figure 2.40: Assigning a trigger to the pipeline*

9. Publish all your changes.
10. Run the pl_orchestration_recipe_1 pipeline. That should create the backup files in the data container. The trigger we designed will invoke the pl_orchestration_recipe_7 pipeline and move the files from the data container to the backups container.

## How it works...

Under the hood, Azure Data Factory uses a service called Event Grid to detect changes in the blob (that is why we had to register the Microsoft.EventGrid provider before starting with the recipe). Event Grid is a Microsoft service that allows you to send events from a source to a destination. Right now, only blob addition and deletion events are integrated.

The trigger configuration options offer us fine-grained control over what files we want to monitor. In the recipe, we specified that the pipeline should be triggered when a new file with the `.backup` extension is created in the data container in our storage account. We can monitor the following, for example:

- **Subfolders within a container**: The trigger will be invoked whenever a file is created within a subfolder. To do this, specify a particular folder within the container by providing values for the container (that is, data) and the folder path(s) in the **blob name begins with** field (that is, `airlines/`).
- `.backup` **files within any container**: To accomplish this, select **all containers** in the container field and leave `.backup` in the **blob name ends with** field.

To find out other ways to configure the trigger to monitor files in a way that fulfills your business needs, please refer to the documentation listed in the *See also* section.

## There's more...

In the recipe, we worked with event triggers. The types of events that ADF supports are currently limited to blob creation and deletion; however, this selection may be expanded in the future. If you need to have your pipeline triggered by another type of event, the way to do it is by creating and configuring another Azure service (for example, a function app) to monitor your events and start a pipeline run when an event of interest happens. You will learn more about ADF integration with other services in *Chapter 7, Extending Azure Data Factory with Logic Apps and Azure Functions*.

ADF also offers two other kinds of triggers: a **scheduled** trigger and a **tumbling window** trigger.

A scheduled trigger invokes the pipeline at regular intervals. ADF offers rich configuration options: apart from recurrence (number of times a minute, a day, a week, and so on), you can configure start and end dates and more granular controls for the hour and minute of the run for a daily trigger, the day of the week for weekly triggers, and the day(s) of the month for monthly triggers.

A tumbling window trigger bears many similarities to the scheduled trigger (it will invoke the pipeline at regular intervals), but it has several features that make it well suited to collecting and processing historical data:

- A tumbling window trigger can have a start date in the past.
- A tumbling window trigger allows pipelines to run concurrently (in parallel), which considerably speeds up historical data processing.

- A tumbling window trigger provides access to two variables:

  ```
  trigger().outputs.WindowStartTime
  trigger().outputs.WindowEndTime
  ```

- Those may be used to easily filter the range of the data being processed, for both past and current data.

A tumbling window trigger also offers the ability to specify a dependency between pipelines. This feature allows users to design complex workflows that reuse existing pipelines.

Both event-based and scheduled triggers have a many-to-many relationship with pipelines: one trigger may be assigned to many pipelines, and a pipeline may have more than one trigger. A tumbling window trigger is pipeline-specific: it may only be assigned to one pipeline, and a pipeline may only have one tumbling window trigger.

## See also

To learn more about all three types of ADF triggers, start here:

- https://learn.microsoft.com/en-us/azure/data-factory/concepts-pipeline-execution-triggers#trigger-execution
- https://learn.microsoft.com/en-us/azure/data-factory/how-to-create-event-trigger?tabs=data-factory
- https://learn.microsoft.com/en-us/azure/data-factory/how-to-create-schedule-trigger?tabs=data-factory
- https://learn.microsoft.com/en-us/azure/data-factory/how-to-create-tumbling-window-trigger?tabs=data-factory%2Cazure-powershell

## Join our community on Discord

Join our community's Discord space for discussions with the authors and other readers:

https://discord.gg/U229qmBmT3

# 3

# Setting Up Synapse Analytics

This chapter will cover the key features and benefits of **Azure Synapse Analytics**. You will learn how to connect and configure Azure Synapse Analytics, load data, build transformation processes, and operate pipelines.

You will navigate Azure Synapse Analytics and learn about its key components and benefits.

You will also learn how to create an **Azure Synapse Analytics workspace**, to load and transform data in Azure Synapse Analytics.

Then, you will learn how to develop, execute, and monitor pipelines using Azure Synapse.

Here is a list of recipes that will be covered in this chapter:

- Creating an Azure Synapse workspace
- Loading data to Azure Synapse Analytics using Azure Data Factory
- Loading data to Azure Synapse using Azure Data Studio
- Loading data to Azure Synapse Analytics using bulk load
- Pausing/resuming an Azure Synapse SQL pool from Azure Data Factory
- Working with Azure Purview using Azure Synapse
- Copying data in Azure Synapse Integrate
- Using a Synapse serverless SQL pool

# Technical requirements

For this chapter, you'll need the following:

- **An active Azure account**: This could be either your business account or a personal account. If you don't have an Azure account yet, you can activate an Azure free-trial license through Microsoft's main website: `https://azure.microsoft.com/en-us/free/`.

- **Azure Data Studio**: The latest version can be found at `https://learn.microsoft.com/en-us/sql/azure-data-studio/download-azure-data-studio`.

- **GitHub repository**: You can download the dataset from the book's GitHub repository or you may use your own one: `https://github.com/PacktPublishing/Azure-Data-Factory-Cookbook-Second-Edition/tree/main/Chapter03`.

# Creating an Azure Synapse workspace

Azure Synapse is a combination of capabilities that brings together data integration, SQL analytics that you frequently pair with something such as Power BI, and also Spark for big data processing into a single service for building enterprise analytics solutions. In this recipe, you will learn how to create a new Azure Synapse workspace and migrate your Azure SQL data warehouse into it.

## Getting ready

You need to have an Azure subscription and an Azure resource group.

## How to do it...

To create an Azure Synapse workspace, use the following steps:

1. In the Azure portal, click on **Create new resource**, search for **Azure Synapse Analytics**, and click create. Select your subscription and resource group, enter a new workspace name, and select a region:

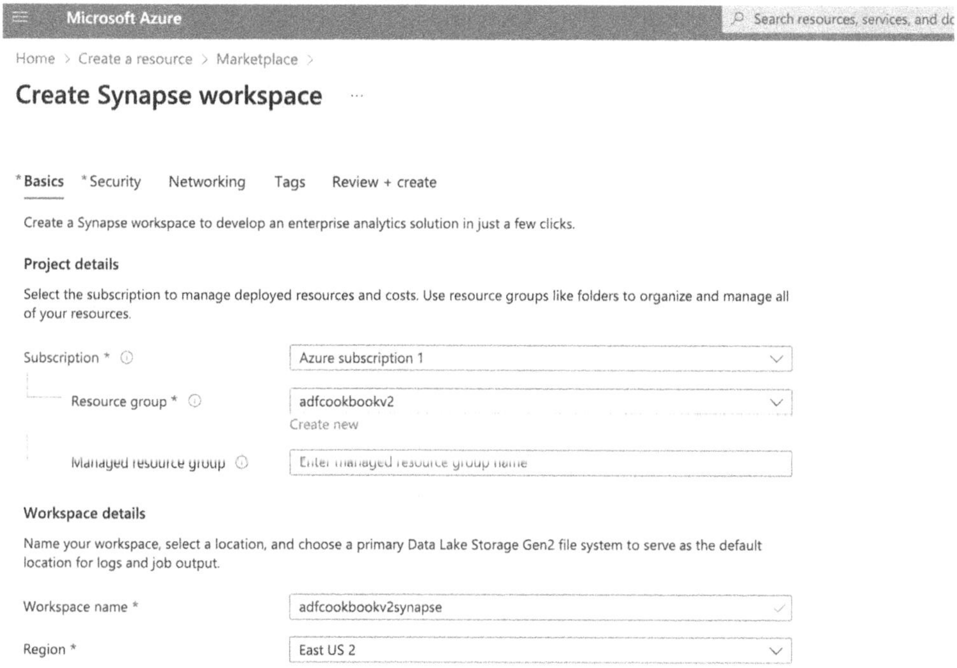

*Figure 3.1: Creating an Azure Synapse workspace*

2.   Enter a new workspace name and select a region. You can either create a new **Azure Data Lake Storage Gen2** account and filename or use existing ones. If you choose to create a new storage account, data access will be automatically granted using the Storage Blob Data Contributor role:

**Workspace details**

Name your workspace, select a location, and choose a primary Data Lake Storage Gen2 file system to serve as the default location for logs and job output.

| | |
|---|---|
| Workspace name * | adfcookbookv2synapse |
| Region * | East US 2 |
| Select Data Lake Storage Gen2 * ⓘ | ◉ From subscription　◯ Manually via URL |
|      Account name * ⓘ | adfcookbookv2 |
| | Create new |
|      File system name * | (New) adfcookbookv2synapsefs |
| | Create new |

☑ Assign myself the Storage Blob Data Contributor role on the Data Lake Storage Gen2 account to interactively query it in the workspace.

ⓘ We will automatically grant the workspace identity data access to the specified Data Lake Storage Gen2 account, using the Storage Blob Data Contributor role. To enable other users to use this storage account after you create your workspace, perform these tasks:

- Assign other users to the **Contributor** role on workspace
- Assign other users the appropriate Synapse RBAC roles using Synapse Studio
- Assign yourself and other users to the **Storage Blob Data Contributor** role on the storage account

Learn more

[ Review + create ]　　[ < Previous ]　　[ Next: Security > ]

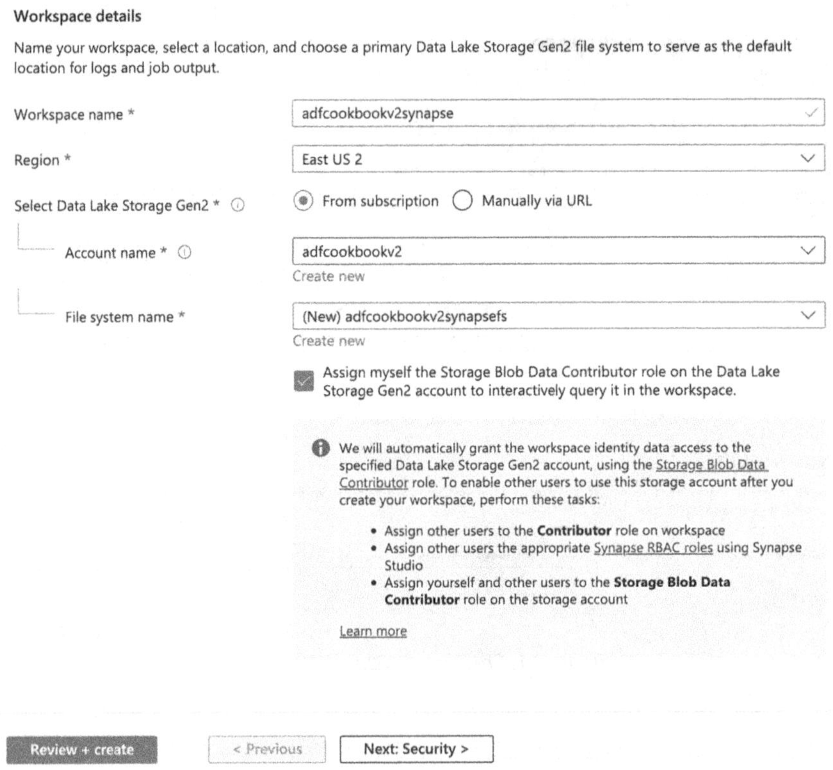

*Figure 3.2: Creating an Azure Synapse workspace – new storage account*

3.   Enter an admin username and password for the Synapse workspace. This could be used to connect to a SQL pool endpoint. Then, click **Review + create**, then **Create**:

## Create Synapse workspace  ···

Configure security options for your workspace.

### Authentication

Choose the authentication method for access to workspace resources such as SQL pools. The authentication method can be changed later on. Learn more ✍

| | |
|---|---|
| Authentication method ⓘ | ● Use both local and Azure Active Directory (Azure AD) authentication |
| | ○ Use only Azure Active Directory (Azure AD) authentication |
| SQL Server admin login * ⓘ | synapseadmin ✓ |
| SQL Password ⓘ | •••••••• ✓ |
| Confirm password | •••••••• ✓ |

### System assigned managed identity permission

Select to grant the workspace network access to the Data Lake Storage Gen2 account using the workspace system identity. Learn more ✍

☐ Allow network access to Data Lake Storage Gen2 account. ⓘ

🛈 The selected Data Lake Storage Gen2 account does not restrict network access using any network access rules, or you selected a storage account manually via URL under Basics tab. Learn more ✍

### Workspace encryption

⚠ Double encryption configuration cannot be changed after opting into using a customer-managed key at the time of

| Review + create | < Previous | Next: Networking > |

*Figure 3.3: Creating an Azure Synapse workspace – security*

The deployment process will take some time, but after it has succeeded, you will get a notification:

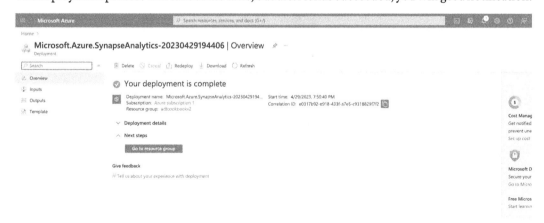

*Figure 3.4: Creating an Azure Synapse workspace – notification on successful deployment*

Once you receive the notification, you have successfully created an Azure Synapse workspace.

## There's more...

If you open the Azure Synapse Analytics workspace created above and go to your SQL pools, you will only see the **Built-in SQL pool**. This is created automatically with the Azure Synapse workspace. But you can migrate your existing Azure Synapse Analytics pool into the workspace to have all the needed resources in one place or create a new SQL pool:

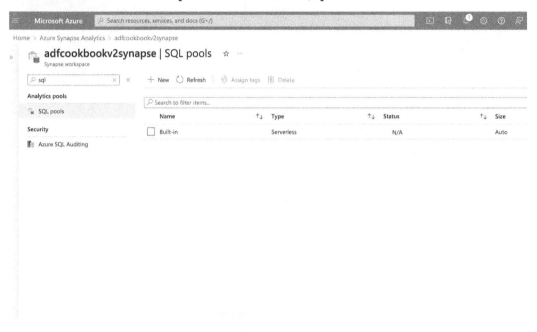

*Figure 3.5: Creating an Azure Synapse workspace – Built-in created automatically*

We will create a new SQL pool. Here is a list of steps that you can follow to create a SQL pool:

1. Click **New** in the SQL Pools menu and enter a SQL pool name – for example, `adfcookbookv2sqlpool`:

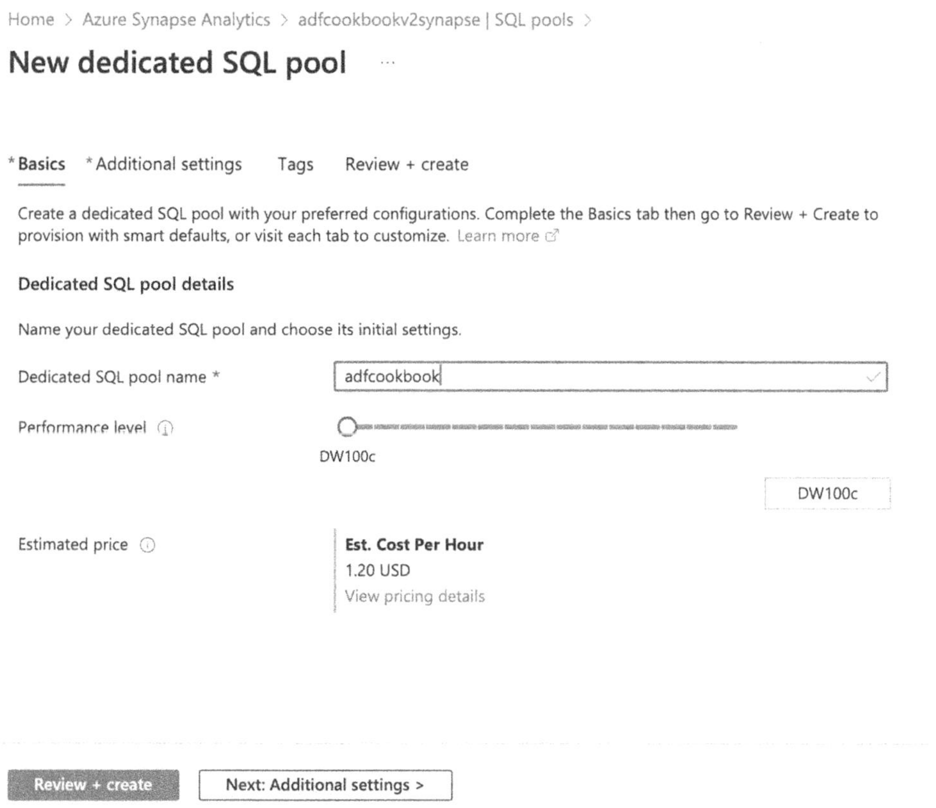

Home > Azure Synapse Analytics > adfcookbookv2synapse | SQL pools >

## New dedicated SQL pool   ⋯

\* **Basics**    \* Additional settings     Tags     Review + create

Create a dedicated SQL pool with your preferred configurations. Complete the Basics tab then go to Review + Create to provision with smart defaults, or visit each tab to customize. Learn more ⬀

### Dedicated SQL pool details

Name your dedicated SQL pool and choose its initial settings.

| | |
|---|---|
| Dedicated SQL pool name * | adfcookbook |
| Performance level ⓘ | |
| | DW100c |
| | DW100c |
| Estimated price ⓘ | **Est. Cost Per Hour**<br>1.20 USD<br>View pricing details |

Review + create     Next: Additional settings >

*Figure 3.6: Creating an Azure Synapse Analytics instance – SQL pool*

2. Choose a performance level (set this to the lowest possible level, DW100c, for this recipe to save costs).

3. In **Additional settings**, we will keep the **None** setting for existing data usage as we will upload our own data to Synapse Analytics.

4. Click **Review + create**, then **Create**. When the deployment process has succeeded, you will get a notification:

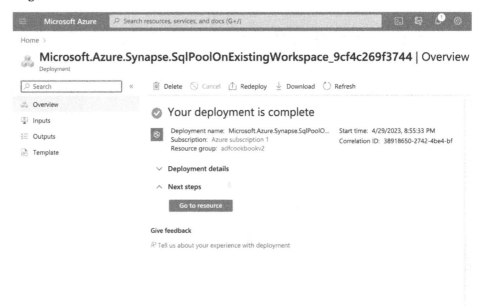

*Figure 3.7: Creating an Azure Synapse Analytics SQL pool instance – notification on successful deployment*

5. Your Azure Synapse Analytics account is billed hourly according to the chosen performance level. So, the best practice is to pause your Azure Synapse Analytics resource when it is not being used to avoid unwanted charges. To do this, simply go to the resource and click **Pause**:

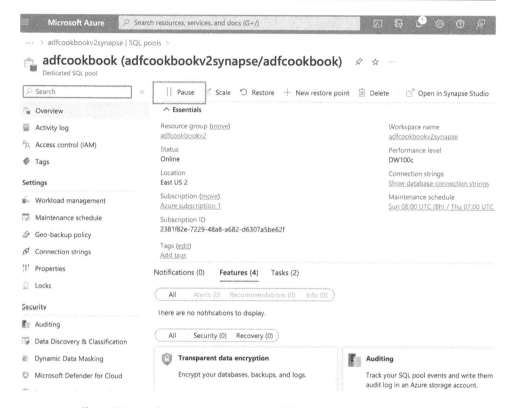

*Figure 3.8: Creating an Azure Synapse Analytics SQL pool instance-- Pause*

Let's learn about loading data to Azure Synapse in the next recipe.

# Loading data to Azure Synapse Analytics using Azure Data Factory

In this recipe, we will look further at how to load data into **Azure Synapse Analytics** using **Azure Data Factory**.

## Getting ready

Before we start, please ensure that you have created a linked service to a Blob storage container and know how to create a Copy Data statement in **Azure Data Factory**. Please refer to *Chapter 2, Orchestration and Control Flow*, for guidelines on how to do that.

# How to do it...

To load data into Azure Synapse Analytics using Azure Data Factory, use the following steps:

1.  Before we create a Copy Data statement in Azure Data Factory, we need to create a new table in Azure Synapse Analytics. To do that, **open Synapse Studio**, go to the **Data** tab on the left side of your screen, and click **New SQL script** on a schema for which you want to create a new table, then click **New table**:

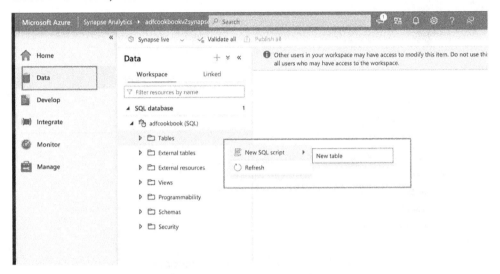

*Figure 3.9: Creating a new table in Azure Synapse Analytics*

2.  Run the following script in the SQL editor and click **Run**:

```
CREATE TABLE [dbo].[Planes]
(
    [Name] varchar(100) NOT NULL,
    [IATA_code] varchar(10) NULL,
    [ICAO_code] varchar(10) NULL
)
```

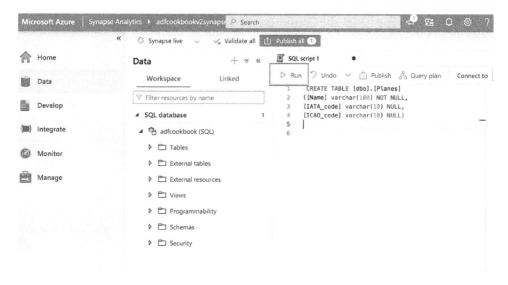

*Figure 3.10: Creating a new table in Azure Synapse Analytics*

3. Go to the home page of Azure Data Factory and select the Ingest tile to start the Copy Data tool, then select the linked service to **Azure Blob storage** or create a new one (refer to *Chapter 2, Orchestration and Control Flow*, if you're facing issues with doing this):

*Figure 3.11: Launching the Copy Data tool*

4. Then we select the **Built-in** copy task, and in the **Source** section, choose the file or folder in Azure Blob storage:

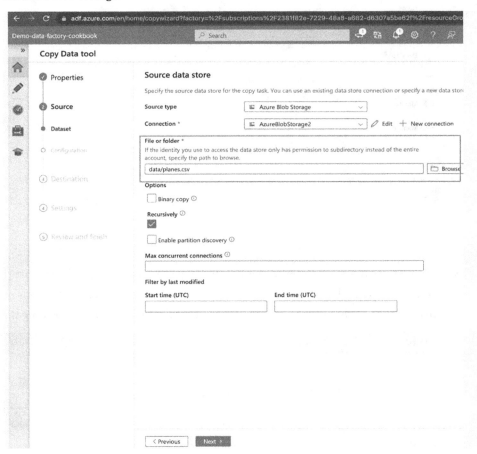

*Figure 3.12: Azure Data Factory Copy Data – Choose the input file*

5.  Usually, file format settings are detected automatically but you can alter these settings:

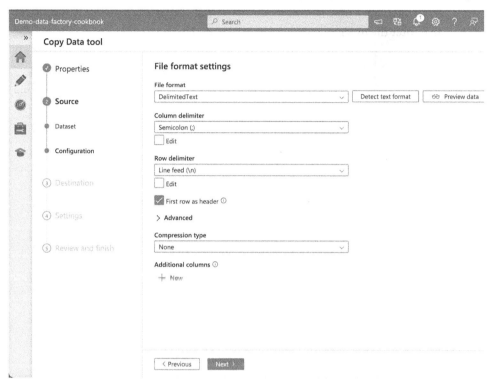

*Figure 3.13: Azure Data Factory Copy Data – File format settings*

6.  In the **Destination** section, you need to choose the linked service to Azure Synapse Analytics or create a new one. You can choose **SQL authentication** for **Authentication type** and enter the username and password created in the previous recipe:

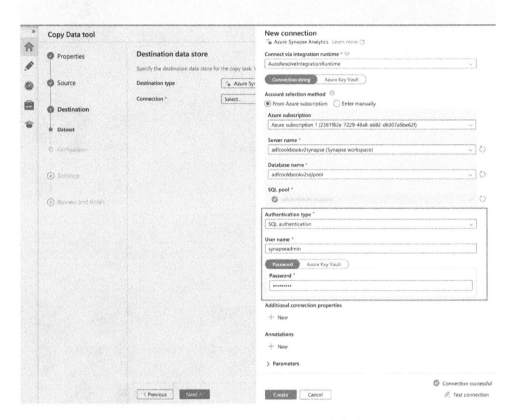

*Figure 3.14: Azure Data Factory Copy Data – linked service*

7.  In **Destination,** choose the table in Azure Synapse Analytics and choose how the source and destination columns are mapped. Click **Next**. Using the Azure Data Factory Copy Data tool doesn't require you to have equally named fields in your dataset. In **Additional settings**, uncheck **Enable staging**, and for the copy method, select **Bulk import**. Then, click **Next** | **Next** | **Finish**.

*Figure 3.15: Azure Data Factory Copy Data – destination table*

8.  When the pipeline is finished, you can debug it and see that the data appears in Azure Synapse Analytics:

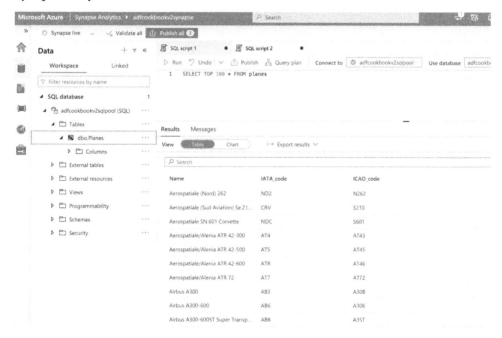

*Figure 3.16: Checking data has appeared in Azure Synapse Analytics*

With that, you have successfully loaded data into Azure Synapse Analytics using Azure Data Factory.

## How it works...

While migrating your data warehouse to Azure Synapse Analytics, configuring automatic pipelines in Azure Data Factory to copy data will save you a lot of time. The Copy Data tool can connect to various dataset types using a service principal or managed identity and push the data into Azure Synapse Analytics.

## There's more...

For loading huge amounts of data, it is better to enable staging. To do this, you need to specify the staging account linked service and storage path:

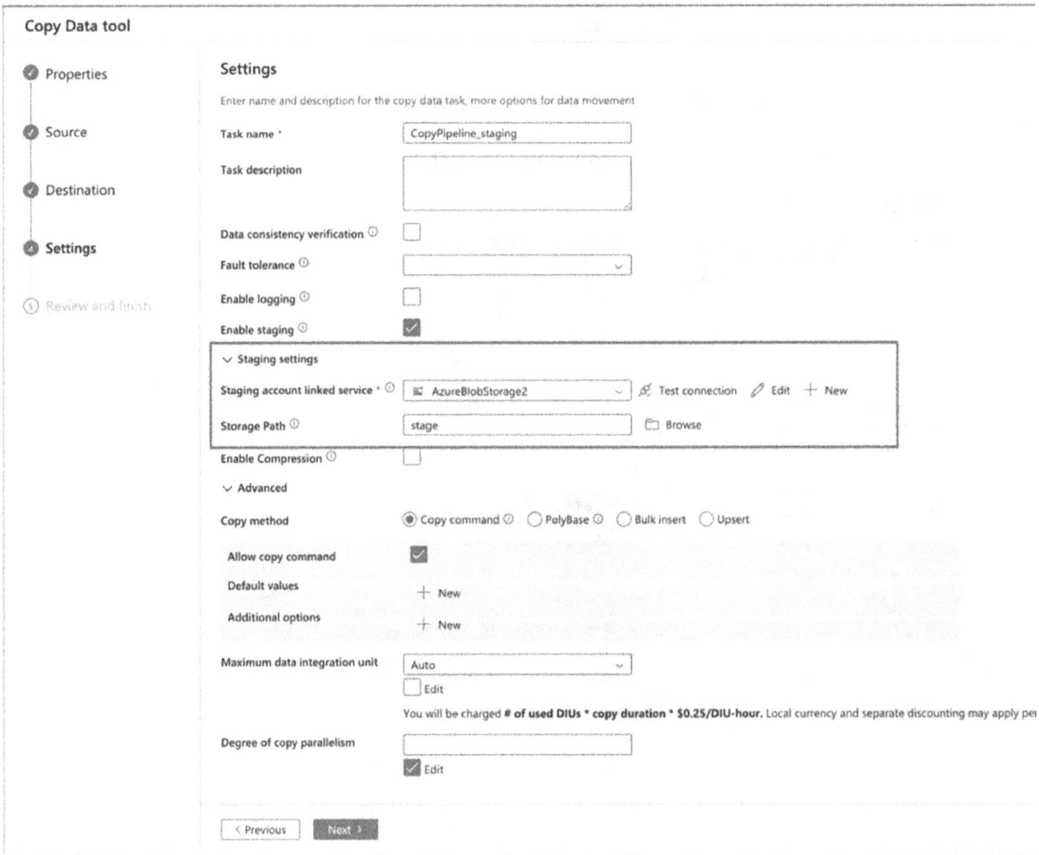

*Figure 3.17: Azure Data Factory Copy data – enabling staging*

When the data loading is done, the temporary data in Blob storage will be automatically deleted.

# Loading data to Azure Synapse Analytics using Azure Data Studio

Azure Data Studio is a cross-platform database tool for data professionals who use on-premises and cloud data platforms on Windows, macOS, and Linux. Azure Data Studio offers a modern editor experience with IntelliSense, code snippets, source control integration, and an integrated terminal. It's engineered with the data platform user in mind, with the built-in charting of query result sets and customizable dashboards.

In this recipe, we are going to configure Azure Data Studio and load data into Azure Synapse Analytics from an external resource.

## Getting ready

You need to have Azure Data Studio installed on your computer.

You need to upload the dataset from this book's GitHub repository to the container. Then, you need to generate shared access signatures to connect blobs via Azure Synapse Analytics.

You can download the dataset from the book's GitHub repository, or you can use your own: `https://github.com/PacktPublishing/Azure-Data-Factory-Cookbook-Second-Edition/tree/main/Chapter03`.

# How to do it...

Open Azure Data Studio. On the welcome page, click on **Create a connection**:

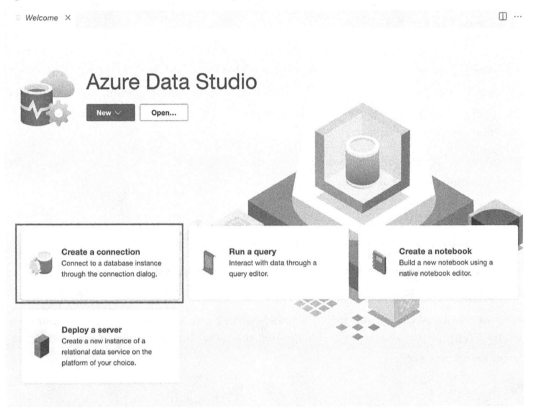

*Figure 3.18: Azure Data Studio – Creating a connection*

You'll be prompted with a form for connection details. Go to **Browse** and choose **Azure**. You need to connect an Azure account. Click on **Sign in to Azure...** and then **Add Account**.

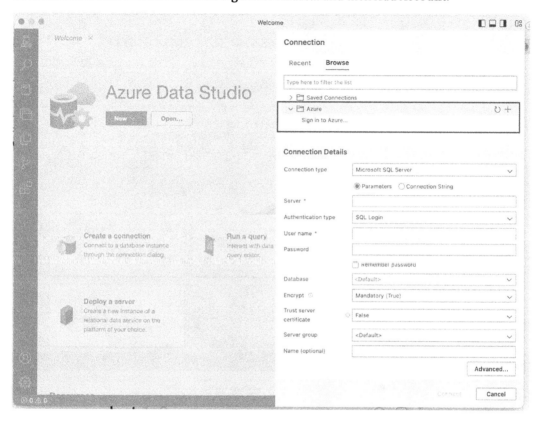

*Figure 3.19: Azure Data Studio – Creating a connection*

Once an account is added, select from the list of servers the Azure Synapse SQL pool created in the previous recipe, choose **SQL authentication** for **Authentication type**, and enter the username and password created in the previous recipe:

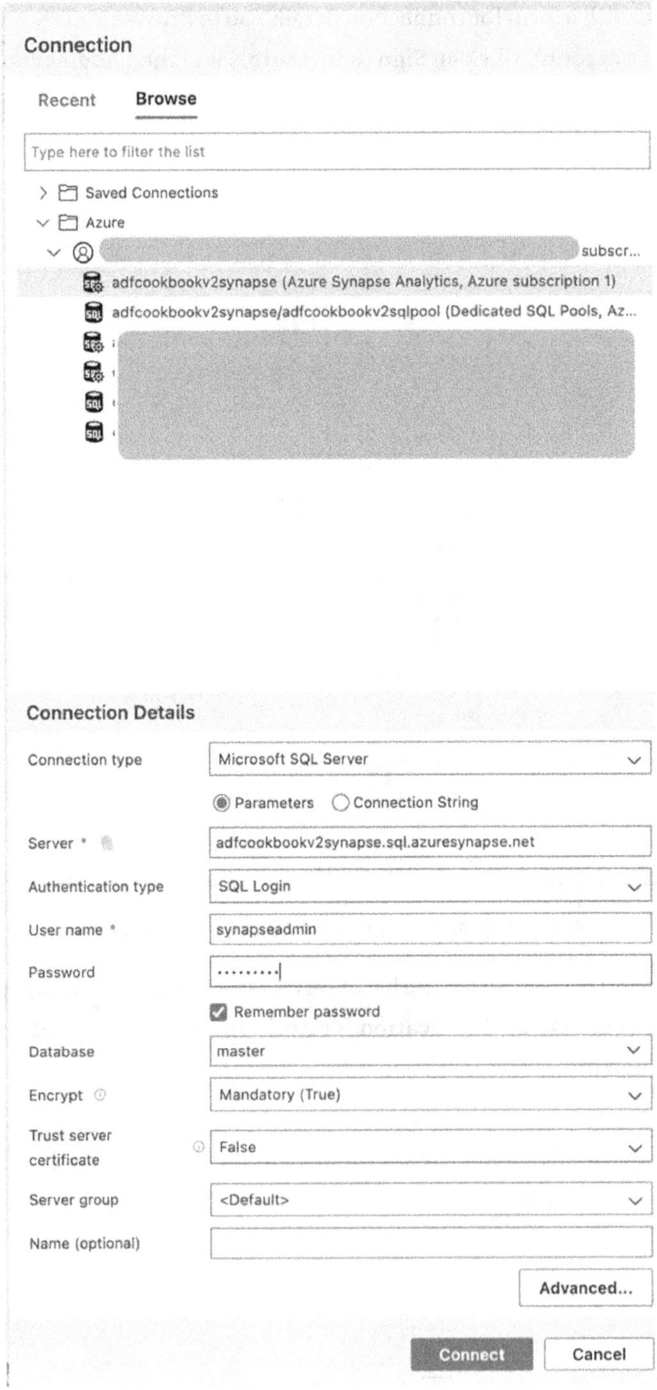

*Figure 3.20: Azure Data Studio – creating a connection*

1.  Loading data into Azure Synapse Analytics is a rather memory-consuming operation. The best practice is to create a new user that will be used for loading data as you can also configure the resource class for maximum memory allocation. **Resource class** refers to the classification or categorization of system resources, such as CPU and memory, to optimize their allocation for different workloads. By assigning a specific resource class to the user responsible for data loading, you gain the flexibility to tailor the allocation of system resources according to the unique demands of this operation.

2.  You need to select **New Query**, enter the following script, and click **Execute**:

```
CREATE LOGIN adfuser WITH PASSWORD = 'ADF3password';
CREATE USER adfuser FOR LOGIN adfuser;
GRANT CONTROL ON DATABASE::[adfcookbookch1devsqldb] to adfuser;
EXEC sp_addrolemember 'staticrc10', 'adfuser';
```

3.  Reconnect to Azure Synapse Analytics as adfuser using the password created in the previous step.

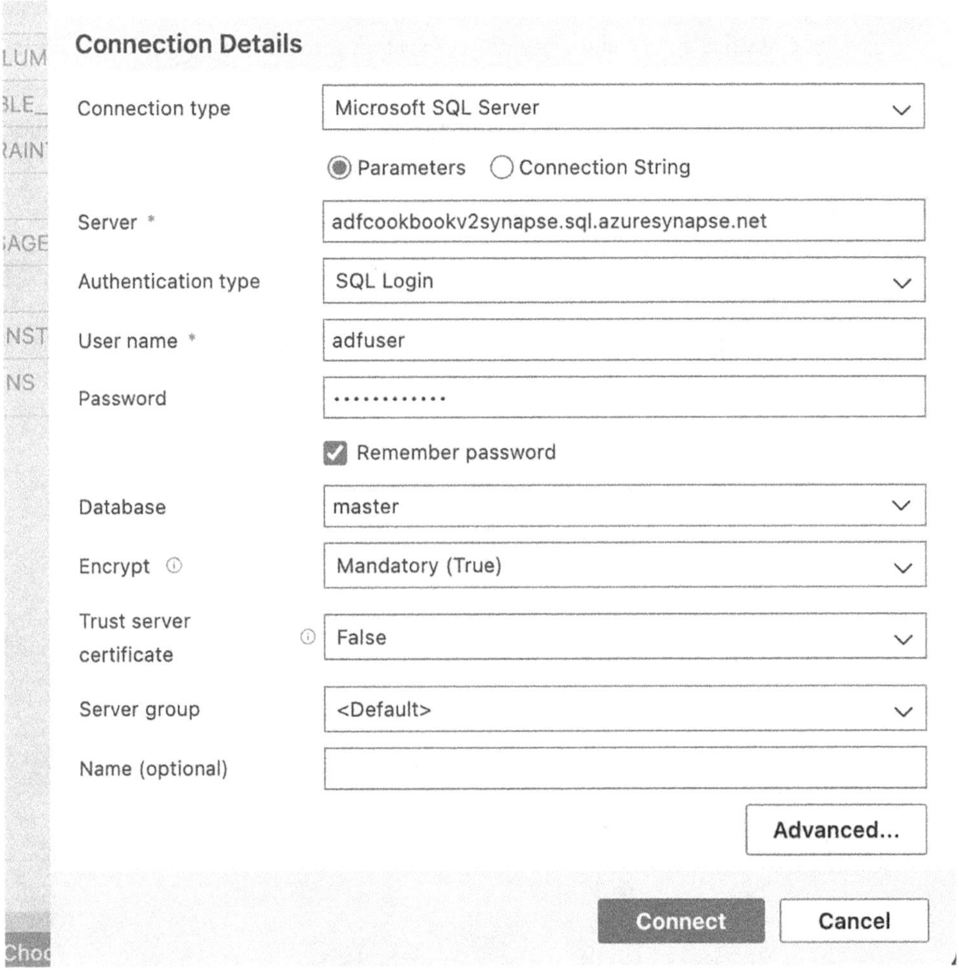

*Figure 3.21: Azure Data Studio – editing connection details*

4.  Create tables that we'll use to load data to Azure Synapse Analytics. This is the SQL script for table creation:

```
CREATE TABLE [dbo].[Countries]
([Name] varchar(50) NOT NULL,
[iso_code] varchar(50) NULL)

CREATE TABLE [dbo].[Airlines]
([Airline_ID] varchar(50) NOT NULL,
```

```
[Name] varchar(50) NULL,
[IATA] varchar(10) NULL,
[Country] varchar(50) NULL)
```

5.  You can load data into created tables using the following SQL script. Please ensure that you've replaced the Blob storage path and **Shared Access Signature (SAS)** secret with your own credentials:

```
COPY INTO dbo.[Countries] FROM 'https://adfcookbookv2.blob.core.
windows.net/data/countries.csv'
WITH
(
CREDENTIAL=(IDENTITY= 'Shared Access Signature', SECRET='?sv=2022-
11-02&ss=bfqt&srt=sco&sp=rwdlacupyx&se=2023-04-30T17:31:49Z&st=2023-
04-30T09:31:49Z&spr=https&sig=9gvX42ymia12CRJ4MOailXsR1aQECg-
I79KBqlOqgJwg%3D'),
FIELDTERMINATOR=','
)
COPY INTO dbo.[Airlines] FROM 'https://adfcookbookv2.blob.core.
windows.net/data/airlines.csv'
WITH
(
CREDENTIAL=(IDENTITY= 'Shared Access Signature', SECRET='?sv=2022-
11-02&ss=bfqt&srt=sco&sp=rwdlacupyx&se=2023-04-30T17:31:49Z&st=2023-
04-30T09:31:49Z&spr=https&sig=9gvX42ymia12CRJ4MOailXsR1aQECg-
I79KBqlOqgJwg%3D'),
FIELDTERMINATOR=','
)
```

## How it works...

The CREATE LOGIN command allows you to create a login with a specified password. The CREATE USER command allows you to create a new user for the created login. The GRANT CONTROL ON DATABASE command allows you to provide access to the database for a specified user. sp_addrolemember is a stored procedure that adds a user to a particular role. CREATE TABLE is a command for creating a new table in the SQL database with specified fields. The COPY INTO command allows you to copy data from the specified file into the created table. You also need to specify the credentials for accessing the file. In this case, the blob is accessed via **Shared Access Signature** with a generated secret.

## There's more...

If you are loading huge amounts of data, that is, migrating your database into the cloud, it would be helpful to use a clustered `columnstore` index in your tables. Even when using that operation, the load could take a lot of time. One more tip is to show the status of the load using the following script:

```
SELECT  t1.[request_id]
,       t1.[status]
,       t1.resource_class
,       t1.command
,       sum(bytes_processed) AS bytes_processed
,       sum(rows_processed) AS rows_processed
FROM    sys.dm_pdw_exec_requests t1
            JOIN sys.dm_pdw_dms_workers t2
                ON t1.[request_id] = t2.request_id
WHERE [label] = 'COPY : Load [dbo].[Countries] - Flights dataset' OR
    [label] = 'COPY : Load [dbo].[Airlines] - Flights dataset'
and session_id <> session_id() and type = 'WRITER'
GROUP BY t1.[request_id]
,       t1.[status]
,       t1.resource_class
,       t1.command;
```

This query returns a table that shows the status of each current `WRITER` request to the database from the system tables.

# Loading data to Azure Synapse Analytics using bulk load

Azure Synapse workspaces allow users to simply load data into a SQL pool with minimal mouse clicks. In this recipe, you will learn how to do this.

## Getting ready

You need to have created an Azure Synapse workspace and a SQL pool, and Azure Data Lake Storage Gen2 should be linked to that workspace. The Customers dataset (or any other dataset) should be uploaded to your storage.

# How to do it...

1. Open the Azure Synapse workspace (also known as **Synapse Studio**).

2. Click on the **Data** tab on the left side of your screen:

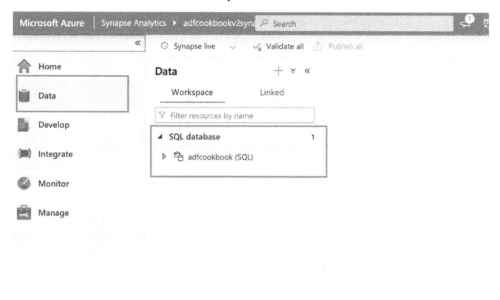

*Figure 3.22: Creating a new SQL script table in the Synapse Analytics workspace*

3. Expand your SQL pool and click on **Actions** to the right of **Tables**. Select **New SQL script** | **New table**:

*Figure 3.23 – Creating a new SQL script table in the Synapse Analytics workspace*

4.  An automatically generated SQL query for a new table will be shown on the canvas. Replace it with the following script:

```
CREATE TABLE [dbo].[Customer]
(
    [CustomerKey] [int]  NOT NULL,
    [CustomerID] [int]  NOT NULL,
    [Customer] [nvarchar](100)  NOT NULL,
    [BillToCustomer] [nvarchar](100)  NOT NULL,
    [Category] [nvarchar](50)  NOT NULL,
    [BuyingGroup] [nvarchar](50)  NOT NULL,
    [PrimaryContact] [nvarchar](50)  NOT NULL,
    [PostalCode] [nvarchar](10)  NOT NULL,
    [ValidFrom] [datetime2](7)  NOT NULL,
    [ValidTo] [datetime2](7)  NOT NULL,
    [LineageKey] [int]  NOT NULL)
WITH
(
        DISTRIBUTION = ROUND_ROBIN,
    CLUSTERED COLUMNSTORE INDEX)
GO
```

5.  Click on **Run**. If you click on **Actions** to the right of **Tables** and choose **Refresh**, you can ensure that a new table has been created:

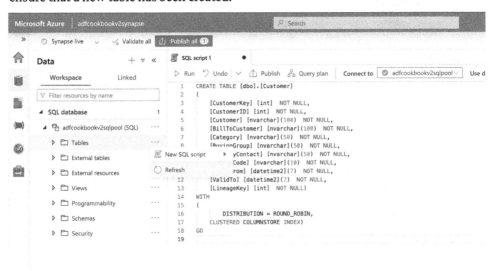

*Figure 3.24: Refreshing the list of tables in an Azure Synapse SQL pool*

6. Go to the **Manage** tab on the left side of your screen, then click on **Linked services** and you'll see all the storage accounts and datasets that are linked to your Synapse workspace:

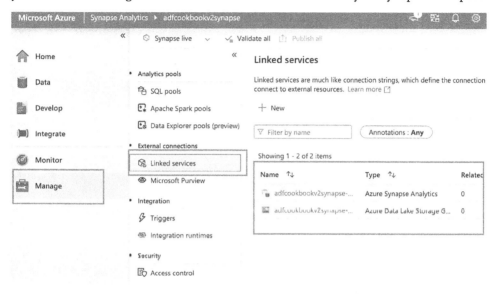

*Figure 3.25: Linked services in Synapse Analytics*

7. Choose the storage in which you uploaded the needed dataset (the storage account should have a hierarchy set in order to be linked).

8. Right-click on the file you are going to load into the Azure SQL pool and select **New SQL script | Bulk load**:

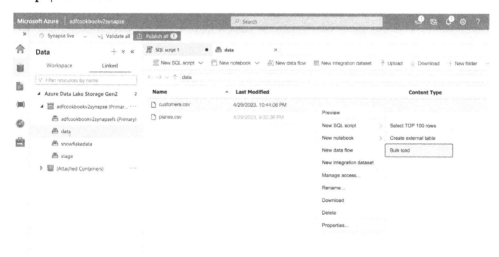

*Figure 3.26: Creating a new SQL script bulk load in the Synapse Analytics workspace*

In the opened **Bulk load** menu, make sure all properties are defined correctly and click **Continue:**

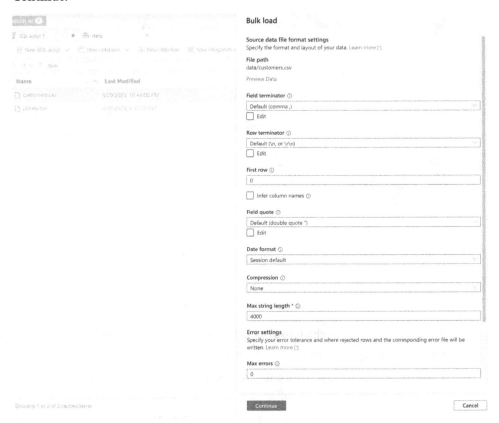

*Figure 3.27: Bulk load settings in the Synapse Analytics workspace*

9. Specify the SQL pool and the target table in which you are going to upload data:

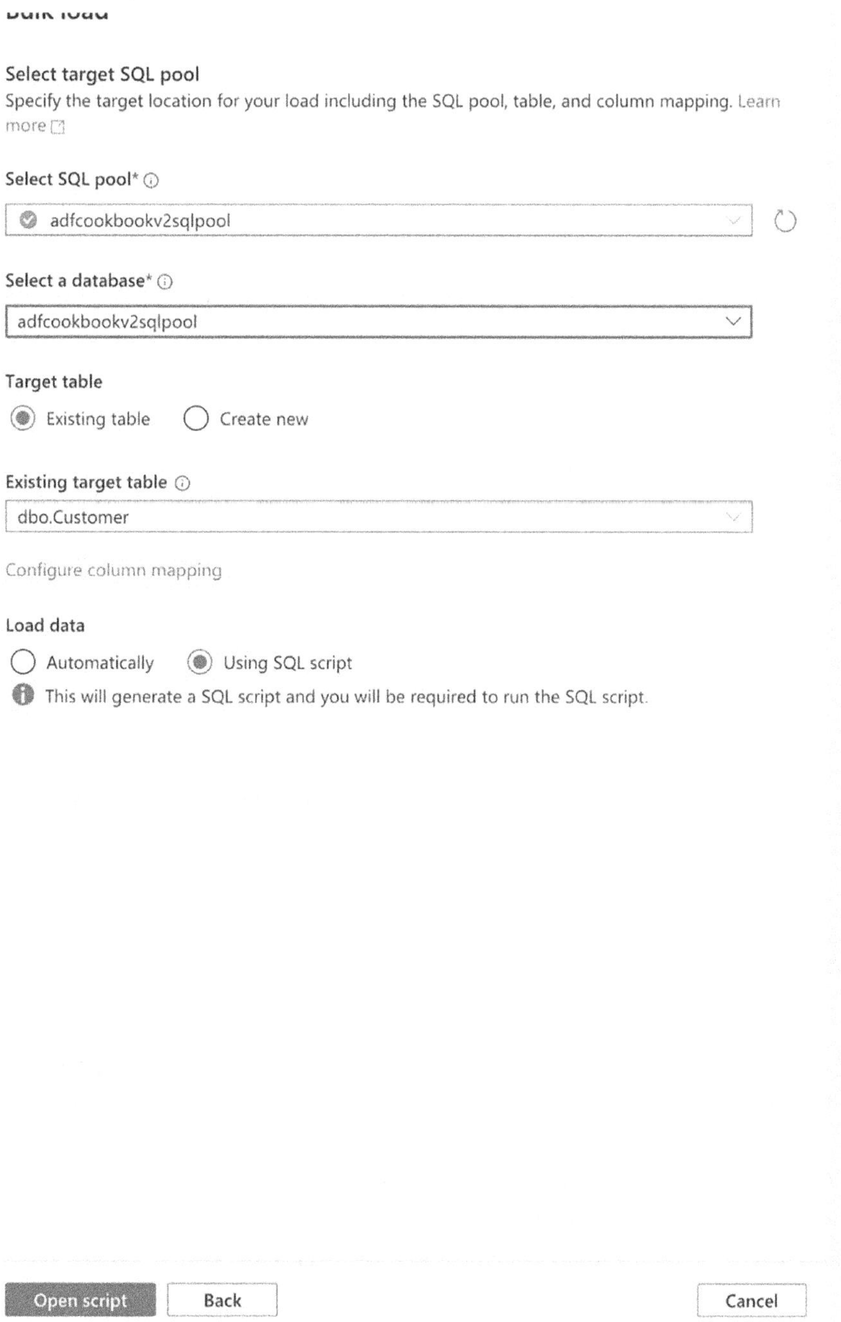

*Figure 3.28: Specifying the target SQL pool in the Synapse Analytics workspace*

10. Click **Open Script** and then **run** the script and you'll see the first 100 rows of the copied data:

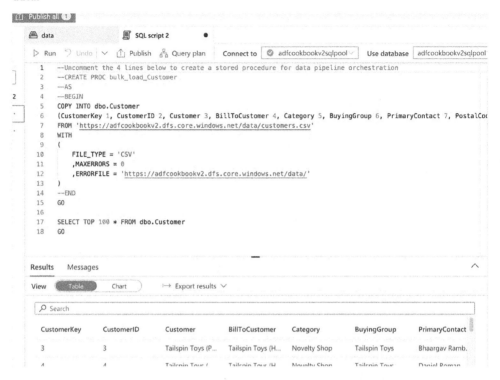

*Figure 3.29: Bulk loading a running script and previewing data in the Synapse Analytics workspace*

11. Publish the script.

## How it works...

The Data Integration tool in the Azure Synapse workspace works like Azure Data Factory but it is built into the workspace and gives users some advantages over Data Factory. You don't need to set up connections and linked services as they are already configured within one Synapse workspace. Furthermore, the Synapse Data Integration tool has the ability to create data pipelines and generate automatic SQL or basic operations, such as creating tables, dropping tables, and copying and loading data. Note that using the bulk load capability, you can load data not only from CSV but also from Parquet file formats, which is rather useful in dealing with data lakes.

# Pausing/resuming an Azure Synapse SQL pool from Azure Data Factory

In this recipe, you will create a new Azure Data Factory pipeline that allows you to automatically pause and resume your Synapse dedicated SQL pool.

## Getting ready

You need access to an Azure Synapse workspace with a dedicated SQL pool for this recipe. Make sure your dedicated SQL pool is paused before starting this recipe as you are going to resume it automatically using Azure Data Factory pipeline.

## How to do it...

We shall start by designing a pipeline to resume a Synapse SQL pool with an Azure Data Factory pipeline, and then create a pipeline to pause it:

1.  Go to your Azure Data Factory studio, open the **Author** section, and create a new pipeline. In the **Activities** section, choose **Web**. Rename the activity and the pipeline:

*Figure 3.30: Azure Data Factory pipeline – Web activity*

Go to the **Settings** tab, then copy and paste the following text into the **URL** textbox:

```
https://management.azure.com/subscriptions/{subscription-id}/
resourceGroups/{resource-group-name}/providers/Microsoft.Synapse/
workspaces/{workspace-name}/sqlPools/{database-name}/resume?api-
version= 2021-06-01
```

2.  As you can see, there are some parameters that you need to change for your values: {subscription-id}, {resource-group-name}, {server-name}, and {database-name}. You can find these values in the **Overview** section of your **dedicated SQL pool**:

    a.  {subscription-id} for **Subscription ID**

    b.  {resource-group-name} for **Resource group**

    c.  {server-name} is your Azure Synapse **Workspace name**

    d.  {database-name} is the name of the SQL pool:

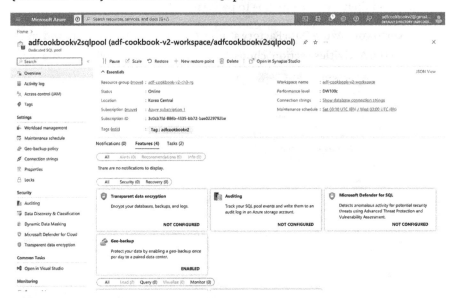

*Figure 3.31: Synapse dedicated SQL pool Overview blade*

If you have the same names as in the preceding screenshot, the text should look like this:

```
https://management.azure.com/subscriptions/3c0cb7fd-886b-4335-
bb72-bae0229792be/resourceGroups/adf-cookbook-v2-ch3-rg/providers/
Microsoft.Synapse/workspaces/adf-cookbook-v2-workspace/sqlPools/
adfcookbookv2sqlpool/resume?api-version=2021-06-01
```

For **Method**, choose **POST**, and for **Body**, type { }. Change the **Authentication** to **System Assigned Managed Identity**, and for **Resource**, type `https://management.core.windows.net`:

*Figure 3.32: Azure Data Factory – Web activity settings*

3.   The next thing to do is to grant permissions to your Azure Data Factory managed identity on your dedicated SQL pool. To do this, navigate to the dedicated SQL pool in the Azure portal, and go to the **Access control (IAM)** tab. Click on the plus sign to add a new role assignment. In the opened blade, select the **Privileged administrator roles** tab, then click on the **Contributor** role and then on the **Next** button.

*Figure 3.33: Assign a Contributor role to your ADF managed identity on your dedi-
cated SQL pool*

On the next page, select **Managed Identity,** and find your Data Factory in the blade on
the right. Press **Select** and your role will be assigned.

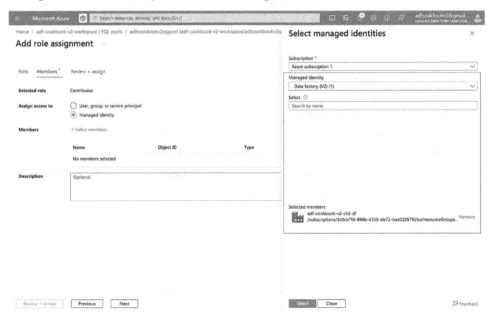

*Figure 3.34: Assign role to selected managed identity*

4. Switch back to **Azure Data Factory Studio**, click **Publish all** to save all the changes to your pipeline, and click **Debug**.

5. If you go to your Azure Synapse SQL pool listings in Synapse Studio, you'll see that the status has changed to **Resuming**. It usually takes a minute or two to fully resume a dedicated SQL pool. Once it is resumed, the status will change to **Online**.

6. Now you can easily create a pipeline for auto-pausing your Synapse SQL pool. You just need to clone the pipeline we created in previous steps and change the word in the URL text from resume to pause:

```
https://management.azure.com/subscriptions/{subscription-id}/
resourceGroups/{resource-group-name}/providers/Microsoft.Synapse/
workspaces/{workspace-name}/sqlPools/{database-name}/pause?api-
version=2021-06-01
```

In our case, the URL text will look like this:

```
https://management.azure.com/subscriptions/3c0cb7fd-886b-4335-
bb72-bae0229792be/resourceGroups/adf-cookbook-v2-ch3-rg/providers/
Microsoft.Synapse/workspaces/adf-cookbook-v2-workspace/sqlPools/
adfcookbookv2sqlpool/pause?api-version=2021-06-01
```

7. Rename the pipeline and leave all the other settings in the pipeline the same as in the previous one. Click **Publish all** to save the new pipeline:

*Figure 3.35: Azure Data Factory – pipeline to pause the SQL pool*

8.  Ensure that your Synapse SQL pool is running now and debug the newly created pipeline
    (I called it *ch3-5-pipeline-pause-sql-pool*). While debugging is in progress, go to the Synapse
    SQL pool listing in your Synapse Studio and verify that the status has changed to **Pausing**:

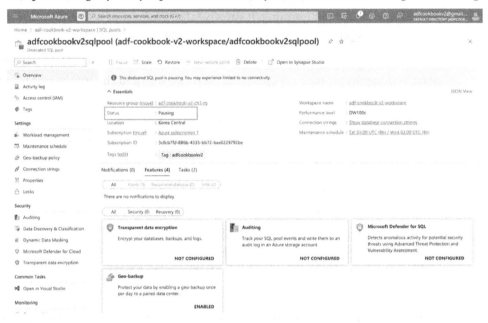

*Figure 3.36: Verifying the SQL pool is Pausing*

## How it works...

Azure Synapse provides the ability to pause or resume its dedicated SQL pools via a REST API. In
this recipe, we took advantage of these REST APIs and invoked them from Azure Data Factory's
Web activity. We had to grant our factory a **Contributor** role on the SQL server that hosts the
SQL pool the Azure Data Factory is accessing. This permitted our instance of Azure Data Factory
to execute the pause and resume actions on the Synapse SQL pool.

## There's more...

The text in the URLs of this recipe is hardcoded in the pipelines, but you can also use dynamic
content to parametrize the pipelines if you have several Azure Synapse Analytics instances in your
organization. You can create similar pipelines to automate your SQL pool in the Azure Synapse
workspace Integrate tool (which is going to be covered later in this chapter).

Also, it's a useful scenario to run these pipelines using different triggers. For example, you can keep
your databases paused outside of working hours if you don't need them (to save costs on running
your Azure SQL pool). Refer to the *Creating event-based triggers* recipe in the *Chapter 2, Orchestration
and Control Flow*, for details on how to configure triggers.

# Working with Azure Purview using Azure Synapse

Azure Purview, Microsoft's cloud-based data governance service, allows organizations to discover, understand, and manage data assets across various environments and clouds. Purview is integrated with Synapse Analytics, and by connecting a Purview account, users can unlock enhanced data governance capabilities: gain insights into stored data assets and metadata extracted from Synapse Analytics objects, understand data lineage, track usage, and enforce robust data governance policies and regulatory compliance – all from within the Synapse Analytics workspace.

In this recipe, we will connect a Microsoft Purview account to our Synapse Analytics workspace, run a scan on our Synapse SQL pool, and view the scan's results right in the Synapse workspace.

## Getting ready

You need access to an Azure Synapse workspace (see the *Creating an Azure Synapse workspace recipe*) and access to a Microsoft Purview account. If you do not have a Microsoft Purview account, create one in the Azure portal:

1. Open `https://portal.azure.com/#create/Microsoft.AzurePurviewGalleryPackage` in your browser.

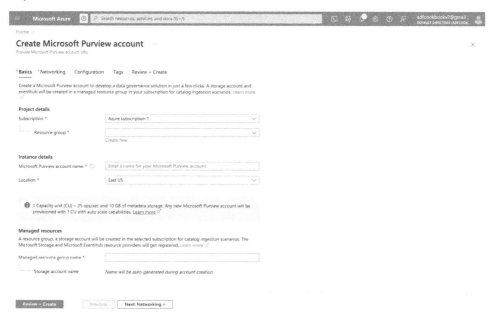

*Figure 3.37: Create a Microsoft Purview account*

2.  Fill in the **Resource group** field and choose a name for your Purview account. Choose the appropriate region. The rest of the settings can be left at the default. Press the **Review + Create** button, review your selections, and finalize them by pressing the **Create** button. Wait until the deployment completes – and now you have a Purview account.

## How to do it...

1.  First, add your Purview account to your instance of Synapse Analytics: open **Synapse Analytics Studio**, and in the **Manage** tab, select **Microsoft Purview**:

*Figure 3.38: Connect Microsoft Purview to a Synapse Analytics workspace*

2. Click on the **Connect to a Purview account** button, select your Purview account in the drop-down list, and click **Apply**. Once your Purview account is linked, your screen should look like this:

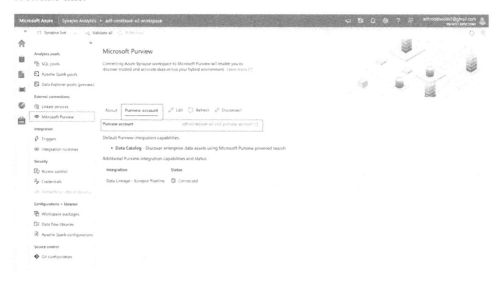

*Figure 3.39: Microsoft Purview is connected*

3. Now you need to register the managed identity of your Purview account as a user of your dedicated SQL pool in the Synapse workspace. In the **Data** tab, right-click next to your SQL pool to create a new SQL script, and enter the following code:

```
CREATE USER [<your-purview-managed-identity-name>] FROM EXTERNAL
PROVIDER
GO

EXEC sp_addrolemember 'db_datareader', [<your-purview-managed-
identity-name>]
GO
```

Here, `<your-purview-managed-identity-name>` is the name you gave to your Purview instance. For example, in the screenshot above, our Purview instance name is `adf-cookbook-v2-ch3-purview-account`, so the script will look like this:

```
CREATE USER [adf-cookbook-v2-ch3-purview-account] FROM EXTERNAL
PROVIDER
GO
EXEC sp_addrolemember 'db_datareader', [adf-cookbook-v2-purview-
account]
GO
```

Run this script to add your Purview instance as a user on your SQL pool. This is necessary to perform the scan.

4.   Now, we shall configure our dedicated **Synapse SQL Pool** as a data source to **Purview**. Find your Purview instance in the Azure portal, and then open **Microsoft Purview governance portal**:

*Figure 3.40: Open Microsoft Purview Governance Portal*

5.   In the **Purview governance portal**, in the **Data Map** tab, select **Sources**. You will see that you have one main "root" collection. It is named the same as your Purview account. Click on **Register**:

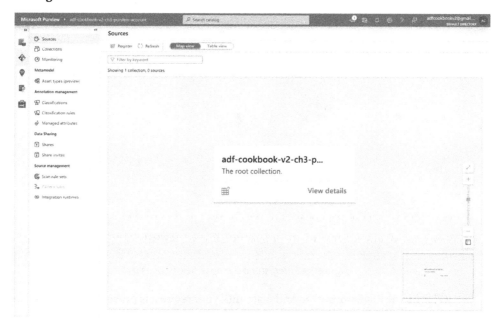

*Figure 3.41: Microsoft Purview Data Map*

In the **Registration** blade, select **Azure Dedicated SQL Pool (formerly SQL DW)** and click **Continue**. Then, choose an appropriate name and your desired Azure subscription. Select your Synapse workspace as a **Server** name from the dropdown. The **Endpoint** and default collection fields will be filled in automatically.

*Figure 3.42: Register a Synapse SQL pool as a data source*

Click on the **Register** button and wait until your request is processed. You should see your workspace in the map:

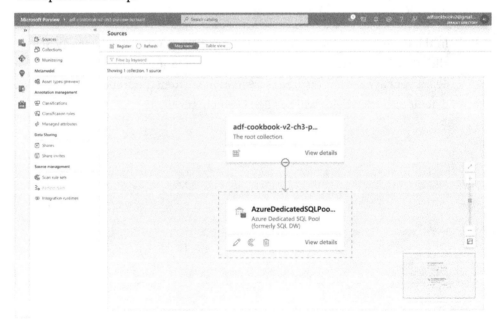

*Figure 3.43: Data map: Synapse SQL pool is registered*

6. In the added tile, click on the **New Scan** icon, and configure a scan by filling in the requested field as shown: you database in your Synapse dedicated SQL pool, and the collection is the root collection.

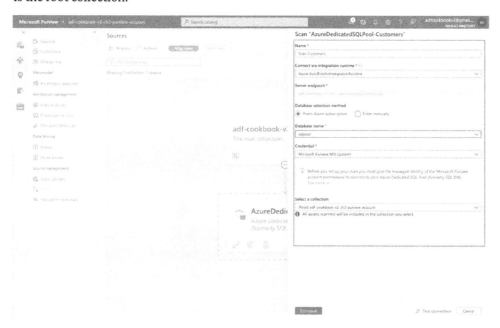

*Figure 3.44: Create a new scan in Microsoft Purview*

The blade displays a hint to grant Purview appropriate managed identity permissions on your data source. Note that we already added the Purview managed identity to the dedicated SQL pool by running a SQL script in *step 2*. Be sure to click the **Test Connection** button to verify that Purview can connect to your SQL pool.

Click on the **Continue** button, and leave the pre-selected values in the **Scope Your Scan** and **Select a Scan Rule Set** blades (those will be the next two blades). On the next blade, set a **Scan Trigger** to only run the scan once. Finally, review your scan settings, and click **Save** and run.

Scans run asynchronously, so it might take a few minutes. This is a good time to take a break!

7. When the scan completes, an overview of your data will be available to you directly in Synapse. Let us look at it. In **Synapse Studio**, in the **Data** tab, locate the **Search** window in the top bar. When you place your cursor in the search window, you will see a dropdown with the word **Purview**:

*Figure 3.45: Search window in Synapse Studio after connecting Microsoft Purview*

8.  Enter the search term Customers in the **Search** field, and Synapse Studio will open a Purview **Search** tab, where you have the results of Purview data analysis – metadata, classifications, glossary, lineage, etc. – at your fingertips.

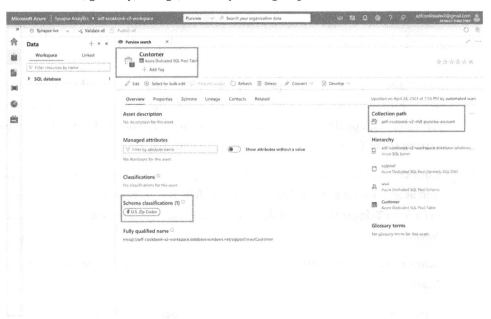

*Figure 3.46: Microsoft Purview scan results in Synapse Studio*

# How it works...

In this recipe, we integrated two tools: **Microsoft Purview**, a data governance tool, and Azure Synapse, a data analytics environment. In order for integration to be useful, we need to properly configure permissions to allow Purview to access data in our database (dedicated SQL pool). On the Purview side, this is configured automatically when you connect your Purview account to a Synapse workspace. Purview has its own system of user permissions, and our Azure workspace was assigned a Data Contributor role in Purview. However, we had to grant Purview a data reader role manually in the SQL database.

After granting appropriate roles to the Purview managed identity on the SQL pool Customers database, and registering the data source in the Purview data map, we configured and ran a scan on our database. Purview scans data in your SQL pool and reports the data landscape to you: your schemas, lineage, classifications, etc. You can view this report both in the Microsoft Purview governance portal and, as we saw in this recipe, directly in Azure Synapse Studio.

## There's more...

- You can register and scan data sources across your Azure tenant in Purview and, if your Purview account is connected, you can view the results of your scans directly in Synapse Studio

- You can also edit your metadata directly in Synapse Studio: annotate schemas, classifications, label data, etc.

# Copying data in Azure Synapse Integrate

In this recipe, you will create a Copy Data pipeline using the Azure Synapse Integrate tool and export data from a dedicated SQL pool into a data lake.

## Getting ready

You need to have access to an **Azure Synapse workspace** that has a dedicated **SQL pool**. The SQL pool should have the table Customer (refer to the *Loading data to Azure Synapse Analytics using bulk load* recipe for instructions on how to create this table and load data).

## How to do it...

To export data using **Azure Synapse Integrate**, follow these steps:

1.   Open your Azure Synapse workspace and go to the **Integrate** tab.

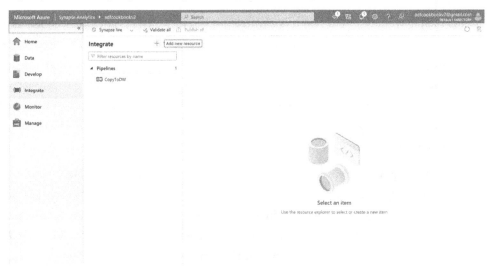

*Figure 3.47: Synapse Analytics: Integrate tool*

2.   Select **Add new resource**, choose **Pipeline**, and then add a **Copy data** activity to your pipeline and rename it:

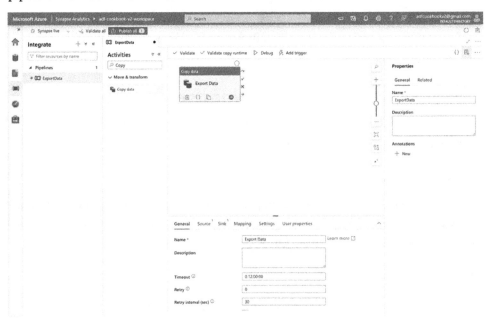

*Figure 3.48: Creating a new pipeline with the Integrate tool of the Synapse Analytics workspace*

3. In the **Source** section, create a new source dataset with **Azure Synapse Dedicated SQL Pool** as a data store. Configure dataset properties by giving it an appropriate name and selecting your dedicated SQL pool and the `Customer` table:

*Figure 3.49: Source dataset in the Integrate tool of the Synapse Analytics workspace*

4. In the sink section, create a new sink dataset. Select **Azure Data Lake Storage Gen2** and choose the **Parquet** format. Choose an existing linked service and specify the target file path:

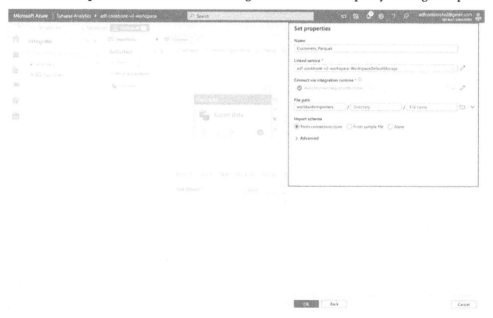

*Figure 3.50: Setting target dataset properties in the Integrate tool of the Synapse Analytics workspace*

5.   Make sure your dedicated SQL pool is not paused, and run your pipeline in Debug mode.

6.   If you go to the **Monitor** tool of the Synapse workspace, and then to the **Pipeline runs** section, you should see the status of your pipeline as **Succeeded**:

*Figure 3.51: Monitoring runs in the Synapse Analytics workspace*

7.   If you go to the **Data** tool of the Synapse workspace, and then the **Linked** section, you'll see the copied Parquet file:

*Figure 3.52: Result of pipeline execution*

8.   Be sure to publish your changes so that your pipeline is saved for future use.

9.   Now you can pause your dedicated SQL pool to save money.

## How it works...

The Integrate tool in the Azure Synapse workspace allows you to perform common data processing operations. Creating pipelines and monitoring them works pretty much the same as in Azure Data Factory (see *Chapter 2, Orchestration and Control Flow*). Note that your dedicated SQL pool must be running for the pipeline to execute successfully.

# Using a Synapse serverless SQL pool

In this recipe, you will learn how to leverage **a serverless SQL pool** in an Azure Synapse workspace to analyze data in your data lake.

## Getting ready

You need to have access to an Azure Synapse workspace. You should also have a file in Parquet format stored in your Azure Synapse storage account. If you do not have one, refer to the *Copying data in Azure Synapse Integrate* recipe to create it.

## How to do it...

Open your Azure Synapse workspace, go to the **Data** tab, then **Linked**, and open the folder that contains the **Parquet** format file:

1. Right-click on the file (we selected **Customers.Parquet**) and choose **New SQL script | Select TOP 100 rows**:

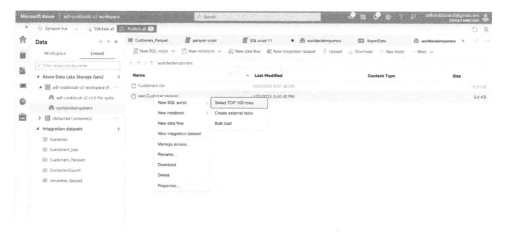

*Figure 3.53: Creating a new SQL script for a file in a storage account*

A new script is created for connecting to the file using a serverless SQL pool. Run it to see the first 100 rows of your Customer table.

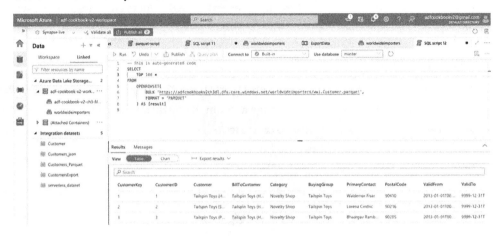

*Figure 3.54: Connecting to the file from the Synapse workspace using a serverless SQL pool*

### NOTE

The query executes within several seconds; you don't need to wait several minutes for the cluster to start.

2.  Now, we are going to leverage the power of serverless SQL to query a very large dataset: data collected for New York City taxi cab rides over several years. This is a public dataset.

Go to the **Scripts** tab and select **New SQL Script**. Make sure to select **Built In** in the **Connect To** dropdown. We are going to run a script that will show us how many rides per day NYC yellow cabs delivered in 2017 through 2019. Enter the following code:

```
SELECT
    CAST([tpepPickupDateTime] AS DATE) AS [tripday],
    COUNT(*) as num_trips
FROM
    OPENROWSET(
BULK 'https://azureopendatastorage.blob.core.windows.net/nyctlc/
yellow/puYear=*/puMonth=*/*.parquet',
```

```
        FORMAT='PARQUET'
    ) AS [NYTaxi]
WHERE NYTaxi.filepath(1) >= '2017' and NYTaxi.filepath(1) <= '2019'
GROUP BY CAST([tpepPickupDateTime] AS DATE)
ORDER BY tripday ASC
```

Run this code, and you will see the data representing the number of New York City yellow cab rides per day between 2017 and 2019:

*Figure 3.55: Running a query on a big Parquet dataset with an Azure Synapse server-less SQL pool*

In this interface, you can also visualize the results in the chart. All you have to do is switch to the **Chart** tab in the results window:

*Figure 3.56: Viewing results as a chart in a Synapse workspace*

3. You can also use a Synapse serverless SQL pool to connect from SSMS or a visualization tool (such as Power BI or Tableau). For this, you need to use a serverless SQL pool endpoint as a server name. This can be copied from the Synapse workspace overview:

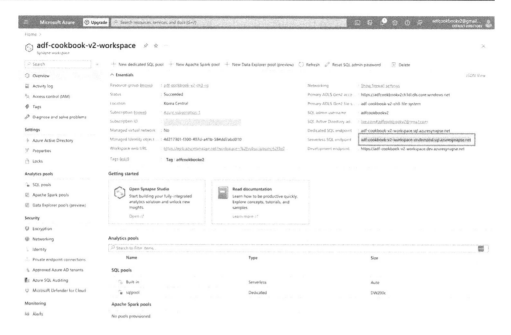

*Figure 3.57: Synapse workspace overview*

4. Open SSMS and paste the SQL serverless endpoint as the server name. You can use your admin credentials for the Synapse workspace as the login and password:

*Figure 3.58: Connecting to a SQL on-demand endpoint from SSMS*

5.  Paste the query below in the query window and run it (note that this is the same query as in *step 3*):

```
SELECT
    CAST([tpepPickupDateTime] AS DATE) AS [tripday],
    COUNT(*) as num_trips
FROM
    OPENROWSET(
BULK 'https://azureopendatastorage.blob.core.windows.net/nyctlc/
yellow/puYear=*/puMonth=*/*.parquet',
        FORMAT='PARQUET'
    ) AS [NYTaxi]
WHERE NYTaxi.filepath(1) >= '2017' and NYTaxi.filepath(1) <= '2019'
GROUP BY CAST([tpepPickupDateTime] AS DATE)
ORDER BY tripday ASC
```

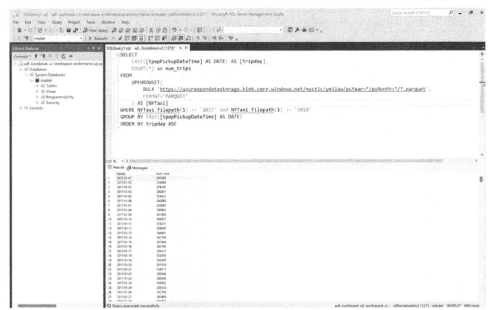

*Figure 3.59: Reading data from a big Parquet dataset from SSMS using SQL serverless*

You can also use the same query to connect to this file from BI systems such as Power BI or Tableau. Serverless SQL pools make it easy for you to analyze data in your Azure data lake.

# How it works...

A serverless SQL pool is provisioned automatically for every Azure Synapse workspace. It allows you to query the contents of your data lake with SQL without the need to spin up a Spark cluster or SQL warehouse. In this recipe, we analyzed a huge public dataset with minimal preparation or effort, leveraging serverless SQL pool capabilities.

# There's more...

Synapse serverless SQL pools offer users many advantages, but you have to evaluate your business intelligence solution on a case-by-case basis. While there are no infrastructure costs associated with serverless SQL pools, you will be charged for the data processed by your queries, which may run up costs if the queries are expensive. Refer to the resources below for best practices and cost management advice:

- Best practices for using serverless SQL pools: `https://learn.microsoft.com/en-us/azure/synapse-analytics/sql/best-practices-serverless-sql-pool`

- Cost management with Synapse serverless SQL pools: `https://learn.microsoft.com/en-us/azure/synapse-analytics/sql/data-processed`

# Join our community on Discord

Join our community's Discord space for discussions with the authors and other readers:

`https://discord.gg/U229qmBmT3`

# 4

# Working with Data Lake and Spark Pools

A **data lake** is a central storage system that stores data in its raw format. It is used to collect huge amounts of data that are yet to be analyzed by analysts and data scientists or for regulatory purposes. As the amount of information and the variety of data that a company operates with increase, it gets increasingly difficult to preprocess and store it in a traditional data warehouse. By design, data lakes are built to handle unstructured and semi-structured data with no pre-defined schema.

On-premises data lakes are difficult to scale and require thorough requirements and cost estimations. Cloud data lakes are often considered an easier-to-use and easier-to-scale alternative. In this chapter, we will go through a set of recipes that will help you to launch a data lake, load data from external storage, and build ETL/ELT pipelines around it.

Azure Data Lake Gen2 can store both structured and unstructured data. In this chapter, we will load and manage our datasets in Azure Data Lake Gen2. These datasets will then be used for analytics in the next chapter.

This chapter covers the following recipes:

- Setting up Azure Data Lake Storage Gen2
- Creating a Synapse Analytics Spark pool
- Integrating Azure Data Lake and running Spark pool jobs
- Building and orchestrating a data pipeline for Data Lake and Spark

Azure Synapse Analytics is a cloud-based analytics service that enables businesses to easily ingest, prepare, manage, and serve data for immediate business intelligence and machine learning needs. Within this service, a Spark pool refers to a dedicated Apache Spark compute environment that provides on-demand processing of big data workloads.

By using a Synapse Analytics Spark pool, businesses can efficiently process large datasets and run distributed computing workloads in a scalable and secure Apache Spark environment. Spark pools are built on top of Azure Data Lake Storage Gen2, which offers high-performance storage and data access. With Spark pools, users can run Spark jobs, Spark SQL queries, and Spark streaming applications.

In addition to being a scalable and secure environment for Spark workloads, Synapse Analytics Spark pools come with built-in integration with other Azure services, such as Azure Data Factory and Azure Machine Learning, making it easy to build end-to-end analytics pipelines. These Spark pools can also be easily integrated with Power BI, enabling users to create compelling visualizations and reports based on their Spark data.

Overall, Synapse Analytics Spark pools are a valuable tool for big data processing and analytics in the cloud. They offer a fully managed Spark environment that can be easily scaled up or down as needed to meet the dynamic needs of modern businesses.

By the end of this chapter, you will have gained the knowledge and skills to design, build, and orchestrate robust data pipelines for your organization, harnessing the power of Data Lake and Spark within Azure Synapse Analytics.

# Technical requirements

You need to have access to Microsoft Azure with a Synapse workspace resource created. An Azure free account is sufficient for all recipes in this chapter. To create an account, use the following link: `https://azure.microsoft.com/free/`. To create a Synapse workspace resource, please refer to *Chapter 3*.

# Setting up Azure Data Lake Storage Gen2

Azure Data Lake Storage Gen2 is a versatile solution that can be used as a single storage platform.

It is Hadoop compatible, so you can use it with HDInsights and Databricks, which we will cover in the next chapter.

Setting up properly configured storage is a critical operation for developers and data engineers. In this section, we will set up and configure a scalable Azure data lake to be used with Azure Data Factory and Azure Synapse Analytics.

# Getting ready

To get started with the recipe, log in to your Microsoft Azure account.

# How to do it...

Azure Data Lake Gen2 uses hierarchical namespaces to organize and manage data in a way that is more efficient and scalable. The hierarchical namespace feature provides a hierarchical file system that allows you to organize data into directories and subdirectories. Unless you already have a storage account with hierarchical namespaces, you will have to create a new one.

Now that we have set up the resource group, let's create a storage account:

1. Search for **Storage accounts** in the Azure search bar and click on it.
2. To add a new storage account, click + **Add**.
3. Select **Azure Subscription** and **Resource Group**.
4. Add a storage account name. This needs to be globally unique. See `https://docs.microsoft.com/en-us/azure/azure-resource-manager/management/resource-name-rules`, and set a data center location as shown in the following screenshot. In order to minimize latency, pick a region close to the location of your servers:

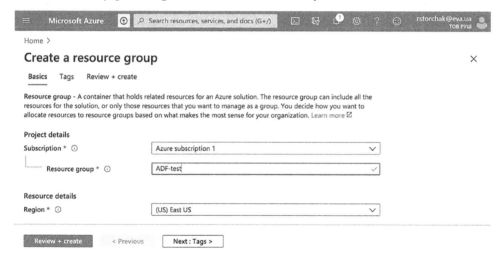

*Figure 4.1: Creating a storage account*

5. Pick **Standard** or **Premium** performance. Use the **Standard** option for cheaper and slower hard drive-based storage. Premium performance may be used for higher and consistent performance for large-scale analytics as well as low-latency access and enhanced SLA.

6.  Select **StorageV2 (general purpose v2)** for **Account kind.**

> IMPORTANT NOTE
>
> Note that **StorageV1 (general purpose v1)** is deprecated. **BlobStorage** is a specialized type that stores only blobs and can also be considered outdated.

7.  For **Replication**, select **Locally-redundant storage (LRS).**
8.  Set **Access tier(default)** to **Cool** and click **Next: Networking.**
9.  Let's configure network connectivity for our new storage account. You can connect to your storage account either publicly or privately. Select **Public endpoint (all networks)** and **Microsoft network routing (default)** as shown in the following screenshot:

*Figure 4.2: Configure network connectivity*

10. Click **Next: Data protection.** On this tab, we have to set up policies for soft delete and blob versioning, which can help us recover files after overwrites and file share data. We are not going to track changes, so we will keep the default settings:

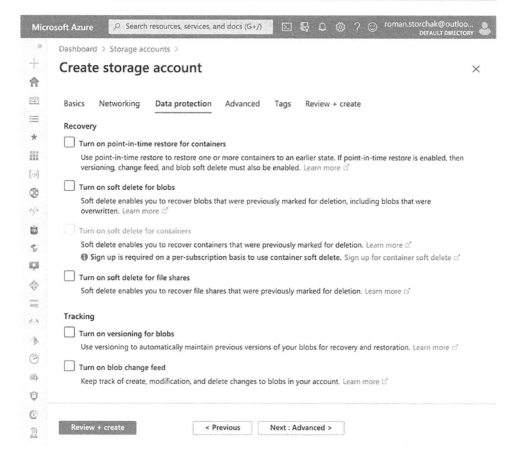

*Figure 4.3: Setting up data protection*

11. For the current exercise, we don't need any recovery or tracking, so we can set everything to disabled and click **Next: Advanced** to move to the next tab.

12. Set up the following parameters on the **Advanced** tab:

    a.  Set **Secure transfer required** to **Enabled**.

    b.  Set an appropriate **Minimum TLS version** (the default version is fine for this recipe and most cases of production usage).

    c.  Leave **Infrastructure encryption** as **Disabled**.

    d.  Set **Allow Blob public access** to **Enabled**.

e.   Set **Blob access tier (default)** to **Hot**.

f.   Leave **NFS v3** as **Disabled**.

g.   Set **Hierarchical namespace** to **Enabled**. Please note that **Hierarchical namespace** is a feature of Data Lake Storage Gen2 and has to be enabled.

h.   Leave **Large file shares** as **Disabled**. If you are planning to use files bigger than 5 TiB, then you will need to reconfigure storage options.

i.   Leave **Customer-managed keys support** as **Disabled**.

j.   You will see the settings as shown in the following screenshot:

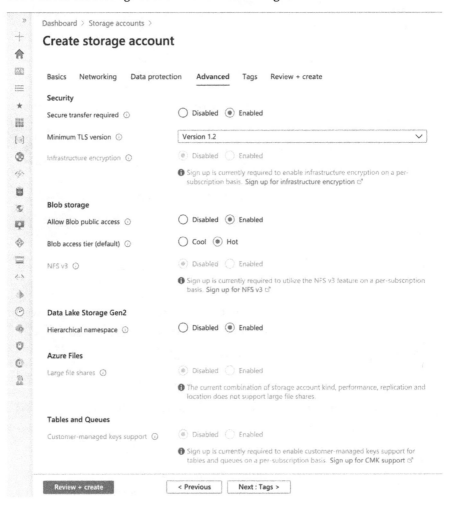

*Figure 4.4: Setting advanced features*

13. Proceed to the **Tags** tab. Fill tags and add appropriate tags as per your requirements.

14. After checking all inputs on the **Review + create** tab, click **Create**.

15. After a short wait, we will have our storage account created and ready for use with Azure Data Factory. Don't forget to delete unused storage accounts.

## There's more...

For a more detailed explanation, go to the official Microsoft documentation: `https://learn.microsoft.com/en-us/azure/storage/blobs/create-data-lake-storage-account`.

# Creating a Synapse Analytics Spark pool

A Spark pool is a fundamental component that provides the computing resources for running large-scale Apache Spark jobs within Synapse Analytics.

In this recipe, we'll guide you through the process of creating a Spark pool in Azure Synapse. You'll learn how to configure pool settings, customize resource allocation, manage credentials, and monitor job progress.

By the end, you'll have the knowledge to provision and configure a Spark pool in Azure Synapse, enabling you to harness the power of Apache Spark for high-performance data processing and analytics.

## Getting ready

To get started with the recipe, log in to your Microsoft Azure account. You need to have a Synapse workspace created.

## How to do it...

To create a Synapse Analytics Spark pool, follow these steps:

1. Log in to the Azure portal and navigate to your Synapse Analytics workspace.

2. Click on the **Manage** button in the left-hand menu and select **Apache Spark pools** from the drop-down menu. This will take you to the Apache Spark pool page.

3.  Click on the **New** button to create a new Spark pool.

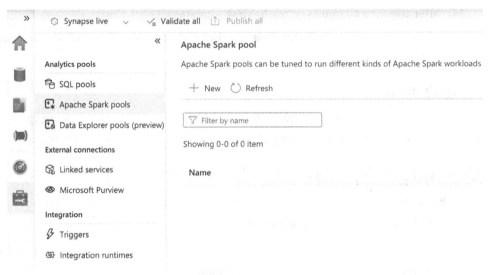

*Figure 4.5: Creating an Apache Spark pool*

4.  In the Create Apache Spark pool form, enter a name for the pool and select the subscription, resource group, and region where the pool will be deployed.

5.  Choose a node size based on your data volume and complexity. Customize other advanced settings as needed. It's OK to disable the isolated compute for now unless you plan to carry out a heavy task.

6. Auto-scale automatically uses nodes based on current memory requirements and processing load.

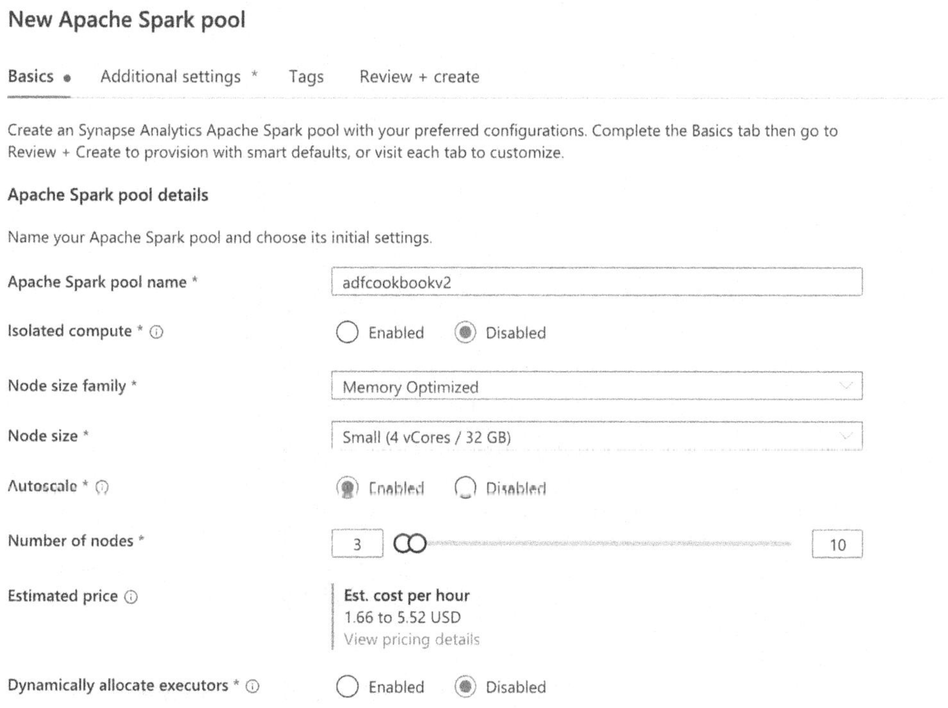

## New Apache Spark pool

Basics ●    Additional settings *    Tags    Review + create

Create an Synapse Analytics Apache Spark pool with your preferred configurations. Complete the Basics tab then go to Review + Create to provision with smart defaults, or visit each tab to customize.

### Apache Spark pool details

Name your Apache Spark pool and choose its initial settings.

| | |
|---|---|
| Apache Spark pool name * | adfcookbookv2 |
| Isolated compute * ⓘ | ◯ Enabled    ⦿ Disabled |
| Node size family * | Memory Optimized |
| Node size * | Small (4 vCores / 32 GB) |
| Autoscale * ⓘ | ⦿ Enabled    ◯ Disabled |
| Number of nodes * | 3   ∞     10 |
| Estimated price ⓘ | **Est. cost per hour** <br> 1.66 to 5.52 USD <br> View pricing details |
| Dynamically allocate executors * ⓘ | ◯ Enabled    ⦿ Disabled |

*Figure 4.6: Configure your Apache Spark pool*

7.  In Additional settings, select the version of Apache Spark you want to use and set the number of nodes you want in the pool. Also, make sure to use automatic pausing as it will help you to save costs and pause the pool after the selected idle time.

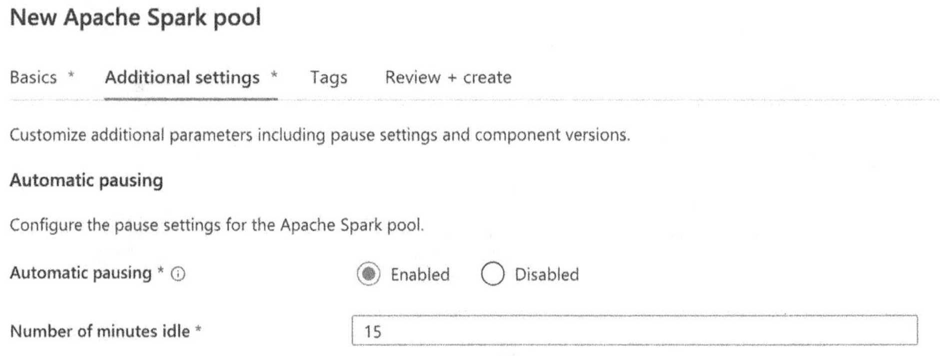

**New Apache Spark pool**

Basics *    **Additional settings** *    Tags    Review + create

Customize additional parameters including pause settings and component versions.

**Automatic pausing**

Configure the pause settings for the Apache Spark pool.

Automatic pausing * ⓘ              ⦿ Enabled      ○ Disabled

Number of minutes idle *          | 15                                        |

*Figure 4.7: Automatic pausing of an Apache Spark pool*

8.  You may want to enable **Allow session level packages** if you would like to install libraries during notebook sessions.

9.  Review and validate your settings, and then click the **Create** button to create the new Spark pool.

After completing these steps, the new Spark pool will be created, and you can start submitting Spark jobs and running Spark SQL queries using the Synapse Analytics workspace. Additionally, you can monitor the performance and usage of the Spark pool through the Azure portal.

## How it works...

By following the steps outlined in this recipe, you can configure the pool settings, customize resource allocation, and establish the necessary credentials to access and manage the Spark pool. With your Spark pool created, you can submit and execute Spark jobs to process and analyze large volumes of data efficiently.

## There's more...

For a good explanation of Apache Spark pools, see `https://learn.microsoft.com/en-us/azure/synapse-analytics/spark/apache-spark-overview`.

You can learn more about creating a new serverless Apache Spark pool using the Azure portal WITH the following link: `https://learn.microsoft.com/en-us/azure/synapse-analytics/quickstart-create-apache-spark-pool-portal`.

# Integrating Azure Data Lake and running Spark pool jobs

In this recipe, we'll explore how to integrate Azure Data Lake with a Spark pool in Azure Synapse Analytics. By combining these services, we can unlock powerful data processing and analysis workflows. We'll cover the steps to establish the connection, run Spark jobs, and leverage the capabilities of both services. Get ready to harness the potential of Azure Data Lake and Spark pools for efficient and scalable data processing.

## Getting ready

Let's load and preprocess the **MovieLens** dataset (F. Maxwell Harper and Joseph A. Konstan. 2015. *The MovieLens Datasets: History and Context*. ACM Transactions on **Interactive Intelligent Systems (TiiS)** 5, 4: 19:1–19:19. `https://doi.org/10.1145/2827872`). It contains ratings and free-text tagging activity from a movie recommendation service.

The **MovieLens** dataset exists in a few sizes, which have the same structure. The smallest one has 100,000 ratings, 600 users, and 9,000 movies. The biggest one can be as big as 1.2 billion reviews, 2.2 million users, and 855,000 items.

**MovieLens** is distributed as a set of `.csv` files. Go to `https://grouplens.org/datasets/movielens/` and download a dataset that seems to be appropriate for your practice and Azure budget.

Make sure you have set up Azure Data Lake Gen2. You can use the *Setting up Azure Data Lake Storage Gen2* recipe.

## How to do it...

1.  Before running Spark pool jobs in Synapse, we should first upload data to the storage account. This ensures that the data is accessible and available for processing by Spark in the Synapse environment. Log in to your Synapse Analytics workspace account, navigate to **Data**, choose the primary storage account, create a new container under its file system, and name the container **movielens**.

2.  Upload files to the **movielens** container via the Azure Data Lake UI. See the following
    screenshot:

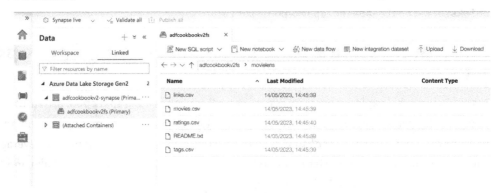

*Figure 4.8: Upload data to a storage account from a Synapse Analytics workspace*

3.  To create a new notebook, you can follow these steps. Click on the **Develop** button in the
    left-hand menu, then select Workspace from the drop-down menu. On the workspace
    page, click on the **New** button, then select **Notebook** from the drop-down menu. In the
    **New Notebook** form, specify the job name, select the **Spark pool** you want to use, and
    choose the language (Python, Scala, C#, SQL, or R).

*Figure 4.9: Create a new notebook*

4.  If you'd like to load the file into a DataFrame, you can go straight from the storage account,
    right-click on the **ratings.csv** file, and choose **New notebook – Load to DataFrame**. Syn-
    apse will create a notebook with the loading Python script.

5.   Just attach the notebook to the created Apache Spark pool, uncomment **header=True**, and press **Run all**. Synapse will start the Spark pool (it usually takes some time) and execute the Python script. The output of the script will be shown below the notebook cell. It will show the first 10 rows of the file.

*Figure 4.10: Run Python script with Apache Spark pool*

6.   Click **Publish** to save the notebook. It will be saved under **Develop/Notebooks**.

7.   You can monitor the progress and view the output of Apache Spark applications on the Monitor page of a Synapse workspace.

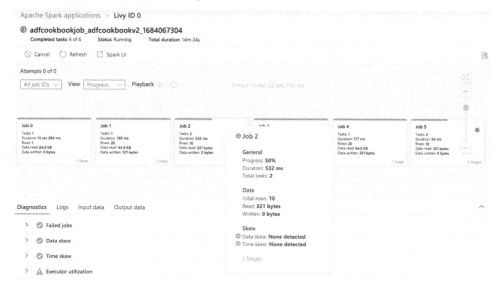

*Figure 4.11: Run a Python script with an Apache Spark pool*

8.  If you're not going to use the Spark pool longer during the session, it makes sense to cancel it. You will find the **Cancel** button in the top-left corner.

# How it works...

In Synapse Analytics, Apache Spark executes Python scripts using its built-in support for the Python programming language. When you submit a Python script to be executed in Synapse Analytics, here's a simplified explanation of what happens:

1.  **Script Submission**: You write your Python script that contains the data processing or analysis logic. The script can use the PySpark API, which is a Python library provided by Apache Spark, to interact with Spark and perform distributed data processing tasks.

2.  **Spark Context Initialization**: When you submit the script, Spark initializes a SparkContext. The SparkContext is the entry point for interacting with Spark and provides the necessary functionality for executing distributed computations.

3.  **Data Processing**: Spark splits the data into partitions and distributes them across the available compute resources. It then applies the operations defined in your script to each partition of the data in a parallel and distributed manner. This parallel processing allows Spark to handle large datasets efficiently.

4.  **Execution Plan**: Before executing the script, Spark analyzes the operations defined in your code and creates an optimized execution plan. This plan determines the most efficient way to execute the operations based on the data layout and available resources.

5.  **Execution**: Spark's execution engine takes the optimized execution plan and coordinates the execution of tasks across the distributed environment. Each task processes a subset of the data on a separate worker node, and the results are combined to form the final result.

6.  **Result Collection**: Once the execution is complete, the results are collected and returned to the client. Depending on the nature of your script, the result can be saved to a file, displayed on the screen, or further processed within your script.

It's important to note that Synapse Analytics also provides integration with other languages like Scala and SQL, allowing you to choose the most suitable language for your data processing needs. However, the steps mentioned above specifically outline the execution of Python scripts in Apache Spark within Synapse Analytics.

# Building and orchestrating a data pipeline for Data Lake and Spark

In this recipe, we will explore the process of constructing and orchestrating data pipelines using Data Lake and Spark in Azure Synapse Analytics. By leveraging the capabilities of these services, you can efficiently manage and process large amounts of data for analysis and insights.

We will improve the code in the notebook from the previous recipe to create a data transformation job and orchestrate it from Synapse Integrate. You'll learn how to extract, transform, and load data into a data lake using Spark, building efficient and scalable pipelines.

Additionally, we'll cover the crucial aspect of orchestration, where you'll discover how to schedule, monitor, and manage the execution of your data pipelines using Azure Synapse's orchestration capabilities.

## Getting ready

To get started with the recipe, log in to your Synapse Analytics workspace. You'll need to have the notebook created in the previous recipe.

## How to do it...

1.  Open the **adfcookbookjob** notebook created in the previous recipe and modify it with the code below. Set the language of the notebook to PySpark (Python) and attach it to the created Spark pool.

2.  In the first cell, we will import the required libraries and assign the storage_account variable. Make sure that you use the name of your storage account along with the file system:

    ```
    import datetime
    from pyspark.sql.functions import *


    storage_account = 'adfcookbookv2fs@adfcookbookv2storage'
    ```

3.  Use the code from the previous recipe to load the ratings.csv file:

    ```
    ratings_df = spark.read.load(f'abfss://{storage_account}.dfs.core.
    windows.net/movielens/ratings.csv'
    , format='csv'
    ## If header exists uncomment line below
    , header=True
    )
    ```

4.  Transform the unix `timestamp` column into date using the code below:

```
ratings_df = ratings_df.withColumn("date", from_
unixtime(col("timestamp"),"yyyy-MM-dd")).drop(col("timestamp"))
```

5.  Add a new cell to aggregate ratings by `movieid` using the code below:

```
group_cols = ["movieid"]
agg_df = ratings_df.groupBy(group_cols) \
                    .agg(count("rating").alias("count_rating"), \
                        avg("rating").alias("avg_rating") \
                    )
```

6.  Add a new cell to load the `movies.csv` file using the code below:

```
movie_df = spark.read.load('abfss://adfcookbookv2fs@
adfcookbookv2storage.dfs.core.windows.net/movielens/movies.csv'
, format='csv'
## If header exists uncomment Line below
, header=True
)
```

7.  Add a new cell to join aggregated ratings with movie DataFrames using the code below:

```
output_df = movie_df.join(agg_df, 'movieid', 'inner')
```

8.  In the new cell, we'll write the output of the DataDrames to curated and enriched folders using the code below:

```
ratings_df.write.mode("overwrite").parquet(f'abfss://{storage_
account}.dfs.core.windows.net/curated/rating/')
output_df.write.mode("overwrite").parquet(f'abfss://{storage_
account}.dfs.core.windows.net/enriched/movies_rating/')
```

9.  Now click on the **Add to pipeline** button on the top right of your screen and choose **New pipeline**.

*Figure 4.12: Add job to pipeline*

10. Name it `pl_sparkpool_receipt3` and click **Publish all** to save your progress. A notebook will be attached to your pipeline.

*Figure 4.13: Create a new pipeline*

11. Go to the settings of the notebook activity, choose the existing Spark pool and executor size, disable dynamically allocated executors, and choose the driver size, as below:

*Figure 4.14: Notebook activity settings*

12. Now debug the **pl_sparkpool_receipt3** pipeline. After the execution of the notebook, two new Parquet files should be created in your storage account.

*Figure 4.15: New files created after pipeline execution*

## How it works...

When running a Synapse pipeline with a Spark notebook, the following process takes place:

1.  **Pipeline definition and compilation**: You define the pipeline using the Azure Synapse pipeline SDK or relevant libraries. This code defines the pipeline activities, their dependencies, and any data transformations or processing steps required. The pipeline code is compiled into an execution graph that represents the logical flow of activities.

2.  **Pipeline submission**: The compiled pipeline is submitted to the Azure Synapse orchestration service. The orchestration service takes the execution graph and creates an instance of the pipeline run.

3.  **Activity execution**: The orchestration service schedules and manages the execution of pipeline activities based on their dependencies and defined schedule. Each activity within the pipeline is executed as a separate task. In our case, the activity is a notebook with PySpark (Python) code.

4.  **Activity execution environment**: For each activity, an appropriate execution environment is provisioned. This environment can be a dedicated Spark cluster, a Data Lake analytics job, or another service depending on the activity type and configuration.

5.  **Data movement and processing**: Data movement and processing operations, such as data ingestion, transformation, and analytics, are performed within the execution environments. For example, if an activity involves running a Spark job, the necessary data is read from the data lake and processed using Spark, and the results are stored back in the data lake.

## There's more...

For a good explanation of Synapse Analytics Integrate with pipelines, see `https://learn.microsoft.com/en-us/azure/synapse-analytics/get-started-pipelines`.

To learn more about how to transform data using an Apache Spark job definition, see `https://learn.microsoft.com/en-us/azure/synapse-analytics/quickstart-transform-data-using-spark-job-definition`.

## Join our community on Discord

Join our community's Discord space for discussions with the authors and other readers:

`https://discord.gg/U229qmBmT3`

# 5

# Working with Big Data and Databricks

This chapter covers the following recipes:

- Setting up an HDInsight cluster
- Processing data from Azure Data Lake with HDInsight and Hive
- Building data models in Delta Lake and data pipeline jobs with Databricks
- Ingesting data into Delta Lake using Mapping data flows
- External integrations with other compute engines (Snowflake)

## Introduction

**Azure Data Factory (ADF)** stands out for its adept use of big data tools, facilitating the creation of rapid and scalable ETL/ELT pipelines while seamlessly managing petabytes of data storage. However, venturing into the realm of establishing a production-ready data engineering cluster without the support of Azure's specialized services unveils significant challenges. The intricacies of manual configuration, fine-tuning processes, and resource management become formidable tasks for practitioners navigating this journey. Setting up Apache Hive, Apache Spark, or Apache Kafka clusters demands meticulous attention to hardware specifications, software compatibility, and networking intricacies.

Estimating workloads and planning for autoscaling capacity without the aid of Azure HDInsight clusters and Databricks introduces complexities, making practitioners grapple with issues ranging from performance optimization to ensuring fault tolerance in dynamic workloads. Troubleshooting and maintaining clusters without the streamlined tools provided by Azure become time-consuming endeavors. Scalability challenges and manual monitoring further compound the difficulties.

In this chapter, we delve into the intricate challenges encountered when setting up production-ready clusters without Azure's specialized support. By comprehending the complexities users may face, we aim to deepen the reader's appreciation for the transformative solutions offered by Azure HDInsight and Databricks. These Azure services, through seamless deployment and integrated management tools, empower any Azure practitioner to establish robust clusters in a matter of minutes.

# Technical requirements

You need to have access to Microsoft Azure. You will be able to run HDInsight clusters with Azure credits, but running Databricks requires a pay-as-you-go account. Also, you can use the code from `https://github.com/PacktPublishing/Azure-Data-Factory-Cookbook/`.

# Setting up an HDInsight cluster

HDInsight is a comprehensive solution based on a diverse list of open source platforms. It includes Apache Hadoop, Apache Spark, Apache Kafka, Apache HBase, Apache Hive, and Apache Storm. Solutions based on HDInsight can be integrated with ADF, Azure Data Lake, Cosmos DB, and so on.

In this section, we will set up the HDInsight service, build a basic pipeline, and deploy it to ADF.

## Getting ready

Before getting started with the recipe, log in to your Microsoft Azure account.

We assume you have a pre-configured resource group and storage account with Azure Data Lake Gen2. If you don't know how to create a resource group and a storage account, please refer to *Chapter 1, Getting Started with ADF*.

## How to do it...

We will go through the process of creating an HDInsight cluster using the Azure portal and its web interface. Follow these instructions:

1.  Create a user-assigned managed identity. We will need it in the next step, to set up HDInsight cluster access to Data Lake v2. Find **Managed Identities** in Azure and click **+Add**.

2.  Fill in the appropriate details, such as **Resource group**, **Region**, and **Name**, as shown in the following screenshot:

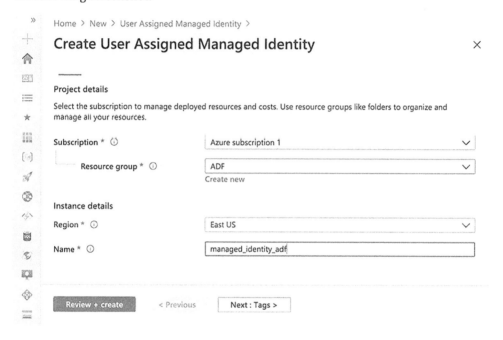

*Figure 5.1: Create User Assigned Managed Identity*

3.  Click on **Next : Tags >** and fill in tags that will help you with tracking this managed identity.

4.  Now, click **Create** and wait for a few seconds while the identity is created.

5.  Once the managed identity is created, go to **Storage accounts** and select an appropriate storage account that you will use with the HDInsight cluster.

6.   Click **Access Control (IAM)** | **+ Add** | **Add role assignment**, as shown in the following screenshot:

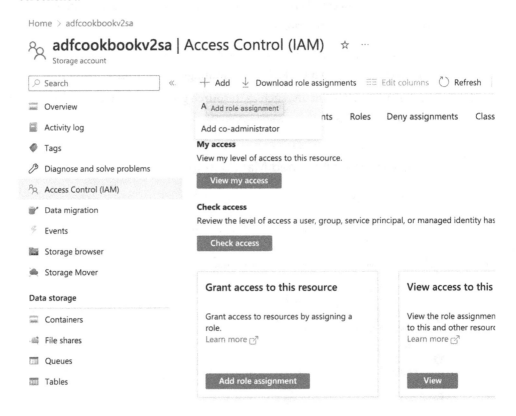

*Figure 5.2: Adding a role assignment*

7.   Select the **Storage Blob Data Owner** role, assign access to **User assigned managed identity**, which is in the following dropdown, and select your subscription, as shown in *Figure 5.3*.

8. Click **Review + assign** to finalize the role assignment:

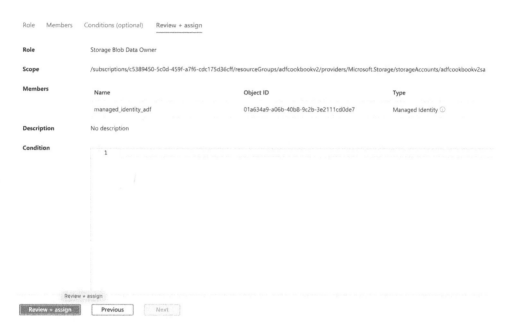

*Figure 5.3: Setting up a role assignment*

9. Now you need to register a resource provider in the Azure portal:

   a. Select your subscription

   b. Under **Settings,** select **Resource Providers**

   c. Search **Microsoft.HDInsight**

   d. Click on **Register**

10. Go to **HD Insight clusters** and click **+ Add**.

11. Select your subscription and resource group.

12. Name your cluster, select the region, and select a cluster type, as shown in the following screenshot. For this recipe, we will select Hadoop version 3.1.0, which is the default choice as of June 2023:

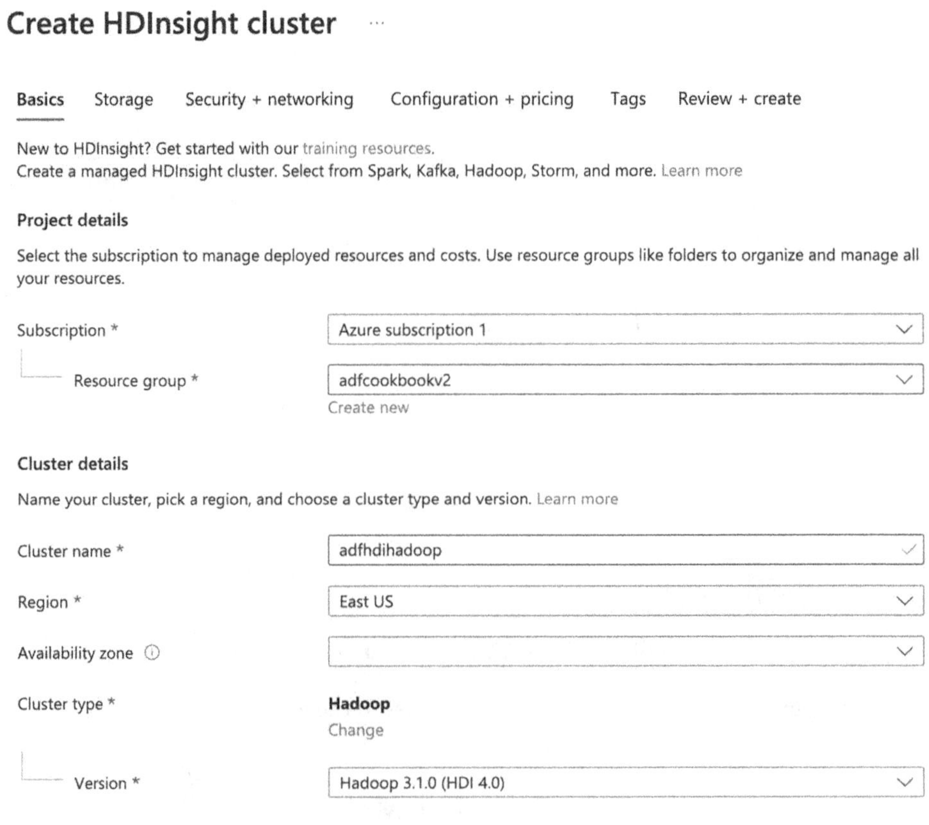

## Create HDInsight cluster     ⋯

Basics    Storage    Security + networking    Configuration + pricing    Tags    Review + create

New to HDInsight? Get started with our training resources.
Create a managed HDInsight cluster. Select from Spark, Kafka, Hadoop, Storm, and more. Learn more

### Project details

Select the subscription to manage deployed resources and costs. Use resource groups like folders to organize and manage all your resources.

| | |
|---|---|
| Subscription * | Azure subscription 1 |
| Resource group * | adfcookbookv2 |
| | Create new |

### Cluster details

Name your cluster, pick a region, and choose a cluster type and version. Learn more

| | |
|---|---|
| Cluster name * | adfhdihadoop |
| Region * | East US |
| Availability zone ⓘ | |
| Cluster type * | **Hadoop** Change |
| Version * | Hadoop 3.1.0 (HDI 4.0) |

*Figure 5.4: Creating an HDInsight cluster*

13. Set your details for the **Cluster login username** and **Cluster login password** fields and confirm the password (*Figure 5.5*).

14. Fill in the **Secure Shell (SSH) username** field and allow the cluster login password to be used for SSH:

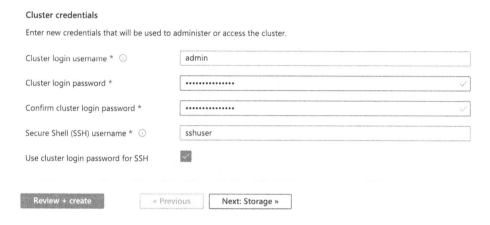

*Figure 5.5: Adding HDInsight cluster credentials*

15. Click **Next: Storage >>** to set up the storage options.

16. Select **Primary storage type.** Be aware that Azure Data Lake Storage Gen2 is not yet the default choice despite all of its advantages, as shown in the following screenshot:

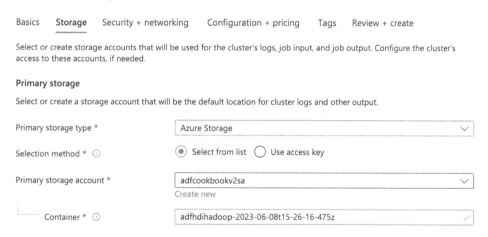

*Figure 5.6: Setting up storage for an HDInsight cluster*

17. Select a primary storage account, which is our Data Lake Gen2 storage, and its filesystem. The HDInsight cluster will use this storage and filesystem as its main storage. Even if you decide to delete your cluster, the data will stay intact.

18. In **Security + networking**, select the user-assigned managed identity that we created during *steps 1* to *4* and granted necessary rights to during *steps 5* to *8* of this recipe.

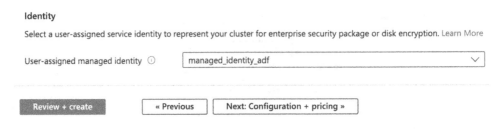

*Figure 5.7: User-assigned managed identity*

19. You can add additional Azure storage, an external Ambari database, and external metadata stores for Hive and Oozie. For our setup, those fields should be blank.

20. Leave **Enable enterprise security package** not selected.

21. Set **Minimum TLS version** to its default: **1.2**.

22. In our setup, we do not need to connect our cluster to a virtual network and provide our own disk encryption settings. Select **User-assigned managed identity** to represent our cluster for the enterprise security package.

23. Click **Next: Configuration + pricing**.

24. Select the appropriate node types and the price for the task you are intending to use this cluster for, as shown in the following screenshot:

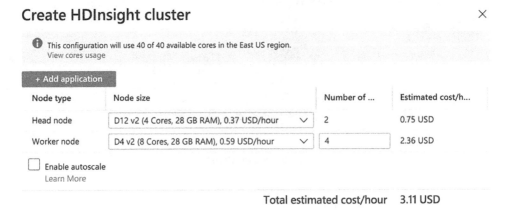

*Figure 5.8: Configuring hardware*

25. Click **Next** and add appropriate tags that will help you to track your resources.

26. Click the **Review + create** button to finalize cluster creation. Check whether everything is correct.

27. The Azure portal will forward you to the **Deployment** page. After a short wait, you will see that your cluster is created and functional, as seen in the following screenshot. You can use it with ADF or directly:

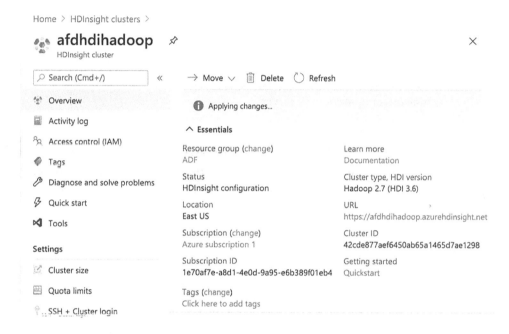

*Figure 5.9: The HDInsight cluster is ready*

IMPORTANT NOTE

Azure charges for the HDInsight cluster even if it is not used. So, you have to programmatically create clusters, execute jobs, and delete clusters. To automate the creation, execution, and deletion of HDInsight clusters on Azure, you can use Azure PowerShell, the Azure CLI, or one of the Azure SDKs for your preferred programming language (such as Python or .NET).

## How it works...

HDInsight clusters are a versatile service that allow the easy deployment of various open source technologies. They allow running the following:

- Hadoop
- Spark
- Kafka
- HBase
- Interactive Query (Hive)
- Storm
- Machine learning services (R server)

In this recipe, we built a managed Hadoop cluster that is ready to be used with ADF. Hadoop requires permission to access storage accounts. In our case, it is Azure Data Lake Storage (Gen2). To grant this access, we have to create a user-assigned managed identity and grant the appropriate rights (Storage Blob Data Owner for our storage). Then, the Hadoop cluster uses this managed identity to access the storage.

## There is more...

For more information on managed identities in Azure HDInsight, check out the following link: `https://learn.microsoft.com/en-us/azure/hdinsight/hdinsight-managed-identities`. Microsoft documentation on setting up clusters in HDInsight: `https://learn.microsoft.com/en-us/azure/hdinsight/hdinsight-hadoop-provision-linux-clusters`.

Having set up the HDInsight cluster, let's learn how to build an ADF pipeline and make use of the benefits of HDInsight.

# Processing data from Azure Data Lake with HDInsight and Hive

In this recipe, we will learn how to create an Azure Data Factory pipeline with an HDInsight job and run HQL queries to process data from Azure Data Lake.

HDInsight clusters are versatile open source tools that can handle ETL/ELT and data analytics and scientific tasks at scale. Unfortunately, usage of Azure HDInsight is chargeable even when the cluster is inactive or not loaded. But ADF can create and manage short-lived HDInsight clusters. These clusters ensure efficient resource utilization, allocating resources only during active processing tasks and automatically de-provisioning afterward.

The parallel creation of multiple short-lived clusters by ADF enhances scalability, enabling the processing of concurrent tasks. Isolation and clean environments are maintained, preventing interference between tasks. ADF's automation of cluster lifecycles simplifies management, adapting to variable workloads and fluctuating processing demands.

The integration of ADF with HDInsight clusters facilitates the incorporation of data processing tasks into larger ETL/ELT workflows. This adaptability to changing requirements and the ability to dynamically create clusters as needed make ADF a flexible solution for end-to-end data processing pipelines. Additionally, short-lived clusters provide resource isolation for improved security and compliance. In summary, utilizing short-lived HDInsight clusters with ADF optimizes costs, ensures resource efficiency, scales processing tasks, and simplifies management, making it a versatile solution for dynamic data processing workloads. Let's build one.

## Getting ready

Ensure that you have a pre-configured resource group and storage account with Azure Data Lake Gen2. Now, log in to your Microsoft Azure account.

## How to do it...

To process data from Azure Data Lake with HDInsight and Hive, use the following steps:

1. Go to the Azure portal and find **Azure Active Directory**.
2. Click **App registrations**, as shown in the following screenshot:

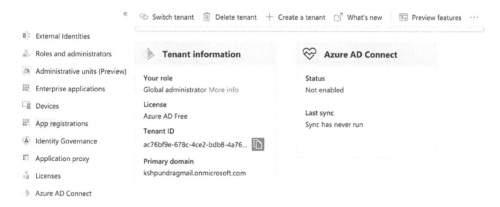

*Figure 5.10: App registrations*

3.  Then, click **+ New registration** and fill in the name of your app, as shown in the following screenshot:

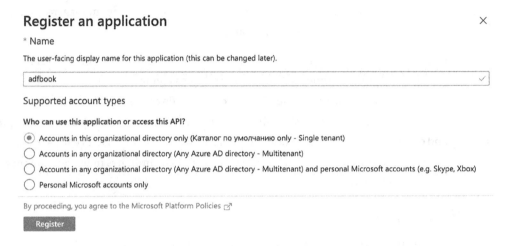

*Figure 5.11: Registering an app*

4.  Leave the default answer to **Who can use this application or access this API?** and click **Register**.

5.  Go to the Azure portal and then to **Subscriptions**. Select a subscription that you will use to run your app, as shown in the following screenshot:

*Figure 5.12: Selecting subscriptions*

6.  Click **Access control (IAM) | + Add role**, as shown in the following screenshot:

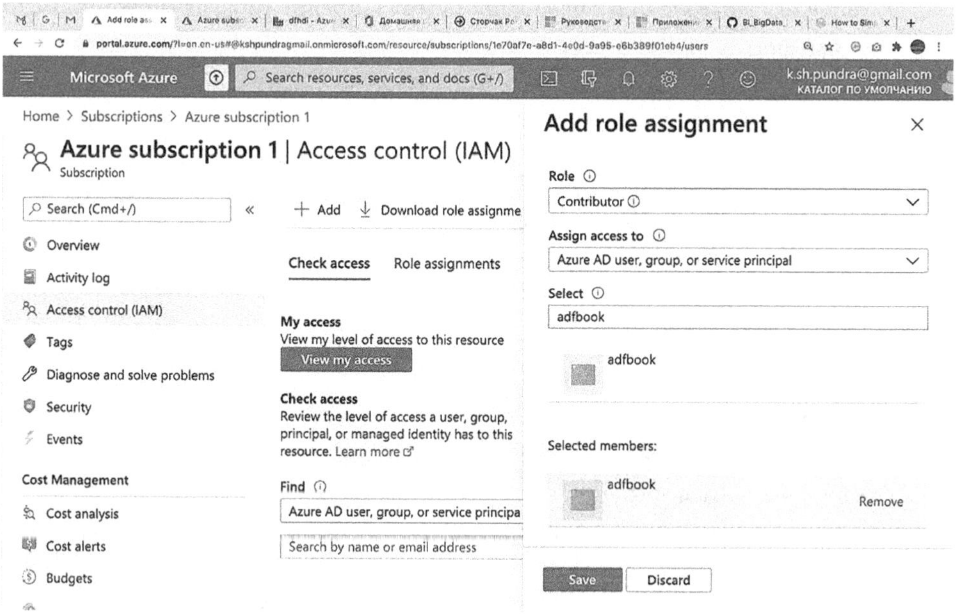

*Figure 5.13: Adding a role assignment*

7.  Assign the **Contributor** role to the app that you have created. Select **Azure AD user, group, or service principal** for **Assign access to** and select your app by its name.

Congratulations, you have registered an app and added the necessary role to use it with an on-demand HDInsight cluster in ADF!

8.  Go to the ADF interface. Click **Create Pipeline**. Add a name and description. Set **Concurrency** to **1** since we don't need simultaneous pipeline runs, as shown in the following screenshot:

*Figure 5.14: Creating a Hive pipeline*

9.  Click on **HDInsight** and drag and drop **Hive** to the workspace.

10. Set the name as HiveJob, add a description, and set **Timeout**, the number of retries, and **Retry interval** (*Figure 5.15*).

11. Leave **Secure input** and **Secure output** unchecked:

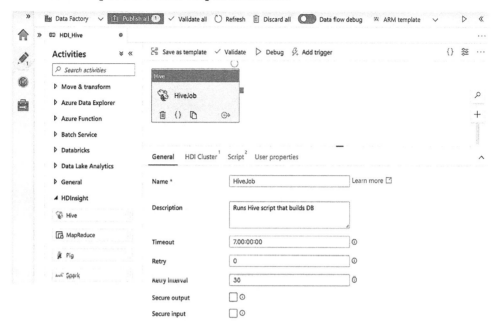

*Figure 5.15: Setting up a Hive job*

12. Go to the **HDI Cluster** tab. Click to create a new HDInsight linked service.

13. Add a name and description for the linked service, as shown in the following screenshot:

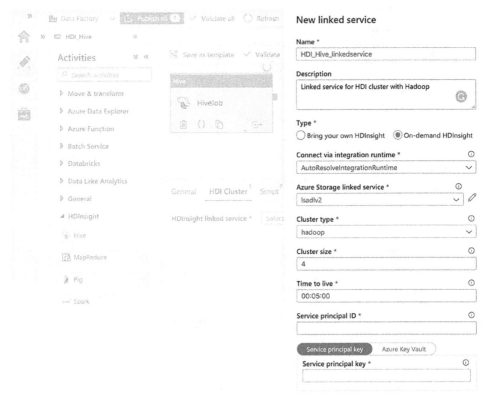

*Figure 5.16: Setting up a Hive linked service*

14. Select **On-demand HDInsight**.

15. Leave the default **Connection via integration runtime** setting (**AutoResolveIntegrationRuntime**).

16. Select an existing or create a new Azure Storage linked service (we created linked services in *Chapter 4, Working with Data Lake and Spark Pools*).

17. Set **Cluster type** to **hadoop** and **Cluster size** to **1**. The smallest cluster size will be enough for testing purposes.

18. **Time to live** specifies the amount of time that a cluster can be inactive for. Then, it will be deleted. Please note that data is stored separately in Azure Storage, so it will be available after cluster deletion.

19. Switch to **Active Directory** | **App Registrations** and click on the app page. Copy the **Application (client) ID** value, as shown in the following screenshot, and insert it into the **Service principal ID** field (that you can see in *Figure 5.16*):

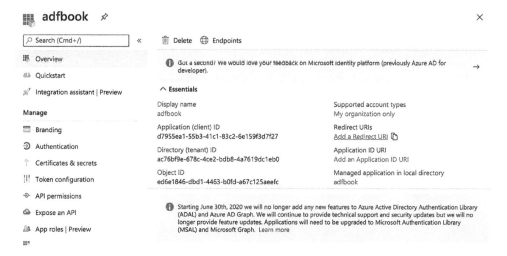

*Figure 5.17: Getting the application ID*

20. Go to **Certificates & secrets** and click **+ New client secret**. Set the password time and copy the password value.

21. Paste the password into **Service principal key** on the **New linked service** interface in ADF, as shown in the following screenshot:

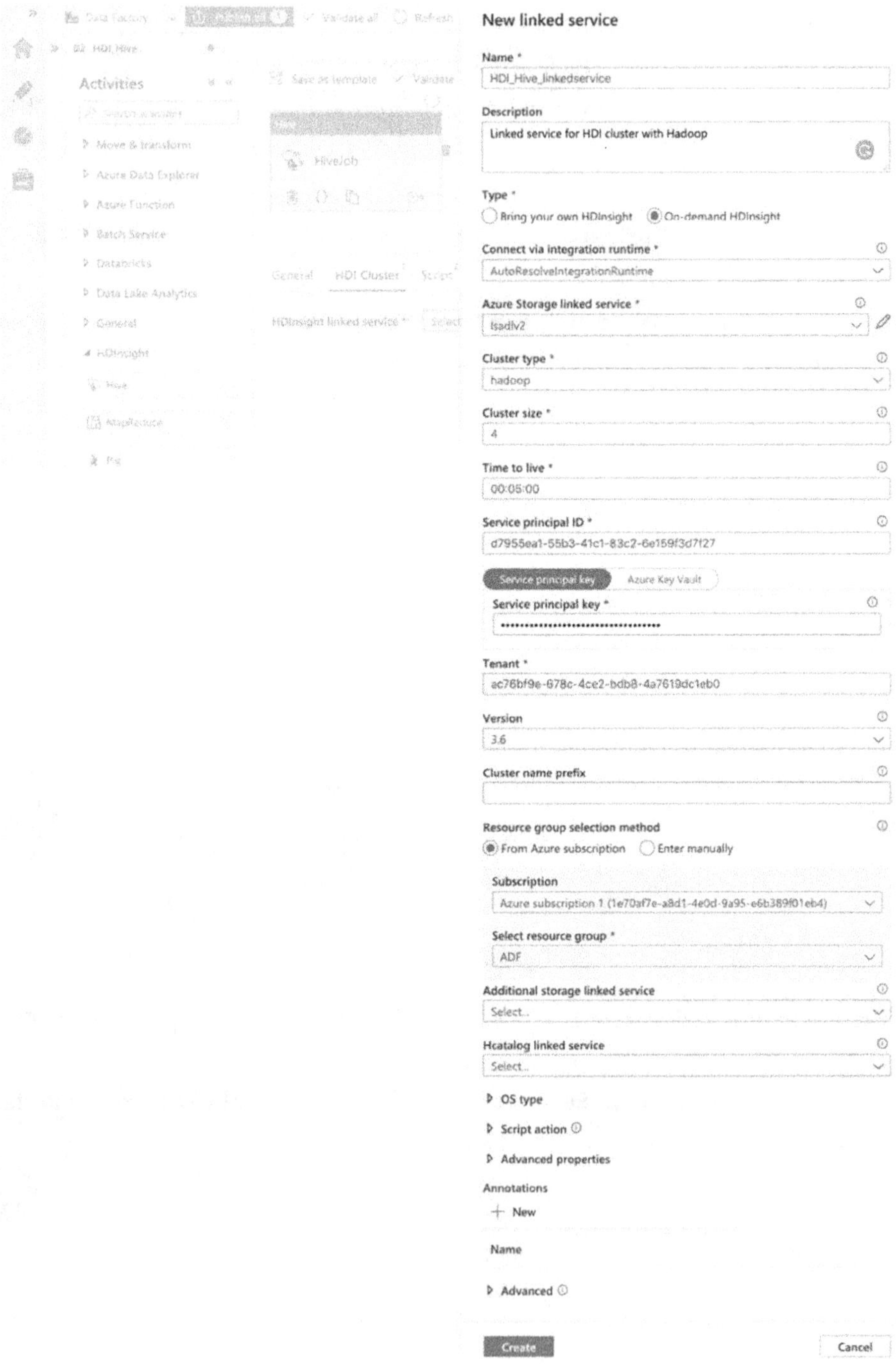

*Figure 5.18: Creating an HDInsight Hive cluster linked service*

22. The **Tenant** field should be generated automatically. Otherwise, copy-paste it from **Active Directory | App Registrations** and the app page.

23. Leave the default version of the HDInsight cluster.

24. Leave **Cluster name prefix** blank.

25. Select your subscription and resource group.

26. Click on **OS type** and fill **Cluster SSH user name** with `sshuser` and a password.

27. Add details for the **Cluster user name** and **Cluster password** fields. They will be useful for cluster monitoring and troubleshooting.

28. Click **Create**.

29. Switch to the **Script** tab.

30. Add a script-linked service. This is a linked service that allows access to the storage where the Hive script is stored.

31. Copy or clone the `query.hql` file from `https://github.com/PacktPublishing/Azure-Data-Factory-Cookbook/`. It contains a toy query that we will run.

32. Upload `query.hql` to Azure Data Lake Storage (Gen2) to the same folder where the MovieLens dataset files are stored.

33. Fill in placeholders for the Azure storage account name and container name where you store a dataset. Then, specify the location of the `movies.csv` file.

34. Add a Hive script file path that will be executed, as shown in the following screenshot:

*Figure 5.19: Adding a Hive script to ADF*

35. Don't forget to save a pipeline by clicking **Publish all** and confirming it. Please be aware that ADF does not allow publishing pipelines with activities that contain empty fields.

36. Manually trigger a pipeline to run it. Please note that launching a cluster takes about 10 minutes.

37. After some time, you can check that your job was successful, as shown in the following screenshot. Keep in mind that Hive stores its data in your Azure Data Lake (Gen2) area, so you can log in to your storage account and visually inspect tables and so on. So, when the HDInsight cluster is deleted, you still have access to its data:

*Figure 5.20: Hive job details*

If the job failed with a user config error, try restarting your HDInsight cluster. Sometimes, issues related to user configurations can be resolved by restarting the cluster. Also, it's worth verifying that your authentication configuration is accurate. Make sure that the credentials for accessing Azure Data Lake Storage Gen2 are correctly configured in your Hive script or cluster.

## How it works...

Apache Hive is a piece of data warehouse software that can run SQL queries. The HDInsight Hive cluster stores the data in Azure Data Lake Storage (Gen2). ADF can create a temporary HDInsight Hive cluster, run queries, and delete unused clusters.

In order to allow ADF to create and kill HDInsight Hive clusters, we need to create an Azure Active Directory app. Then, we assign a Contributor role to the app, allowing it to manage resources in Azure. Later, when we use Hive jobs from ADF, an application with proper permissions is needed to automatically create a cluster.

During the execution, these ADF pipelines create a cluster, run Hive scripts, store Hive query outputs, and kill the cluster.

Creating temporary HDInsight Hive clusters for specific tasks, as opposed to maintaining persistent clusters, provides distinct advantages in various scenarios:

- **Cost Efficiency**: Temporary clusters are provisioned only when needed, minimizing idle time and resulting in cost savings. This approach aligns costs directly with active processing periods, making it more economical than maintaining persistent clusters that incur charges continuously.

- **Resource Optimization**: Temporary clusters enable efficient resource utilization, allocating compute resources precisely for the duration of the specific Hive task. This prevents over-provisioning and ensures that resources are dedicated to the task at hand, enhancing overall resource optimization.

- **Isolation and Cleanliness**: Each temporary cluster provides a clean and isolated environment for the specific Hive task. This isolation helps avoid potential conflicts with configurations or data artifacts from previous tasks, ensuring a consistent and controlled processing environment.

- **Scalability on Demand**: Provisioning temporary clusters as needed allows for seamless scalability to handle varying workloads. Tasks can be processed concurrently with separate clusters, providing flexibility in scaling resources based on the demands of specific jobs.

- **Automated Lifecycle Management**: Automating the lifecycle of temporary clusters, as facilitated by Azure Data Factory or similar orchestration tools, streamlines management tasks. Clusters are automatically created, scaled, and de-provisioned, reducing manual intervention and administrative overhead.

- **Adaptability to Dynamic Workflows**: In dynamic data processing workflows where tasks vary in complexity and scale, the ability to create temporary clusters on demand ensures adaptability. It accommodates changes in processing requirements without the need for maintaining a constant, potentially over-dimensioned infrastructure.

Having efficiently processed data from Azure Data Lake with HDInsight, we now shift our focus to building a robust data model in Delta Lake and executing data pipeline jobs with the powerful capabilities of Databricks.

# Building data models in Delta Lake and data pipeline jobs with Databricks

In this recipe, we will learn how to set up a new Azure Databricks service, create a new Databricks cluster, create delta tables using Python scripts, and create an ADF pipeline running a Databricks notebook.

Apache Spark is a well-known big data framework that is often used for big data ETL/ELT jobs and machine learning tasks. ADF allows us to utilize its capabilities in two different ways:

- Running Spark in an HDInsight cluster
- Running Databricks notebooks and JAR and Python files

Running Spark in an HDInsight cluster is very similar to the previous recipe. So, we will concentrate on the Databricks service. It also allows running interactive notebooks, which significantly simplifies the development of the ETL/ELT pipelines and machine learning tasks.

In this recipe, we will connect Azure Data Lake Storage to Databricks, ingest the MovieLens dataset, transform the data, and store the resulting dataset as a delta table in Azure Data Lake Storage. Using Databricks for running Spark is preferable when seeking a unified, user-friendly, and collaborative platform with features like auto-scaling, integrated workspaces, performance optimization, serverless execution, and cost-effective pricing, making it a compelling choice for diverse data processing scenarios.

## Getting ready

First, log in to your Microsoft Azure account. We assume you have a pre-configured resource group and storage account with Azure Data Lake Gen2 and the Azure Databricks service from the previous recipe.

Hence, we assume the following:

- ADF has a linked service for Azure Data Lake Storage
- The MovieLens dataset (used in *Chapter 4, Working with Data Lake and Spark Pools*) is loaded in Azure Data Lake Storage (Gen2)

# How to do it...

Use the following steps to create a delta table with Databricks and Azure Data Factory:

1. Go to the Azure portal and find **Databricks**.

2. Click **+ Add** and fill in the project details.

3. Select your subscription and resource group, as shown in the following screenshot:

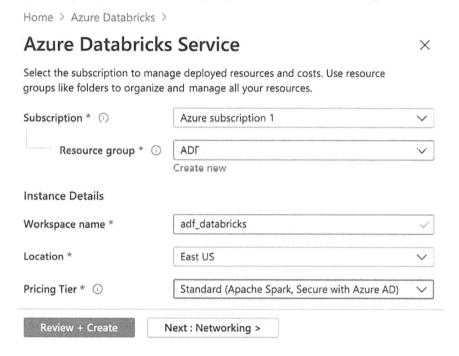

*Figure 5.21: Setting up Azure Databricks*

4. Name your Databricks workspace and select a location.

5. Pick **Standard** for **Pricing Tier** as it is more than enough for our application.

6. Click **Next: Networking**.

7. Now, select **No** for **Deploy Azure Databricks workspace in your own Virtual Network (VNet)**.

8. Click **Next: Tags** and add appropriate tags to simplify recourse tracking and management.

9. Click **Review + Create**, and then **Create**. After a short deployment process, Databricks will be operational.

10. Log in to your Databricks web UI. Go to the **Compute** page and select **Create compute**.

11. Add a cluster name and set **Cluster Mode** to **Single Node**. Leave the **Pool** setting as **None**. Select the default Databricks runtime version. At the time of writing, it is **Runtime: 13.0 (Scala 2.12, Spark 3.4.0)**.

    Check **Terminate after** and set **10** minutes of inactivity. Select an appropriate node type. We are testing Databricks with a small dataset, so the **Standard_DS3_v2** node fits our recipe, as shown in the following screenshot:

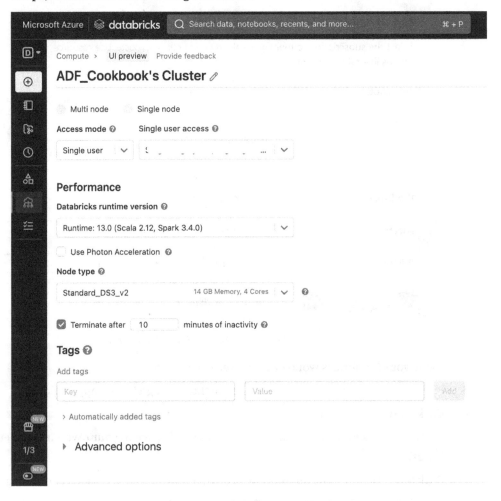

*Figure 5.22: Creating a new cluster*

12. Click **Create**.

13. Go to the Databricks main page, **Workspace | Shared,** and click on **Create | Notebook.**

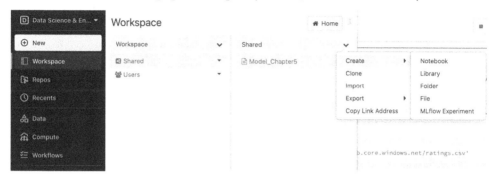

*Figure 5.23: Creating a new Databricks notebook*

14. Fill in the notebook name, set **Default Language** to **Python.**

15. In order to connect to ADLS Gen2 from a Databricks notebook and load the data, you need a storage account access key. Navigate to the Azure portal, your storage account, **Security + Networking, Access keys,** and copy the key from either of the two existing keys.

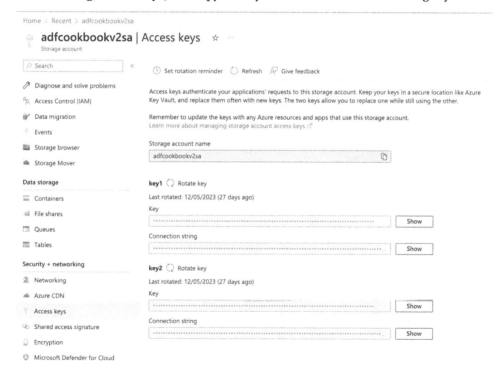

*Figure 5.24: Storage account access key*

16. In the Databricks notebook, you need to create new variables for `storage_account_name` and `storage_account_access_key` and set the Spark configuration:

```
storage_account_name = "adfcookbookv2sa"
storage_account_access_key = "xxxx"
spark.conf.set(
  "fs.azure.account.key."+storage_account_name+".blob.core.windows.
net",
  storage_account_access_key)
```

17. Now you can assign the file location variables and load data to Spark dataframes as follows:

```
raw_container = 'raw'
ratings_location = f'wasbs://{raw_container}@{storage_account_name}.
blob.core.windows.net/ratings.csv'
movies_location = f'wasbs://{raw_container}@{storage_account_name}.
blob.core.windows.net/movies.csv'
links_location = f'wasbs://{raw_container}@{storage_account_name}.
blob.core.windows.net/links.csv'
tags_location = f'wasbs://{raw_container}@{storage_account_name}.
blob.core.windows.net/links.csv'
ratingsDF = spark.read.format("csv").option("inferSchema", "true").
option("header", "true").load(ratings_location)
linksDF = spark.read.format("csv").option("inferSchema", "true").
option("header", "true").load(links_location)
moviesDF = spark.read.format("csv").option("inferSchema", "true").
option("header", "true").load(movies_location)
tagsDF = spark.read.format("csv").option("inferSchema", "true").
option("header", "true").load(tags_location)
```

18. Now, let's use a simple data transformation Python script to prepare the resulting dataframe. First, let's import the needed functions:

```
from pyspark.sql.functions import avg, round, current_timestamp,
concat_ws, collect_set, from_unixtime, max, date_format, to_date
```

19. The following code will aggregate the ratings dataframe to get the average rating by movie, and aggregate the tags to get all tags related to a particular movie:

```
agg_ratingsDF = ratingsDF.groupBy("movieId").
agg(round(avg("rating"), 2).alias("avg_rating"), max("timestamp").
alias("unix_timestamp"))
```

```
agg_tagsDF = tagsDF.groupBy('movieId').agg(concat_ws(" | ", collect_
set("tag")).alias("agg_tags"))
```

20. The next command will join movies with aggregated ratings, aggregated tags, and links in order to get all the information in one dataset. Also, it will modify the timestamp to get the date, which will be used later for partitioning and load_timestamp:

```
resultDF = (moviesDF.join(agg_ratingsDF, ['movieId'], 'left')
                    .join(linksDF, ['movieId'], 'left')
                    .join(agg_tagsDF, ['movieId'], 'left')
                    .withColumn("rating_datetime", to_date(date_
format(from_unixtime("unix_timestamp"), "yyyy-MM-dd")))
                    .withColumn('load_timestamp', current_timestamp())
                    .drop('unix_timestamp')
)
```

21. The next command will write the resulting dataframe as a delta table to the Azure storage account:

```
target_container = 'curated'
target_path = f'wasbs://{target_container}@{storage_account_name}.
blob.core.windows.net/movie_lens'
resultDF.write.format("delta").mode("overwrite").
partitionBy('rating_datetime').saveAsTable(path=target_path,
name='movie_lens')
```

22. Once you have created the table, with the next run you may want to update it without overwriting it. To do this, you can use the merge method from Spark:

```
from delta.tables import *
from pyspark.sql import SparkSession
spark = SparkSession.builder.appName("app").getOrCreate()
target_table = DeltaTable.forPath(spark, target_path)

key_column = "movieId"

(target_table.alias("target")
    .merge(resultDF.alias("source"), f"source.{key_column} = target.
{key_column}")
```

```
    .whenMatchedUpdateAll()
    .whenNotMatchedInsertAll()
    .execute())
```

23. Go to the ADF UI, then click on **Manage | Linked services | + New**.

24. Select the **Compute** tab and click on **Azure Databricks** and **Continue**, as shown in the following screenshot:

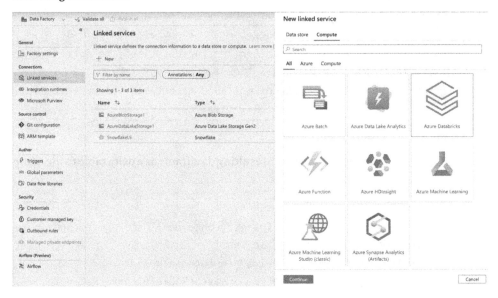

*Figure 5.25: Selecting Azure Databricks*

1. Fill in the **Name** and **Description** fields for the linked service.

2. Select **AutoRevolveIntegrationRuntime** for the **Connect via integration runtime** field.

3. Select your subscription from the **Azure subscription** drop-down menu in the Databricks workspace that we created in *steps 1* to *9* of this recipe.

4. In **Select cluster**, pick **New job cluster**. This option will allow you to start Spark clusters, process the data, and stop them.

5. Log in to your Databricks workspace. If you're logging in to the Azure Databricks service for the first time, click on your service and click **Launch Workspace**.

6. Click on the user icon in the top-right corner and select **User Settings**, as shown in the following screenshot:

*Figure 5.26: Generating a new token*

7. Click **Generate new token** and enter an appropriate lifetime and a comment.

8. Copy the token and paste it into the **Access token** field in **New Linked Service (Azure Databricks)**.

9. Click **Create**. Congratulations, you have created a linked service to a Databricks cluster!

10. Navigate to Data Factory, create a new pipeline, and drag and drop the **Notebook** activity from the **Databricks** section. In Azure Databricks, select the linked service you created previously.

*Figure 5.27: Creating a new pipeline*

11. In **Settings**, select the notebook you created in the Azure Databricks workspace:

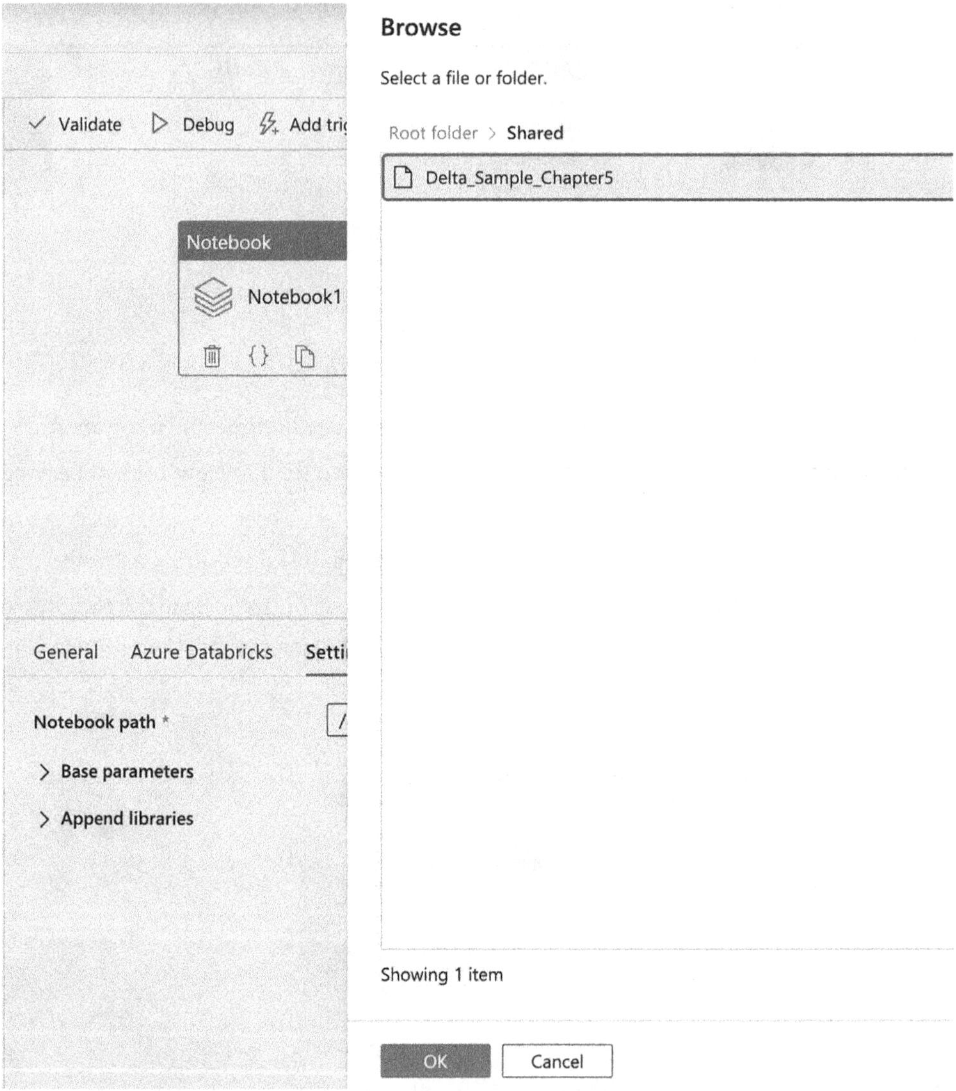

*Figure 5.28: Setting up notebook activity*

12. In the **General** tab, fill in the **Name** and **Description** fields.

13. For this recipe, leave **Timeout, Retry, Retry interval, Secure output,** and **Secure input** at their default values.

14. Go to the **Azure Databricks** tab. Select your linked service and test the connection.

15. Save your pipeline by clicking **Publish all**.

16. Now you can run or debug your notebook activity within ADF.

17. Our cluster is fully functional and executes Spark jobs that ingest the data and transform and write the data as a delta table. In the following screenshot, you can see a list of the jobs and their IDs, as well as stages, statuses, and durations:

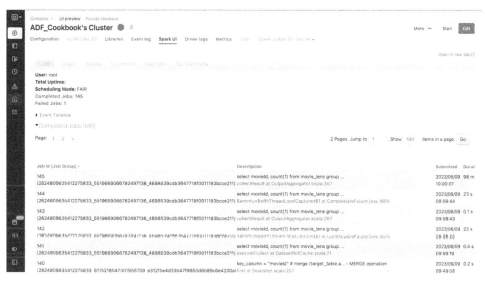

*Figure 5.29: Spark UI and jobs list*

18. You can go to **Clusters**, click on your cluster, then **Metrics**, and download a snapshot of the cluster overview, which includes load statistics, memory, network, CPU usage in the last hour, and so on. A partial view of this snapshot is presented in the following screenshot:

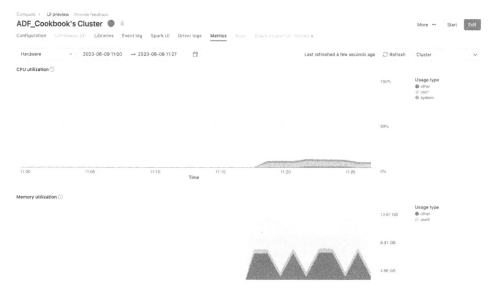

*Figure 5.30: Cluster metrics snapshot*

19. Let's move to our Azure Data Lake Storage interface and check the outcomes of the job. Go to **Storage Accounts**, click on your account with the data and model, and then **Containers**. Then, click on the container name and check what is inside. We can see that Databricks stored the model in the pre-defined location, as shown in the following screenshot:

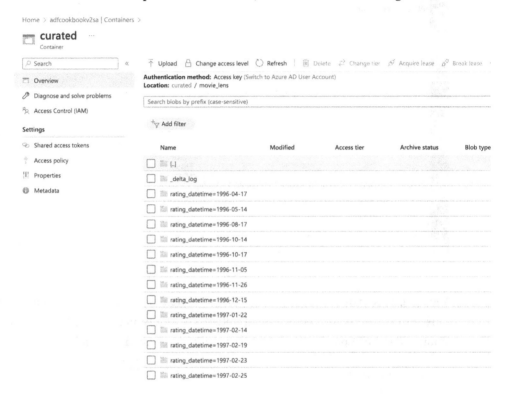

*Figure 5.31: Checking out outputs to Azure Data Lake Storage*

## How it works...

Azure Databricks is a managed solution that runs Spark clusters in a convenient way. These clusters use an internal filesystem. ADF can forward parameters and credentials and trigger the execution of notebooks and JAR and Python files. Later, when we run Spark jobs, we can securely mount Azure Data Lake Storage and both read data that we process and write process outputs.

ADF can create new Databricks clusters or utilize existing ones. Using a linked service, ADF connects to the external service and programmatically triggers the execution of Databricks notebooks and JAR and Python files. You can create extremely complex pipelines using ADF and Databricks.

Using Databricks for running Spark provides several advantages and is preferred over running Spark in an HDInsight cluster in certain scenarios:

- **Unified Platform**: Databricks offers a unified platform that seamlessly integrates data engineering, machine learning, and collaborative analytics, providing a consolidated environment for end-to-end data processing.

- **Ease of Use**: Databricks simplifies the deployment and management of Spark clusters, eliminating the administrative overhead associated with HDInsight, and making it more user-friendly and accessible.

- **Interactive Collaboration**: Databricks facilitates interactive and collaborative data analysis, allowing teams to work on notebooks simultaneously, fostering real-time collaboration and enhancing productivity.

- **Auto-Scaling and Dynamic Resource Management**: Databricks provides built-in auto-scaling, allowing clusters to automatically adapt to varying workloads, ensuring optimal resource utilization without manual intervention.

- **Integrated Workspace**: Databricks features an integrated workspace with version control, enabling seamless collaboration on code and notebooks, making it easier to manage and maintain Spark jobs.

- **Performance Optimization**: Databricks optimizes Spark performance through features like Delta Lake for efficient storage and caching, resulting in improved query speeds and overall job performance.

- **Serverless Execution**: With Databricks' serverless execution, users can run Spark workloads without the need to manage or provision clusters explicitly, enhancing resource efficiency and reducing operational complexities.

- **Managed Spark Environment**: Databricks manages the Spark environment, ensuring the latest Spark versions, security updates, and optimizations are automatically applied, reducing the burden on users for maintenance tasks.

- **Cost-Effective Pricing Model**: Databricks offers a cost-effective pricing model, providing flexibility in resource allocation and cost management, particularly beneficial for variable workloads.

- **Integration with Other Azure Services**: Databricks seamlessly integrates with various Azure services, promoting interoperability and enhancing the overall Azure ecosystem's capabilities.

## There is more...

For more information, check out the Microsoft documentation on running a Databricks notebook with the Databricks Notebook activity in Azure Data Factory: `https://learn.microsoft.com/en-us/azure/data-factory/transform-data-using-databricks-notebook`.

Having established a robust data model in Delta Lake and executed efficient data pipeline jobs with Databricks, our focus now shifts to the seamless ingestion of data into Delta Lake through the utilization of Mapping data flows.

# Ingesting data into Delta Lake using Mapping Data Flows

In the realm of data management, **Atomicity, Consistency, Isolation, Durability (ACID)** is a foundational set of principles ensuring the reliability and integrity of database transactions. Let's break down the significance of each component:

- **Atomicity**: Guarantees that a transaction is treated as a single, indivisible unit. It either executes in its entirety, or not at all. This ensures that even if a system failure occurs mid-transaction, the database remains in a consistent state.

- **Consistency**: Enforces that a transaction brings the database from one valid state to another. Inconsistent states are avoided, providing a reliable and predictable environment for data operations.

- **Isolation**: Ensures that transactions operate independently of each other, preventing interference. Isolation safeguards against concurrent transactions affecting each other's outcomes, maintaining data integrity.

- **Durability**: Guarantees that once a transaction is committed, its changes are permanent and survive any subsequent system failures. This ensures data persistence and reliability in the face of unexpected events.

Delta Lake is a cutting-edge open source storage layer that ensures the atomicity, consistency, isolation, and durability of data within a lake. Essentially, Delta Lake conforms to ACID standards, making it an ideal solution for data management.

In addition to offering scalable metadata handling and support for ACID transactions, Delta Lake integrates seamlessly with existing data lakes and Apache Spark APIs. If you're interested in exploring Delta Lake, there are several options available to you. Databricks provides notebooks, along with compatible Apache Spark APIs, to create and manage delta lakes. On the other hand, Azure Data Factory's Mapping data flows allow for ACID-compliant CRUD operations through simplified ETL pipelines using scaled-out Apache Spark clusters. This recipe will walk you through how to get started with Delta Lake using Azure Data Factory's new Delta Lake connector, demonstrating how to create, insert, update, and delete data in a delta lake.

## Getting ready

Ensure that you have a pre-configured resource group and storage account with Azure Data Lake Gen2 and Azure Data Factory. In ADLS Gen2, you'll need to have raw, staging, and curated containers. One of the fundamental components of any modern data architecture is the Raw zone, which serves as a repository for storing source data in its original form. In addition to the Raw zone, there is also the Staging zone, which is designed to house delta updates, inserts, deletes, and other transformations. The Curated zone acts as a refined, curated repository that bridges the gap between raw, unprocessed data and the finalized, business-ready data, facilitating a structured and well-maintained foundation for downstream analytical processes. While this particular demonstration won't make use of the Curated zone, it's worth noting that this section of the architecture often contains the final ETL pipelines, advanced analytics, and data science models that have been further refined and curated from the Staging zone.

## How to do it...

We will go through the process of creating a Snowflake account and a new database, loading data into a new table, then connecting ADF to the Snowflake table and loading the data to ADLS. Follow these instructions:

1.  In ADF, go to the **Author** page and create a new **Data Flow**. Name it **Load_DeltaLake_DF**.

2.  Under **Source settings,** Enter:

    a.  **Output stream name** – RawSource

    b.  **Source type** – **Dataset**

    c.  **Dataset** – Choose a dataset with CSV data from the Raw zone of your ADLS Gen2

    d.  If your dataset is huge, you can enable sampling to limit the number of rows for testing purposes, otherwise choose **Disable**

*Figure 5.32: Creating a new data flow*

3. Add a new sink. Under the **Sink** options, choose:

    a. **Output stream name** – DeltaSink

    b. **Incoming stream – RawSource**

    c. **Sink type – Inline**

    d. **Inline dataset type – Delta**

    e. **Linked service – AzureBlobStorage1**

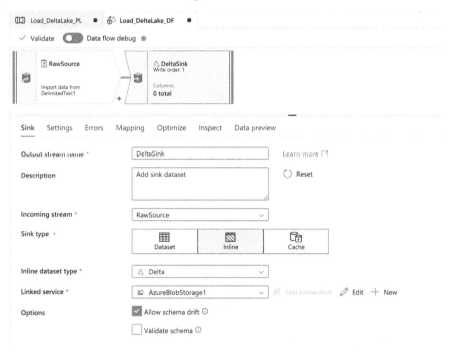

*Figure 5.33: Setting up the sink*

4.  In **Settings**, choose the container and folder path where you want to store the output delta table. In our case, it's `staging/ratings`, as `ratings.csv` is a source file. You need to check **Allow insert** in **Update method:**

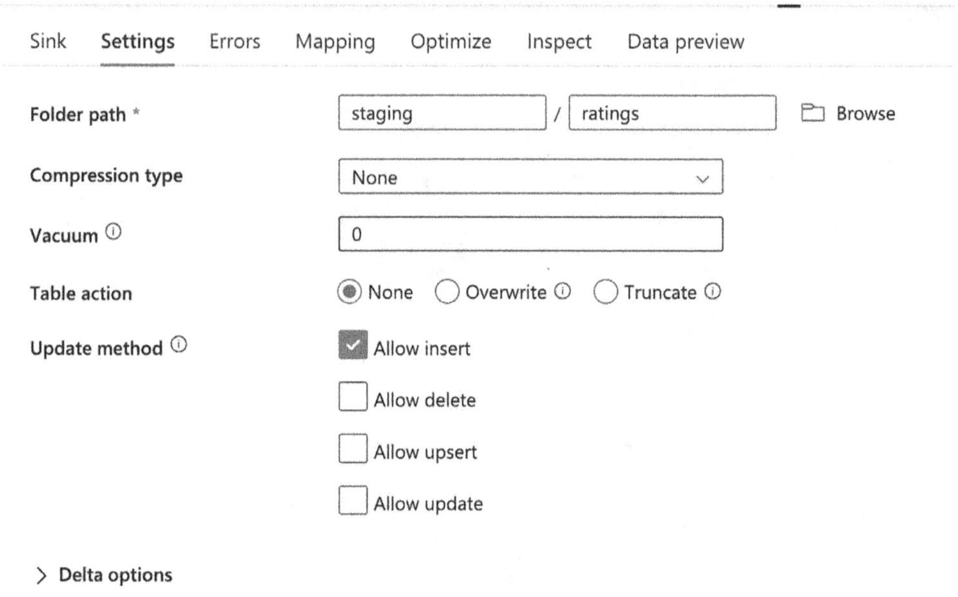

| Sink | **Settings** | Errors | Mapping | Optimize | Inspect | Data preview |
|------|--------------|--------|---------|----------|---------|--------------|

Folder path *                    staging          /  ratings              📁 Browse

Compression type               None                                 ⌄

Vacuum ⓘ                       0

Table action                   ⦿ None   ◯ Overwrite ⓘ   ◯ Truncate ⓘ

Update method ⓘ                ☑ Allow insert

                               ☐ Allow delete

                               ☐ Allow upsert

                               ☐ Allow update

› Delta options

*Figure 5.34: Configuring data flow settings*

5.  Create a new Data Factory pipeline and add a data flow activity from **Move & Transform**. Name it `Load_DeltaLake_PL`. In **Settings**, choose:

    a.  **Data Flow – Load_DeltaLake_DF**

    b.  **Run on (Azure IR) – AutoResolveIntegrationRuntime**

    c.  **Compute size – Small**

    d.  **Logging level – Verbose**

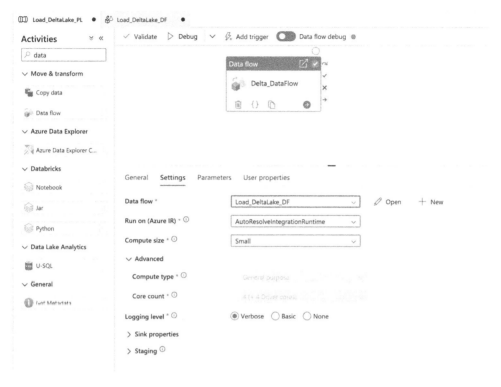

*Figure 5.35: Creating a new pipeline with data flow activity*

6.  Debug the pipeline. It will ask you to turn on the data flow debug. You need to make a choice for **Integration runtime** and **Debug time to live** (which is needed for cluster autotermination in order to save costs). It will spin up the cluster and run the data flow.

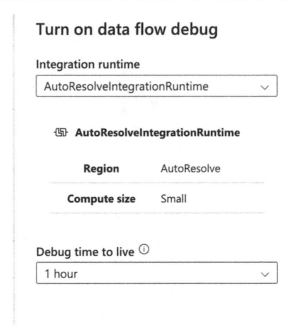

*Figure 5.36: Turning on data flow debug*

7.  When the pipeline succeeds, you can go to the storage account and check the specified folder has the data and **_delta_log** files.

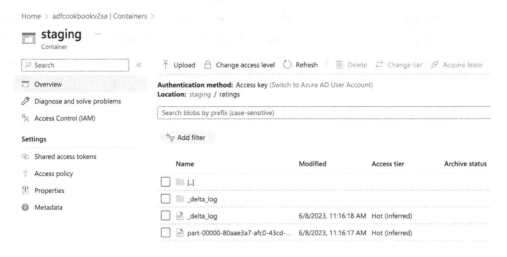

*Figure 5.37: Checking the delta table in the storage account*

8. Now let's add some transformations to our dataset and update the delta table. We will update the **timestamp** column to convert it from Unix timestamp to **yyyy-MM-dd HH:mm:ss** datetime format. Add a new derived column as follows:

   a. **Output stream name** – AddDatetime

   b. **Incoming stream** – RawSource

   c. **Columns** – timestamp

   d. **Expression** – toString(toTimestamp(toInteger(byName('TIME-STAMP'))*1000l,'yyyy-MM-dd HH:mm:ss'), 'yyyy-MM-dd HH:mm:ss')

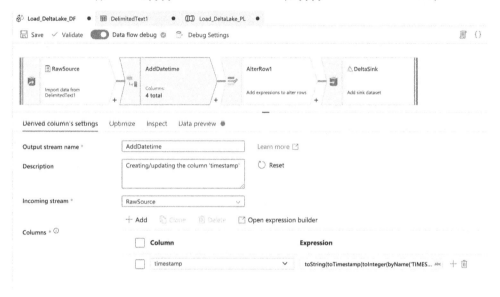

*Figure 5.38: Adding transformations*

9.  To allow **Update operation**, you need an **AlterRow** transformation to set row policies. Add it as follows. In **Alter row conditions**, select **Update if**. Under **Expression**, add **true()**. You can also specify **Insert If, Delete If,** and **Upsert If** conditions if needed.

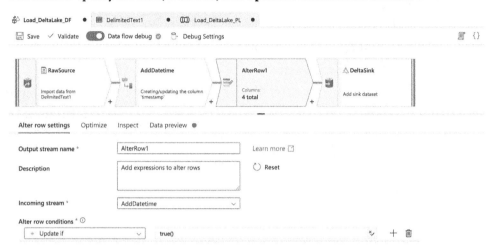

*Figure 5.39: Adding alter row*

10. In the **DeltaSink** activity, for **Update method,** select **Allow insert, Allow upsert, Allow update**. For **Key columns,** choose **List of columns** and select **userId** and **movieId** as they represent the unique key of the table.

*Figure 5.40: Setting up merge*

11. Debug the pipeline and check the results of the delta table in the ADLS Gen2 folder.

# How it works...

The Delta file format is a proprietary format developed by Databricks that provides improved reliability, performance, and scalability for large-scale data processing workflows. When you execute the data flow, ADF generates code that runs on Apache Spark clusters to perform the data transformation and writing to ADLS Gen2 in the Delta format. As data is written to ADLS Gen2, it is automatically partitioned into multiple smaller files called Delta files. These files are organized based on the partitioning scheme defined in the data flow mapping. Each Delta file contains a header that describes the data schema, metadata, and transaction log information for the file. Each subsequent write operation to the same Delta file adds new records to the existing data, rather than overwriting or duplicating it. This allows efficient updates and incremental processing of the data.

Overall, using Mapping data flows in ADF to write data to Delta files in ADLS Gen2 provides a scalable and reliable way to process large volumes of data with built-in support for data versioning, change tracking, and data lineage.

## There is more...

For more information, check out Microsoft documentation on Delta format in Azure Data Factory: `https://learn.microsoft.com/en-us/azure/data-factory/format-delta`.

Having explored the seamless process of ingesting data into Delta Lake using Mapping data flows, we will now pivot toward external integrations. In the next section, we delve into the intricacies of connecting Delta Lake with other compute engines, with a specific focus on integration with Snowflake.

# External integrations with other compute engines (Snowflake)

**Azure Data Factory** (**ADF**), a powerful cloud-based data integration service from Microsoft, has emerged as the go-to solution for enterprises seeking efficient and scalable data movement across various platforms. With its extensive capabilities, ADF not only enables seamless data integration within the Azure ecosystem but also offers external integrations with leading compute engines such as Snowflake.

Azure Data Factory's integration with Snowflake enables enterprises to seamlessly leverage cloud data warehousing capabilities. Snowflake's architecture, built for the cloud, complements Azure's cloud-native approach, offering a scalable and elastic solution for storing and processing vast amounts of data. The integration supports the creation of cost-effective and scalable data solutions. Azure Data Factory's ability to dynamically manage resources and Snowflake's virtual warehouse architecture contribute to cost optimization, ensuring enterprises only pay for the resources they consume.

This recipe will explore the integration between Azure Data Factory and Snowflake, an advanced cloud-based data warehousing platform. We will delve into the benefits and possibilities of combining these two technologies, showcasing how they harmonize to streamline data workflows, optimize processing, and facilitate insightful analytics.

Through this recipe, you will learn how to create, configure, and load data into Snowflake and gain insights into the steps involved in integrating Azure Data Factory with Snowflake, empowering you to effortlessly orchestrate data movement, transformations, and analytics across diverse sources and targets.

# Getting ready

Ensure that you have a pre-configured resource group and storage account with Azure Data Lake Gen2 and Azure Data Factory. Now, log in to your Microsoft Azure account.

# How to do it...

We will go through the process of creating a Snowflake account and a new database, loading data into a new table, and then connecting ADF to the Snowflake table and loading data to ADLS. Follow these instructions:

1. Create a new free account within **Snowflake** (or you can use an existing one if you already have one).

2. Go to **Data | Databases** and add a new database. Name it adfcookbookv2 and click **Create**.

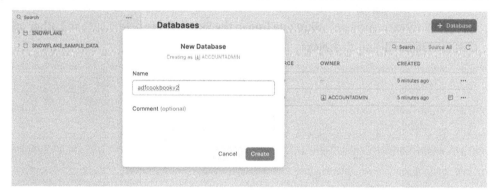

*Figure 5.41: Creating a database in Snowflake*

3. Go to your new database, select **PUBLIC**, and click **Create | Table | Standard**.

*Figure 5.42: Creating a table in Snowflake*

4.  Create a new table named tags in the database as follows:

*Figure 5.43: SQL script for creating a table in Snowflake*

5.  Select the **tags** table, click on **Load Data** in the top-right corner of your screen, choose **CSV** format, and select **Skip one line** in the **Skip header** field. Leave the other options as the defaults and click **Next**.

*Figure 5.44: Loading data into a table in Snowflake*

6. You will see a new window showing that data has been loaded. If you click on **Data Preview**, you can see the data in the **tags** table.

Figure 5.15: Preview table data in Snowflake

7. Now you can go to **Azure Data Factory** and create a new linked service in order to connect to **Snowflake**:

    a. **Name** – SnowflakeLS

    b. **Connect via integration runtime** – **AutoResolveIntegrationRuntime**

    c. **Account name** – full name of your Snowflake account

    d. **User name** – login name of the user used for connection

    e. **Password** – password for the specified user name

    f. **Database** – name of the created database in Snowflake **ADFCOOKBOOKV2**

    g. **Warehouse** – you can find it in your Snowflake account settings under **Admin | Warehouses**.

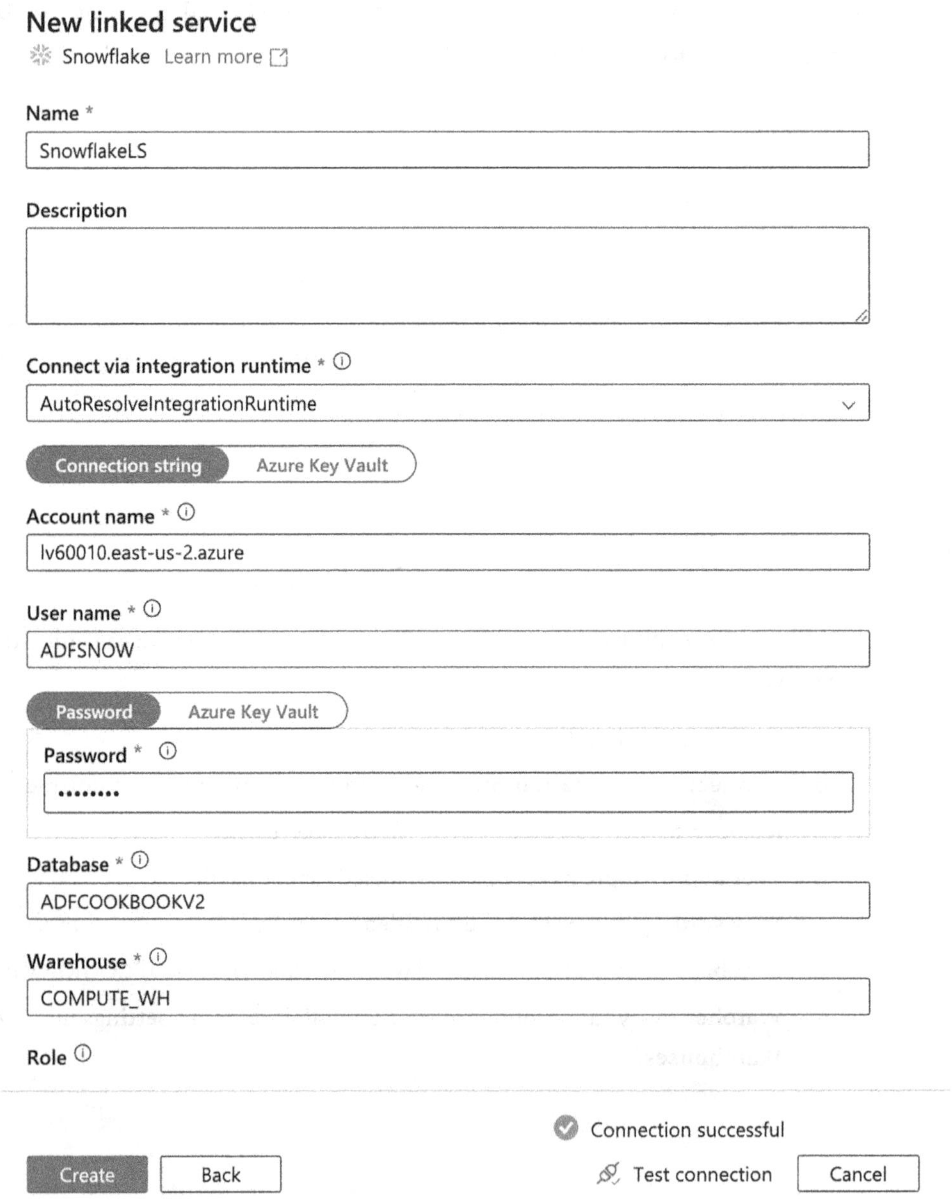

# New linked service

❄ Snowflake   Learn more ☐

**Name** *

SnowflakeLS

**Description**

**Connect via integration runtime** * ⓘ

AutoResolveIntegrationRuntime                                                      ⌄

( **Connection string**    Azure Key Vault )

**Account name** * ⓘ

lv60010.east-us-2.azure

**User name** * ⓘ

ADFSNOW

( **Password**    Azure Key Vault )

**Password** * ⓘ

••••••••

**Database** * ⓘ

ADFCOOKBOOKV2

**Warehouse** * ⓘ

COMPUTE_WH

**Role** ⓘ

                                                              ✅ Connection successful

[ Create ]  [ Back ]                               ✐ Test connection   [ Cancel ]

*Figure 5.46: Creating a linked service from Azure Data Factory to Snowflake*

Test the connection and click **Create**.

8.  You can find the account name for the previous step in **Admin – Account**, under **Locator**. You have to use it without **https://** and without **snowlakecomputing.com**.

*Figure 5.47: Finding account name in Snowflake*

9.  Now create a new dataset with **Snowflake** as the selected data store.

*Figure 5.48: Creating a Snowflake dataset in ADF*

10. Create a new ADF pipeline. Select **SnowflakeTable1** as the source dataset, and select **CSV** or the Parquet dataset linked to your Azure Blob Storage. If you haven't created a dataset, please refer to the previous chapter. Note that in order to write data in Parquet format, you will have to enable staging in the **Copy activity** settings. You can create a container named **staging** in your Azure Blob Storage for that.

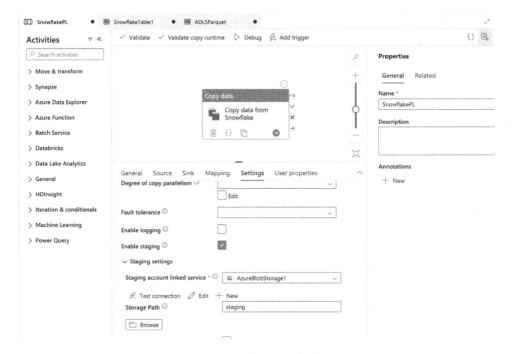

*Figure 5.49: Creating a pipeline in ADF*

11. Also, in order to copy data from Snowflake to Azure Blob Storage, you have to configure your linked service using SAS URI authentication. Go to your storage account settings, select **Shared access signature**, **Create SAS token**, and copy **Blob Service SAS URL**.

*Figure 5.50: Creating a Shared access signature in ADF*

12. In your Data Factory linked service configuration, select **Authentication type** as **SAS URI**. For the SAS URL, paste the Blob Service SAS URL. Test the connection to make sure it works.

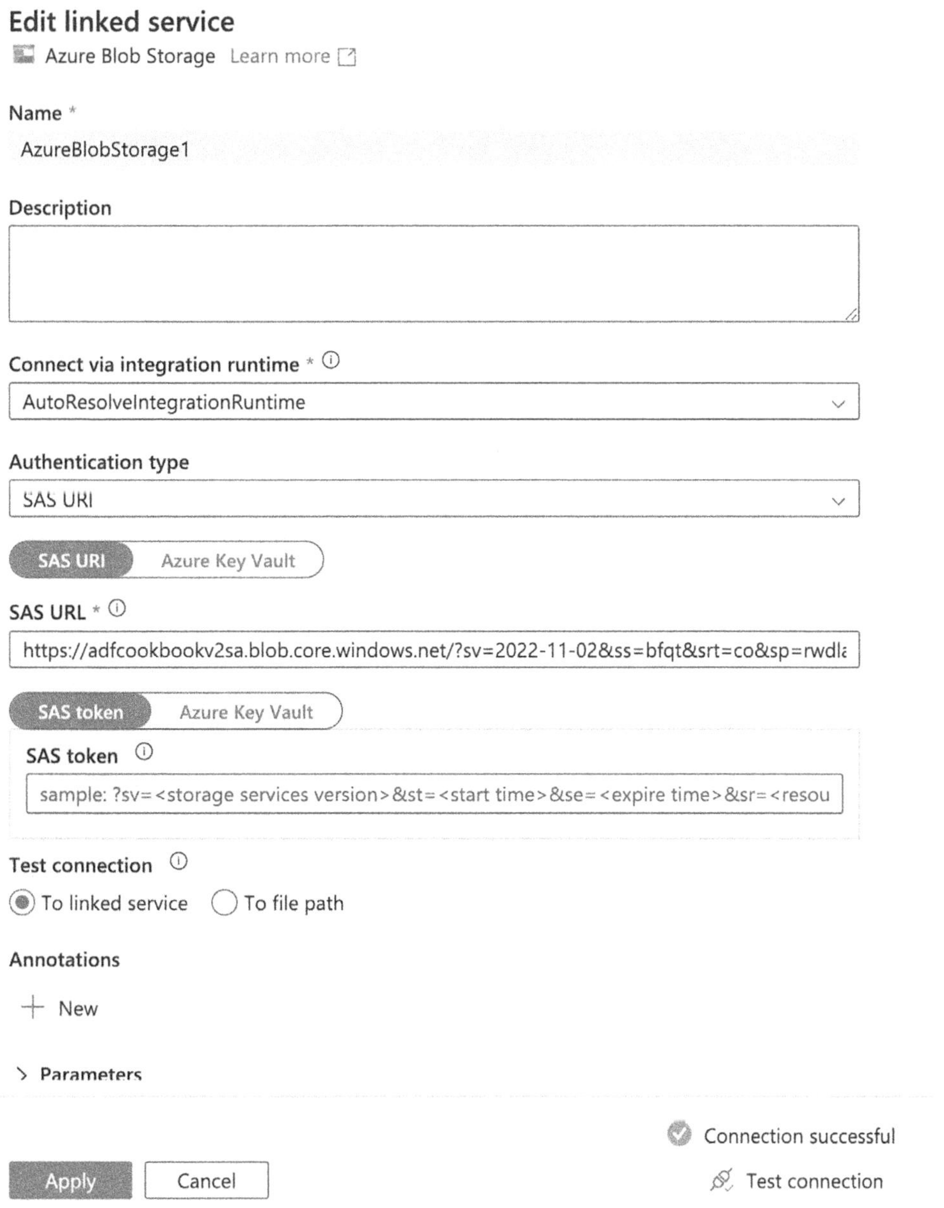

### Edit linked service
Azure Blob Storage  Learn more

Name *

AzureBlobStorage1

Description

Connect via integration runtime *

AutoResolveIntegrationRuntime

Authentication type

SAS URI

**SAS URI** | Azure Key Vault

SAS URL *

https://adfcookbookv2sa.blob.core.windows.net/?sv=2022-11-02&ss=bfqt&srt=co&sp=rwdla

**SAS token** | Azure Key Vault

SAS token

sample: ?sv=<storage services version>&st=<start time>&se=<expire time>&sr=<resou

Test connection

(•) To linked service   ( ) To file path

Annotations

+ New

> Parameters

| Apply | Cancel |

✔ Connection successful

Test connection

*Figure 5.51: Creating a linked service with SAS URL in ADF*

13. You will also need to assign your Data Factory a **Contributor** role in your storage account. To do this, you can go to the **Access Control (IAM)** section of your storage account, select **Add role assignment**, select the **Storage Blob Data Contributor** role and **Assign access to Managed Identity**, then members. Then add your Data Factory name (in our case, it's **adfcookbookch5**).

*Figure 5.52: Adding role assignment in access control*

14. Debug the pipeline and click on the googles to check the details of the run. If you selected Parquet as a sink, you'll see three stages of the copy activity, meaning that the one in the middle is for staging. You can also check the results in Azure Blob storage.

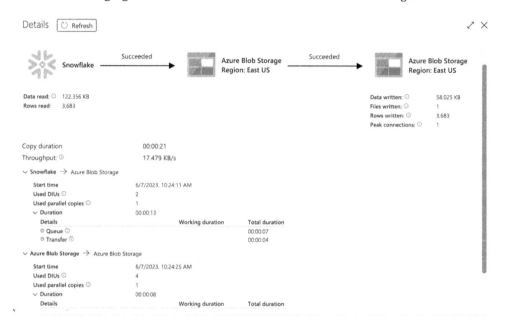

*Figure 5.53: Details of ADF pipeline execution*

## How it works...

When configuring the ADF pipeline, the data movement between Snowflake and Azure Blob storage happens through the Azure Integration Runtime (IR). In this configuration, the Azure IR handles the orchestration and execution of the pipeline, but Snowflake performs the necessary computations and data extraction from its storage to transfer the data to Azure Blob storage. The Azure IR is responsible for managing the data transfer process, including authentication, data movement, and error handling.

By configuring the pipeline to use the Snowflake computational resources, you can take advantage of Snowflake's parallel processing capabilities and optimizations for data extraction. The data will be transferred directly from Snowflake to Azure Blob storage using the staging layer, leveraging Snowflake's computational resources for efficient data movement.

## There is more...

Microsoft documentation on copying and transforming data in Snowflake using Azure Data Factory or Azure Synapse Analytics: `https://learn.microsoft.com/en-us/azure/data-factory/connector-snowflake?tabs=data-factory`

## Join our community on Discord

Join our community's Discord space for discussions with the authors and other readers:

`https://discord.gg/U229qmBmT3`

# 6

# Data Migration – Azure Data Factory and Other Cloud Services

When your business needs to move data between cloud providers, Azure Data Factory presents a convenient and robust interface for this task. Microsoft provides connectors to integrate Data Factory with multiple third-party services, including **Amazon Web Services** (**AWS**) and **Google Cloud**. In this chapter, we will walk through several illustrative examples of migrating data from these two cloud providers. In addition, you will learn how to use Azure Data Factory's Custom Activity to work with providers who are not supported by Microsoft's built-in connectors. Utilizing Azure Data Factory's Custom Activity not only empowers users to seamlessly integrate with data providers beyond Microsoft's native connectors but also underscores the platform's adaptability, allowing organizations to tailor their data workflows to unique business needs and leverage a broader spectrum of data sources.

In this chapter, we will cover the following recipes:

- Copying data from Amazon S3 to Azure Blob storage
- Copying large datasets from S3 to ADLS
- Copying data from Google Cloud Storage to Azure Data Lake
- Copying data from Google BigQuery to Azure Data Lake Storage
- Migrating data from Google BigQuery to Azure Synapse

# Technical requirements

All recipes in this chapter assume that you have a Microsoft Azure account and a Data Factory instance. Refer to *Chapter 1, Getting Started with ADF*, for instructions on how to set up your Azure account and create a Data Factory instance.

For the recipes in this chapter, you will need accounts with sufficient permissions on third-party services. For the first and second recipes, you will need to set up an account with AWS. For the third, fourth, and fifth recipes, you will need a Google Cloud account. For the final recipe, you will need a Snowflake account.

If you do not have accounts already set up with the aforementioned services, you can do this for free:

- Go to https://aws.amazon.com/console/ to sign up for a free AWS account. You will need to know this account's access key ID and secret access key. How you get this information will depend on how your account is set up (in other words, is this a root account or an IAM user?). Refer to https://aws.amazon.com/blogs/security/wheres-my-secret-access-key/ for instructions on how to obtain this information.

- Go to https://cloud.google.com/ to sign up for a free Google Cloud account and create your first project.

- Go to https://signup.snowflake.com/ to sign up for a Snowflake account.

# Copying data from Amazon S3 to Azure Blob storage

In this recipe, you will learn how to copy data from an AWS S3 bucket to the Azure Blob storage container using a data factory.

# Getting ready

This recipe requires you to have an AWS account and an S3 bucket. Refer to the *Technical require-ments* section to find out how to set up a new AWS account if you do not have one. Once you have your AWS account set up, go to `https://s3.console.aws.amazon.com/s3/` to create a bucket. Upload the sample CSV files from `https://github.com/PacktPublishing/Azure-Data-Factory-Cookbook-Second-Edition/tree/main/Chapter06/datasets` to your bucket.

# How to do it...

Rather than designing the pipeline in the **Author** tab, we will use the Copy Data wizard. The Copy Data wizard in Azure Data Factory is recommended for pipeline creation due to its user-friendly interface, quick setup with built-in templates, automatic mapping, support for various connectors, and seamless integration with monitoring and management features. It simplifies the pipeline creation process, making it accessible to users with varying levels of technical expertise.

The Copy Data wizard will walk you through pipeline creation step by step, and will create and run the pipeline for you:

1. Go to the home page of Azure Data Factory and select the **Ingest** tile to start the Copy Data wizard.

*Figure 6.1: Copy Data Wizard interface*

2.  We need to define the properties of the data pipeline. We will start by selecting **Task type** and **Task cadence or task schedule**:

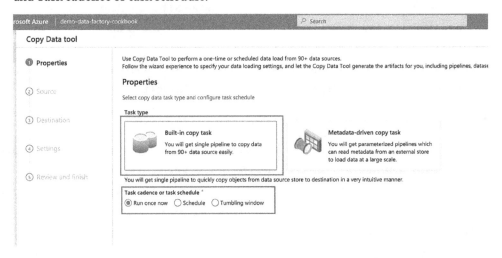

*Figure 6.2: Copy Data wizard properties*

3.  The Copy Data wizard will help us define the properties of the source (connection and the dataset). We will start by configuring the connection properties. In the interface, select **Create New Connection**, and then, in the **New connection** blade, select **Amazon S3** as the connector. Then, fill in the name of your connector as well as the access key ID and secret access key. It is crucial to prioritize the security of your data by treating the access key ID and secret access key information with the utmost confidentiality. Ensure that these credentials are securely stored and managed, following best practices for access control and encryption to safeguard sensitive data and prevent unauthorized access. Refer to the *Getting ready* section on how to obtain the credentials if you do not have them to hand.

    Your **New linked service** blade should look like this:

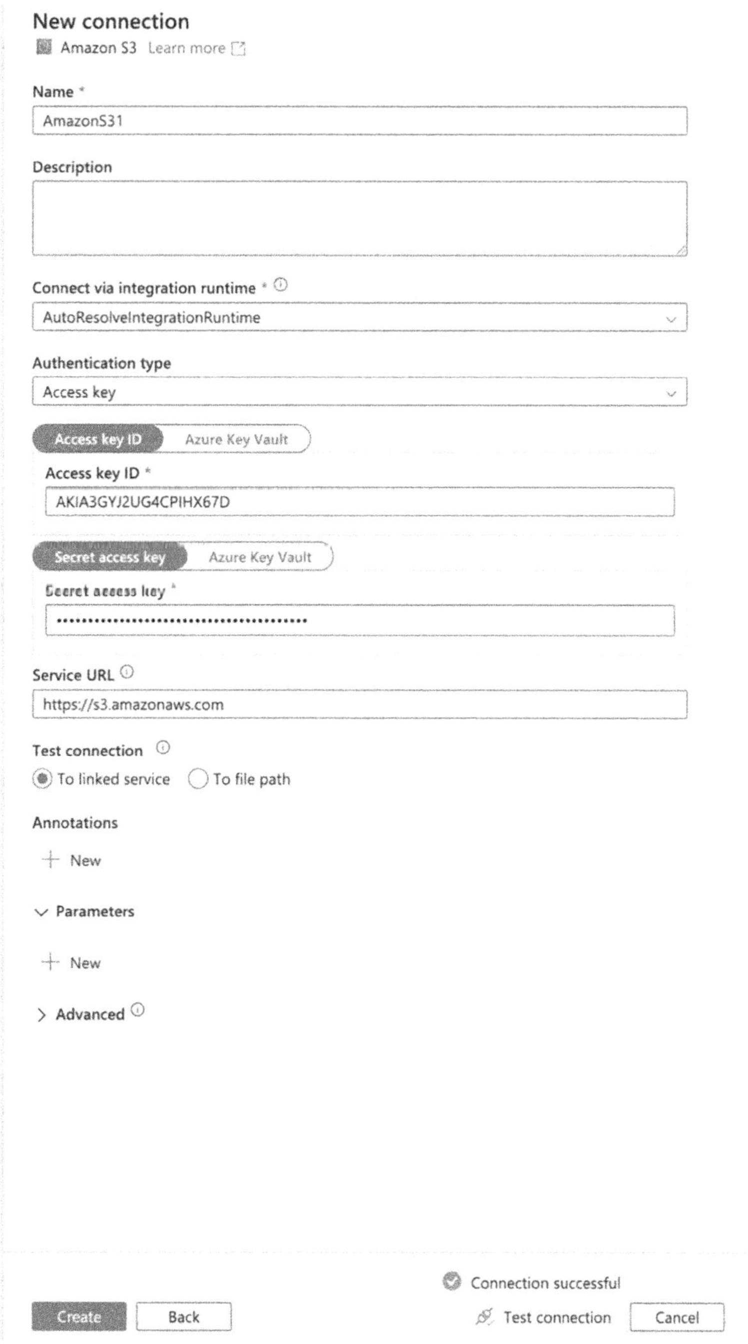

## New connection

Amazon S3   Learn more ☐

Name *

AmazonS31

Description

Connect via integration runtime * ⓘ

AutoResolveIntegrationRuntime ⌄

Authentication type

Access key ⌄

**Access key ID**   Azure Key Vault

Access key ID *

AKIA3GYJ2UG4CPIHX67D

**Secret access key**   Azure Key Vault

Secret access key *

••••••••••••••••••••••••••••••••

Service URL ⓘ

https://s3.amazonaws.com

Test connection ⓘ

◉ To linked service   ◯ To file path

Annotations

+ New

⌄ Parameters

+ New

⟩ Advanced ⓘ

✅ Connection successful

Create   Back           🖊 Test connection   Cancel

*Figure 6.3: Creating a linked service for AWS S3*

4.  Test the connection and create the linked service. Click on **Next** to move to the next step.

5.  Now we need to configure the dataset for our source. In the interface presented, enter the name of your S3 bucket (`adf-migration-to-azure-demo` in our example). Use the **Browse** button to visualize the folder structure. Leave the recursive checked (we do want to copy the contents of the directory recursively), and set **Max concurrent connections** to 1. Then, hit **Next**.

6.  The Copy Data wizard will test the connection and will present you with the **File format settings** interface. Click on **Detect text format** and then check the **First row as header** checkbox to allow the Copy Data wizard to configure the dataset for you:

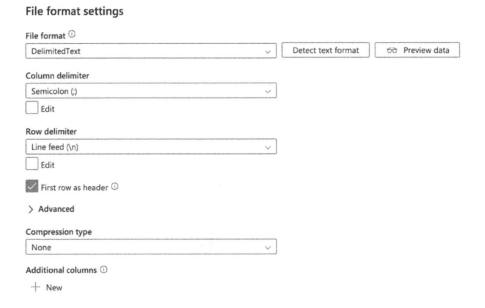

*Figure 6.4: Configuring the file format in the Copy Data wizard*

With the source dataset formatted, we are ready to go to the next step.

7.  Now we need to configure the **Destination** properties (as with **Source**, both for the connection and the dataset). Let's configure the connection. Select a linked service for the Azure blob where you intend to store the data from your S3 bucket. You may have one already available if you followed one of the recipes in previous chapters. If you do not have one configured, follow the instructions in the *Using parameters and built-in functions* recipe in *Chapter 2, Orchestration and Control Flow,* for detailed instructions on how to create a linked service for an Azure blob.

Configuring a linked service for Azure Blob storage is essential as it establishes a secure and managed connection between Azure Data Factory and the storage account. This linked service not only streamlines the configuration process but also ensures that credentials and connection details are centrally managed, promoting best practices in security, governance, and centralized administration for storing and retrieving data in Azure Blob storage.

8.  After you have selected your connection, you will see an interface to choose the output location, as shown in the following screenshot. Type in the full path to the folder within your Azure storage account where you want to import the files. Again, use the **Browse** button for ease of navigation:

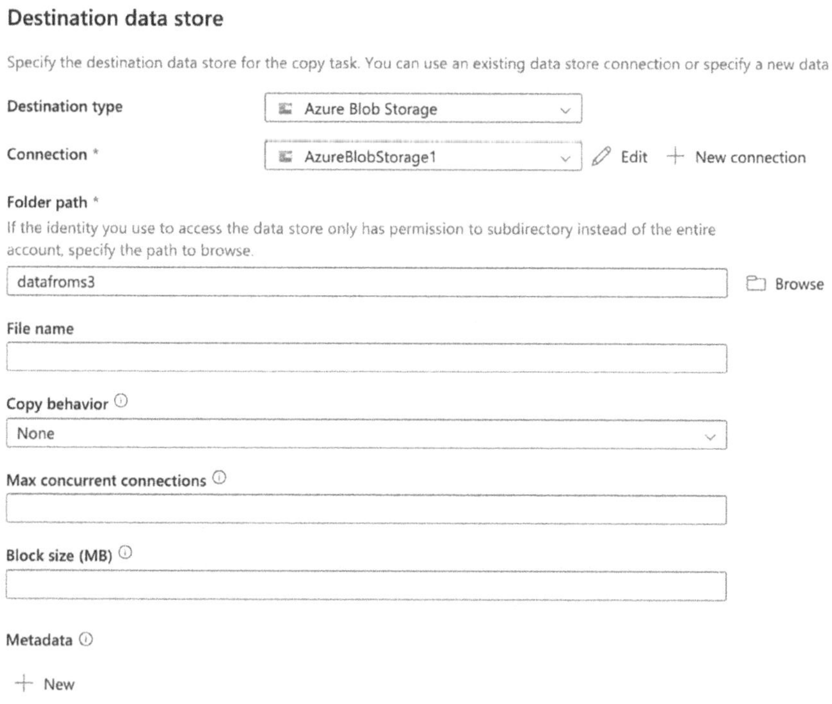

### Destination data store

Specify the destination data store for the copy task. You can use an existing data store connection or specify a new data store.

| | |
|---|---|
| Destination type | 🖳 Azure Blob Storage ⌄ |
| Connection * | 🖳 AzureBlobStorage1 ⌄  ✎ Edit  + New connection |

**Folder path ***

If the identity you use to access the data store only has permission to subdirectory instead of the entire account, specify the path to browse.

datafroms3                                            📁 Browse

**File name**

**Copy behavior** ⓘ

None                                                  ⌄

**Max concurrent connections** ⓘ

**Block size (MB)** ⓘ

**Metadata** ⓘ

+ New

*Figure 6.5: Specifying the location of your files*

9.  You have set up the connection. The Copy Data wizard will verify the connection and present you with two consecutive screens – **File Format Settings** and **Settings**. Click through both. No additional configuration is needed.

10. We have filled in the connection and dataset information for both the source (Amazon S3 bucket) and destination (Azure Blob storage) of our pipeline. Review the summary that the Copy Data wizard presents, and verify that all the settings are correct:

*Figure 6.6: Copy Data wizard – Summary*

11. When you go to the next step, the Copy Data wizard will run the validation to ensure that all the configurations are correct, and then run the pipeline. Click on the **Monitor** button to see your pipeline status. Once the pipeline completes execution, you should see the files in your Azure Blob storage.

## How it works...

The Copy Data wizard is simply an application that assists you in designing a simple data movement pipeline. It presents you with a series of steps, and once you have filled them all in, it creates and publishes the pipeline for you. After you have gone through the steps in this recipe, go to the **Monitor** tab. Monitoring the pipeline is essential for tracking the execution status and performance metrics of your pipeline. It consists of a single Copy activity that we configured with the Copy Data wizard. This provides real-time insights into the health of your data movement tasks, enabling proactive troubleshooting, ensuring successful execution, and facilitating timely response to any potential issues that may arise during the data integration process.

# Copying large datasets from S3 to ADLS

Azure Data Factory can help you move very large datasets into the Azure ecosystem with speed and efficiency. The key to achieving this efficiency lies in data partitioning. Data partitioning optimizes the movement process by breaking down the dataset into smaller, manageable chunks, allowing for parallel processing and increased performance. The specific way you partition your data depends heavily on the nature and characteristics of your dataset, ensuring that the movement process is tailored to maximize efficiency.

In the following recipe, we will illustrate a methodology to utilize a data partitioning table for moving a large dataset. We will use a public Common Crawl dataset, which contains petabytes of web crawl data from 2008 to the present day. It is a public dataset hosted on the AWS S3 platform. We will only use a small subset of this data for our example, enough to illustrate the power of data factory parallel processing.

## Getting ready

In order to access AWS, such as an S3 bucket, you need to have proper credentials. These credentials consist of an access key ID (for example, *AKFAGOKFOLNN7EXAMPL8*) and the secret access key itself (for example, *pUgkrUXtPFEer/PO9rbNG/bPxRgiMYEXAMPLEKEY*). In this book, we will refer to these credentials as your **AWS Account key** and **Secret**.

Even though Common Crawl data is hosted in a public repository, you will still need an AWS account and your own **Account key** and **Secret**. Refer to the instructions in the *Technical requirements* section at the beginning of the chapter on how to obtain these credentials.

We will need to create a partition table in our SQL database. Download the script to create the partitions from `https://github.com/PacktPublishing/Azure-Data-Factory-Cookbook-Second-Edition/blob/main/Chapter06/CreateCommonCrawlPartitionsTable.sql`.

You will also need access to an Azure Gen2 storage account where you plan to copy the data. Refer to the document at `https://docs.microsoft.com/azure/storage/common/storage-account-create?tabs=azure-portal` if you need to create one.

Finally, we will need an instance of the Azure SQL Database, and the linked service for this instance. Refer to the *Using parameters and built-in functions* recipe in *Chapter 2, Orchestration and Control Flow*, for detailed instructions on how to create this resource and configure the connection.

> Note that moving large datasets can be very expensive. We suggest that you opt for local redundancy when you create your Azure Data Lake account, and delete data that is not required as a cost-saving measure. Additionally, it's crucial to proactively manage and monitor your usage to avoid unexpected charges. Once you construct your pipeline and verify that it works as expected, do not run it repeatedly: you might incur considerable charges. Regularly check your Azure consumption and usage metrics to strike a balance between utilizing Azure services effectively and managing expenses responsibly.

## How to do it...

In order to copy the large dataset, we will first create a database table that will define how we partition our data. Then, we will create an outer pipeline, which will read information from the partition table and pass it to a **ForEach** activity. The **ForEach** activity will invoke an inner pipeline that will perform the data movement:

In the Azure portal, go to your Azure SQL Database and open **Query Editor**, logging in with the credentials you specified when you were creating the resource. In the **Query** window, enter the following query. The text of this query is available in the `CreateCommon CrawlPartitionsTable.sql` file that you downloaded in the *Getting ready* section. We strongly advise you to copy text from the file downloaded from GitHub:

```
CREATE TABLE [dbo].[CommonCrawlPartitions](
    [YearAndMonth][varchar](255) NULL,
    [Path] [varchar](255) NULL,
```

```
    [UpdatedAt] [Datetime]
)
INSERT INTO CommonCrawlPartitions (YearAndMonth, Path, UpdatedAt)
VALUES
('01-2022', 'cc-index/collections/CC-MAIN-2022-05/indexes', GetDate()),
('05-2022', 'cc-index/collections/CC-MAIN-2022-21/indexes', GetDate()),
('06-2022', 'cc-index/collections/CC-MAIN-2022-27/indexes', GetDate()),
('08-2022', 'cc-index/collections/CC-MAIN-2022-33/indexes', GetDate()),
('09-2022', 'cc-index/collections/CC-MAIN-2022-40/indexes', GetDate()),
('11-2022', 'cc-index/collections/CC-MAIN-2022-49/indexes', GetDate()),
('06-2023', 'cc-index/collections/CC-MAIN-2023-06/indexes', GetDate()),
('03-2023', 'cc-index/collections/CC-MAIN-2023-14/indexes', GetDate());
```

Run the query to create and populate the dbo.Common CrawlPartitions table.

## Creating the linked services and dataset for the pipeline

Once we have created the dbo.Common CrawlPartitions table, we are ready to create the linked services and dataset for our pipeline. Perform the following steps to do so:

1. You can reuse the Azure SQL linked service and dataset that you created in one of the previous recipes. If you have not created any, or do not wish to reuse them, create a new one.

   Go to your **Data Factory** instance and open the **Author** interface. Create a dataset to store the data from the partition table. From **Factory Resources** (on the left), select **New Dataset**. In the **New Dataset** blade, select **Azure SQL**. Select the appropriate subscription and test connection, and then click on **Create**.

2. Create a linked service to connect to **S3**: from the **Manage** tab, select **Linked Services**, and then click on **New**. This step is similar to *step 3* in the previous recipe (*Copying data from Amazon S3 to Azure Blob storage*), and you may reuse that connection here as well.

3.  Create a dataset to refer to the **S3 Common Crawl** repository. Specify **S3** as the data store and **Binary** as the file format. Select the **S3** linked service we created in the previous step as the linked service. For the file path, enter Common Crawl as a bucket. Do not enter anything in the *folder* or *file* text fields:

*Figure 6.7: S3 Common Crawl dataset configuration*

4.  Create a linked service and a dataset for the ADLS account to which you will be moving data. The steps are similar to those that you perform when creating a linked service and dataset for a common Azure Blob storage account, but instead of **DelimitedText**, select **Binary** for **Format Type**. Make the dataset parameterized (refer to the *Using parameters and built-in functions* recipe in *Chapter 2, Orchestration and Control Flow*, for instructions on how to create a parameterized dataset). Parameterizing the dataset enhances flexibility and facilitates dynamic data movement. Specify a single parameter, DirName, of the **String** type. In the **Connection** tab, enter the following text in the **Directory** part of the file path:

```
@dataset().DirName
```

The **Connection** tab for your dataset configuration window should look similar to the following screenshot:

*Figure 6.8: ADLS dataset configuration*

## Creating the inner pipeline

We now have all the components to design the inner pipeline, the pipeline that will actually copy chunks of data (defined in our partition table) from the **S3 Common Crawl** dataset into our Azure storage account. An inner pipeline is instrumental in orchestrating and optimizing the data movement process, allowing for efficient handling of partitioned data and enhancing the overall performance of the data transfer:

1. Create a new pipeline. For this example, we will call this pipeline pl_Common Crawl_ data_inner.

2. Add the **Path** parameter to the inner pipeline. Click anywhere on the white canvas, and in the **Parameters** tab at the bottom, add a new parameter with the name **Path** of the **String** type.

   Your inner pipeline **Parameters** tab should look similar to the following screenshot:

*Figure 6.9: Adding a path parameter to the inner pipeline*

3.  Add a Copy activity to this pipeline and name it `Copy Common Crawl from S3 to ADLS`.
    Next, configure the source for this Copy activity. Specify the **S3 Common Crawl** dataset we
    created in *step 3* (in the previous section) as the data source. In the **File Path Type** section,
    select the **Wildcard file path** radio button. This configuration is crucial for enhancing
    flexibility and accommodating varying file paths. By choosing the **Wildcard file path**
    option, the pipeline becomes adaptable to dynamic changes in file naming or directory
    structures. This is particularly valuable in scenarios where the dataset's organization
    may evolve over time.

    In the **Wildcard Paths** section, fill in the value using the dynamic content interface. Click
    inside the **Wildcard folder path** text field and then select the **Add dynamic content** link
    to bring up the interface. In that interface, scroll down to find the **Parameters** section and
    select the **Path** parameter. Click the **Finish** button to finalize your choice.

    Finally, in the **Wildcard file name** text field, enter *.gz.

4.  Configure the sink for the Copy activity. Select **ADLS dataset** from *step 4* of the previous
    recipe. Then, follow the instructions from *step 3* in this section, to use dynamic content
    to fill in the **Path** parameter text field.

## Creating the outer pipeline

Next, we will build the outer pipeline. The outer pipeline reads the data partitions from the table
and invokes the inner pipeline:

1.  Create one more pipeline. In this example, we will refer to it by the name `pl_Common
    Crawl_data_outer`.

2.  Add a **Lookup activity** from the **Activities** pane on the main canvas, and name it `Get
    Partitions`. In **Settings**, specify the **Source** dataset that we created in *step 1* of the *Creating the linked services and dataset for the pipeline* section (which represents the Azure SQL
    table). Click **preview data** to make sure the table is connected.

3.  Add a **ForEach** activity from the **Activities** pane and name it `For Each Partition`. In
    the **Settings** tab, set the batch count as 8 (the number of folders to load), and enter the
    following text in the **Items** text field:

    ```
    @activity('Get Partitions').output.value
    ```

    Make sure that the **Sequential** checkbox is not checked.

4.  Click inside the **ForEach** activity to open the **ForEach** activity canvas. Place an **Execute Pipeline** activity on this canvas and configure it to call the pl_Common Crawl_data_inner pipeline. Use the dynamic content interface to fill in the **Path** parameter value. Click inside the **Value** text field for the **Path** parameter, and select the **Add dynamic content** link. In the interface, scroll down to see the **ForEach Iterator** section. Select **Current item**. This will place the word @item() in the textbox on top of the dynamic content interface. Append the word Path to it. As a result, the text in the dynamic content textbox should read @item().Path. Click **Finish** to finalize your choice.

Your **Execute Pipeline** activity configuration settings should look similar to the following screenshot:

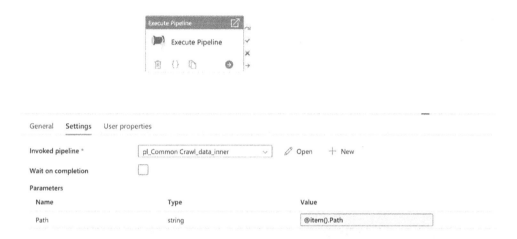

*Figure 6.10: Executing the pipeline activity configuration*

5.  Connect the **Lookup** activity and the **ForEach** activity.

6.  Publish your pipelines and run the outer pipeline. Click on **Add trigger** and select the **Trigger Now** option. If you run it in debug mode, you will not see parallelism.

7. Go to the **Monitor** tab and verify that you have one instance of the outer pipeline and two instances of the inner pipeline running, similar to the following screenshot:

*Figure 6.11: Monitor tab*

## How it works...

In this recipe, we have constructed a pipeline that is capable of moving very large datasets from S3 to an Azure storage account. For our example, we used one year of Common Crawl data. We then created the **Common CrawlPartitions** table in which we listed our partitions. This table also contained paths to the data locations.

Next, we created the inner and outer pipelines to ingest this data from locations provided in the **Common CrawlPartitions** table and copy it over to the Azure Data Lake Storage. The key to parallel execution is the design of the outer pipeline: it is the **ForEach** activity that allows us to execute activities in parallel by allowing us to specify the batch count. The ForEach activity is crucial for parallel execution as it acts as a container, managing the specified batch count and orchestrating the parallel processing of multiple sub-pipelines. Note that there is a limitation in terms of the degree of parallelism. If your batch count is more than 40, it is better to enhance the design by further partitioning the data and having multiple **ForEach** activities, each executing a subset of parallel sub-pipelines.

One thing to notice is that we have limited our dataset further by specifying the query in **Look-upActivity** as a **select top 2** path from [dbo][Common CrawlPartitioning]. We can regulate the size of our data pull by tweaking this query and, of course, by adding data to our data partitioning table.

## See also

If you are interested in the Common Crawl dataset, which contains web crawl data from 2008, you can obtain more information at https://Common Crawl.org/the-data/.

Microsoft offers guidance on pricing for Azure Data Factory. We strongly suggest that you familiarize yourself with this information before copying large datasets: `https://docs.microsoft.com//azure/data-factory/pricing-concepts`.

# Copying data from Google Cloud Storage to Azure Data Lake

In this recipe, we will use the built-in Microsoft connectors to copy the data from Google Cloud Storage to an Azure storage account. You will learn how to configure the Google Storage account and grant permissions to allow your data factory to connect and import the files.

## Getting ready

For this recipe, you will need to have a Google Cloud account and at least one Google Cloud Storage bucket:

1. To set up a free Google Cloud account and create your first project, refer to the *Technical requirements* section. Once your project is set up, go to your dashboard and copy your project ID.

2. Then, go to the Google Storage browser. It can be accessed at this URL: `https://console.cloud.google.com/storage/browser?<your-project-id>`. Be sure to replace the your-project-id field in the URL with the correct value.

3. In the Google Storage browser, create a new bucket. Once the bucket is created, upload the CSV files from the GitHub account (`https://github.com/PacktPublishing/Azure-Data-Factory-Cookbook-Second-Edition/tree/main/Chapter06/datasets`) to your bucket.

4. If you do not have an Azure storage account already available, follow the instructions at `https://docs.microsoft.com/azure/storage/common/storage-account-create?tabs=azure-portal` to set one up.

## How to do it...

In order to import the data, we will first set up the Google Storage account with the correct permissions. Ensuring the correct permissions for the Google Storage account is crucial, as it establishes the necessary access controls for a secure and smooth data import process. Once permissions are set, we will use the built-in Data Factory connectors to configure the linked services and datasets, connecting seamlessly to both the Google Cloud Storage bucket and the Azure storage account:

1. Start by generating credentials to access your Google Storage bucket. The credentials are called **Access Key** and **Secret**.

Log in to your Google Cloud Storage account and select the bucket that you want to export to Azure Storage. Select **Settings** from the menu on the left, and then go to the **INTEROPERABILITY** tab in the main blade. In the **INTEROPERABILITY** tab, click on the **CREATE A KEY FOR A SERVICE ACCOUNT** button:

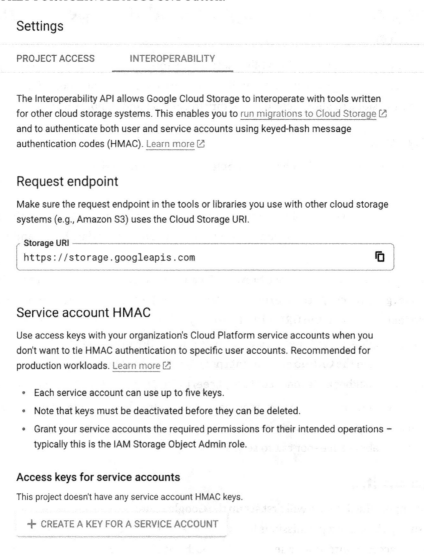

## Settings

| PROJECT ACCESS | INTEROPERABILITY |
|---|---|

The Interoperability API allows Google Cloud Storage to interoperate with tools written for other cloud storage systems. This enables you to run migrations to Cloud Storage [↗] and to authenticate both user and service accounts using keyed-hash message authentication codes (HMAC). Learn more [↗]

### Request endpoint

Make sure the request endpoint in the tools or libraries you use with other cloud storage systems (e.g., Amazon S3) uses the Cloud Storage URI.

```
Storage URI
https://storage.googleapis.com
```

### Service account HMAC

Use access keys with your organization's Cloud Platform service accounts when you don't want to tie HMAC authentication to specific user accounts. Recommended for production workloads. Learn more [↗]

- Each service account can use up to five keys.
- Note that keys must be deactivated before they can be deleted.
- Grant your service accounts the required permissions for their intended operations – typically this is the IAM Storage Object Admin role.

#### Access keys for service accounts

This project doesn't have any service account HMAC keys.

    + CREATE A KEY FOR A SERVICE ACCOUNT

*Figure 6.12: Settings menu*

2.  If you do not have a service account available, you have an option to create one at this point. Make sure to assign the **Storage Object Admin** role to this service account to grant permissions to transfer data.

    If you have an existing service account, you can view and change its access permissions here: `https://console.cloud.google.com/iam-admin/serviceaccounts?project=<your-project-id>` (replace `<your-project-id>` with the correct value for your project).

    Select your desired service account and then click on **CREATE KEY**:

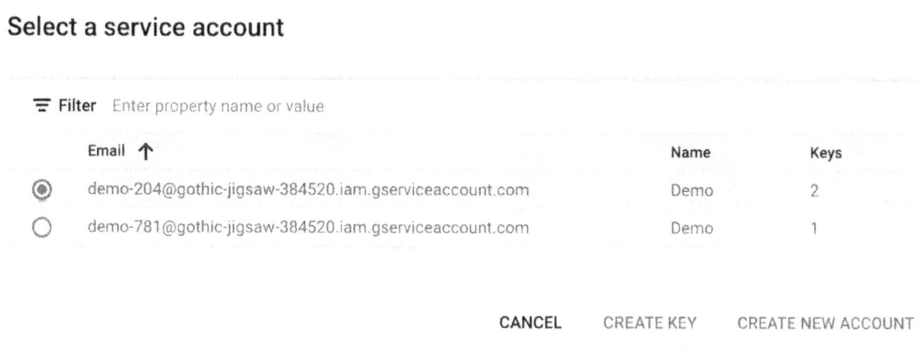

    ### Select a service account

    | ☰ Filter  Enter property name or value | | | |
    | --- | --- | --- | --- |
    | | Email ↑ | Name | Keys |
    | ◉ | demo-204@gothic-jigsaw-384520.iam.gserviceaccount.com | Demo | 2 |
    | ○ | demo-781@gothic-jigsaw-384520.iam.gserviceaccount.com | Demo | 1 |

    CANCEL    CREATE KEY    CREATE NEW ACCOUNT

    *Figure 6.13: Creating an access key and secret*

    Make a note of your account key and secret; you will need these values later to create a linked service.

    We have set up the access policies on the Google Cloud service account to allow the data factory to perform a data pull. Now we can design the pipeline.

3.  In the Azure portal, open the **Monitor** interface of your data factory. Start by creating a linked service and the dataset for the Google Cloud Storage bucket.

4.  In the **Manage** tab, add a new linked service. Specify its type as **Google Cloud Storage (S3 API)**. Fill in the next blade, using the access key ID and secret access key values you obtained in *step 2*. In the **Service URL** field, enter `https://storage.googleapis.com`.

The following is an example of a filled-out Google Cloud Storage linked service creation blade:

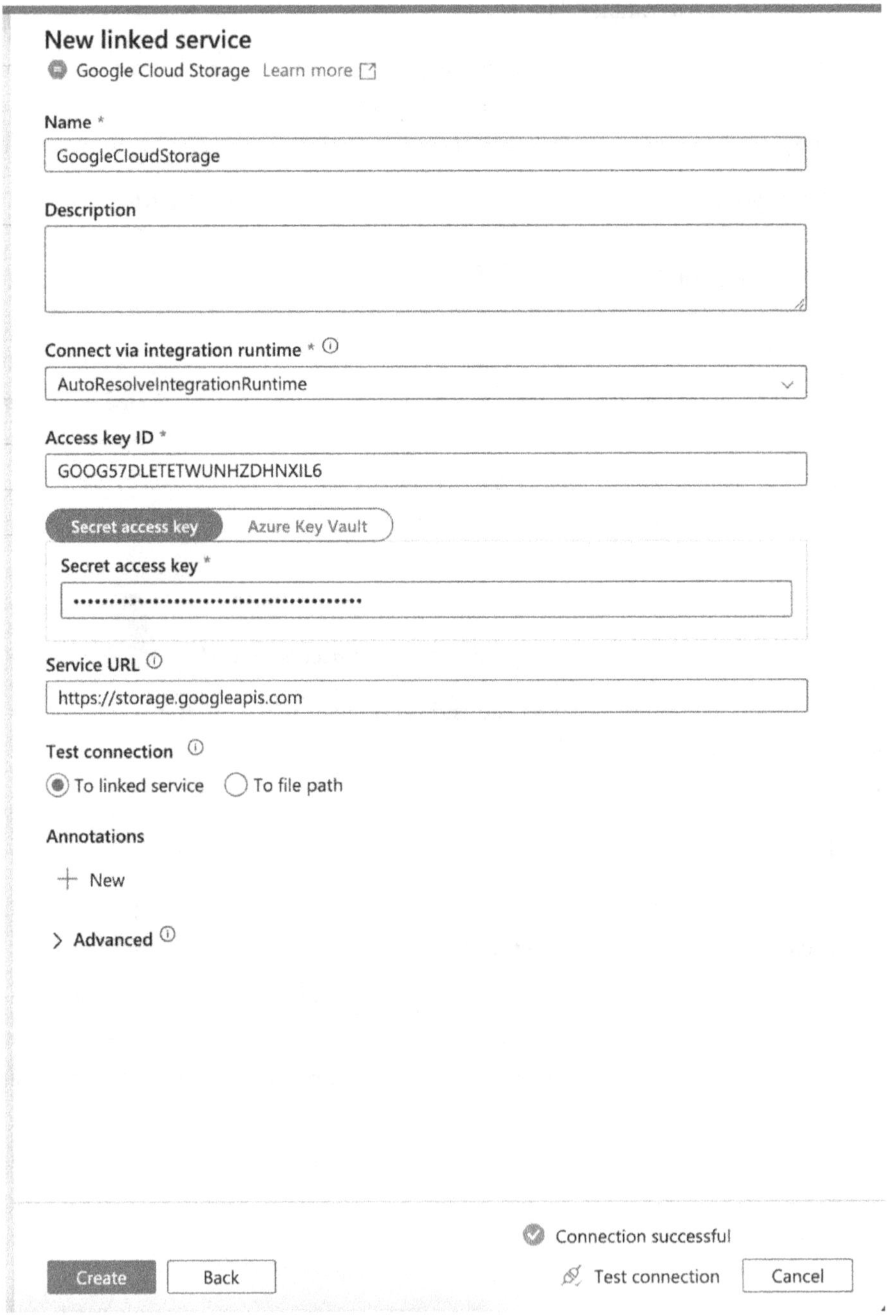

**New linked service**

🌐 Google Cloud Storage   Learn more ☐

Name *

| GoogleCloudStorage |

Description

| |

Connect via integration runtime * ⓘ

| AutoResolveIntegrationRuntime ⌄ |

Access key ID *

| GOOG57DLETETWUNHZDHNXIL6 |

( **Secret access key**   Azure Key Vault )

Secret access key *

| ••••••••••••••••••••••••••••••••••••••• |

Service URL ⓘ

| https://storage.googleapis.com |

Test connection ⓘ

◉ To linked service   ○ To file path

Annotations

＋ New

❯ Advanced ⓘ

✅ Connection successful

Create    Back              ⚡ Test connection    Cancel

*Figure 6.14: Google Cloud linked service*

5. In the **Author** tab, create a new dataset. Select **Google Storage (S3 API)** as the type, **De-limitedText** as the format, and specify the Google Storage linked service we just created as the linked service. In the **File path** text field, specify the Google Storage bucket name.

6. Create a linked service and a dataset for the Azure Blob storage account where you want to store the data from the Google Cloud bucket. In the **File path** section of the dataset, specify a container where you want to transfer the files. We'll call it **datafromgoogle**. If the container does not exist, it will be created during the transfer. Your resulting dataset should look similar to *Figure 6.15*:

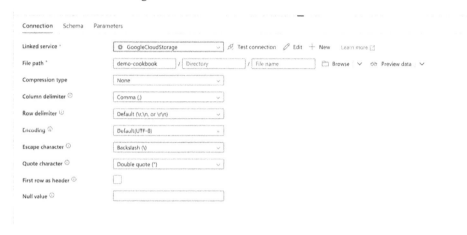

*Figure 6.15: Dataset for the Azure storage account*

7. Refer to the *Using parameters and built-in functions* recipe in *Chapter 2, Orchestration and Control Flow*, for detailed instructions.

NOTE

You can also use an **Azure Data Lake Storage V2 (ADLS)** account for this recipe. If you choose to do that (for example, if you want to reuse the ADLS account from the previous *Copying large datasets from S3 to ADLS* recipe), you will have to create a linked service and dataset with corresponding connectors. Refer to the previous recipe for detailed instructions on how to do that.

8.  In the **Author** tab, create a new pipeline. We will call it pl_transfer_from_gcs. Add a Copy activity to it and name this activity Copy From GC To Azure Storage. Configure **Source** and **Sink**. In **Source**, select the Google Storage dataset we created in *step 6*. For **File path type**, select **Wildcard file path** to copy all the files in the dataset. In **Sink**, select the Azure Blob dataset we created in *step 7*. In the **Sink** tab, make sure that the **File Extension** text field is empty. Ensuring the **File Extension** text field is empty is important as it allows the Copy activity to transfer the files without modifying their extensions, preserving the original file format. Leave all the other options as their default settings.

9.  Run your pipeline in debug mode. Once it is done, you should see that the CSV files were copied from your Google bucket to the Azure storage account.

10. Publish your changes to save them.

## How it works...

In this recipe, the main challenge is to configure the Google Storage access permissions correctly. The pipeline is simple and follows all the pipeline design principles we have covered in previous recipes.

## See also

Google Cloud is a vast and nimble ecosystem. To learn more about Google Cloud Storage and access management on this platform, refer to the current Google documentation at https:// cloud.google.com/iam/docs/granting-changing-revoking-access?.

# Copying data from Google BigQuery to Azure Data Lake Store

In this recipe, we will use Azure Data Factory to import a subset of a public fdic_banks.locations dataset from the Google BigQuery service (a cloud data warehouse) into an Azure Data Lake store. We will write the data into the destination storage in Parquet format for convenience. Choosing the Parquet format offers benefits such as efficient storage, columnar compression, and compatibility with various analytics and processing tools. It enhances data query performance and provides a flexible and optimized solution for data storage and analysis in Azure Data Lake.

# Getting ready

For this recipe, we assume that you have a Google Cloud account and a project, as well as an Azure account and a Data Lake Storage account (ADLS Gen2). The following is a list of additional preparatory work:

1. You need to enable the BigQuery API for your Google Cloud project. You can enable this API here: `https://console.developers.google.com/apis/api/bigquery.googleapis.com/overview`.

2. You will require information for the **Project ID**, **Client ID**, **Client Secret**, and **Refresh Token** fields for the BigQuery API app. If you are not familiar with how to set up a Google Cloud app and obtain these tokens, you can find detailed instructions at the following community blog: `https://jpda.dev/getting-your-bigquery-refresh-token-for-azure-datafactory-f884ff815a59`.

3. Note that these instructions include consent given by the Azure Data Factory user. Make sure that this user (the Data Factory user, the account that is signed into the Azure portal) has the correct permissions to run BigQuery user jobs. Azure Data Factory will not be able to access data in Google Cloud otherwise. To assign the correct permissions, perform the following steps:

4. Go to `https://console.cloud.google.com/iam-admin/iam?project=<your-project-name>`.

5. In the **IAM & Admin** section and **Permissions** tab, click on **Grant Access** and fill in the necessary information (email and role):

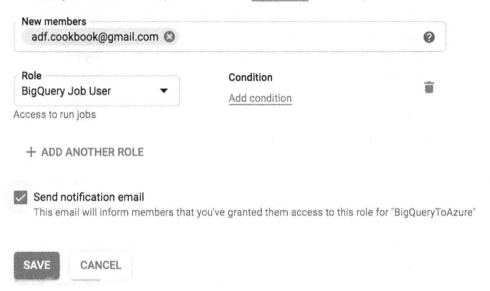

Figure 6.16: Adding a BigQuery Job User role

6.  Save the assignment.

## How to do it...

Microsoft provides connectors to both Google BigQuery and Azure Data Lake Storage. We will create a simple pipeline with a Copy activity utilizing these built-in connectors:

1.  Create a linked service for BigQuery Connection.

    From the **Manage** tab, select **Linked Services** and then click on **New**. In the **New Linked Service** blade, search for BigQuery and then enter the **Project ID**, **Client ID**, **Client secret**, and **Refresh Token** information that you obtained previously (refer to the *Getting ready* section) in the blade presented. The blade should look similar to the following screenshot:

## New linked service (Google BigQuery)

Name *

```
GoogleBigQueryToAzure
```

Description

```

```

Connect via integration runtime *                                    ⓘ

```
AutoResolveIntegrationRuntime                                    ⌄
```

Project ID *

```
bigquerytoazure-287414
```

Additional project IDs

```

```

Request access to Google Drive

◯ True   ◉ False

Authentication type *

```
User authentication                                             ⌄
```

Client ID

```
                                                    ercontent.com
```

( **Client secret**   Azure Key Vault )

Client secret

```
••••••••••••••••••••••
```

( **Refresh Token**   Azure Key Vault )

Refresh Token

```
••••••••••••••••••••••••••••••••••••••••••••••••••••••••••••••••
```

Annotations

.

☑ Connection successful

**Create**   Back        🔌 Test connection   Cancel

*Figure 6.17: Creating a BigQuery linked service*

Test your connection and click on **Create** to save the linked service.

2.  Create the BigQuery dataset. From the **Author** tab, select **Datasets** and then click on **New**. In the **New Dataset** blade, search for **BigQuery**. Finally, enter a name for your dataset (for this example, we named it GoogleBigQueryDS) and select the **BigQuery** linked service we created in the previous step in the dropdown.

3.  Create a linked service and the dataset for the **ADLS Gen 2** account where you intend to store the data. In **Select format blade**, choose **Parquet**. Opting for the Parquet format is recommended as it offers advantages such as efficient compression, columnar storage, and compatibility with various analytics tools. Parquet format enhances data query performance, reduces storage costs, and provides a versatile and optimized solution for storing and processing data in Azure Data Lake Storage Gen2. You can find detailed instructions on creating linked services and datasets in the *Using parameters and built-in functions* recipe in *Chapter 2, Orchestration and Control Flow*.

4.  We have all the components necessary to design the pipeline. Now, create a new pipeline, pl_bigquery_to_storage. Add a single **Copy** activity to this pipeline and rename it Copy from BigQuery To Storage.

    Configure **Source** and **Sink** for the Copy activity. In **Source**, select the **GoogleBigQueryDS** dataset we created in *step 2*. Check the **Query** radio button in the **Use Query** section, and enter the following query:

    ```
    select * from bigquery-public-data.fdic_banks.locations LIMIT 3000
    ```

    In **Sink**, select the **ADLS2** Parquet dataset we created in *step 3*. Leave all the other options as their default settings.

    Run your pipeline in debug mode. Once the run is complete, you will see new Parquet files in your ADLS account. You can use a tool such as http://Parquet-viewer-online.com/ to verify that this is the data from the BigQuery dataset.

5.  Publish your pipeline to save the changes.

# Migrating data from Google BigQuery to Azure Synapse

In this recipe, we will import a public dataset, github_repo.files, from Google BigQuery into Azure Synapse: formerly Azure Data Warehouse. We will create a SQL data pool, create the table to store our imported data, and configure the pipeline to migrate data from a public dataset hosted at Google BigQuery.

# Getting ready

To complete this recipe, you will need a Google Cloud project with the BigQuery API enabled. Refer to the *Getting ready* section in the previous recipe for instructions on how to set those up and obtain your **Project ID**, **Client ID**, **Client secret**, and **Refresh Token** fields.

You will also need an instance of an Azure Synapse SQL pool to import the data. Refer to the chapter on Azure Synapse on how to create and configure a SQL pool. Have the login credentials for this SQL pool to hand.

You will also need to create a table in your database to store the data we import. Download the script to create the table from `https://github.com/PacktPublishing/Azure-Data-Factory-Cookbook-Second-Edition/blob/main/Chapter06/CreateGithubRepoTable.sql`.

# How to do it...

We will create a simple pipeline consisting of just one Copy activity, which will use the **BigQuery** connector and **Azure Synapse** connector (both provided by Microsoft) to migrate the data from one cloud provider to the other:

1. First, let's create a table to hold the data. From the Azure portal, go to your **Azure Synapse** account and find the SQL pool where you intend to store the data. From the menu on the left, select **Query Editor** (preview), and, when prompted, log in with your credentials.

2. In **Query Editor**, execute the following script (you downloaded it from the GitHub repo in the *Getting ready* section):

```
CREATE SCHEMA github_repo
GO
CREATE TABLE github_repo.files(
   repo_name       VARCHAR(200) NOT NULL
  ,ref             VARCHAR(17) NULL
  ,path            VARCHAR(200) NULL
  ,mode            INTEGER   NULL
  ,id              VARCHAR(64) NOT NULL
  ,symlink_target VARCHAR(200) NULL
);
```

This will create a table with an appropriate schema to load data from BigQuery data.

3. Create a linked service for the **BigQuery** connection. Refer to the previous recipe (*step 1*) for detailed instructions on how to configure a linked service for BigQuery. We named our linked service `GoogleBigQueryToAzure2`.

4. Create a dataset that uses this linked service and name it `GoogleBigQueryDataSet`. When specifying the table, check the **Edit** checkbox and then enter `bigquery-public-data.github_repos.sample_files` as the table name.

   Your dataset **Connection** configuration should look similar to the following screenshot:

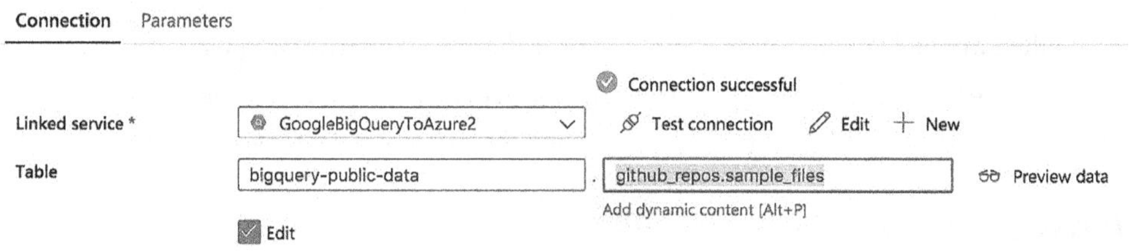

*Figure 6.18: Configuration for the BigQuery dataset*

Create a linked service to connect to the Azure Synapse SQL pool. Refer to *Chapter 3*, *Setting Up Synapse Analytics*, on how to obtain credentials and create the linked service. Name your linked service `AzureSynapseLinkedService`.

5. Create a dataset using `AzureSynapseLinkedService` and name it `AzureSynapseDataset`. Specify `github_repo.files` for **Table**.

6. We are ready to create the pipeline. Create a new pipeline, name it `pl_bigquery_to_synapse`, and then add a Copy activity to it. Specify the `GoogleBigQueryDataSet` dataset as the source and check the **Query** radio button. Enter the following query in the textbox:

   ```
   select * from bigquery-public-data.github_repos.sample_files limit
   30
   ```

   **IMPORTANT NOTE**

   In order to configure and test our pipeline, we will limit the import to 30 records. Once we are sure that the pipeline works correctly, we can expand our selection.

7. Configure **Sink**. Select **AzureSynapseDataset** for the dataset. Select **Bulk Insert** as the Copy method, leaving all the other fields blank.

IMPORTANT NOTE

The Copy activity supports three methods for copying data to Azure Synapse Analytics: **PolyBase**, **Copy Command** (**preview**), and **Bulk Insert**. While PolyBase and Copy Command are more efficient options, their usage is limited to specific services at the time of writing. For our use case involving the loading of data from Google **BigQuery**, Bulk Insert is the most straightforward option. The simplicity arises because Bulk Insert is a native operation supported by Azure Synapse Analytics, requiring no additional setup. This makes it a convenient and efficient choice for seamlessly transferring data in our specific scenario.

In a production environment, where efficiency is of paramount importance, you will want to explore the **PolyBase** and **Copy** options. References to resources are included in the *See also* section of this recipe.

8.  In the **Mapping** tab, click on **Import Schema** and verify that the mappings are correct.

9.  Run the pipeline in debug mode. Once it completes, you should see 30 records in your Azure Synapse table.

10. We have built the pipeline and verified that it works, loading 30 records. If desired, we can now load the full dataset. To do this, just replace the query in the **Source** tab with the following:

```
select * from bigquery-public-data.github_repos.sample_files
```

However, this is optional and can be done at your discretion.

11. Publish your pipeline to save it.

## See also

To learn more about the copy methods supported by the data factory's Azure Synapse connector, refer to the following resources:

*   https://docs.microsoft.com/en-us/azure/data-factory/connector-azure-sql-data-warehouse#use-polybase-to-load-data-into-azure-synapse-analytics
*   https://docs.microsoft.com/en-us/azure/data-factory/connector-azure-sql-data-warehouse#use-copy-statement
*   https://docs.microsoft.com/en-us/azure/data-factory/load-azure-sql-data-warehouse

# Leave a review!

Enjoying this book? Help readers like you by leaving an Amazon review. Scan the QR code below for a 20% discount code.

# 7

# Extending Azure Data Factory with Logic Apps and Azure Functions

The Azure ecosystem comprises a variety of different services. Most of them can be integrated with and connected to **Azure Data Factory (ADF)**. In this chapter, we will show you how to harness the power of serverless execution by integrating some of the most commonly used Azure services: Azure Logic Apps and Azure Functions. These recipes will help you understand how Azure services can be useful in designing **Extract, Transform, Load (ETL)** pipelines.

We will cover the following recipes in this chapter:

- Triggering your data processing with Logic Apps
- Using the Web activity to call an Azure logic app
- Adding flexibility to your pipelines with Azure Functions

## Technical requirements

For this chapter, you will need the following:

- **An active Azure account**: It could be either your business account or a personal account. If you don't have an Azure account yet, you can activate an Azure free-trial license through Microsoft's main website: https://azure.microsoft.com/en-us/free/.

- **GitHub repository**: You can download the dataset from this book's GitHub repo or use your own: `https://github.com/PacktPublishing/Azure-Data-Factory-Cookbook-Second-Edition/tree/main/Chapter10/data`.

# Triggering your data processing with Logic Apps

In this recipe, you will learn how to create an **Azure logic app** and trigger your ADF pipeline with it. One of the biggest use cases is when you need to use a custom event-based trigger. Microsoft provides built-in event-based triggers in Azure Data Factory; however, they are limited to storage events (i.e., *When a blob is created* or *When a blob is deleted*), or a custom event for which you'd have to set up an Event Grid instance – which can be expensive and inconvenient. Frequently, it is much easier to leverage Azure Logic Apps and build a lightweight custom trigger. Azure Logic Apps opens up a world of possibilities for executing your ADF pipelines using built-in integration.

## Getting ready

Before we start, ensure that you have an Azure license and are familiar with basic operations on an Azure resource, such as finding resources in the Azure portal, creating and deleting resources, and creating pipelines in ADF. You also need to know how to assign roles to managed identities and have sufficient privileges on the account to do so. You can find more information about Azure resources in *Chapter 1, Getting Started with ADF*, and *Chapter 2, Orchestration and Control Flow*, of this book. Detailed instructions on how to do role assignments to managed identities can be found in *Chapter 12, The Best Practices of Working with ADF*, in the recipe *Setting up roles and permissions with access levels for working with ADF*.

## How to do it...

We are going to create a new Azure logic app with the create a new data factory pipeline action running inside of it. To trigger the logic app, we will use a **Hypertext Transfer Protocol (HTTP)** request with a **Uniform Resource Locator (URL)**:

1. Navigate to the Azure portal and create a new **Logic App** resource.
2. Select an active subscription and resource group, write the name of your logic app, choose the same region as the region of your data factory, and click **Review + create**, then **Create**:

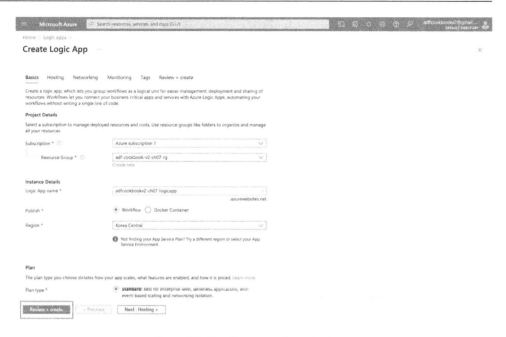

*Figure 7.1: Creating a new Azure logic app*

3. After deployment completes, click on the **Go to resource** button to open the Logic Apps portal view. In the portal, first go to the **Identity** tab:

*Figure 7.2: Identity tab*

Examine the status of your system-assigned identity. If it is **Off**, turn it **On** and click on the **Save** button to create a system-assigned identity for your logic app if you do not have one already.

4. Next, select **Logic app designer** from the menu on the left.

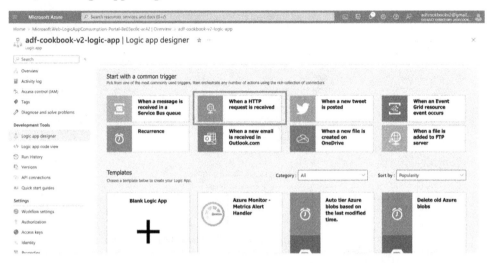

*Figure 7.3: Logic app designer*

5. In the logic app designer, we shall proceed to build the logic app. First, we specify the trigger for the logic app. Search for **When a HTTP request is received**. This is one of the most popular triggers for testing purposes as you don't need any additional systems set up and integrated.

6. Add a new parameter called **Method** and select **GET** from the drop-down list for **Method**:

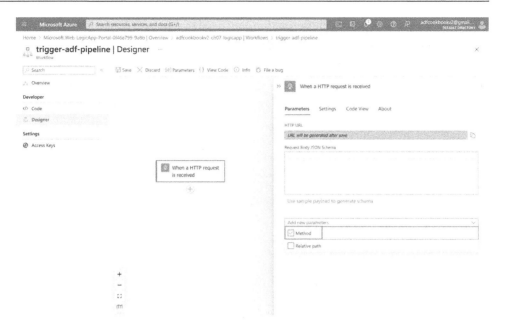

*Figure 7.4: Selecting a trigger for a logic app*

7.   Click on **New step** (the + sign under the **When HTTP request is received** tile) to add a
     new action. Search for **Azure Data Factory** and select **Create a pipeline run**. This action
     is used to trigger your Data Factory pipeline:

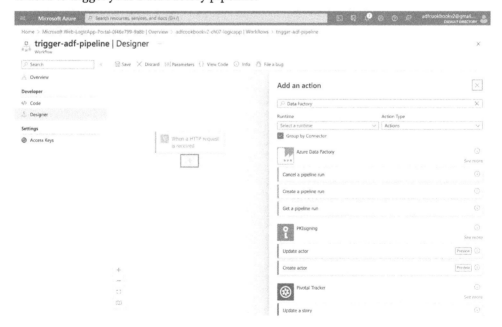

*Figure 7.5: Selecting an action for a logic app*

In the settings of your chosen action, you need to sign in to ADF with your account. Then, you need to fill in all the required fields with your information from the following drop-down lists: **Subscription**, **Resource Group**, **Data Factory Name**, and **Data Factory Pipeline Name**. Choose an existing simple pipeline (we advise a pipeline consisting of one activity, like the one created in *Chapter 1*, *Getting Started with ADF*, in the recipe *Creating an ADF pipeline by using the Copy Data tool*):

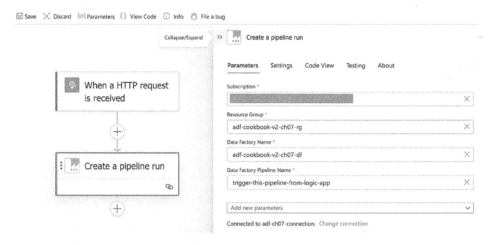

*Figure 7.6: Setting up an action for a logic app*

8. After you save your workflow, a value in the **HTTP GET URL** field will be auto-generated. Copy this value by clicking on the **Copy URL** button to the right of **HTTP GET URL**:

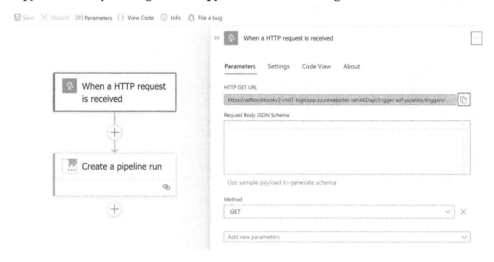

*Figure 7.7: Copying the value in the HTTP GET URL field*

In the preceding screenshot, you can see that the URL has appeared in the trigger step after the logic app is saved.

9. Assign a Contributor role on **Data Factory** to this logic app workflow's **Managed System Identity (MSI)**.

10. Paste the copied URL path into a browser search bar and press *Enter*. Though you see a blank window, your logic app has been triggered.

You can check this if you go to the **Overview** tab of your workflow, and from there, select the **Run History** tab in the center.

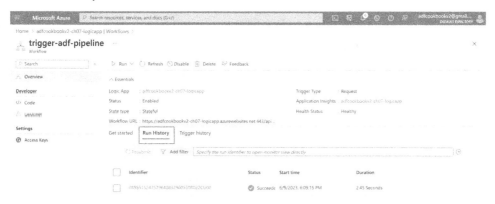

*Figure 7.8: Monitoring logic app runs*

From the preceding screenshot, you can see that the logic app was fired at a specific start time. If the status is **Succeeded**, it means that all the logic app steps worked correctly, and your Data Factory pipeline was triggered.

You can also check this in the **Monitor** section of ADF. Detailed information on how to monitor ADF pipelines is provided in *Chapter 10*, *Monitoring and Troubleshooting Data Pipelines*, in the recipe *Monitoring pipeline runs and integration runtimes*.

Now that we have created an Azure logic app, let's have a look at how these steps work.

## How it works...

When you create and save a logic app workflow with the **When a HTTP request is received** trigger, a callback URL is created. It is stored in the logic app settings. Every time you send a request to the callback URL (like we did in the browser in *step 9* in the *How to do it...* section), a **Logic Apps** instance is created, and it starts executing the actions of the workflow one by one.

In our logic app, we have only one action, which is **Create a pipeline run**, in ADF. When the workflow instance runs this action, it uses the pre-built **Application Programming Interface (API)** connector, which uses the specified MSI account to log in to your ADF instance and run the configured pipeline. You can also use this action to pass parameters to your ADF pipeline via JSON code in the **Parameters** field.

## There's more...

You can choose different triggers for your logic apps. Here are a few such triggers you can choose from:

- When an item is modified on SQL Server
- When code is pushed to Azure DevOps
- When there are messages in Azure Queue Storage
- When a rule is fired in Azure IoT
- When a file is created in a SharePoint folder
- When an email is received
- When a resource event occurs in Azure Event Grid

You can also use other actions for ADF in Logic Apps, such as **Cancel a pipeline run** or **Get a pipeline run**.

As there are no activities in ADF that can cancel an ADF pipeline run, the **Cancel a pipeline run** action from the Logic Apps workflow comes in handy. It can help you both reduce costs from unnecessary runs and avoid different logical errors in your pipelines. To build a logic app that incorporates the **Cancel a pipeline run** action, you will need to capture the **Data Factory Pipeline Run Id** from the response to the **Create a pipeline run** step.

**Get a pipeline run** becomes a really useful action in building a solution where the next logic app step will wait until the ADF pipeline executes completely before proceeding. For example, it could be helpful when you want to update your Power BI dataset after data preparation is completed. To do this, you need to follow these steps:

1. Initialize a variable named **Status** after the **Create a pipeline run** action and set its value as **InProgress**. This variable will be updated when our pipeline run completes.

2. Create a new **Until** action and add the **Status is equal to Succeeded** break condition.

3. Inside the **Until** action, create a new **Get a pipeline run** action. Set **Data Factory Pipeline Run Id** as **runID** from the **Create a pipeline run** action.

4. Inside the **Until** action, add a **Set variable** action, choose your **Status** variable, and put the ADF status from the previous step into **Value**.

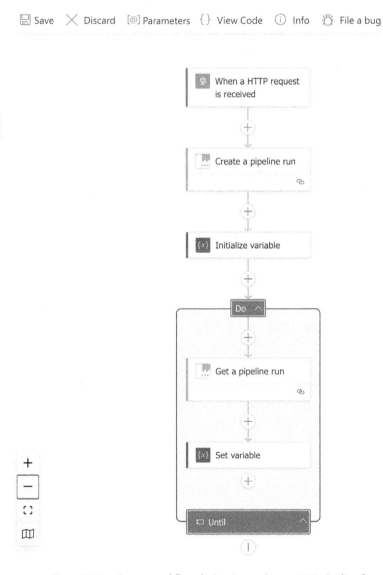

*Figure 7.9: Logic app workflow design to monitor an ADF pipeline for completion*

This means that the next steps of the logic app will continue only after the status of the pipeline changes to **Succeeded**.

# Using the Web activity to call an Azure logic app

Azure Logic Apps allows you to extend the capabilities of ADF in numerous ways; many tasks that either can't be done or are very difficult to do in ADF at this point in time can be accomplished with the help of custom-built logic apps.

In this recipe, you will learn how to call an Azure logic app from ADF and how to pass parameters between them to archive files from a folder in **Blob storage** and delete those files from the original location.

## Getting ready

You need to have access to an Azure Data Factory instance and an Azure Data Lake Storage Gen2 account. Set up your storage account in the following way: you should have a container called `flights` with one file inside (we have uploaded `airports.csv`; you can use any file), and a container called `archive`, as in the example shown in the screenshot below:

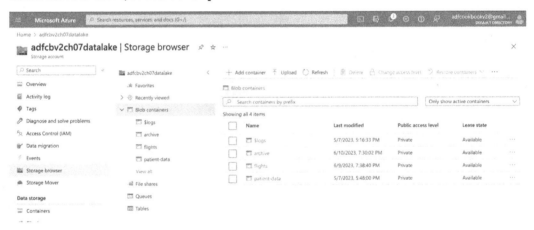

*Figure 7.10: ADLS Gen2 container setup*

In ADF, create a `Flights` dataset with the `flights` container and the CSV file.

You need to be familiar with creating ADF pipelines containing the **Get Metadata, Filter**, and **For Each** activities. Refer to *Chapter 2, Orchestration and Control Flow*, for guidelines on how to do that.

## How to do it...

We are going to create a new Azure logic app workflow and an ADF pipeline. The **logic app** will have Azure Blob storage actions (**Copy Blob (V2)** and **Delete Blob (V2)**) and will be triggered by an HTTP request. The ADF pipeline will get information about blobs in storage and pass it to the **logic app** via a Web activity:

1. Create a new logic app. You can find instructions on how to do this in the previous recipe, *Triggering your data processing with Logic Apps*.

2. After the resource is created, click **Go to Resource** and select **When a HTTP request is received** from the trigger list.

3. Inside the **When a HTTP request is received** trigger, find the **Request Body JSON Schema** field and paste the following script:

```
{
    "properties": {
        "Container": {
            "type": "string"
        },
        "FileName": {
            "type": "string"
        }
    },
    "type": "object"
}
```

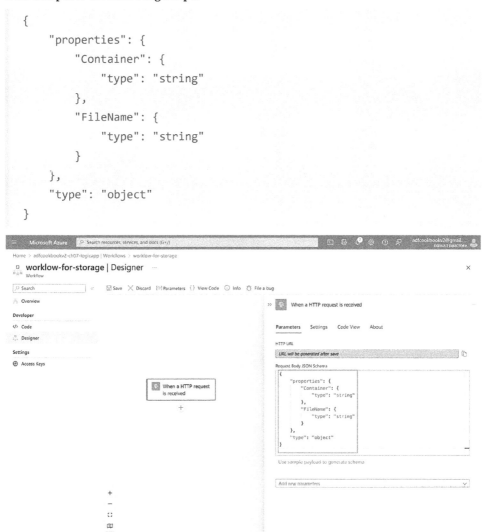

*Figure 7.11: Adding parameters to a logic app trigger*

4.  Add a new **Copy blob** step from the **Azure Blob Storage** actions. To do this, click on **New step**, then select **All** and search for copy blob in the logic app actions and click on it:

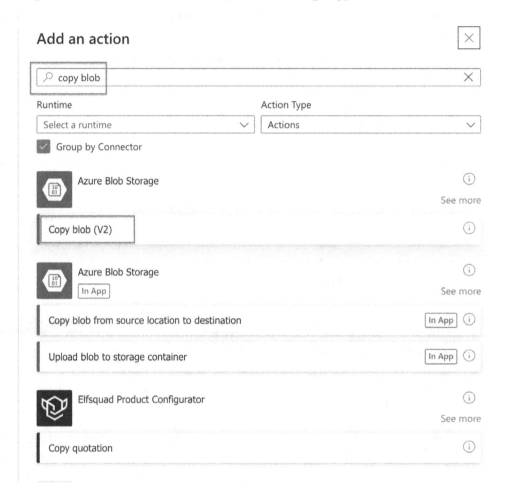

*Figure 7.12: Selecting the Copy blob action for a logic app*

5.  You will see the form as in the screenshot below. Fill in the information to create a new connection:

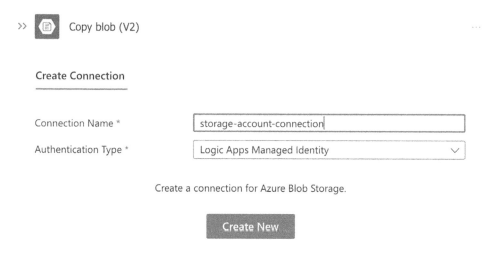

*Figure 7.13: Creating a new Azure Blob connection*

6.  Go to your ADLS Gen2 account's **Access Control (IAM)** section and assign a **Storage Blob Data Contributor** role to the logic app. Then go to the **Access Control (IAM)** section in the logic app and assign a Contributor role to ADF.

7.  After creating the Azure Blob storage connection, fill in the fields as follows:

    -   **Storage Account Name Or Blob Endpoint:** The name of your storage account.
    -   **Source Url:** Choose the **Container** and **FileName** variables.
    -   **Destination Blob Path:** Enter archive/ and choose **FileName** from the dynamic content.

To enter variables like Container, put your cursor inside of the text field and click on the lightning icon in the blue button that appears on the right:

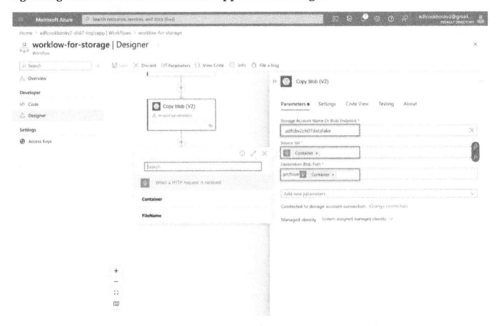

*Figure 7.14: Adding dynamic content to a logic app activity*

8. Then select appropriate variables from the popup.

9. The screenshot below will help you to fill the fields in correctly:

*Figure 7.15: Copy blob activity configuration*

10. Create a new **Delete blob (V2)** step and select **Container** and **FileName** in the **Blob** section.

The screenshot below shows the correct setup:

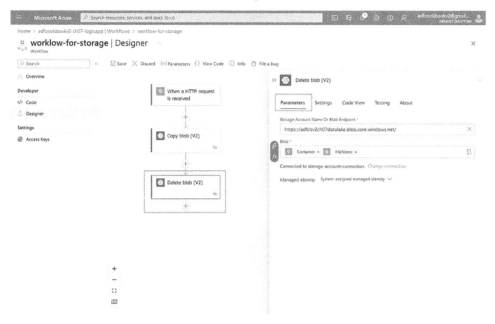

*Figure 7.16: Setting up the Delete blob activity of the logic app*

11. Save your **logic app** and copy the value of the HTTP POST URL field.

12. Create a new pipeline in ADF and add a **Get Metadata** activity.

13. In the settings, choose a dataset from your storage account that you would like to archive. The dataset should point to a file in your storage (for instance, `Flights_Dataset` in the following screenshot contains a CSV file in ADLS Gen2 in the `flights` container: this is the file we are going to archive). Under **Field list**, add an **Item name** argument:

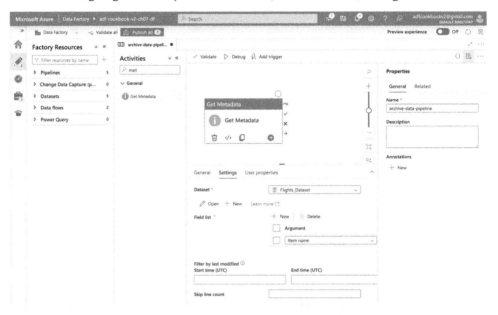

*Figure 7.17: Creating the Get Metadata activity in an ADF pipeline*

14. Add a **Web Activity** to your canvas, and connect it to **on success** of **Get Metadata**. Fill in the fields in the settings as follows:

    - **URL**: Paste the HTTP POST URL from your logic app.
    - **Method**: Select **POST**.
    - **Body**: Add the following script:

```
{
    "Container":"@{pipeline().parameters.Container}",
    "FileName":"@{activity('Get Metadata').output.itemName}"
}
```

After you complete this step, your canvas should look similar to this screenshot:

*Figure 7.18: Setting up a web activity in an ADF pipeline*

15. Create a new parameter for the pipeline. To do this, you need to left-click on the blank pipeline canvas. Name it `Container` and set the default value as your container name with a backslash:

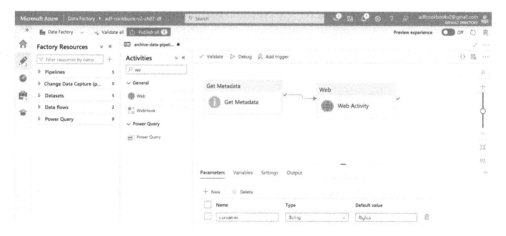

*Figure 7.19: Adding a new parameter to an ADF pipeline*

16. Publish the pipeline and click **Debug**. Let your ADF pipeline run to the end, and go to your logic app workflow. You should see a successful run in the run history:

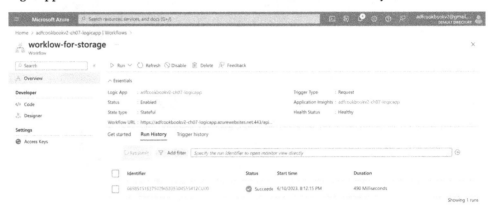

*Figure 7.20: Monitoring logic app runs*

If you go to your storage account, you will see that the blob you specified in the dataset has moved from the flights container to the archive container.

## How it works...

We have created an ADF pipeline with two parameters: Container and FileName. The Container parameter is a global parameter for the pipeline; we hardcoded its value. The **Get Metadata** activity retrieves the value of the FileName parameter, which, of course, represents the file in the storage we are archiving. We configured the **Body** section (key-value pairs) of the Web activity to pass the parameters **Container** and **FileName** in JSON format to the logic app.

The **Web activity** is configured to make a POST API call to the **logic app** workflow using that workflow HTTP URL (it was auto-generated after we saved the workflow for the first time) and pass the parameters in the body of the request.

We also have created a **logic app** workflow with an HTTP request trigger with JSON code included. This code helps us retrieve the ADF pipeline parameters and push them as dynamic content for Azure Blob storage activities in the workflow.

At first, parameters inside our logic app workflow do not have values. When we execute the ADF pipeline, it sets the container parameter to `flights` and the `FileName` parameter to `airports.csv`. These parameters are sent to the logic app in the HTTP request body. The workflow fires the activity to copy the `flights/airports.csv` blob to `archive/airports.csv`, and the next activity deletes the older version of the blob from `flights/airports.csv`.

## There's more...

Instead of moving just one file, you can set up your pipeline to process multiple files at once. To do this, replace your one-file dataset in the **Get Metadata** activity's **Settings** with an ADLS Gen2 `folder` dataset. Then, instead of setting **Item name** as a **Field list** argument, select **Child items**:

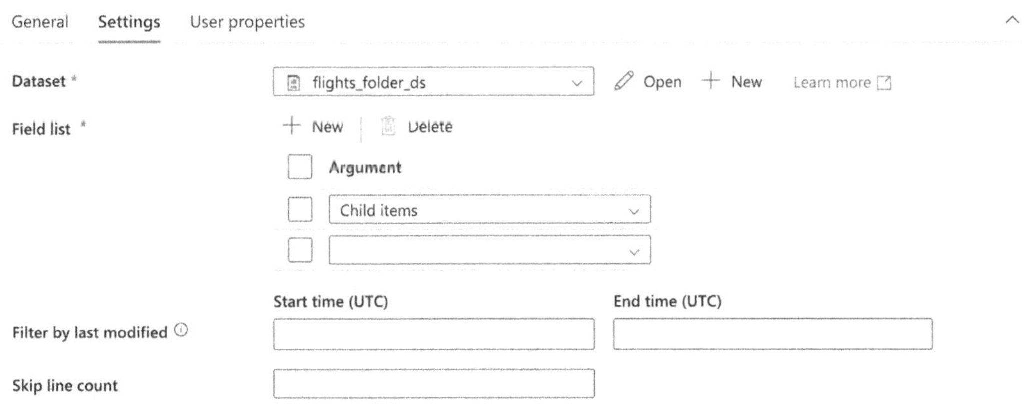

*Figure 7.21: Retrieving metadata for multiple items*

Then, add a **ForEach** activity and add the following code in the **Items** text field (in the **Settings** tab):

```
@activity('Get Metadata').output.childItems
```

Finally, add a **Web** activity inside your **ForEach** activity, and configure it the same way as we did in the recipe, except in the **Body**, enter the modified script below:

```
{
    "Container":"@{pipeline().parameters.Container}",
    "FileName" :"@{item().name}"
}
```

Below is a snapshot of such a pipeline:

*Figure 7.22: ADF pipeline to archive files in a folder with a logic app workflow*

# Adding flexibility to your pipelines with Azure Functions

In this recipe, you will learn how to create an Azure Functions app and an Azure function and call it from ADF. Azure Functions enables users to create and execute small/moderate programs in C#, Java, JavaScript, Python, or PowerShell with no complex infrastructure setup; you just need to provision an Azure Storage account and App Insights to store your Azure Functions code and collect its execution metrics.

## Getting ready...

Before we start, ensure that you have an Azure license. You should be familiar with the basics of Azure resources, such as the Azure portal, creating and deleting Azure resources, and creating pipelines in ADF. You can find more information about Azure resources in *Chapter 1, Getting Started with ADF*, and *Chapter 2, Orchestration and Control Flow*, of this book.

## How to do it...

We are going to create a Functions app, add a new Azure function, and then create a new ADF pipeline that calls this function:

1. First, you need to create a Functions app. Go to the **Resources** page, search for **Function App,** and choose **Create new**.

2. Fill in the fields as follows:

    • **Subscription**: Select your desired subscription.

    • **Resource Group**: Select your desired resource group.

    • **Function App name**: Set the name you prefer.

    • **Publish**: Choose **Code**.

    • **Runtime stack**: Choose **.NET**.

    • **Version**: Select the current version (6 LTS, or whatever is the currently supported version).

    • **Region**: Select a region of your choice.

    • **Operating System: Windows.**

    • **Hosting options and plans: Consumption.**

*Figure 7.23: Creating a Functions app*

In the next tab, **Storage**, select the desired storage account. You can leave all the other values as the default. Click on **Review + create**, review the presented configuration summary, and click on **Create to deploy.**

Wait until the resource is deployed.

3.  Go to **your Azure Functions** portal, click on **Functions**, and click **Create**. In the **Create function** blade, choose the following:

    -   **Development environment: Develop in portal**

    -   **Template: HTTP trigger**

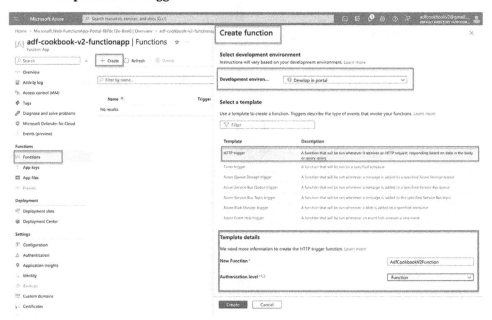

*Figure 7.24: Creating a new Azure function*

4.  Set the name of the new function and set **Authorization level** as **Function**, then press **Create**.

5.  Once your function has been created, click on it to go to the **Functions** interface. Select the **Code + Test** tab on the left, enter the following code in the editor, and select **Save**:

```
#r "Newtonsoft.Json"
using System.Net;
using Microsoft.AspNetCore.Mvc;
using Microsoft.Extensions.Primitives;
using Newtonsoft.Json;
using System.Text;
public static async Task<HttpResponseMessage> Run(HttpRequest req,
ILogger log)
```

```
{
    log.LogInformation("C# HTTP trigger function processed a
request.");
    string name = req.Query["name"];
    string requestBody = await new StreamReader(req.Body).
ReadToEndAsync();
    dynamic data = JsonConvert.DeserializeObject(requestBody);
    name = name ?? data?.name;
    string responseMessage = string.IsNullOrEmpty(name)
        ? "This HTTP triggered function executed successfully. Pass
a name in the query string or in the request body for a personalized
response."
                : $"Hello, {name}. This HTTP triggered function
executed successfully.";
    var responseObj = new {result = responseMessage};
    var responseJson = JsonConvert.SerializeObject(responseObj);
    return new HttpResponseMessage(HttpStatusCode.OK) {
        Content = new StringContent(responseJson, Encoding.UTF8,
"application/json")};
}
```

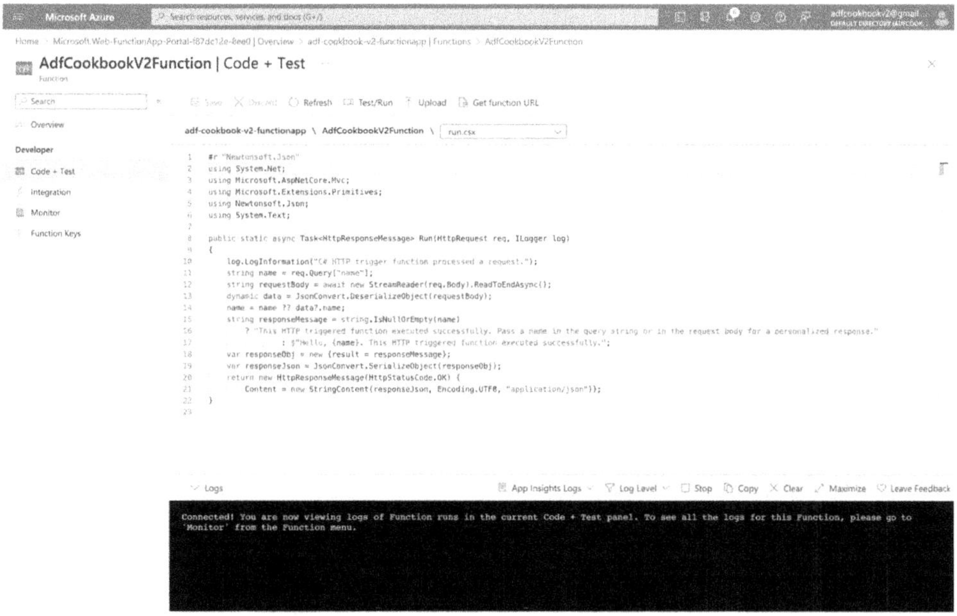

*Figure 7.25: Code editor window in the Azure Functions portal*

6. Now, go to the **Function Keys** tab and generate a new key. This key will be used by ADF **Azure Function Linked Service** to access this function.

*Figure 7.26: Creating a new function key*

7. Go to ADF and create a new pipeline. Add an **Azure Function** activity to it.

8. In the **Azure Function** activity's **Settings**, create a new **Azure Function linked service** with the following values:

   a. **Name:** Enter your desired name.

   b. **Azure subscription:** Select your subscription.

   c. **Azure Function App url:** Select your Azure Function App.

   d. **Function Key:** Enter the function key that you generated in *step 6*.

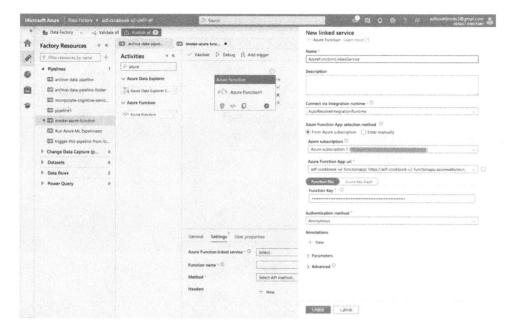

*Figure 7.27: Creating a new Azure Function linked service*

9.   After creating the linked service, fill in the rest of the **Settings** fields as follows:

   a.   **Function name:** Enter the name of your Azure function.

   b.   **Method: POST**.

   c.   **Body:** Add this script: { "name":"@{pipeline().Pipeline}" }.

Publish your changes.

*Figure 7.28: Setting up an Azure Function activity*

10. Click on the **Debug** button to run the pipeline. Once it has finished running, go to your Azure Function App portal, open your function, and examine the **Monitor** tab:

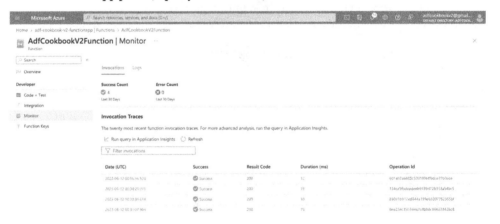

*Figure 7.29: Monitoring Azure function runs*

In the next section, we will see how these steps work in the background.

## How it works...

We used an **Azure Function App** service to host our function app, running our C# code snippet on pre-built and pre-deployed infrastructure. We chose an **HTTP request trigger** for the function, to execute this code whenever somebody sends an HTTP request.

In **Data Factory**, we built a simple pipeline utilizing a pre-built connector – an **Azure Function activity** – to send HTTP requests. We defined a linked service to access the Azure function and protected it with the function key that we created for our specific function. The Azure Function activity sends simple JSON in its request body. This JSON contains the name of the pipeline that we are running. The function's code parses the request body, extracts the name of the pipeline, and outputs it to the log.

## There's more...

You can use an Azure function to dynamically update ADF's settings. For example, it could change the schedule of pipelines or activities. To trigger an Azure function, it is helpful to use its own scheduler, which has the much more powerful and really flexible **CRON** syntax (scripts for a time-based job scheduler). With the addition of Azure Functions, ADF's potential greatly increases; we can configure functions to connect to databases for which Microsoft does not provide pre-built connectors.

## Join our community on Discord

Join our community's Discord space for discussions with the authors and other readers:

```
https://discord.gg/U229qmBmT3
```

# 8

# Microsoft Fabric and Power BI, Azure ML, and Cognitive Services

One of the benefits of Azure Cloud Services is the opportunity to leverage the latest technological innovations without investing additional resources. In this chapter, we delve into several services that provide access to state-of-the-art technologies. Azure **Machine Learning** (**ML**) equips data engineers and data scientists with the tools necessary to create, deploy, and manage complex data models. Azure Cognitive Services offers a collection of APIs that grant access to a range of artificial intelligence algorithms (various image classification, natural language processing, and speech recognition algorithms to name just a few areas), which are tailored for business use. Finally, in May 2023, Microsoft unveiled Fabric, a comprehensive integrated analytics solution. Fabric contains a suite of services for data storage, data movement, and data analytics.

**Azure Data Factory** (**ADF**) serves as a bridge for integration with both Azure ML and Azure AI (formerly Azure Cognitive Services). Microsoft Fabric incorporates its own Data Factory, which has many similarities with ADF.

You will learn how to build an ADF pipeline that operates on a prebuilt Azure ML model. We will also create and run an ADF pipeline that leverages Azure AI for text data analysis. In the last three recipes, you'll familiarize yourself with the primary components of Microsoft Fabric Data Factory.

This chapter covers the following recipes:

- Introducing Microsoft Fabric and Data Factory
- Microsoft Fabric Data Factory: A closer look at the pipelines
- Loading data with Microsoft Fabric Datafllows
- Automatically building ML models with speed and scale
- Analyzing and transforming data with Azure AI and prebuilt ML models

# Technical requirements

For this chapter, you will need the following:

- For the first three recipes, you will need a Power BI or a Fabric subscription. If you do not have one, you can activate a free trial subscription by following these steps:

  1. Navigate to `https://app.fabric.microsoft.com/home` and sign up for a free Power BI license.

  > **Note**
  >
  > You need a business email address to do this.

  2. Once on the Fabric portal, go to the account manager in the top-right corner and click on the **Start Trial** button in the popup. Your trial should be activated after this, and your account manager should look similar to the following snapshot:

*Figure 8.1: Activated Fabric trial*

If you do not see the **Start Trial** button, you need to work with your Power BI tenant administrator to enable user access to Fabric. Instructions for administrators can be found on the Microsoft site at `https://learn.microsoft.com/en-us/fabric/get-started/fabric-trial#administer-user-access-to-a-fabric-preview-trial`.

- For the last two recipes you will need an Azure account. It could be either your business account or a personal account. If you don't have an Azure account yet, you can activate an Azure free-trial license through Microsoft's main website: `https://azure.microsoft.com/en-us/free/`.

- You can download the dataset from this book's GitHub repository: `https://github.com/PacktPublishing/Azure-Data-Factory-Cookbook-Second-Edition/tree/main/Chapter08`.

Some recipes have additional requirements, which will be discussed in the *Getting ready* section of the recipe.

# Introducing Microsoft Fabric and Data Factory

Microsoft unveiled its unified business analytics platform Fabric in Spring 2023. Fabric combines the capabilities of Power BI, Azure Synapse, and ADF in one integrated environment.

In this recipe, our goal is to get acquainted with the Microsoft Fabric environment, where we will create the infrastructure and data store necessary for working in Fabric, and load some data from remote storage into the newly created data store.

## Getting ready

For this recipe, you need an active Power BI account and Microsoft Fabric activated. Follow the steps described in the *Technical requirements* section of this chapter to activate the Fabric trial license if you have not done so already.

## How to do it...

We shall start by creating a Microsoft Fabric workspace, then we'll instantiate a Lakehouse and load data using the Microsoft Fabric Copy data wizard:

1. Open Fabric at `https://app.fabric.microsoft.com/home` and log in to your account. You should see the main panel, with vertical tabs on the left. Select the **Workspaces** tab.

*Figure 8.2: Create a new workspace in the Microsoft Fabric studio*

Click on the **+ New workspace** button and fill in the desired workspace name in the presented form. Leave all other fields with the preselected options. After you click on the **Apply** button at the bottom, your workspace will be created.

 Since Fabric was in preview at the time of writing this book, there have been significant changes to the **User Interface (UI)** as it transitioned to **General Availability (GA)**. While we strive to provide accurate representations, some screenshots may no longer reflect the current UI layout or features. We recommend referring to the latest documentation or platform interface for the most up-to-date information.

2. Next, we shall create a Lakehouse within this workspace. Your workspace should be open from the previous step; if you closed it, select the **Workspaces** tab again and then click on the newly created **workspace**.

When you are within your workspace, click on the **Create** tab on the left. You will see several tiles displaying items you can create:

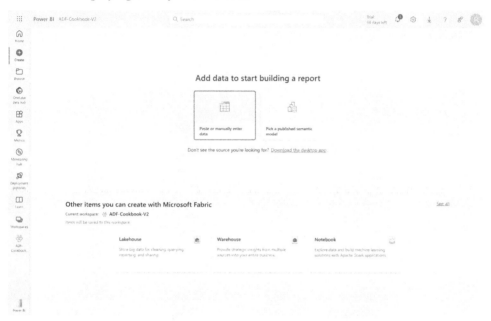

*Figure 8.3: Create interface in the Microsoft Fabric studio*

When you select the **Lakehouse** tile, you will see a popup asking for the Lakehouse name. Enter a name for your lakehouse. We named our lakehouse ADFCookbookV2_LH.

Your lakehouse should be created within a minute or two. Once it is created, you will see the Lakehouse interface:

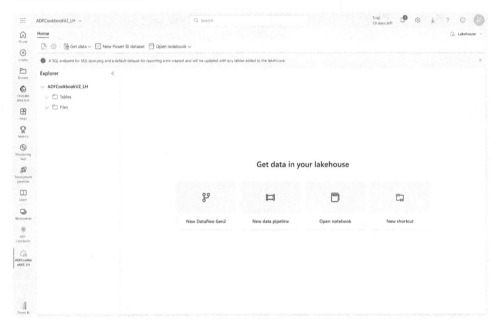

*Figure 8.4: Creating a Lakehouse*

In the Lakehouse Explorer pane, you will see that the new lakehouse has no tables or files. Create a new subfolder: right-click on **Files** and select the **New Subfolder** option. Give your subfolder the name data.

3.  Click on the **Get data** dropdown in the ribbon at the top of your Lakehouse interface and select **New data pipeline**. Alternatively, you can click on the **New data pipeline** tile in the center (as shown in *Figure 8.5*). Enter your pipeline name in the presented popup.

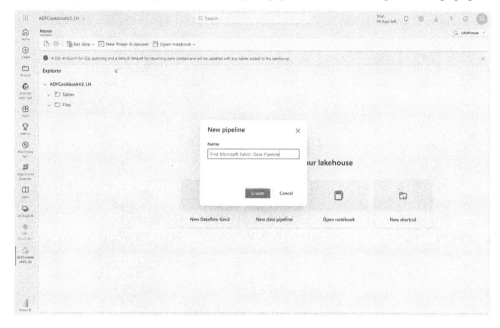

*Figure 8.5: Creating a Microsoft Fabric data pipeline*

Next, you will see the **Copy data** wizard.

We start by selecting a data source for the data import. Scroll down to view the available data sources, and select the **Generic protocol** tab:

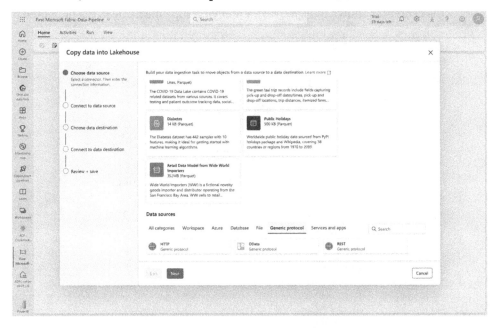

*Figure 8.6: Select a data source in the Copy data wizard*

Select **HTTP**, and hit **Next**.

4.  Select **New connection** and enter the following URL: `https://raw.githubusercontent.com/PacktPublishing/Azure-Data-Factory-Cookbook-Second-Edition/main/Chapter08/Customers.csv`.

Give your connection a name so that you can easily identify it when you look for it later. We named this connection data connection 1.

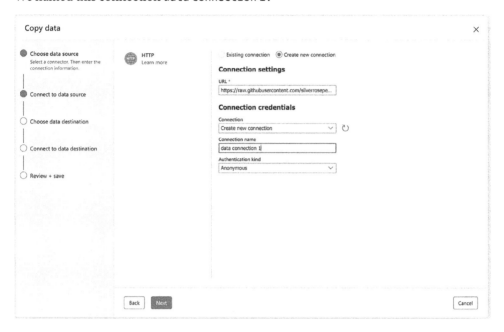

*Figure 8.7: Specify a connection in the Copy data wizard*

On the next screen, leave all fields (**Base URL, Request Method, Request Timeout**, etc.) with their default values: we do not need to change anything there. Click **Next**.

5.  This is the screen that will describe your data. Wait until the wizard connects to the source and samples your data. Then, you should see a screen similar to the following screenshot:

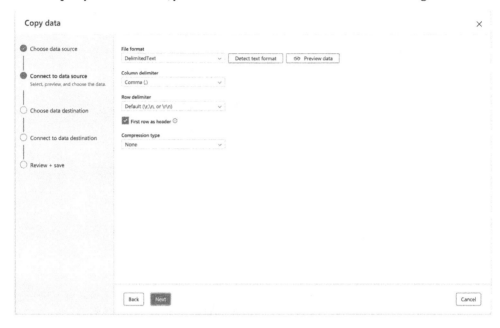

*Figure 8.8: Inspecting data format in the Copy data wizard*

Make sure that **First row as header** is checked, and that **File format** and **Row delimiter** are **filled in similarly to** in the screenshot. Then, click **Next**.

6.  The next screen will show you the possible destinations for our data. We want to import the data into the lakehouse we created in *step 2*, so select the **Lakehouse** tile:

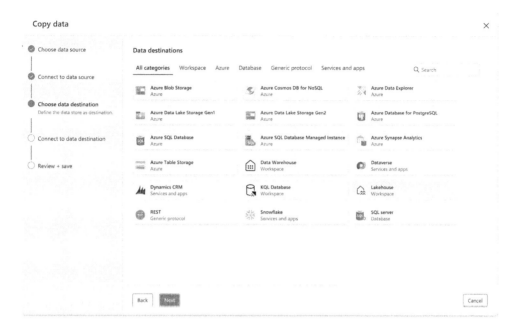

*Figure 8.9: Select Lakehouse as the data destination*

Click on **Next**, and on the next screen select the **Existing Lakehouse** radio button and the Lakehouse we created in *step 2* in the dropdown.

*Figure 8.10: Selecting an existing Lakehouse as the destination*

7.  We are almost done! In the next screen, specify **Files** as the root folder, then click on **Browse** to select the subfolder that we created in *step 2*, and finally type the file name (Customers. csv) in the **File name** text field.

*Figure 8.11: Specify the destination file path in the Copy data wizard*

8.  Click **Next** and review the destination file format settings. They should be similar to the source file settings (*Figure 8.7*).

9. Finally, click **Next** to navigate to the **Review + save** screen.

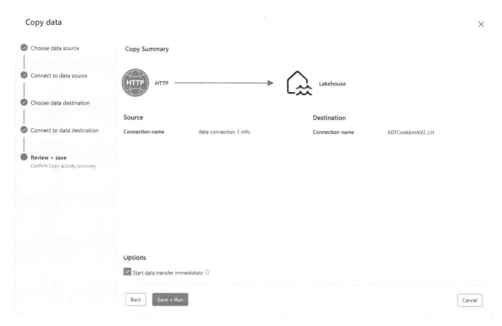

*Figure 8.12: Review + save screen in Copy data wizard*

On this screen, you will see the summary of the data transfer configuration: the source is the HTTP connection data connection 1 and the destination is the Lakehouse ADFCookbookV2_LH. Make sure the **Start data transfer immediately** checkbox is checked and click on **Save + Run** to start the pipeline.

Your pipeline will run for a minute or two, and you will see a pipeline interface screen similar to the following screenshot:

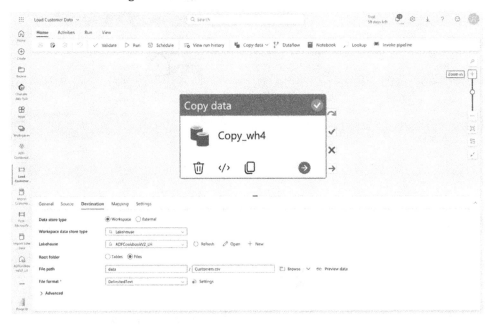

*Figure 8.13: Microsoft Fabric data pipeline interface*

If you went through the chapters describing ADF pipelines, you will see the similarities between this interface and the ADF interface: the **canvas**, the **Activities library** (at the top), and the **Configuration panel** at the bottom are all present both in ADF and the Fabric Data Factory. Note that because we used the wizard and ran the pipeline, this pipeline is already configured and saved, and we can run it any time again and again.

10. After the pipeline run has been completed, we can view the file we imported in the `ADFCookbookV2_LH` lakehouse. Navigate back to the lakehouse by selecting **Lakehouse** tab on the left panel, and in the Lakehouse Explorer click on the `data` subfolder in the `Files` folder. You should see the file we uploaded in the center panel:

*Figure 8.14: Imported data file in Lakehouse Explorer*

# How it works...

In this recipe, we have set up our own Microsoft Fabric workspace, created a **Lakehouse**, and utilized the Copy data wizard to transfer data from external storage. Microsoft Fabric workspaces are containers for storage and compute platforms such as lakehouses, warehouses, and notebooks. You can also associate assets such as datasets and reports with workspaces. Fabric workspaces allow you to manage access permission to the assets, providing isolation environments within the same tenant.

Microsoft Fabric Lakehouse is a data platform for storing both structured and unstructured data (the very name "lakehouse" alludes to the combination of a **delta lake** and a **warehouse**). In this recipe, we stored unstructured data – a file – in the lakehouse we created.

Finally, we leveraged the Copy data wizard to import data into the lakehouse. The Copy data wizard guided us step by step through choosing data sources and a data destination, describing the data format, and creating linked service connections for us under the hood. After we completed the setup with the Copy data wizard, it created a data pipeline for us, fully set up with a Copy activity and all the required settings. This pipeline can be used and re-used as necessary.

# Microsoft Fabric Data Factory: A closer look at the pipelines

Microsoft Fabric Data Factory pipelines have many similarities with ADF pipelines. Many activities that are available in ADF (such as control flow and move and transform activities) are also available in Fabric Data Factory, and as time goes by more and more activities (such as data transformation activities) will be available on the Fabric platform.

In this recipe, we shall build a more complex pipeline to parse and load data from a file into a table in the lakehouse storage.

## Getting ready

For this recipe, you need an active Power BI account and Microsoft Fabric activated. Follow the steps described in the *Technical requirements* section of this chapter to activate a Fabric trial license if you have not done so already.

This recipe builds upon the pipeline that we built in the previous recipe. If you do not have the pipeline or did not upload the data, please make sure to complete the previous recipe.

## How to do it...

Here, we shall build upon the knowledge from the previous recipe *Introducing Microsoft Fabric and Data Factory*. Open Fabric at https://app.fabric.microsoft.com/home and log in to your account. You should have a workspace and a lakehouse with an uploaded data file already available.

1. Go to your lakehouse and select **New notebook** from the **Open notebook** dropdown in the top menu ribbon:

*Figure 8.15: Create a new notebook*

Fabric will create a new **notebook** – an interactive programming environment – for you. You will see the notebook interface with one single cell and cell menu in the upper-right corner of the cell. Click on the **ellipsis** (...), and select **Toggle parameter cell** from that menu:

*Figure 8.16: Select Toggle parameter cell from the cell menu*

Now, you should see that your cell is designated as a **Parameters** cell:

```
1   # Welcome to your new notebook
2   # Type here in the cell editor to add code!
3
```

Parameters  PySpark (Python)

*Figure 8.17: Cell is designated as a Parameters cell*

Enter the following code in the first cell:

```
table_name = "customers"
```

2.  Next, create a new **notebook cell** by hovering your cursor over the bottom of the existing cell and choosing **+ Code**:

```
1   # Welcome to your new notebook
2   # Type here in the cell editor to add code!
3   table_name = "Customers"
```

PySpark (Python)

+ Code    + Markdown

*Figure 8.18: Create a new Code cell*

In the second cell, enter the following code:

```
from pyspark.sql.functions import *

# Read the Customers.csv file in Files/data folder
```

```
df = spark.read.format("csv").option("header","true").load("Files/
data/Customers.csv")

# Split the CustomerName column into FirstName and LastName columns
df = df.withColumn("FirstName", split(col("CustomerName"), "
").getItem(0)).withColumn("LastName", split(col("CustomerName"), "
").getItem(1))

# Include FirstName and LastName columns into the dataframe
# Reorder Columns
df = df["CustomerId", "FirstName", "LastName", "Email", "PhoneNum",
"Address1", "Address2", "City", "State", "Zipcode"]

# Load dataframe into the table
df.write.format("delta").mode("append").saveAsTable(table_name)
```

Your notebook should look similar to the following screenshot:

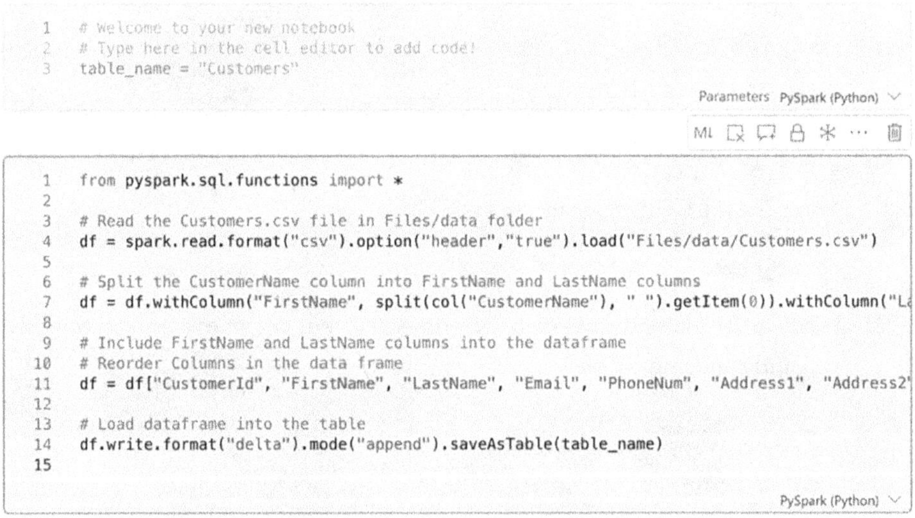

*Figure 8.19: Complete notebook code*

3.   Save your notebook, giving it the name Import Customer Data.

Click on the **Browse** tab on the left hub menu, and select the pipeline you designed in the previous recipe. Switch to the **Activities** tab at the top of the **canvas** and select **Notebook activity** to add it to the canvas. Position it to the right of the **Copy data activity** and connect the activities as shown in the following screenshot:

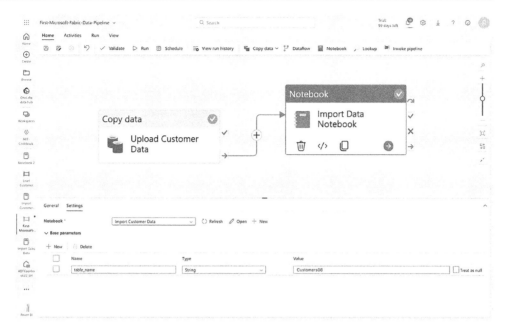

*Figure 8.20: Add a Notebook activity to the existing pipeline*

4.  In the configuration panel at the bottom, fill in the desired notebook activity name in the **General** tab. Next, in the **Settings** tab, select the **Import Customer Data** notebook we created in *step 1* for the **Notebook** dropdown. Then, in **Base parameters**, create a new base parameter called table_name of type **String**. The value of this parameter will be the name of the table (it will override the table_name variable we specified in the first cell of the **Import Customer Data** notebook). Enter the desired name in the **Value** field as shown in *Figure 8.20*.

 Lakehouse table names can only contain letters a through z or underscores _. If you enter invalid characters as part of your table name, your pipeline will fail.

5.  Navigate to the **Home** tab at the top of the canvas and save your pipeline. Then, click on the **Run** button to execute it. You can monitor the progress in the **Output** tab of the Configuration panel at the bottom:

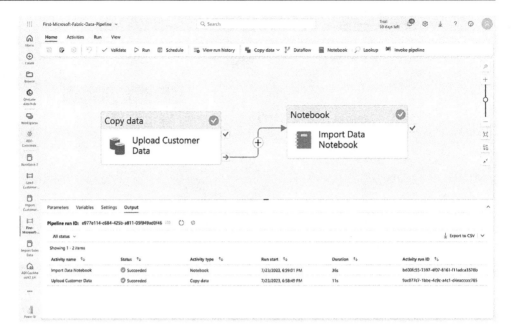

*Figure 8.21: Monitor pipeline progress*

6.  Go back to the Lakehouse ADFCookbookV2_LH and examine the **Tables** folder. You should see a new table with the name you specified in the **Base** parameters configuration of your **Notebook** activity in *step 3*.

*Figure 8.22: Lakehouse tables after loading the data from the file*

# How it works...

In this recipe, we created a pipeline to load data from a file residing in the lakehouse into a table in the same warehouse.

We started by writing a PySpark script to read the CSV file (unstructured data we imported into the lakehouse), load data into memory, apply some light transformations (we split the field **CustomerName** into two fields, **FirstName** and **LastName**), and then write this data into a structured table **Customers** in the same lakehouse. We used a Microsoft Fabric notebook – a web-based interactive programming interface – to write and edit our code and then ultimately run it.

We then enhanced the pipeline from the previous recipe by adding a **Notebook** activity to it. The Notebook activity allowed us to specify a custom table name to store the data. Of course, we could have just run the notebook by itself – since the file was already imported, the code would have executed and the notebook would have created the **Customers** table – but having it as part of a data pipeline has multiple advantages: just like ADF pipelines, we can execute this pipeline again and again on demand, we could set a schedule to run it automatically, and, of course, having a data pipeline gives us flexibility to design the ETL process according to our specifications.

# Loading data with Microsoft Fabric Dataflows

Fabric Data Factory has another data transformation tool in its arsenal: **Dataflow Gen2**. Readers who have worked with Power BI will be familiar with the concept of Dataflows. While there are many similarities between Data Factory Dataflow Gen2 and Power BI Dataflows (they both allow users to ingest, transform, and combine data from various sources to create reusable and scalable data preparation processes), it's important to note that as of the time of writing, they are not interchangeable.

> If you went through previous chapters of this book, you will remember that ADF also has a concept of Dataflows – a tool to perform common data transformations without writing code. In Fabric, Dataflow Gen2 is considered a Data Factory component, but it has a distinctive interface and allows users to leverage Power Query when designing transformations.

We shall use an instance of Dataflow Gen2 to import data from a data source directly into the lakehouse, enriching it along the way.

# Getting ready

For this recipe, you need an active Power BI account with a Microsoft Fabric license activated. Follow the steps described in the *Technical requirements* section of this chapter to activate the Fabric trial license if you have not done so already.

This recipe assumes that you followed the first recipe in the chapter and already have a workspace and a lakehouse created. If you do not have this set up, please follow *steps 1* and *2* in the first recipe, *Introducing Microsoft Fabric* and Data Fabric, to prepare for this recipe.

# How to do it...

Before starting the recipe, open Fabric at `https://app.fabric.microsoft.com/home` and log in to your account. Navigate to your workspace and then to your lakehouse.

1.  In the lakehouse interface, click on **Get data** from the menu ribbon at the top, and then select **New Dataflow Gen2**. This will open the Dataflow Gen2/Power Query interface.

*Figure 8.23: Dataflow Gen2 user interface*

2.  Rename the data flow: click on the **Dataflow Gen2** name (default is **data flow 1**) in the upper-left corner, and in the field **Name** enter Load Order Data.

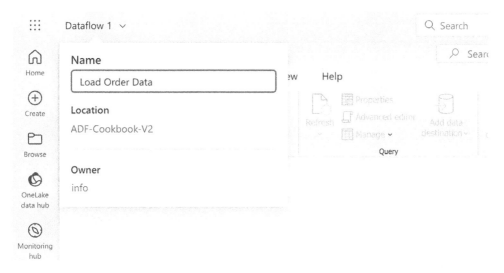

*Figure 8.24: Rename Dataflow Gen2*

3.  Select the **Import from Text/CSV file** tile. You will see the configuration wizard. On the first screen, **Connect to data source**, select the **Link to file** radio button, and enter the text https://raw.githubusercontent.com/PacktPublishing/Azure-Data-Factory-Cookbook-Second-Edition/main/Chapter08/Orders.csv in the **File Path or URL** field. **Connection type** should be set to **Anonymous**. Click **Next**.

4.  Wait until a connection is established and the data preview loads on the next screen. You should see a view similar to the following screenshot:

*Figure 8.25: Dataflow Gen2 data preview*

Click on **Create** to create this dataset.

5.  You will see the Power Query interface again, but now it will display a data preview and show some tools for query manipulation and transformation:

*Figure 8.26: The Power Query interface*

 Your interface might look different from this screenshot, depending on what segments are selected or expanded/collapsed. The main sections of the interface are:

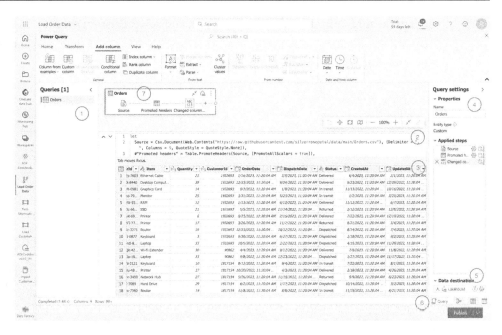

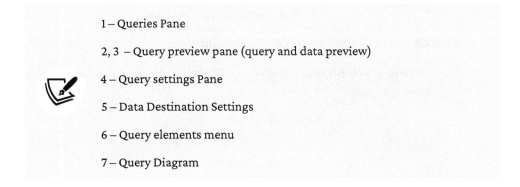

*Figure 8.27: Annotated Power Query interface*

1 – Queries Pane

2, 3 – Query preview pane (query and data preview)

4 – Query settings Pane

5 – Data Destination Settings

6 – Query elements menu

7 – Query Diagram

6. Switch to the **Add Column** tab in the top menu, and select **Custom column**. In the pop-up, enter the column name as `ImportedAt`, set **Date/Time** for **Data type**, and in **Custom column formula** enter the following code: `DateTime.FixedLocalNow()`.

*Figure 8.28: Add a custom column*

Click **OK** to add this custom column to your data.

7. Click **Publish** to publish your **Dataflow Gen2**, and then refresh the data flow by clicking the refresh button.

*Figure 8.29: Refreshing the Dataflow Gen2*

Refreshing the dataflow will load this data directly into the **Orders** table in your lakehouse. It might take a minute or two to process.

8. To view the results of running this data flow, go to your lakehouse and refresh the **Tables** folder. You should see a new table called `Orders`, which contains the data we just loaded:

Figure 8.30: Lakehouse: Orders table

# How it works...

In this recipe, we used a feature of Fabric Data Factory called Dataflow Gen2 to connect to a data source, preview data, apply some simple transformations, and import data into a table in our lakehouse.

 When we create our first Dataflow Gen2 in a workspace, a few special system entities are provisioned: **DataflowsStagingLakehouse** (lakehouse, default dataset, and SQL endpoint) and **DataflowsStagingWarehouse** (dataset and warehouse). You can see them in your workspace. Those are internal system data stores; they should not be deleted.

When you use Dataflow Gen2 to import your data, you can use a multitude of various data sources. At the time of writing, Dataflow Gen2 has more than 120 data source connectors, both internal to Microsoft (i.e., Azure storage accounts and KQL Database) and external, such as Google BigQuery, Amazon Athena, Snowflake, and Databricks.

After specifying the data source and ensuring that the connection was successful, we worked with Power Query – a tool with a graphical interface for data transformation and data preparation. We applied a simple transformation – a column recording was added when data was imported. Of course, it is possible to do much more complex transformations in this tool: we could have filtered our data based on some row value, merged or split rows, transposed rows and columns, changed data types and primary keys, and so on – the possibilities are endless. Every step in the applied transformations was recorded in the query script as well as reflected in the Applied Steps table, so that we can easily see the sequence of steps, rearrange them, or remove unnecessary or erroneous steps.

> Since we started loading data by clicking the Get data button in the Lakehouse Explorer, the destination for our Dataflow Gen2 is already configured – it is our lakehouse. Additionally, the Power Query engine analyzed the data and suggested the column name for us – although the user is free to update or change it if they so choose.

We can also open a new Dataflow Gen2 from a **Data Engineering** menu by clicking on **Create** button in the menu hub on the left panel and choosing Dataflow Gen2 in the **Data Factory** section. If we start our design there, we need to explicitly assign a data destination. Currently, four data stores are supported as a destination for Dataflow Gen2: a Lakehouse, Azure SQL database, Azure Data Explorer (Kusto), and a Data Warehouse, all from the Fabric ecosystem.

We published our dataflow to finalize it (in Fabric Dataflow Gen2, you do not have to explicitly save your design as you apply changes – changes are saved automatically), and when we re-freshed it for the first time, data was loaded into a table. In practice, we probably would want to update our table data regularly by scheduling a periodic dataflow refresh. We can do this from the workspace interface by locating our dataflow, clicking on the ellipsis (**...**) button, selecting **Settings**, and then editing the dataflow refresh schedule.

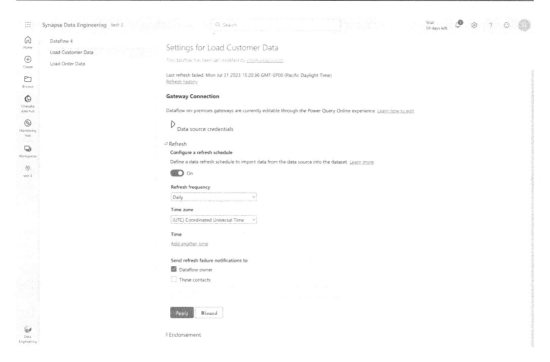

*Figure 8.31: Edit schedule for dataflow refresh*

# There's more...

As you saw, the Lakehouse platform is fundamental to the Fabric experience: it is a multi-purpose data store for both structured and unstructured data.

When a lakehouse is set up, two additional structures are created along with it: an **SQL endpoint** and a **default dataset**.

**SQL endpoint** allows users to interact with structured lakehouse data using SQL. You can experiment with it: navigate to your lakehouse and switch to the SQL endpoint view using the button in the upper right corner:

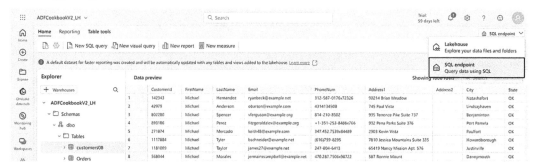

*Figure 8.32: Switch to the SQL Endpoint view in the Lakehouse*

Note, SQL endpoint was renamed as SQL Analytics Endpoint after release to general availability.

Now, you can examine your data with an SQL query. Click on the **New SQL Query** button, and write the following sample query:

```
SELECT top 100 FirstName, LastName, OrderId, OrderDate, Status
from Orders
join customers08 on Orders.CustomerId = customers08.CustomerId
where Status = 'Returned'
Order by OrderDate desc
```

This shows you information on the 100 most recent returned orders.

**SQL endpoint** also lets you connect to your lakehouse from a tool like SSMS or Visual Studio. Click on the gear icon in your lakehouse menu and copy the SQL connection string from the popup:

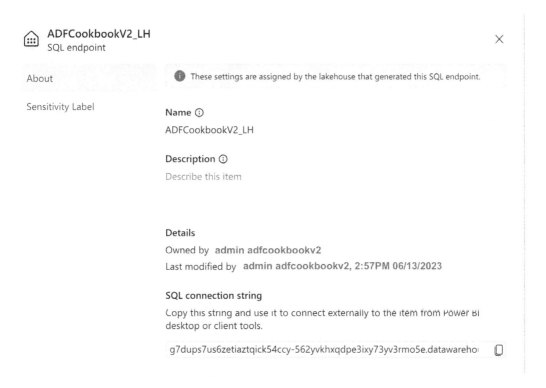

With this connection string, you'll be able to connect to the lakehouse as you would to a regular MSSQL database or a data warehouse.

Currently, the Fabric lakehouse SQL endpoint exposes only read-only capability. Another limitation is that only tables stored in Delta Lake (i.e., not in CSV or Parquet format) are available via SQL endpoint.

The **default dataset**, also auto-provisioned together with the lakehouse, is named the same as your lakehouse. Initially, it is populated with all the tables and views contained in your lakehouse's warehouse, but you can edit the dataset's models to suit your business needs.

Having a default dataset allows you to create Power BI reports directly from the Fabric UI. For example, you can **auto-create** a report for fast visualization by following these steps:

- Locate the default dataset in your workspace

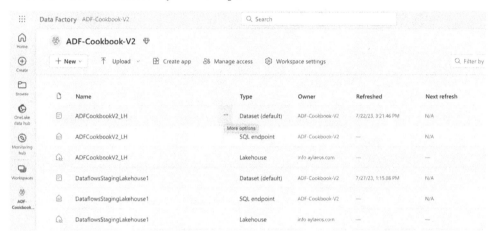

*Figure 8.34: Default dataset in workspace*

 After release to general availability the default dataset was renamed as semantic model.

- Click on it to load the **Dataset** interface
- In the **Visualize this data** tile, click **+ Create a report** and select **Auto-create**

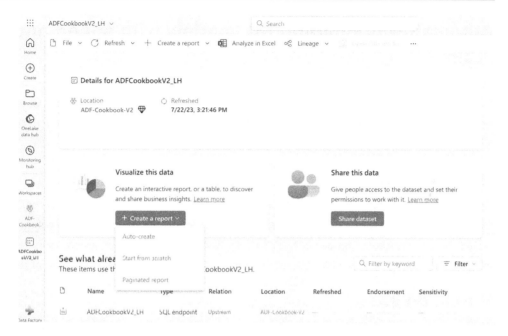

*Figure 8.35: Auto-create a report*

In a few seconds, you will see a visualization of your data in the Power BI report.

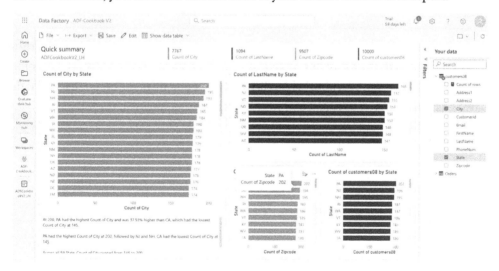

*Figure 8.36: Sample Power BI visual report*

# Automatically building ML models with speed and scale

The Azure ML cloud service provides data scientists and developers with easy-to-use tools to build, train, and deploy ML models. ADF allows you to invoke Azure ML pipelines to carry out predictive analytics as part of your data workflow. In this recipe, you will learn how to create an Azure ML workspace and call an Azure ML pipeline from ADF.

## Getting ready

Before we start, make sure you have access to an Azure license. You should be familiar with the basics of working with Azure, such as navigating within the Azure portal, creating and deleting Azure resources, and creating pipelines in ADF. You can find more information about Azure resources in *Chapter 1*, *Getting Started with ADF*, and *Chapter 2*, *Orchestration and Control Flow*, of this book.

## How to do it...

We are going to use the Azure ML cloud service to create and train a model, and then run it from a Data Factory pipeline.

Note: If you already have an Azure ML pipeline, you can skip to step 8 and use your own pipeline in the ADF.

1.  Before we can create an ML model, we need to have an **Azure Machine Learning** workspace. Go to the Azure **Resources** page, and search for **Azure Machine Learning**. In the **Azure Machine Learning** blade, click on **Create** and fill in the required information, such as resource group, region, and workspace name, as shown in the following:

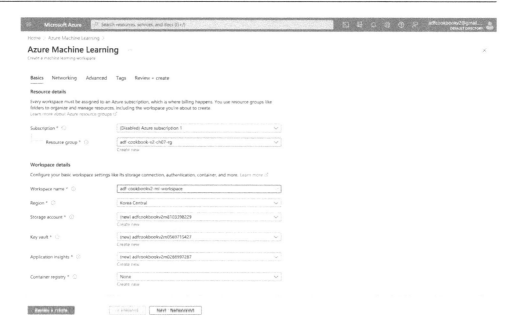

*Figure 8.37: Create an Azure ML workspace*

You can leave the default settings in all other tabs. Click on **Review + create** to validate and create your workspace.

After your workspace has been created, click on the **Go to Resource** button to navigate to the Azure ML workspace overview page, and from there click on the **Launch studio** button.

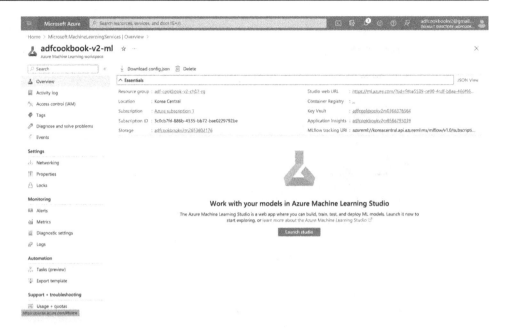

Figure 8.38: Azure ML workspace overview in the Azure portal

2.  Next, we shall create a **Compute** resource. In **Azure ML Studio**, select **Compute** from the tabs on the left, and choose the **Compute clusters** tab in the center.

Figure 8.39: Compute interface in Azure ML Studio

Click on **New** to create a new **cluster**. In the **Create compute cluster** blade, select the desired parameters.

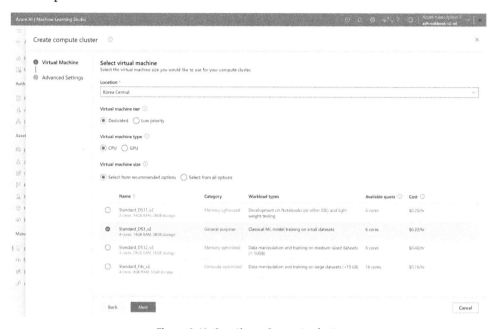

*Figure 8.40: Creating a Compute cluster*

In the preceding example, we selected a dedicated virtual machine tier, of the size Standard_ DS3_v2.

On the next screen, fill in your desired cluster name. All other values are prepopulated, and we can leave them as is.

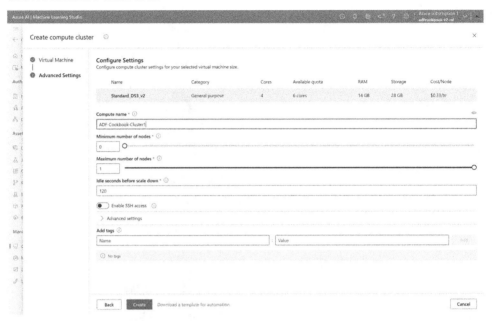

*Figure 8.41: Finishing Compute cluster creation*

Click on **Create** and wait for the deployment to finish.

3.  After the cluster has been successfully provisioned, we shall create our model.

Note

In Azure ML, workflows (preprocessing data, training, and evaluating models) are also called pipelines. To distinguish them from ADF pipelines, I shall refer to them as Azure ML pipelines.

From the **Authoring** section on the left, choose **Designer**. You will see a selection of sample pipelines, similar to the following snapshot.

*Figure 8.42: Designer interface: sample Azure ML pipelines*

Click on the **Show samples** link in the upper-right corner, and from the displayed pipelines, select **Recommendation - Movie Rating Tweets**.

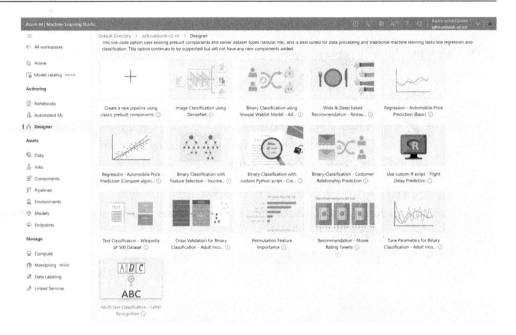

*Figure 8.43: Designer interface: additional sample pipelines*

This will take you to the **Designer** panel, which will be prepopulated with the sample Azure ML pipeline.

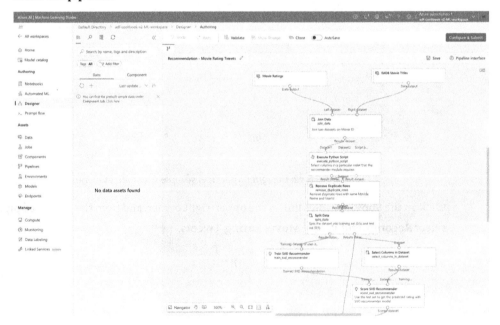

*Figure 8.44: Sample Azure ML pipeline Multiclass Classification - Letter Recognition*

Click on **Configure and Submit** in the upper-left corner and fill in the required information:

- In the **Basics** tab, create a new experiment and give it the desired name:

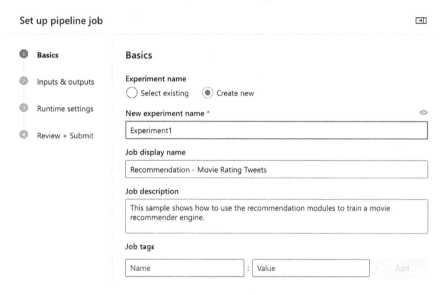

*Figure 8.45: Create a new experiment*

- In the **Runtime Settings** tab, set the cluster we created in the previous step as **Default compute**:

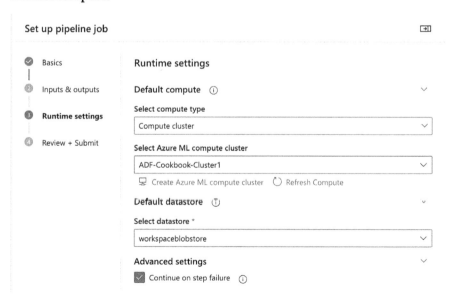

*Figure 8.46: Select compute cluster*

Leave all other settings with the default values.

4. Click on the **Review+Submit** button, review your settings, and click on **Submit**. Your pipeline will be automatically created and submitted.

5. Wait for your **Azure ML job** to complete. This will take several minutes. You can view the progress of your Azure ML pipeline in the **Pipelines** tab:

*Figure 8.47: Monitoring Azure ML pipeline job*

When your Azure ML pipeline job completes, go to the **Jobs** tab and click on your pipeline name. This will take you back to the **Designer** panel. You should see that all the components in your pipeline have green edges, indicating successful completion.

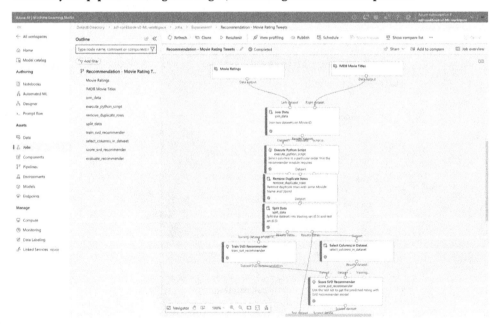

*Figure 8.48: Azure ML pipeline job successfully completed*

6.  Click the **Publish** button. You will see a popup inviting you to specify a pipeline endpoint. Select **Create New**, fill in the desired endpoint name, and click **Publish** in the popup.

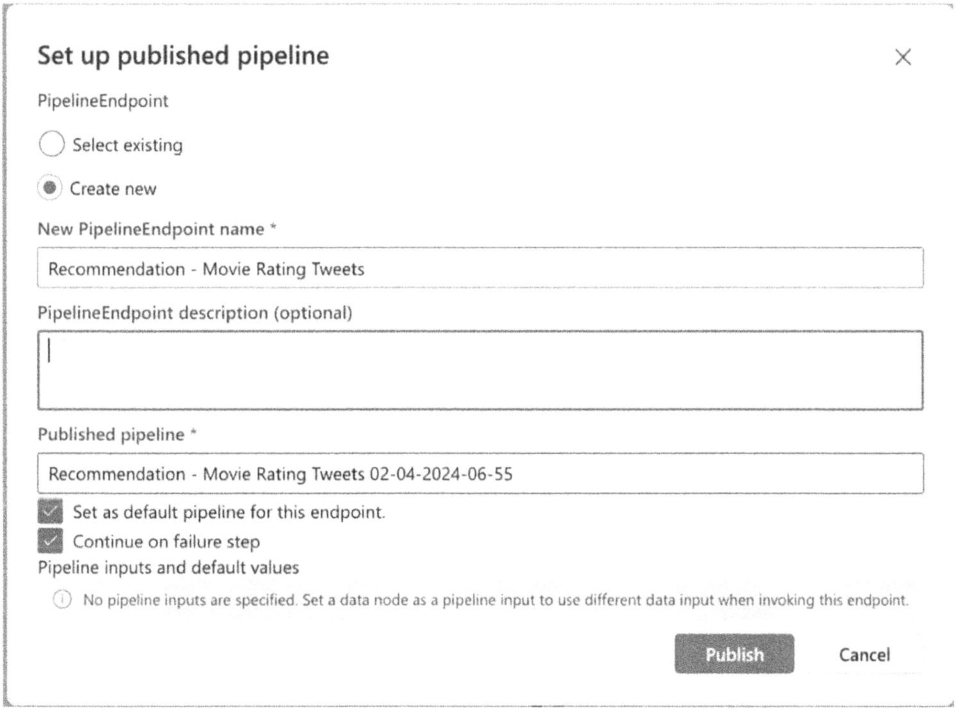

## Set up published pipeline ✕

PipelineEndpoint

◯ Select existing

◉ Create new

New PipelineEndpoint name *

> Recommendation - Movie Rating Tweets

PipelineEndpoint description (optional)

> |

Published pipeline *

> Recommendation - Movie Rating Tweets 02-04-2024-06-55

☑ Set as default pipeline for this endpoint.
☑ Continue on failure step

Pipeline inputs and default values

ⓘ No pipeline inputs are specified. Set a data node as a pipeline input to use different data input when invoking this endpoint.

**Publish**    Cancel

*Figure 8.49: Publishing your Azure ML pipeline*

7.  Go to the **Pipelines** tab in **Azure ML Studio**. In the **Pipeline jobs** tab (the first tab), take note of the experiment name.

*Figure 8.50: Azure ML Studio: Pipeline information*

Next, navigate to the **Pipeline endpoints** tab in the center. You should see the endpoint that was created when we published our pipeline.

*Figure 8.51: Azure ML Studio: Pipeline endpoints*

Click on it. This will open the Designer screen, with the **Pipeline Endpoint Overview** popup on the right. Take note of the **PipelineEndpoint ID** in that popup – we shall need it when we create the Data Factory pipeline to run the Azure ML experiment.

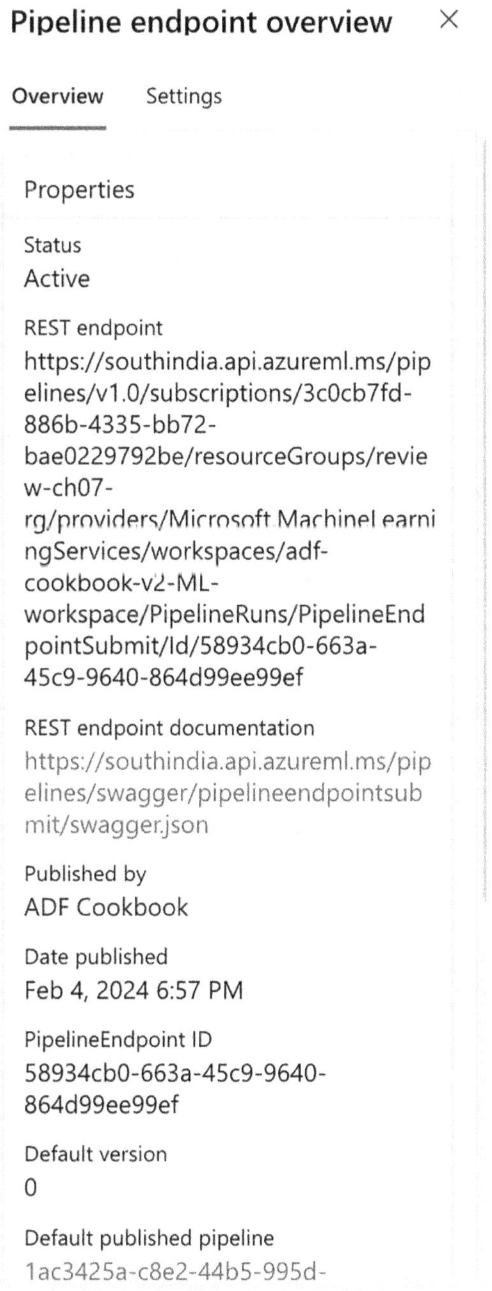

# Pipeline endpoint overview    ✕

**Overview**    Settings

---

Properties

Status
Active

REST endpoint
https://southindia.api.azureml.ms/pip
elines/v1.0/subscriptions/3c0cb7fd-
886b-4335-bb72-
bae0229792be/resourceGroups/revie
w-ch07-
rg/providers/Microsoft.MachineLearni
ngServices/workspaces/adf-
cookbook-v2-ML-
workspace/PipelineRuns/PipelineEnd
pointSubmit/Id/58934cb0-663a-
45c9-9640-864d99ee99ef

REST endpoint documentation
https://southindia.api.azureml.ms/pip
elines/swagger/pipelineendpointsub
mit/swagger.json

Published by
ADF Cookbook

Date published
Feb 4, 2024 6:57 PM

PipelineEndpoint ID
58934cb0-663a-45c9-9640-
864d99ee99ef

Default version
0

Default published pipeline
1ac3425a-c8e2-44b5-995d-

*Figure 8.52: Pipeline endpoint overview*

8.   We have created and trained an Azure ML model and published an Azure ML experiment and pipeline. Let us create a Data Factory pipeline to invoke it.

First, we shall assign the **Azure ML Data Scientist** role to the managed identity of the Data Factory we are going to use. To do this, find your Azure ML workspace in the Azure portal, and go to the **Access Control (IAM)** tab. Click on **Add**, then **Add Role Assignment**. From the list of roles, select **Azure ML Data Scientist**, and click **Next**. On the next screen, check the **Managed Identity** radio button and then click **+Select Members**. Find your Data Factory name in the presented list and press the **Select** button. Finally, click on **Review+Create** to create this role assignment.

9.   Launch your **Azure Data Factory Studio**. If you have more than one Data Factory, make sure that you are opening the one that has the **Azure ML Data Scientist** role with the Azure ML workspace.

In the Data Factory studio, go to the **Author** tab and create a new pipeline. In the **Activities** section, go to the **Machine Learning** section and place the **Machine Learning Execute Pipeline** activity on the canvas. In the **Configuration** panel, rename the activity in the **General** tab.

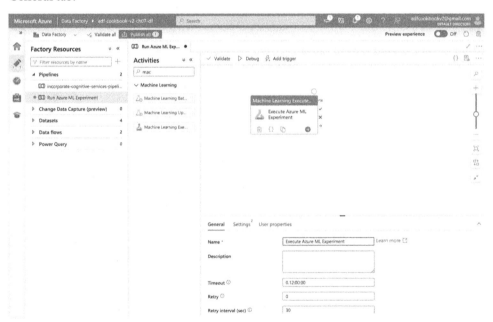

*Figure 8.53: Adding the Machine Learning Execute Pipeline activity*

In the **Settings** tab, select **+New** next to the **Azure ML Linked Service**. You should see the **New linked service** blade. Fill in the required information, such as your subscription and the correct workspace name. Note that we already assigned the appropriate role to the Data Factory-managed identity in *step 7*.

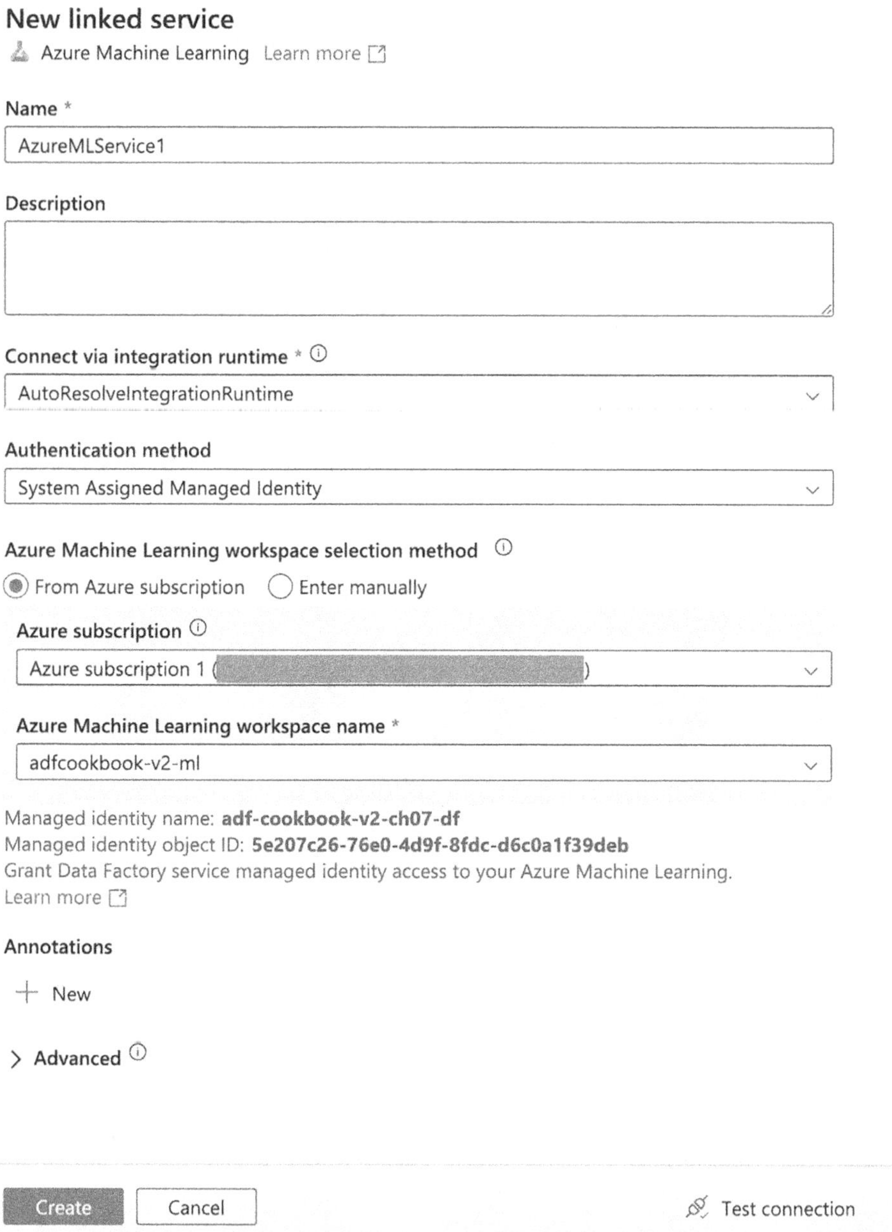

### New linked service

Azure Machine Learning   Learn more

**Name** *

> AzureMLService1

**Description**

> [                                                                                    ]

**Connect via integration runtime** *

> AutoResolveIntegrationRuntime                                             ∨

**Authentication method**

> System Assigned Managed Identity                                           ∨

**Azure Machine Learning workspace selection method**

◉ From Azure subscription   ◯ Enter manually

**Azure subscription**

> Azure subscription 1 (                                              )         ∨

**Azure Machine Learning workspace name** *

> adfcookbook-v2-ml                                                          ∨

Managed identity name: **adf-cookbook-v2-ch07-df**
Managed identity object ID: **5e207c26-76e0-4d9f-8fdc-d6c0a1f39deb**
Grant Data Factory service managed identity access to your Azure Machine Learning.
Learn more

**Annotations**

+ New

> **Advanced**

| Create |   Cancel                                                   ✑ Test connection

*Figure 8.54: Create an Azure ML linked service*

Make sure to test the connection – if your connection test fails, go back to the Azure ML workspace IAM configurations and verify that the Data Factory MSI has the correct role assignment, as explained in *step 7*.

Click on **Create** to create your linked service.

10. After this, in the configuration panel, for **Machine Learning pipeline ID type** select **Pipeline endpoint ID**, and for **Select pipeline endpoint via**, select **Endpoint name**. From the drop-down menu, select the endpoint that we created earlier in this recipe. This should populate the **Pipeline endpoint ID** text field.

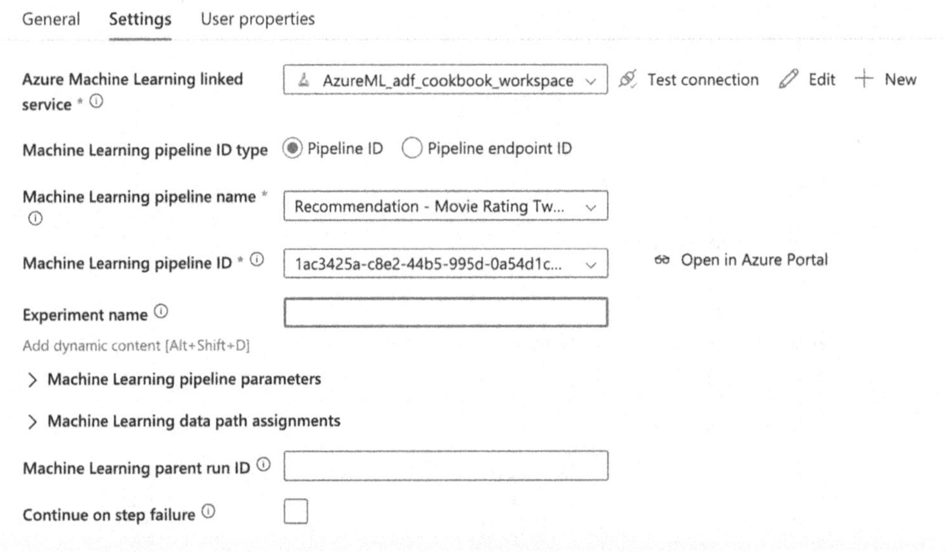

General   **Settings**   User properties

| Azure Machine Learning linked service * ⓘ | ⚗ AzureML_adf_cookbook_workspace ⌄ | ✎ Test connection   ✎ Edit   + New |
| --- | --- | --- |
| Machine Learning pipeline ID type | ⦿ Pipeline ID   ○ Pipeline endpoint ID | |
| Machine Learning pipeline name * ⓘ | Recommendation - Movie Rating Tw... ⌄ | |
| Machine Learning pipeline ID * ⓘ | 1ac3425a-c8e2-44b5-995d-0a54d1c... ⌄ | ⬀ Open in Azure Portal |
| Experiment name ⓘ | | |

Add dynamic content [Alt+Shift+D]

> Machine Learning pipeline parameters
> Machine Learning data path assignments

| Machine Learning parent run ID ⓘ | | |
| --- | --- | --- |
| Continue on step failure ⓘ | ☐ | |

*Figure 8.55: Configure the Machine Learning Execute Pipeline activity*

11. We are ready to run our pipeline. Click on the **Debug** button and wait a few minutes for the pipeline to run. While your activity runs, open your **Azure ML Studio** and go to the **Jobs** tab. You should see a new job that has been created by the Data Factory pipeline.

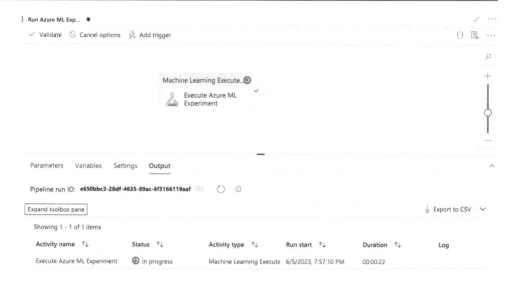

*Figure 8.56: Running the Data Factory pipeline*

*Figure 8.57: Latest job was invoked from the ADF pipeline*

12. Make sure to delete the resources (i.e., compute clusters, etc.) that you used in Azure ML when you no longer need them. Costs can add up quickly when using this service.

## How it works...

In this recipe, we have created an ML training pipeline leveraging a sample provided by Microsoft (*Recommendation - Movie Rating Tweets*). This pipeline prepares the data, defines features, trains, scores, and evaluates the model. We published this pipeline, creating a REST endpoint for this pipeline.

In the ADF pipeline, we used the pre-built **Machine Learning Execute Pipeline** activity. Data Factory provides integration with Azure ML, so we did not have to actually specify the REST endpoint. We just created a linked service to connect to the desired Azure ML workspace and then specified which pipeline endpoint we want our activity to run.

## There's more...

We have created and executed a simple prebuilt Azure ML pipeline that trains a model to predict an English letter category (i.e., classify it as one of the 26 letters of the English alphabet). This pipeline uses a hardcoded data source, and it does not write output.

The set of tools that Azure ML offers deserves a book of its own. If you are using it in production, your Azure ML experiments and pipelines will be much more complex than a sample in this recipe. There is a variety of algorithms at your fingertips: multiple types of text analytics, time series anomaly detection, cleansing data using statistical functions, cascade image classification, and more. You can plug in your own Python and R scripts, combine algorithms and, of course, use various datasets as input. This is where integration with ADF becomes especially useful: you can import, refresh, or transform data from multiple sources, and then pass this data to the **Execute Machine Learning Pipeline** activity to execute your ML models on it.

# Analyzing and transforming data with Azure AI and prebuilt ML models

The Azure AI service offers engineers and data scientists a portfolio of APIs that put the latest in AI research and innovations at their fingertips. This service allows you to access text and speech recognition, image processing, vision, classification, and decision-making AI models via an HTTP call.

In this recipe, we showcase the integration of an ADF mapping data flow and Azure AI Language service. We shall process a file that contains **Personally Identifiable Information** (**PII**), and the result will be a file where fields classified as PII are masked with asterisks.

# Getting ready

Make sure that you have an active Azure subscription. If you do not, follow the instructions in the *Technical requirements* section of this chapter to set up a free trial account.

You will also need access to an instance of ADF and an ADLS Gen2 account.

Before we start working on this recipe, we need to do some preliminary work:

1.  Grant your ADF instance a Data Blob Owner role in the ADLS Gen2 account. Detailed instructions on how to do that can be found in *Chapter 5, Working with Big Data and Databricks*, in the recipe *Setting up an HDInsight cluster*.

2.  Upload the file `https://github.com/PacktPublishing/Azure-Data-Factory-Cookbook-Second-Edition/blob/main/Chapter08/patient-data.csv` to your ADLS Gen2 account

3.  In your ADLS Gen2 account settings, go to the Data protection section, and ensure that all **soft delete** options are off:

*Figure 8.58: ADLS Geb2 Data Protection settings*

- Create a Language resource in Azure AI services by going to the URL `https://portal.azure.com/#create/Microsoft.CognitiveServicesTextAnalytics` and filling out a **Create Language** form similar to the following screenshot:

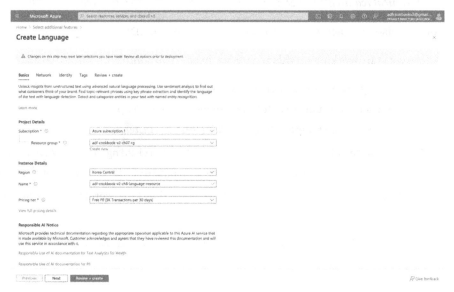

*Figure 8.59: Create a Language resource in Azure AI*

- Deployment will take a minute or two. After the service is deployed, go to the Language service in the Azure portal, search for Cognitive Services, go to **Access Control (IAM)**, add the role **Language Writer**, choose your ADF, and click **Confirm** to save the assignment.

- Finally, go to the **Keys and Endpoint** section, and make a note of the keys and the endpoint. You will need this information in *step 5* in the following recipe:

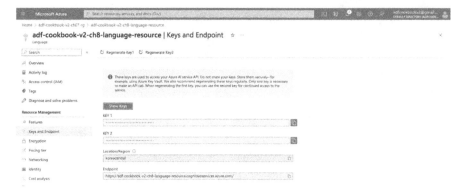

*Figure 8.60: Language resource keys and endpoint*

# How to do it...

In this recipe, we shall construct a pipeline with a Dataflow activity. Core processing and transformation logic is contained in the Dataflow: we shall ingest data from an ADLS Gen2 account, send this data to the Azure AI Language service, and then process the output of that service call to write masked data into another file in the same storage account.

1.  Open your **Azure Data Factory Studio**, go to the **Author** tab, and create a new pipeline.

2.  In the same **Author** tab, in the **Dataflows** section, create a new data flow.

3.  Add **Source** to your data flow and name it IncomingPatientData. Go through the following steps to configure it to load the data that you uploaded to the storage account:

    *   Create a new dataset for the CSV format. When asked to select a **Linked Service** for this dataset, choose **New**.

    *   Create a **linked service** to connect to the ADLS V2 account where your data file is stored. Configure it according to the following figure, and make sure to test the connection.

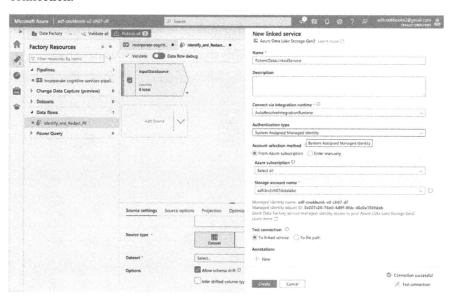

*Figure 8.61: Create a linked service*

    *   After your **lniked service** is configured, finish creating the **dataset**, specifying the path to the data file. Check the **First row as header** checkbox, and select the **Import Schema from | Fonnection/store** radio button.

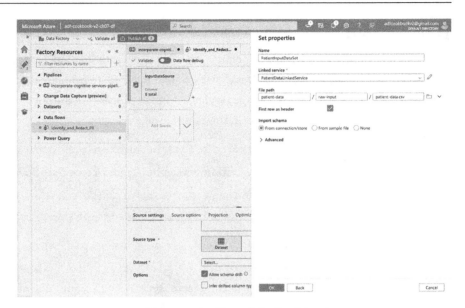

*Figure 8.62: Set file path for the dataset*

- Turn **Data flow debug on** and wait until clusters are running.
- Open your newly created dataset (in the **Datasets** section on the left), and click on **Import schema**. Verify that the schema was imported.

*Figure 8.63: Verify schema was imported in dataset*

- In your pipeline, click on **Source**, go to the **Projection** tab, and verify that the schema is displayed.

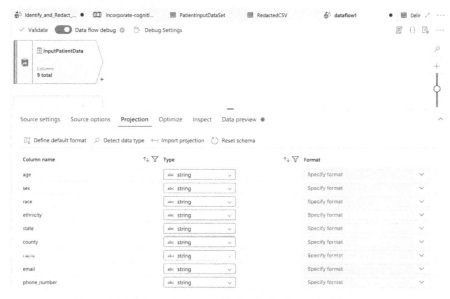

*Figure 8.64: Schema is mapped in the Projection tab of the source*

- Also in **Source**, you should be able to view the data in the **Data preview** tab (hit the **Refresh** button).

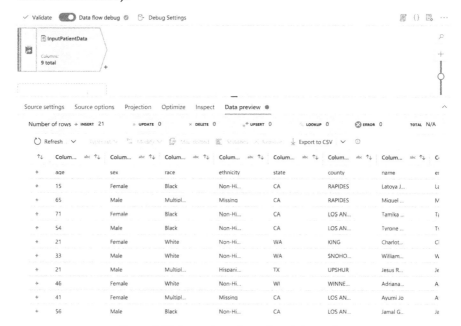

*Figure 8.65: Source transformation data preview*

4. In the data flow, add a **Derive Column** transformation from the **Schema Modifier** section transformation. In the **Configuration** panel, in the **Derived column's settings** tab, add three new columns and configure them exactly as shown in the following list (note that values are case sensitive, so fill the columns and expressions exactly as shown):

- **Column**: kind

  **Expression**: 'PiiEntityRecognition'

- **Column**: parameters

  **Expression**: @(modelVersion='latest')

- **Column**: analysisInput

  **Expression**: @(documents=array(@(id="1", language="en", text=concatWS(', ', age,sex,race,ethnicity,state, county, name, email, phone_number)))))

*Figure 8.66: Adding and configuring a derived column schema modifier transformation*

5. Next, add another transformation, **External Service Call**, to your dataflow graph. In **Settings**, change its name to callCognitiveServices.

Now the **Cognitive Services endpoint** and **account key**, which you obtained in the *Getting ready* section, will come in handy.

In the configuration panel, go to the transformation's **Settings** tab. Create a new **REST linked service** with your **Language Cognitive Service** account information.

- For **Base URL**, enter your **Azure Cognitive Service Endpoint URL** (refer to the *Getting ready* section on how to do so).

- For **Authentication type**, choose **Anonymous**.

- For **Server Certificate Validation**, select **Disable**.

- Create a new **Auth header**. For **Name**, enter Ocp-Apim-Subscription-Key, and for **External Service Call**, enter your Cognitive Services account key.

- Test the connection and create the **linked service**.

*Figure 8.67: Linked service for External Service Call transformation*

Continue configuring your **External Call** transformation: in the **Settings** tab, select **POST** for **Request method,** and enter the following text: `language/:analyze-text?api-version=2022-05-01` for **Relative URL.**

*Figure 8.68: External Call transformation settings*

Next, switch to the **Mapping** tab (same transformation), uncheck **Auto Mapping,** and remove all fields except for **kind, parameters**, and **analysisInput.**

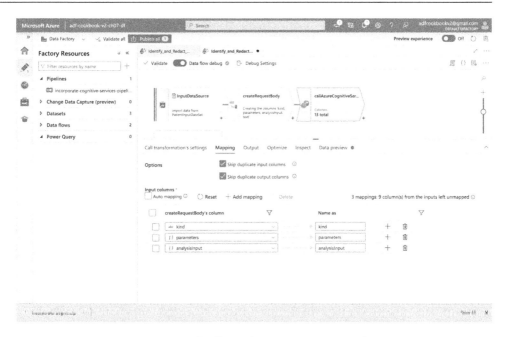

*Figure 8.69: External Call transformation Mapping configuration*

Finally, examine the **Output** tab. Make sure **Body** is checked and that the **Header** and **Status** checkboxes are unchecked. The **Name body as** textbox should have body as its value. In the **Type** textbox, enter the following expression:

```
(kind as string, results as (documents as (redactedText as string, id as
string, entities as (text as string, category as string, offset as integer,
length as integer, confidenceScore as double)[])[]))
```

*Figure 8.70: External Call transformation Output configuration*

6. Now, go back to the **canvas** and add a **Flatten formatter** transformation. Call it flattenOutput. In the **Configuration** panel, in the **Settings** tab, select the path body.result.documents for **Unroll by**.

*Figure 8.71: Flatten formatter transformation settings*

After you've filled in the correct value in **Unroll by**, click the **Reset** button in the same tab. You should see that all input columns changed to reflect the **Unroll by** choice:

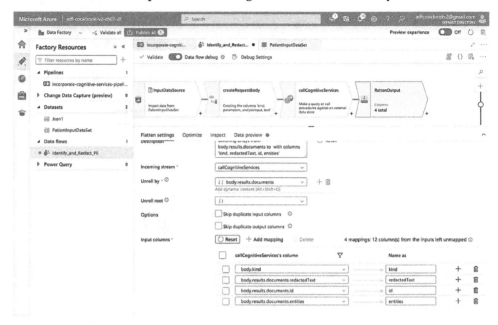

*Figure 8.72: Flatten formatter transformation settings updated settings*

Delete all the new input columns except for `body.results.documents.redactedText`.

7. We are almost done. All we need to do now is to define a **Sink**. In the canvas, add a **Sink** transformation to your data flow, and in the **Configuration** tab, configure a new **CSV dataset**. Give it an appropriate name, and we can use the linked service we created in the previous step (linked service for External Service Call transformation): our transformed data will be stored in the same ADLS Gen2 account as our raw data. Check **First row as header**, and for the **File path**, select the desired path, but do not fill in the file name (the name for the file will be auto-generated).

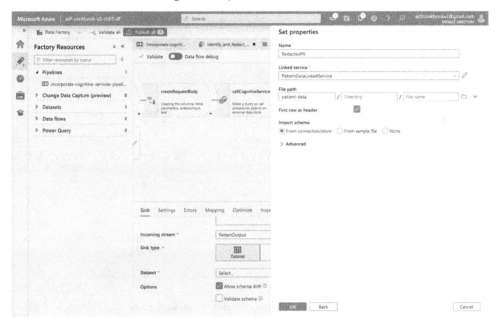

*Figure 8.73: Dataset for the Sink transformation*

All other settings in the **Sink** transformation may be left with the default values. Click **OK** to set up your service.

8.  We have designed the full dataflow, and we are ready to test it. Create a new pipeline, and add a **Dataflow** activity in the **canvas**. Give your **Dataflow** activity an appropriate name, and in the **Settings** section of the **Configurations** panel, select our newly designed dataflow:

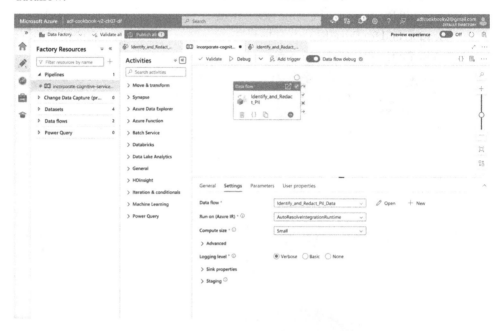

*Figure 8.74: Pipeline with Dataflow activity*

Ensure that your **Data Flow debug** switch is **on**, and click on **Debug**. The pipeline will take a few minutes to run. After it is done, look in the storage account that had your raw data. You should see a new file, named something like `part-00000-abcd`. This is the redacted CSV file that was created by the pipeline. Open this file. You will see that the PII has been removed:

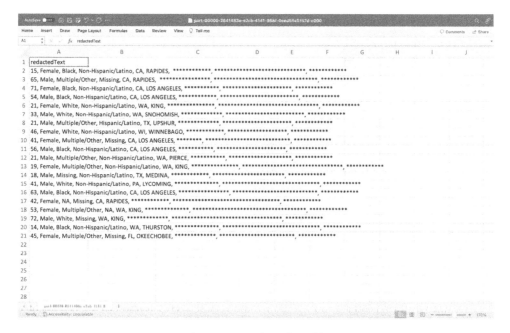

*Figure 8.75: Redacted CSV file*

9.  After you complete the recipe, make sure to turn the dataflow debug off and clean up your resources.

## How it works...

In this recipe, we leveraged the Azure AI Language service to classify and mask PII from a CSV file.

We utilized an ADF Dataflow – a graphical tool for data transformation – to process the file and invoke the Azure AI API on the data.

**Dataflow Source** specified the dataset – a file in the ADLS Gen2 storage – which is the input data for the rest of the flow. The next two transformations are constructing a request body (information that is sent in an HTTP request) and then sending the request to the external service.

These two steps are at the heart of our task: we used the Azure AI Language service to parse and classify the data we sent, identify the PII in it, and return to us the data where those fields are masked (replaced with asterisks).

We used a **Derived Column** transformation (named `createRequestBody`) and we specified the data stream source (previous transformation, called **InputDataSource**). Configured derived columns contain information that we need to provide to the Azure AI Language service for correct processing: the type of processing is `PiiEntityRecognition`, and the `analysisInput` field generates submission text from the input data. We entered the expression `@(documents=array(@(id="1", language="en", text=concatWS(', ', age,sex,race,ethnicity,state, county, name, email, phone_number))))` to concatenate the contents of the columns from the input stream.

As a result, the request body sent to the Azure AI Language will look similar to this:

```
{
    "kind":"PiiEntityRecognition",
    "parameters":
    {
        "modelVersion":"latest"
    },
    "analysisInput":
    {
        "documents":
            [
                {
                    "id":"1",
                    "language":"en",
                    "text":"ddHOmIkIqxve, jrTTsWdoYRov@example.com, 251-647-1890,
2021-07, CA, LOS ANGELES, 50 to 64 years, Unknown, Unknown, NA, Missing,
Missing, Laboratory-confirmed case, Symptomatic, No, Missing, Missing,
Missing"
                }
            ]
    }
}
```

The actual HTTP call happens in the **External Service Call** transformation we named `callCognitiveServices`. The data flow (from the pipeline) will send out a POST request, and the Azure AI Language service will process it and return a response with data looking similar to this:

```
{
    "kind": "PiiEntityRecognitionResults",
    "results": {
```

```
            "documents": [
                {
                    "redactedText": "ddHOmIkIqxve, ***********************,
***********, *******, CA, LOS ANGELES, 50 to ********, Unknown, Unknown,
NA, Missing, Missing, Laboratory-confirmed case, Symptomatic, No, Missing,
Missing, Missing",
                    "id": "1",
                    "entities": [
                        {
                            "text": "jrTTsWdoYRov@example.com",
                            "category": "Email",
                            "offset": 14,
                            "length": 24,
                            "confidenceScore": 0.8
                        },
                        {
                            "text": "251-647-1890",
                            "category": "PhoneNumber",
                            "offset": 40,
                            "length": 12,
                            "confidenceScore": 0.8
                        },
                        {
                            "text": "2021-07",
                            "category": "DateTime",
                            "subcategory": "DateRange",
                            "offset": 54,
                            "length": 7,
                            "confidenceScore": 0.8
                        },
                        {
                            "text": "64 years",
                            "category": "DateTime",
                            "subcategory": "Duration",
                            "offset": 86,
                            "length": 8,
                            "confidenceScore": 0.8
                        }
```

```
                    ],
                    "warnings": []
                }
            ],
            "errors": [],
            "modelVersion": "2021-01-15"
        }
    }
```

This response contains a lot of information. For example, it contains classification of the fields that we sent: it identifies the phone number, email and so on. However, in this recipe, we are only interested in the field redactedText, which contains our input line, masked.

The next transformation in the dataflow, a **Flatten** transformation (named flattenOutput), is used to transform this JSON response similar to the preceding example into a row in a CSV file. This is what the **Unroll by** option is used for.

Finally, in the **Sink**, the dataflow writes processed output into a CSV into data storage (in our case, the same ADLS Gen2 account).

## There's more...

Azure AI is Microsoft's portfolio of production-ready artificial intelligence APIs and models. The range of services is too great to describe here; however, if you are interested, detailed documentation is available at https://learn.microsoft.com/en-us/azure/ai-services/what-are-ai-services#available-azure-ai-services.

In this recipe, we invoked one of the available Azure AI services – a **Language** service – to classify our data in the External Call transformation in the mapping dataflow. The External Call transformation can be adapted to call any other service that has a REST API (most Azure AI services do). Another way to invoke an Azure AI REST API would be by using a Web activity in a data pipeline: this design is more appropriate if you do not need to transform response data.

# Leave a review!

Enjoying this book? Help readers like you by leaving an Amazon review. Scan the QR code below for a 20% discount code.

# 9

# Managing Deployment Processes with Azure DevOps

Azure DevOps offers a comprehensive set of development collaboration, **continuous integration**, and **continuous delivery** tools. With Azure Repos, you can collaborate on code development using free public and private Git repositories, pull requests, and code reviews. Meanwhile, Azure Pipelines enables you to implement a streamlined build, test, and development pipeline for any application.

In this chapter, we will delve into setting up CI and CD for data analytics solutions in **Azure Data Factory** (**ADF**) using Azure DevOps.

**Continuous Integration** (**CI**) is a practice where code changes are regularly integrated into a shared repository, ensuring that each change is automatically built, tested, and validated.

**Continuous Deployment** (**CD**) is the automatic deployment of changes to production or staging environments after they pass CI tests.

By implementing CI/CD in the context of data analytics, you can streamline the development process, reduce manual errors, and accelerate the delivery of new features and updates in **ADF**. This approach enhances efficiency and reliability in managing data analytics solutions, ultimately improving the agility and effectiveness of your data projects.

We'll begin by creating an Azure DevOps account, establishing an organization, and creating projects within it, all while connecting it to ADF. We will then explore how to publish Git changes to ADF and deploy new features using Azure Repos. Additionally, you'll gain insight into preparing and configuring CI/CD processes for Data Factory pipelines using Azure Pipelines. Throughout the process, we will also demonstrate how to use Visual Studio Code to facilitate the deployment of changes to ADF.

We will cover the following list of recipes in this chapter:

- Setting up Azure DevOps
- Publishing changes to ADF
- Deploying your features into the **master branch**
- Getting ready for the CI/CD of ADF
- Creating an Azure pipeline for CD
- Installing and configuring Visual Studio to work with ADF deployment
- Setting up ADF as a Visual Studio project
- Running Airflow DAGs with ADF

# Technical requirements

For this chapter, you will need the following:

- **An active Azure account:** It could be either your business account or a personal account. If you don't have an Azure account yet, you can activate an Azure free trial license through the main Microsoft website: https://azure.microsoft.com/en-us/free/.

- **GitHub repository**: You may download the dataset from the book's Git repo or you may have your own one: https://github.com/PacktPublishing/Azure-Data-Factory-Cookbook-Second-Edition/tree/main.

Now that you've got a sense of what this chapter covers, along with the technical requirements, let's dive into the recipes.

# Setting up Azure DevOps

To get the most out of Azure DevOps integration with ADF, you first need to create an account within Azure DevOps, link it with your Data Factory, and make sure everything is set up and ready to work. This recipe will take you through the steps on how to accomplish that.

## Getting ready

Before we start, please ensure that you have an Azure subscription and are familiar with the basics of Azure resources such as the Azure portal, creating and deleting Azure resources, and creating pipelines in ADF.

## How to do it...

In this recipe, you will learn how to create an Azure DevOps account, create a new project, connect a DevOps organization with Azure Active Directory, link it with your ADF, and set up a code repository:

1. Navigate to `https://azure.microsoft.com/en-us/products/devops/`.

2. You will see the following screen. Click on **Start free** to begin creating your Azure DevOps account:

*Figure 9.1: Starting your free Azure DevOps account*

3. Log in with your Azure account, as we are going to connect Azure DevOps to Azure Active Directory and click **Continue**:

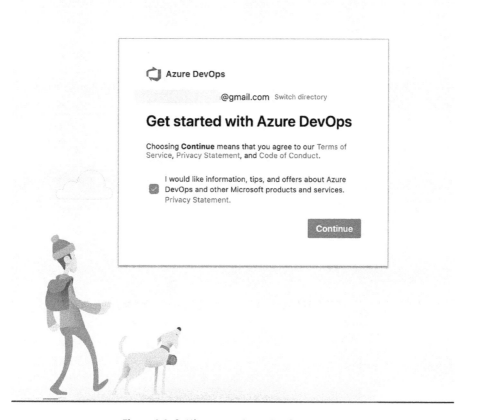

*Figure 9.2: Setting up an Azure DevOps account*

4.  Enter your organization name in the **Name your Azure DevOps organization** field. This name is similar to your account name. If you ever need to change your organization name, you can refer to this document for guidance: `https://learn.microsoft.com/en-us/ azure/devops/organizations/accounts/rename-organization?view=azure-devops`. You also need to select the location for hosting your project. It's recommended to choose the location where your ADF is hosted to avoid potential syncing issues. Once you've made your selection, click on **Continue**:

*Figure 9.3: Creating an Azure DevOps organization*

5. Enter a name in the **Project name** field of the project and click **Create project**:

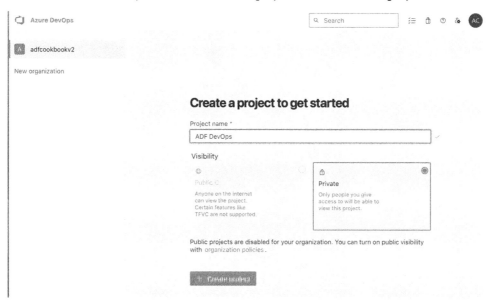

*Figure 9.4: Creating an Azure DevOps project*

6. Go to **Organization page**, and then to **Organization settings** in the bottom-left corner, and you'll see the dialog box shown in the following screenshot. Then, choose the **Default Directory** option in the **Microsoft Entra** dropdown and click **Connect**:

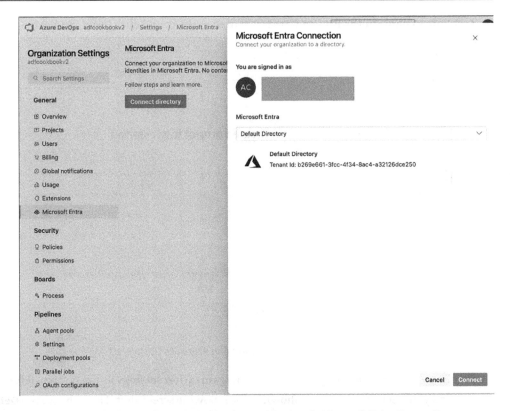

*Figure 9.5: Connecting an organization to Directory in Microsoft Entra Connection*

If you get the connection error shown in the following screenshot, you have to switch **Microsoft Directory** to **Default Directory** in the settings by following this link: `https://aex.dev.azure.com/me`.

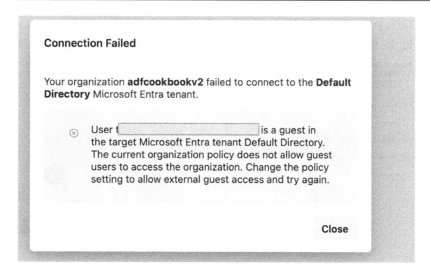

*Figure 9.6: Connection error*

In this step, we have connected our organization to Azure Active Directory. It is a necessary step to link your ADF to an Azure DevOps account.

7.  Then, it's recommended to sign out and sign in again. If you go to the **Microsoft Entra** page of Azure DevOps, you'll see that, now, your organization is connected to **Default Directory**:

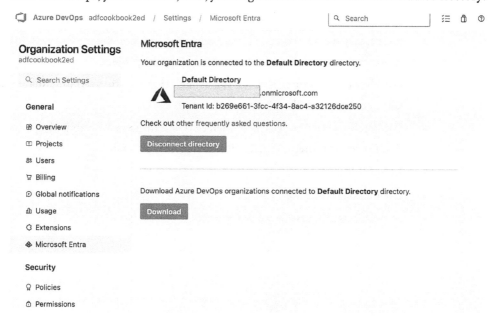

*Figure 9.7: The organization is connected to Default Directory*

8. Go to your ADF and click on **Set up code repository** at the top of the screen, as highlighted in the following screenshot. A dialog box with the repository settings will appear.

*Figure 9.8: Setting up a code repository in ADF*

9. In the open dialog box, you need to have the settings as follows:

- **Azure DevOps Organization name**: Your organization name
- **Azure Active Directory**: Choose your default.
- **Project name**: Your project name.
- **Repository name**: You can create a new repository or choose **Use existing**, which was created by default with the creation of your project.
- **Collaboration branch**: Choose the branch that will be used for collaboration in Git. Usually, it is called the **master branch**.
- **Publish branch**: Choose the branch that will be used for publishing into the production environment. Usually, it is called **adf_publish**.
- **Root folder**: / .
- **Use custom comment**: Check.
- **Import existing resources to repository**: Check.

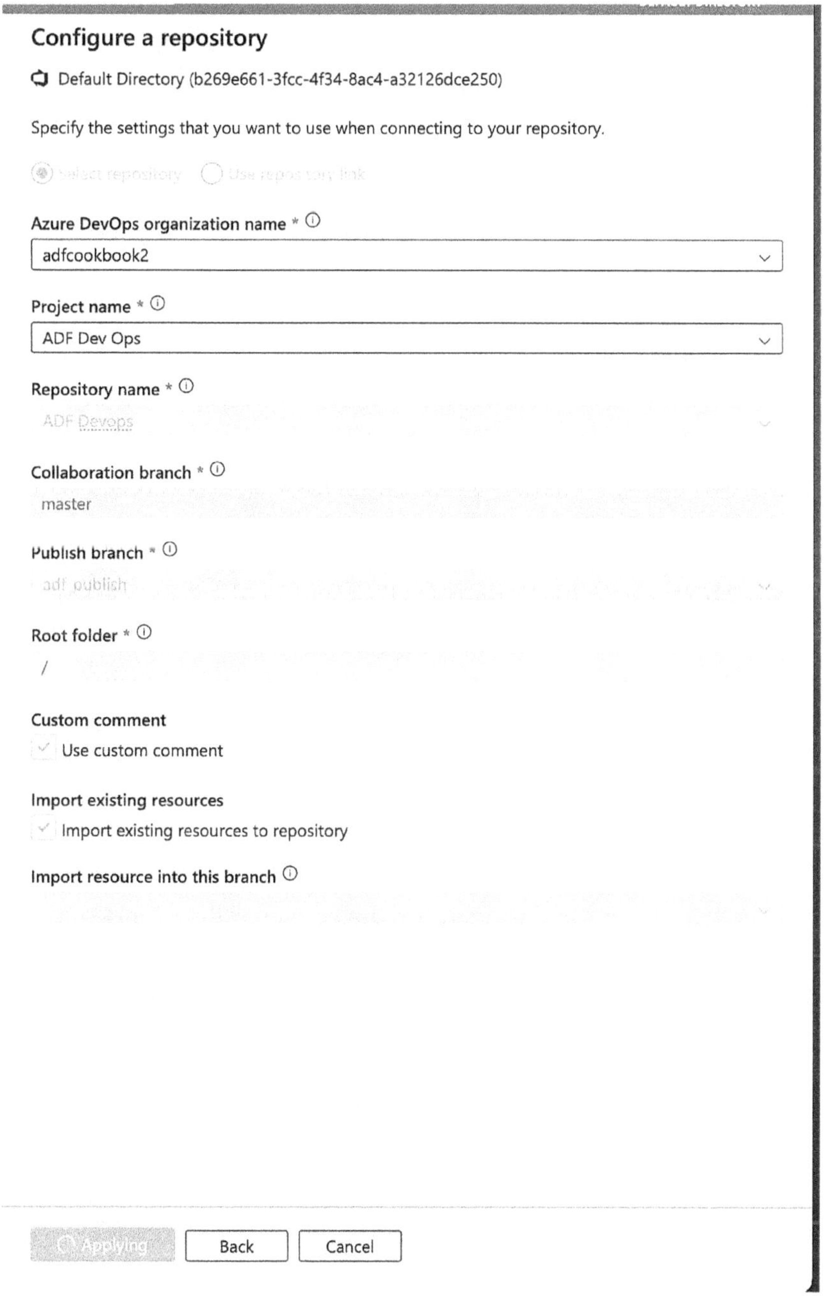

## Configure a repository

◻ Default Directory (b269e661-3fcc-4f34-8ac4-a32126dce250)

Specify the settings that you want to use when connecting to your repository.

⦿ Select repository ◯ Use repository link

**Azure DevOps organization name** * ⓘ

| adfcookbook2 | ⌄ |
|---|---|

**Project name** * ⓘ

| ADF Dev Ops | ⌄ |
|---|---|

**Repository name** * ⓘ

ADF Devops

**Collaboration branch** * ⓘ

master

**Publish branch** * ⓘ

adf_publish

**Root folder** * ⓘ

/

**Custom comment**

☑ Use custom comment

**Import existing resources**

☑ Import existing resources to repository

**Import resource into this branch** ⓘ

⟳ Applying      Back      Cancel

*Figure 9.9: Setting up a Git repository*

10. After you click **Apply**, you will see the **Select working branch** window. Choose **Use existing** to continue your work within the **master branch** and click **Save**. You will see that, now, your ADF is connected to **Azure DevOps Git** and **master branch** is chosen. You can find it highlighted in the following screenshot:

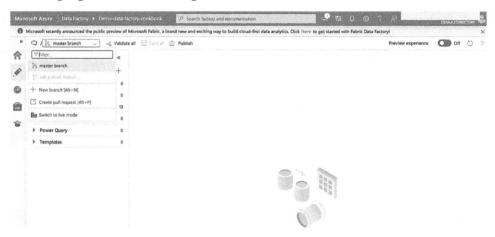

*Figure 9.10: Choosing a branch in Azure DevOps Git*

In this section, we've created an Azure DevOps account with a new project, connected a DevOps organization with Azure Active Directory, linked it with ADF, and set up a code repository. In the next section, we will see how these steps work in the background.

## How it works...

As we have an Azure account and an Azure DevOps account, we can connect them using an Azure Active Directory default directory. This connection is crucial for streamlining the development process by linking Azure DevOps with ADF. It allows for a seamless integration of these services and simplifies the management of your data analytics solutions.

By connecting a DevOps organization to the default Azure Active Directory, we establish a connection that stores the tenant ID necessary for linking these services. This integration not only enhances efficiency but also ensures a secure and controlled environment for your projects.

After setting up the repository in Data Factory, a new repository, ADF DevOps, is automatically created in the Azure DevOps project. Setting the collaboration branch as the master has significance in the context of Azure DevOps and ADF collaboration. It establishes the primary branch for development, making it easier to manage and track changes in your data analytics solution's codebase.

In summary, connecting Azure DevOps with ADF brings benefits such as streamlined development, enhanced security, and simplified project management. Choosing the collaboration branch as the master ensures a clear development path for your data analytics projects.

# Publishing changes to ADF

Collaboration on code development involves using Git. In this recipe, you will learn how to create an ADF pipeline in **Azure DevOps Git** and publish changes from your **master branch** to ADF.

## Getting ready

Before we start, please ensure that you have an Azure subscription and are familiar with the basics of Azure resources, such as navigating the Azure portal, creating and deleting Azure resources, and creating pipelines in **Azure Data Factory** (**ADF**).

Additionally, you will need an Azure DevOps project created and linked to your ADF. If you haven't set up this connection yet, you can refer to the preceding recipe, titled *Setting up Azure DevOps*, for step-by-step instructions on how to do so.

## How to do it...

We are going to create a new ADF pipeline in the master branch of Azure DevOps Git and publish the changes to Data Factory:

1. Create a new ADF pipeline with the **Wait** activity in the **master branch**. Please refer to *Chapter 2, Orchestration and Control Flow*, for guidelines on how to do that. Click **Save all**. Your changes will be saved in the **master branch** of **Azure DevOps Git**:

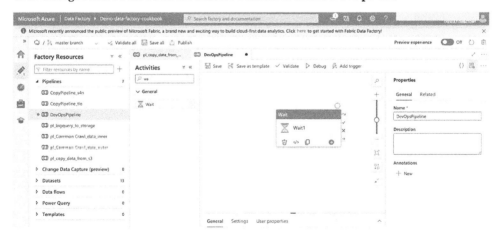

*Figure 9.11: Creating a new pipeline inside the master branch*

2. Now switch from **Azure DevOps Git** to **Live (Data Factory)** mode (in the top-left corner of the following screenshot). You'll see that there are no newly created pipelines:

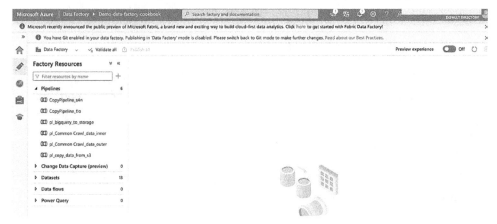

*Figure 9.12: Switching to Data Factory mode*

The blank ADF canvas in the preceding screenshot means that changes have not been deployed to Data Factory yet.

3. Go to Azure DevOps | your project | **Repos** | your repository | **Files** | **Pipeline**. Here, you will see your pipeline created in the **master branch**. It is saved as a JSON file in DevOps. You can also see that there is only the **master branch** created in the current repository:

*Figure 9.13: Azure DevOps repo: a pipeline created in the master branch*

Navigate to your ADF and select **Azure DevOps Git** mode. You will see that your changes are saved in the **master branch** and you can continue working with it. Click **Publish** to publish your DevOps pipeline. **ADF** will create a new branch called **adf_publish** inside your repository and publish the changes to ADF directly. You will see the message about the Publish branch in the **Pending changes** dialog box, as in this screenshot:

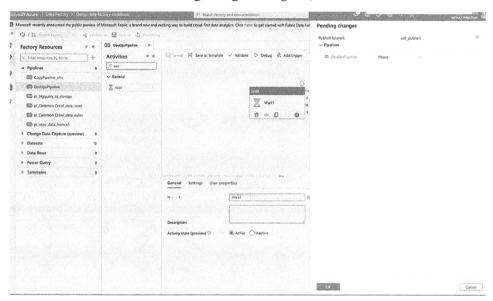

*Figure 9.14: Publishing a pipeline from the master branch*

4.  Click **OK**. While the publishing is being completed, switch to **Data Factory** mode and you will see that the pipeline is deployed to it.

## How it works...

Every activity you do in ADF is saved to a JSON file (there are separate JSON files for datasets, pipelines, linked services, dataflows, and so on), and this file is kept in Azure DevOps.

After publishing your ADF pipeline from the master branch to Data Factory, the adf_publish branch is created automatically in the repository, and the ARM template is created and placed into the adf_publish branch. The adf_publish branch is significant as it is used to store the ARM template, which is crucial for deploying your ADF and its resources. It encapsulates the state of your ADF at a particular point in time and facilitates version control and reproducibility of your data workflows. This branch plays a key role in the deployment process, ensuring that the deployed resources match the desired state defined in the ARM template. The ARM template is a code representation of your **ADF** and Azure resources:

*Figure 9.15: ARM templates are created in the adf_publish branch*

If you go to your project in **DevOps**, you will see that the adf_publish branch has been created and the ARM template of the master branch (ArmTemplateForFactory.json, ARMTemplateParametersForFactory.json) is saved there. The templates highlighted in the preceding screenshot are stored only in the adf_publish branch.

# Deploying your features into the master branch

Now that we have covered how to publish changes from the master branch to Data Factory, we are going to look at how to deploy new branches into the master branch. There are several reasons for creating new branches. While implementing new changes to your project, it is a common practice to create a feature branch, develop your changes there, and then publish them to the master branch. Some teams working in an Agile environment can create branches per story development. Other teams may have branches per developer. In all these situations, the main purpose is to avoid breaking changes during the release into the production environment.

# Getting ready

Before we start, please ensure that you have an Azure subscription and are familiar with the basics of Azure resources such as the Azure portal, creating and deleting Azure resources, and creating pipelines in ADF. Also, you will need an Azure DevOps project created and linked to your ADF; we covered that in the previous recipe, *Publishing changes to ADF*.

# How to do it...

In this recipe, we are going to create a new branch, make changes in this branch, create a pull request, and merge the changes with the **master branch**:

1. To create a new branch, go to your ADF, choose **Azure DevOps Git mode**, then click on **master branch** and then **New branch** (as shown in the following screenshot):

*Figure 9.16: Creating a new branch in Azure DevOps Git*

2.  Type the name of your feature in the field that appears in the dialog box (see the following screenshot) and click **Create**:

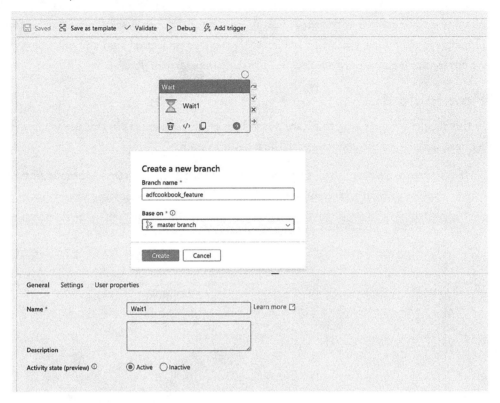

*Figure 9.17: Creating a feature branch in Azure DevOps Git*

3.  Open your **feature branch** and create a new dataset with a CSV file from your **Blob storage**. In the following screenshot, you can see that **adfcookbook_feature** is selected and the changes are made to this branch:

*Figure 9.18: Creating a dataset in the feature branch*

4. Before publishing your changes to ADF, you need to first publish them to the **master branch**. To do so, click **Save all**, then click on your **feature branch**, and choose **Create pull request** (highlighted in the following screenshot):

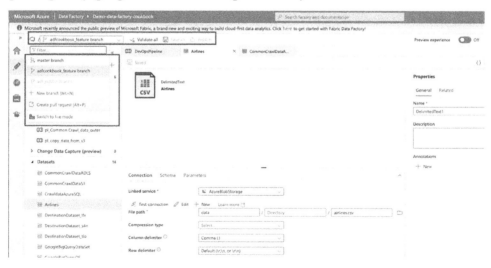

*Figure 9.19: Creating a pull request from ADF*

5.  This option will take you to your Azure DevOps account. We'll navigate the steps of how to do a pull request. You need to enter the title and description (they are created by default). If you're working within an organization, you can also choose **Reviewers** for your deployment (that is, **Team Leader, Senior Engineer, Peers**, and so on):

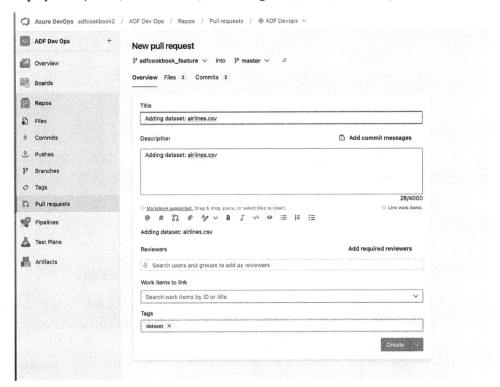

*Figure 9.20: Creating a pull request in Azure DevOps*

In the **Files** tab, you will see the changes that are being deployed as JSON files (as in the following screenshot):

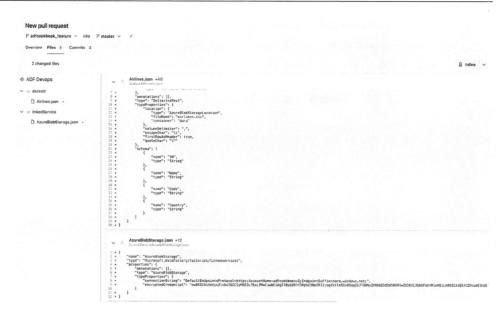

*Figure 9.21: The changes are deployed as JSON files*

To proceed with the pull request, click **Create** on the **Overview** tab.

6. You will see a new active pull request in the **Pull requests** section of your repository:

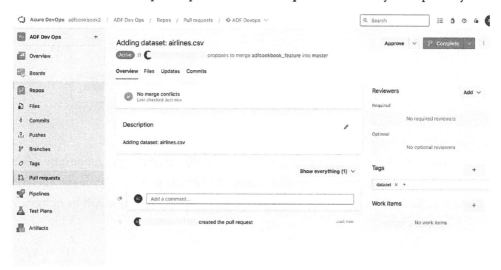

*Figure 9.22: An active pull request form*

7.  You can approve the pull request on your own if you don't have any other approvers (if you have any reviewers, you will need to wait until they approve your pull request before merging). Then, click **Complete**. The dialog box for completing the pull request will appear:

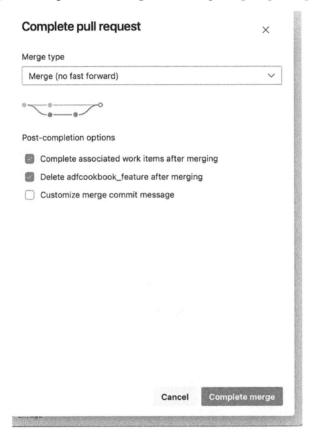

*Figure 9.23: Approving a pull request*

8.  You can delete the source branch on the completion of the pull request by selecting the appropriate checkbox if you don't need this branch anymore. Once you click **Complete merge** (as seen in the preceding screenshot), the feature code will be merged with the **master branch**:

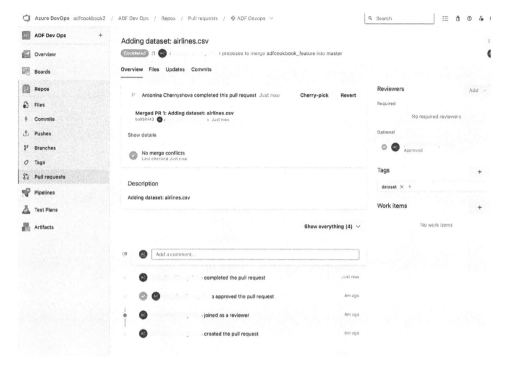

*Figure 9.24: Completing the pull request*

9. Now, if you go to your repository, you can check that you have only two branches as the feature was deleted and your developed dataset is in the **master branch**. You can check the same in the ADF interface:

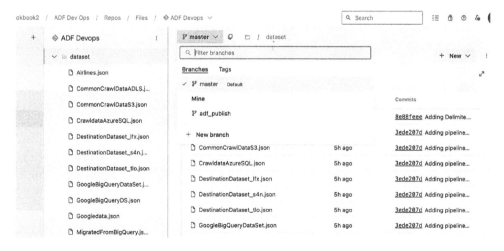

*Figure 9.25: Changes are merged into the master branch*

10. When you go back to ADF, you will see that the current working branch was deleted. To use the existing **master branch**, click **Save**:

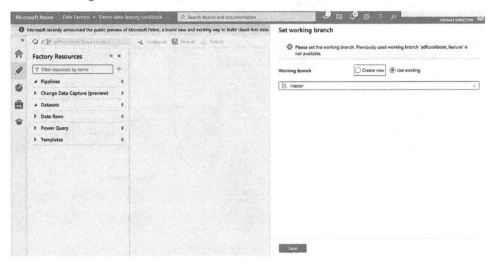

*Figure 9.26: Deleting the feature branch*

11. In the opened **master branch**, click **Publish**, then click **OK**:

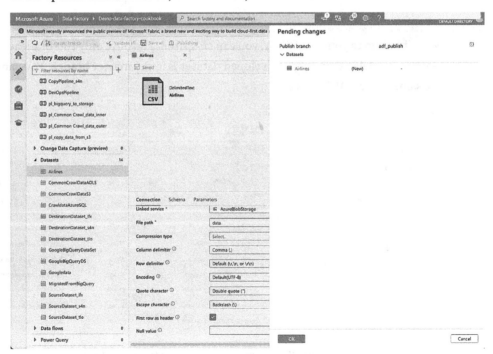

*Figure 9.27: Publishing changes from the master branch to the adf_publish branch*

12. After publishing is completed, you can switch to **Data Factory** mode and check that the dataset has been added to the adf_publish branch.

In this section, we have created a feature branch and successfully merged changes from the new branch to the master branch and publish branch. Now, let's take a look at how it works.

## How it works...

When you click **Create a new branch** in ADF DevOps Git mode, a new branch is created inside the Azure DevOps repository. When you add a new feature in the feature branch, it is saved as a JSON file in this branch of the Azure DevOps repository. In order to release your feature from Git to Data Factory, you need to merge the changes with the master branch first (as it is selected as a collaboration branch) via a pull request. The pull request needs to be approved and completed by a reviewer. After completion of the pull request, the JSON file of the new feature will be copied into the appropriate folder of the master branch. If we tick the **Delete feature** branch after merging checkbox, the feature branch will be deleted.

It's a common practice to delete it after merging changes to keep the repository clean and avoid clutter. However, there may be scenarios where keeping the feature branch is beneficial for future reference or auditing purposes. Whether to delete the branch or not can depend on your organization's policies and workflow preferences.

After publishing the changes from the master branch, the JSON file of the new feature will be copied into the appropriate folder of the publish branch. The publish branch typically represents the deployment or production environment where the finalized changes are stored for execution. It serves as a separation between development and production environments, ensuring that only approved and tested changes are deployed to production. This helps maintain the stability and reliability of your data workflows.

## Getting ready for the CI/CD of ADF

CD includes the deployment of ADF pipelines between different environments - that is, development, testing, and production. The best practice and most secure way of configuring your pipelines in the CI/CD process is using **Azure Key Vault** (**AKV**) instead of a connection string. **AKV** is utilized in Azure Data Factory pipelines for CD because it provides a highly secure and centrally managed solution for storing and safeguarding sensitive information such as connection strings, passwords, and authentication tokens. It ensures controlled access, facilitates secret rotation, enhances auditing capabilities, and seamlessly integrates with ADF, making it the best practice for securing pipelines in the CD process.

In this recipe, you will learn what you need to set up before creating a CD process, and how to establish AKV and connect it with ADF and an Azure storage account.

## Getting ready

Before we start, please ensure that you have an Azure subscription and are familiar with the basics of Azure resources such as the Azure portal, creating and deleting Azure resources, and creating pipelines in ADF.

## How to do it...

In this section, we are going to create and set up two resource groups - development (DEV) and testing (UAT). Inside each resource group, we'll create access policies, secrets on ADF, an Azure storage account, and AKV:

1.  You need to have created two resource groups: ADFCOOKBOOK-DEV-RG and ADFCOOKBOOK-UAT-RG. Please refer to *Chapter 2, Orchestration and Control Flow*, for guidelines on how to do that.

2.  Inside each resource group, there should be these resources: ADF, AKV, and an Azure storage account. Inside the DEV resource group, there will be the following: ADFBOOK-DEV-ADF, ADFBOOK-DEV-AKV, and adfbookdevadls. Inside the UAT resource group, there will be the following: ADFBOOK-UAT-ADF, ADFBOOK-UAT-AKV, and adfbookuatadls.

3.  To create an **AKV** resource, search for it in the Azure portal, choose a **Subscription** option, choose a resource group, fill in the **Key vault name**, and choose a **Region** option and a **Pricing tier** option, as shown in the following screenshot:

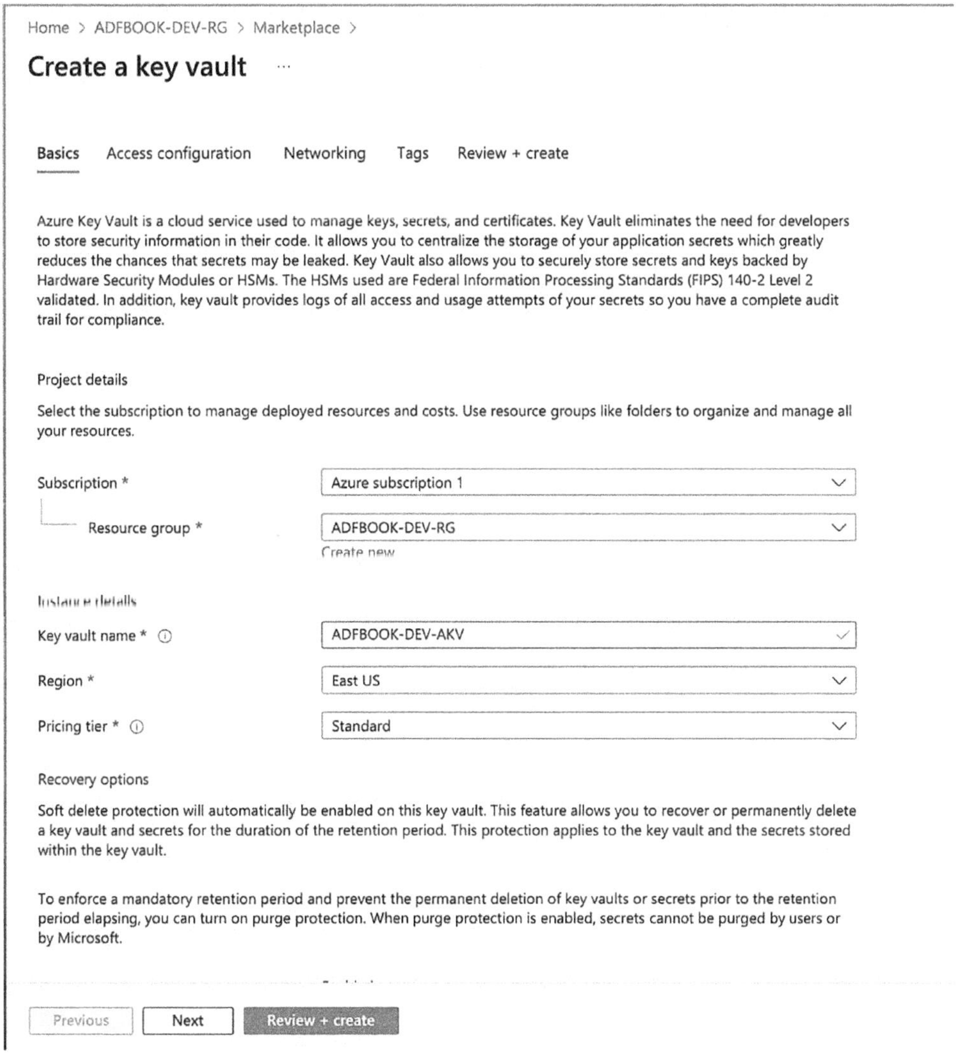

Home > ADFBOOK-DEV-RG > Marketplace >

# Create a key vault  ···

Basics    Access configuration    Networking    Tags    Review + create

Azure Key Vault is a cloud service used to manage keys, secrets, and certificates. Key Vault eliminates the need for developers to store security information in their code. It allows you to centralize the storage of your application secrets which greatly reduces the chances that secrets may be leaked. Key Vault also allows you to securely store secrets and keys backed by Hardware Security Modules or HSMs. The HSMs used are Federal Information Processing Standards (FIPS) 140-2 Level 2 validated. In addition, key vault provides logs of all access and usage attempts of your secrets so you have a complete audit trail for compliance.

## Project details

Select the subscription to manage deployed resources and costs. Use resource groups like folders to organize and manage all your resources.

Subscription *                       | Azure subscription 1                          ⌄ |

    └──── Resource group *            | ADFBOOK-DEV-RG                                 ⌄ |
                                        Create new

Instance details

Key vault name *  ⓘ               | ADFBOOK-DEV-AKV                                 ⌄ |

Region *                          | East US                                         ⌄ |

Pricing tier *  ⓘ                 | Standard                                        ⌄ |

Recovery options

Soft delete protection will automatically be enabled on this key vault. This feature allows you to recover or permanently delete a key vault and secrets for the duration of the retention period. This protection applies to the key vault and the secrets stored within the key vault.

To enforce a mandatory retention period and prevent the permanent deletion of key vaults or secrets prior to the retention period elapsing, you can turn on purge protection. When purge protection is enabled, secrets cannot be purged by users or by Microsoft.

[ Previous ]    [ Next ]    [ Review + create ]

*Figure 9.28: Creating an AKV resource*

4.  In **Access configuration**, you need to create a new access policy for ADF. Click **Vault access policy** and then **Review + create**. For **Secret permissions**, select **Get** and **List**. In the **Select a principal** section, select a principal for your development environment Data Factory. Click **Add**:

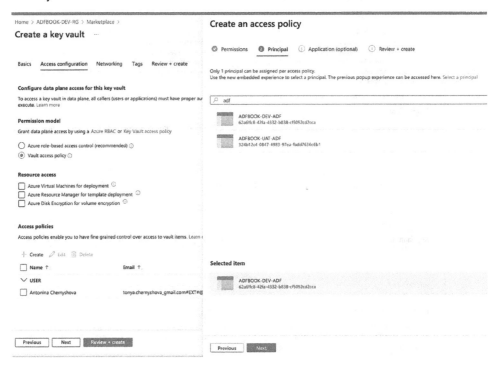

*Figure 9.29: Adding an access policy to Data Factory*

5.  To create a new access policy, click **Create**. Now, when your Dev Data Factory refers to **Dev Key Vault**, it will have access to the stored secrets.

6.  It is common practice when using Azure DevOps pipelines to configure linked services via AKV. To set this up, you need to copy the **connection string** from **Access keys** in your Azure storage account settings and store it in the secret of AKV:

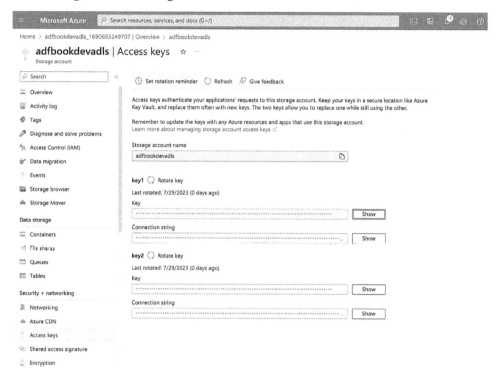

*Figure 9.30: Copying a connection string to an Azure storage account*

7. Go to **AKV** | **Secrets**. Click **Generate/Import**, type the name of the secret, and paste the connection string copied from **Access keys**:

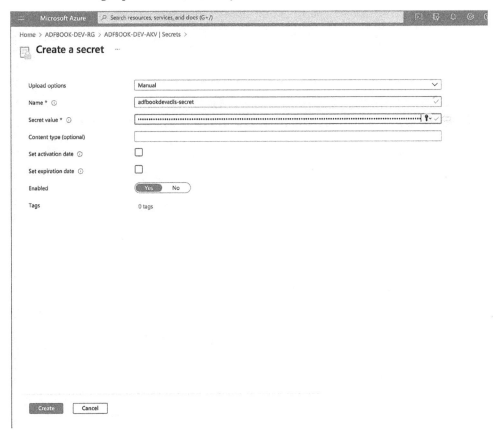

*Figure 9.31: Creating a secret with a connection string in AKV*

8. Link your Dev Data Factory with your DevOps project. Go to **master branch** in your **Azure DevOps Git** and create a linked service for your AKV using an **Azure subscription** method:

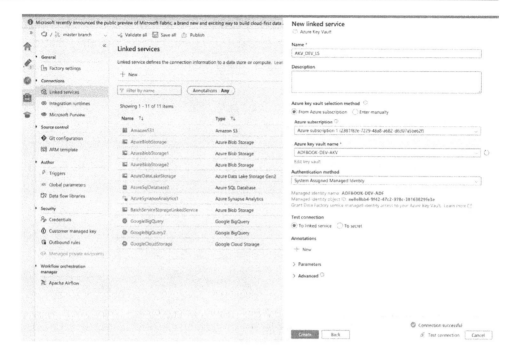

Figure 9.32: Configuring a linked service to AKV

9. Create a linked service to Azure Blob Storage via AKV. Choose your **AKV linked service** and the secret name you created with the connection string to **Azure Blob Storage**:

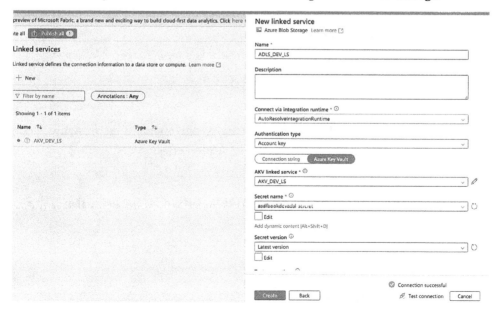

Figure 9.33: Configuring a linked service to Azure Blob Storage via AKV

10. Create a **Copy data** activity in your Dev Data Factory, which will copy a CSV file from the input folder of the Blob container into the output folder. Datasets should be configured via the linked services created in the previous steps:

*Figure 9.34: Creating a pipeline with datasets using the linked services created*

11. In the **Source** tab of the **Copy data** activity, there should be an Azure Blob Storage `DelimitedText` dataset with the following properties:

    a. **Name:** `Input_DS`

    b. **Linked service:** `ADLS_DEV_LS` (the linked service created in *step 9*)

    c. **File path:** `data/input/planes.csv`

    d. **First row as header:** Check

12. In the **Sink** tab of the **Copy data** activity, there should be an Azure Blob Storage `DelimitedText` dataset with the following properties:

    a. **Name:** `Output_DS`

    b. **Linked service:** `ADLS_DEV_LS` (the linked service created in *step 9*)

    c. **File path:** `data/output`

    d. **First row as header:** Check

13. Click **Save all** and **Publish** to publish your developed linked services, datasets, and pipeline to your **ADF**.

Now that we've set up all the necessary resources, you will be able to understand how it works in the following section.

## How it works...

CI/CD processes between two technical environments in Azure usually involve separate resource groups with the same set of resources: ADF, an Azure storage account, and AKV. Using AKV is the best practice for CI/CD as it eliminates the need to store connection strings in your code, allowing you to manage access via parameters and ensuring that connection strings can be automatically updated.

As part of this process, we create secrets within AKV to store connection strings associated with an Azure storage account. These secrets are crucial for configuring linked services between ADF and the storage account.

To enable ADF to access these stored secrets securely, we create a new access policy. This access policy defines the permissions and privileges granted to Data Factory, ensuring it can retrieve and utilize the stored secrets from AKV. This step contributes to the overall security and functionality of the CI/CD processes by ensuring that only authorized entities (in this case, Data Factory) can access and utilize the sensitive connection strings stored in AKV.

# Creating an Azure pipeline for CD

The Pipelines service of Azure DevOps helps you automate your release cycle between different environments - that is, development, testing, and production. In this recipe, you will learn how to create an Azure pipeline and connect it with Azure Data Factories related to different environments.

## Getting ready

Before we start, please ensure that you have an Azure subscription and are familiar with the basics of Azure resources such as the Azure portal, creating and deleting Azure resources, and creating pipelines in ADF. Also, you will need an Azure DevOps project created and linked to your ADF.

## How to do it...

We are going to create a new pipeline in Azure DevOps and set it up to release changes from development to the testing environment:

1. Go to your Azure DevOps account, and click **Pipelines** | **Releases** | **New release pipeline** | **Empty job**. You will see the following screen:

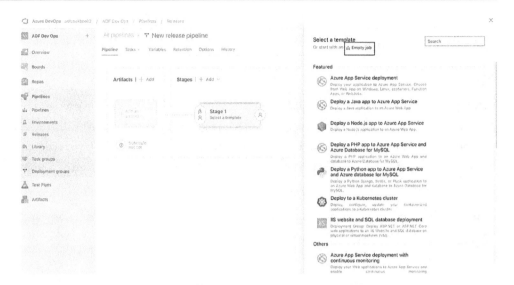

*Figure 9.35: Creating a new release pipeline*

2. You can give a name to your pipeline and set **Stage name** as UAT:

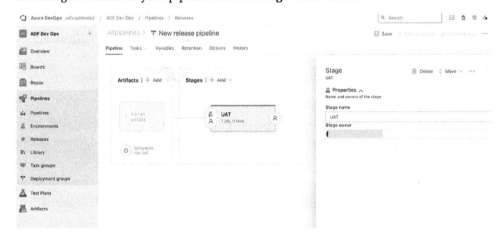

*Figure 9.36: Creating a UAT stage*

3. Click **Add an artifact**. Fill in the fields as follows:

- **Source type: Azure Repos Git**
- **Project:** Your project
- **Source (repository):** Your repository (**ADF Devops**)
- **Default branch:** Your default branch (adf_publish)
- **Default version: Latest from the default branch**

- **Source alias:** _ADF Devops

Click **Add:**

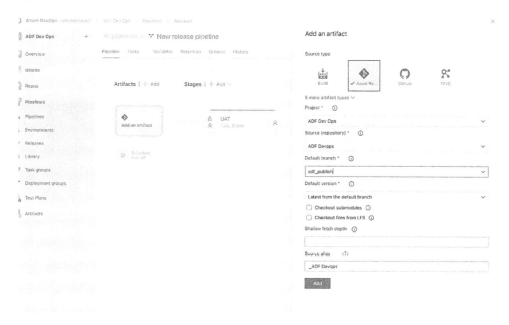

*Figure 9.37: Configuring an artifact*

4.  Click on **1 job, 0 task** (you can find it under the UAT stage of the pipeline in the preceding screenshot). Then, click on the plus sign to the right of **Agent job**, search for ARM Template deployment, and click **Add:**

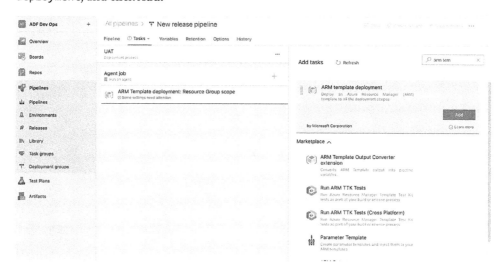

*Figure 9.38: Adding a new task for the job*

5.  Then, you need to change some settings here:

- **Deployment scope: Resource Group.**

- **Azure Resource Manager connection**: Your Azure subscription. Click **Authorize.**

- **Subscription**: Your Azure subscription.

- **Action: Create or update resource group.**

- **Resource group**: ADFCOOKBOOK-UAT-RG.

- **Location:** The location for deploying the resource group.

- **Template location**: Linked artifact:

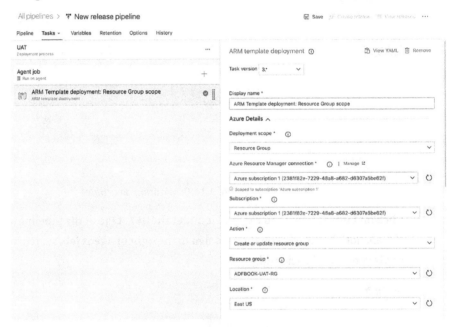

*Figure 9.39: Setting up a task for the job*

- **Template:** Select **Browse template** and the ARMTemplateForFactory.json file from your DevOps project. It should be stored in **Linked artifacts**, as in the following screenshot:

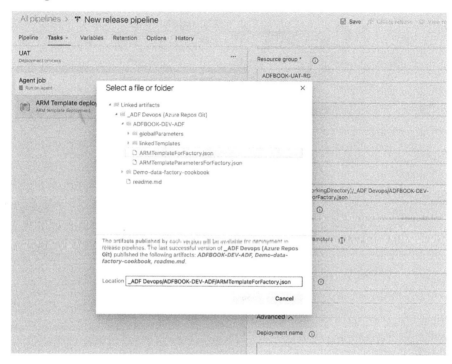

*Figure 9.40: Choosing a file for the template from the DevOps project*

- **Template parameters**: Select **Browse template** and the
  ARMTemplateParametersForFactory.json file from your DevOps project. It should
  be stored in **Linked artifacts,** as in the following screenshot:

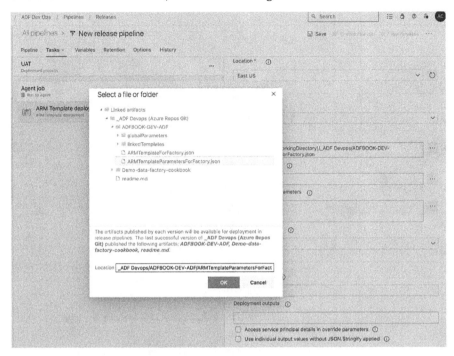

*Figure 9.41: Choosing a file for template parameters from the DevOps project*

- **Override template parameters:** You need to change your DEV parameters to UAT parameters: `ADFCOOKBOOK-UAT-ADF`, `https://ADFCOOKBOOK-UAT-AKV.vault.azure.net/`, and `adfcookbookuatadls-secret`. These parameters should be entered in the **Value** column, as in the following screenshot:

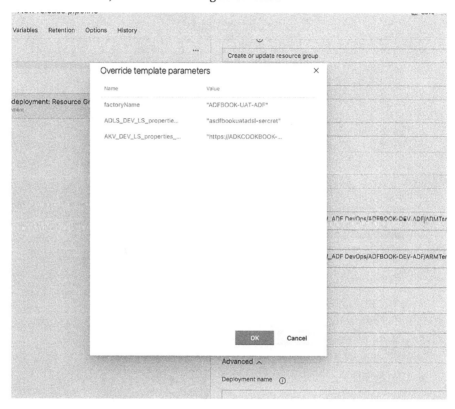

*Figure 9.42: Setting up override template parameters*

6.  Click the **Save** button (at the top of the page below the **Search** box) and **OK**.

7.  To start executing your release pipeline, go to **Releases** and click **Create release** | **Create**:

*Figure 9.43: Creating a release*

8.  You can monitor the status of the release if you click on **Release-1**. Here, you can see how many tasks are deployed already:

*Figure 9.44: Release is completed*

9.  If you go to your UAT Data Factory, you can check that the pipeline and datasets were deployed successfully:

*Figure 9.45: Deployment to the UAT environment is complete*

In the preceding screenshot, you can see that the pipeline is deployed to the UAT environment, as stated in the top-left corner. All the configurations were automatically changed to UAT resources because of the template parameters that were used in the release pipeline.

In the next section, we will see how these steps work in the background.

## How it works...

When the release pipeline executes, it copies JSON files in the publish branch of the development resource group to the production resource group. The publish branch serves as a controlled source of production-ready configurations. Its key role is to ensure that only approved and tested configurations are deployed to the production environment.

To accommodate differences between resource groups, ARM templates often use parameters. These parameters enable the automatic adjustment of configurations when ARM templates are copied from the development resource group to the production resource group, ensuring that configurations match the production environment's naming and settings. The publish branch's use of parameterization and version control helps maintain consistency, reduces errors, and enhances the reliability of your release pipeline.

# There's more...

You can configure more stages in your release pipeline. For example, you can add a production environment. In this case, artifacts from the adf_publish branch will be deployed to the UAT stage, and after that, to the **PROD** stage.

Instead of performing a release manually, you can automate your release pipeline. There are two options for how to do this. The first one is setting up a **Continuous deployment trigger**. If you enable it, a release will be created every time a Git push happens in the selected repository. You can also filter the branch to track **Pushes to**.

Moreover, there is the possibility to enable the **Pull request trigger**, which will perform a release every time an artifact appears in the pull request workflow. Enabling the Pull request trigger enhances the automation process by automatically triggering a release when changes are proposed through a pull request. This can be particularly beneficial in scenarios where changes need to be thoroughly reviewed and tested before deployment, ensuring a controlled and reliable release process. You can find this option in the **Continuous deployment trigger** dialog box in the following screenshot. A dialog box will appear after clicking on the lightning icon on the _ADF DevOps artifact:

*Figure 9.46: Creating a continuous deployment trigger*

The second option for release pipeline automation is enabling **Scheduled release trigger**. This means that the release will be created at the specified time:

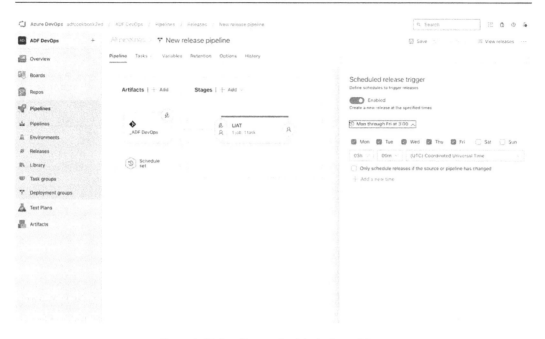

*Figure 9.47: Creating a scheduled release trigger*

The preceding screenshot shows the **Scheduled release trigger** dialog box, which will appear after clicking on **Schedule set** below the _ADF DevOps artifact. You can also set the trigger to work only if the source or pipeline has changed.

# Install and configure Visual Studio to work with ADF deployment

Using Visual Studio for ADF deployment provides a powerful and feature-rich development environment that improves efficiency, collaboration, and code management throughout the ADF development life cycle. In this recipe, you will learn how to install and configure Visual Studio.

## Getting ready

Before we start, please ensure you have an Azure subscription and are familiar with the basics of Azure resources such as the Azure portal, creating and deleting Azure resources, and creating pipelines in ADF. Before moving ahead, make sure you have downloaded and installed Visual Code from the official website: https://code.visualstudio.com/.

# How to do it...

We are going to create a new project in Azure DevOps and Visual Studio:

1.  Let's go to **Azure DevOps** and create a new project. In the **Advanced** settings, choose **Git** and click **Create**:

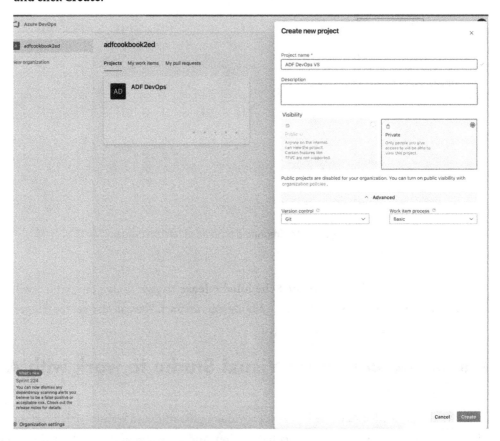

*Figure 9.48: Creating a new project in Azure DevOps*

2. Now, we will go to **Repos | Files**. In the **Initialize main branch with a README or gitignore** section, select **VisualStudio** and click **Initialize**:

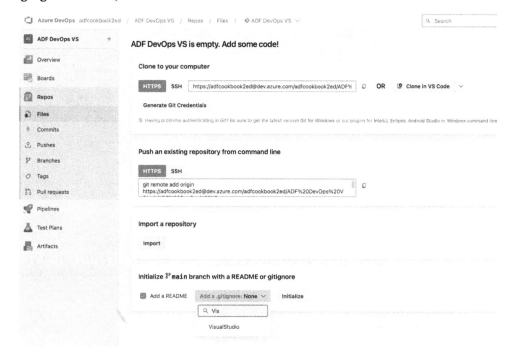

*Figure 9.49: Initializing the main branch in Azure DevOps*

3.  On the next screen in **Repos | Files**, at first, you have to click **Generate Git Credentials** and copy the password, then click Clone, and choose **VS Code** in the IDE drop-down list:

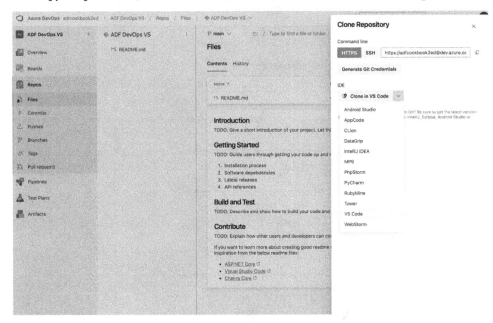

*Figure 9.50: Clone Repository in Azure DevOps*

4.  Visual Studio will open, and you will need to choose the repository destination on your local computer. Next, paste the password generated in *step 3*; the repository will be cloned to the selected location.

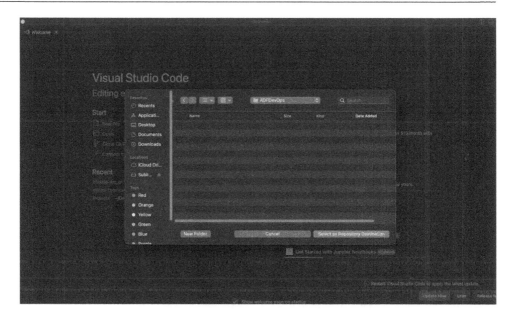

*Figure 9.51: Choosing the repository destination on your local computer*

5.  Now, in VS Code, we can see the cloned repository with the created README file that we initiated from the Azure DevOps UI:

*Figure 9.52: New project in VS Code*

# How it works...

We have cloned the Azure DevOps repository to our local machine and configured it in VS Code to enable us to deploy changes through the IDE, taking advantage of all the benefits it offers. In the next section, we will learn how to deploy ADF pipelines using VS Code.

# Setting up ADF as a Visual Studio project

In this recipe, you will learn how to create an ADF by using Visual Studio and the Azure CLI, define linked services, datasets, and pipelines in the JSON format, and deploy changes to Azure DevOps.

## Getting ready

Before we start, please ensure you have installed Visual Studio and have configured the cloned project from Azure DevOps to your local machine and Visual Studio (the steps described in the previous recipe). Also, download and install the Azure CLI from the official website (`https://docs.microsoft.com/en-us/cli/azure/install-azure-cli`).

## How to do it...

1. Open a terminal in Visual Studio Code by going to **View | Terminal**. Sign in to your Azure account using the Azure CLI by running the following command:

```
az login
```

Follow the instructions to authenticate.

2. In the terminal, use the Azure CLI to create a new ADF instance, such as this example:

```
az datafactory create --location "East US" --name "ADFCookbook-VS"
--resource-group "adfcookbookv2"
```

If you don't have the Data Factory extension installed, you will be prompted to install it.

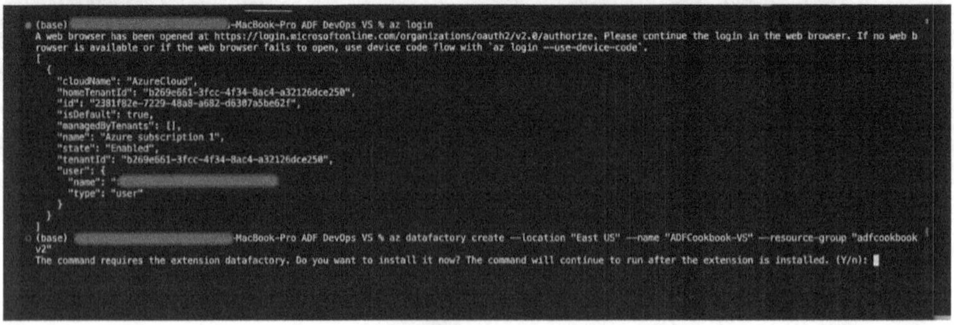

*Figure 9.53: Creating ADF using the CLI*

3.  To configure the Git repository in ADF (which you created in the previous step) on Azure DevOps, you can use the following command:

```
az datafactory configure-factory-repo
--factory-resource-id "/subscriptions/2381f82e-7229-48a8-a682-
d6307a5be62f/resourceGroups/adfcookbookv2/providers/Microsoft.
DataFactory/factories/ADFCookbook-VS"
--factory-vsts-configuration account-name="adfcookbook2ed"
collaboration-branch="main" last-commit-id="" project-name="ADF
DevOps VS" repository-name="ADF DevOps VS" root-folder="/" tenant-
id="b269e661-3fcc-4f34-8ac4-a32126dce250"
--location EastUS
```

Here, the following parameters are used:

- **factory-resource-id**: The resource ID of your ADF. You can find this ID in the Azure portal or by using Azure CLI commands.

- **account-name**: Your Azure DevOps account name.

- **collaboration-branch-name**: The name of the collaboration branch in your Azure DevOps repository.

- **last-commit-id (optional)**: The last commit ID, if needed for specific scenarios.

- **project-name**: The name of your Azure DevOps project where the repository is hosted.

- **repository-name**: The name of your Azure DevOps repository.

- **root-folder**: Set the root folder path for your repository.

- **tenant-id**: The Azure Active Directory tenant ID associated with your Azure DevOps organization. You can find this information in your Azure DevOps account settings.

4.  Now that we have set up ADF and connected the code repository in Azure DevOps, the repository has also been cloned to our local machine from the previous recipe. To stay up to date with the latest changes, we simply need to pull them into the local repository:

```
git pull
```

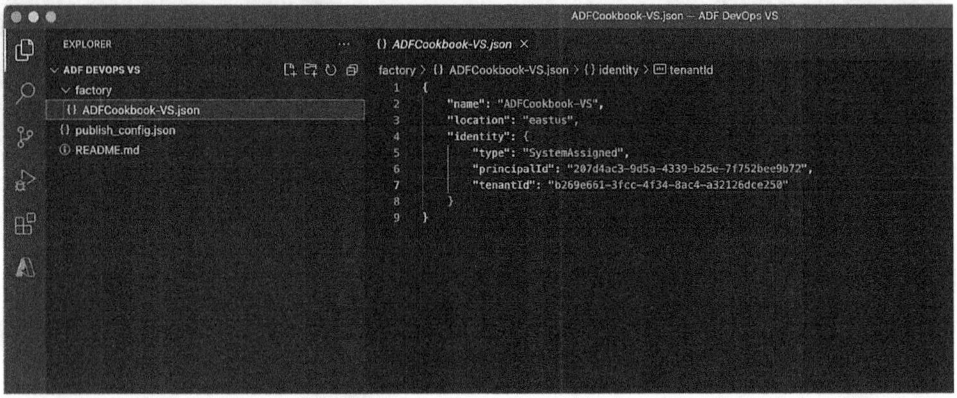

*Figure 9.54: Cloned ADF JSON from the Azure DevOps repository*

5.  Next, create a JSON for the linked service. You can find a code example in the book's GitHub repository at https://github.com/PacktPublishing/Azure-Data-Factory-Cookbook-Second-Edition/tree/main/Chapter09.

*Figure 9.55: Linked service JSON*

6. Create JSONs for input and output datasets:

*Figure 9.56: Input dataset JSON*

7.  And finally, let us create a pipeline JSON to copy data from input_ds to output_ds.

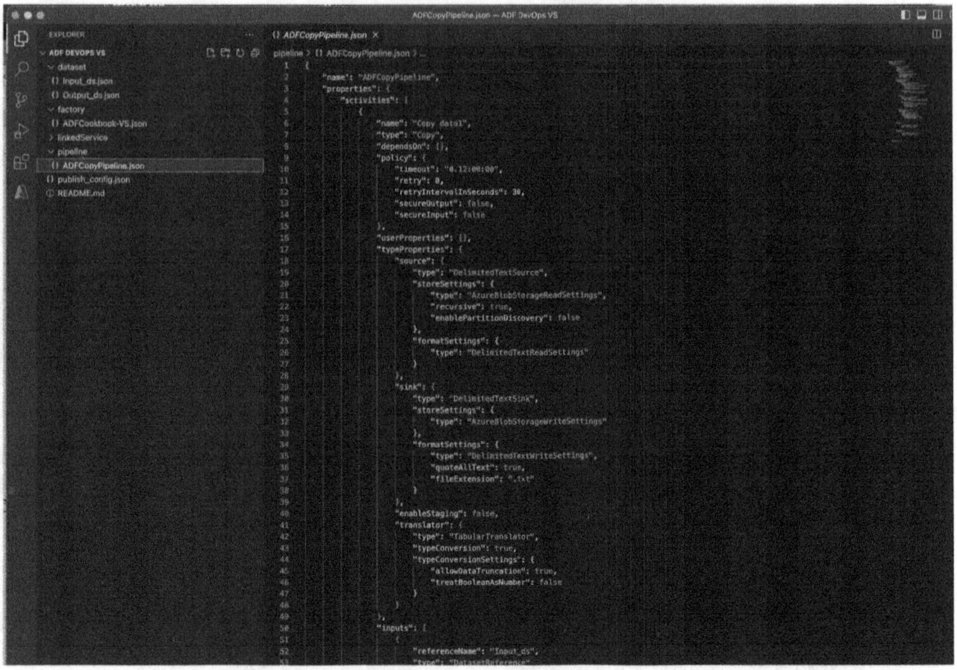

*Figure 9.57: Copy pipeline JSON*

8.  Now that we have all the JSONs ready to be pushed to the repository, the next step is to push changes to the remote repository using the VS Code UI or by running the following Git commands:

```
git add
git commit -m'Description'
git push
```

9.  Now, you can observe that all the data we added in VS Code is accessible in both Azure DevOps and ADF.

Figure 9.58: Files and the pipeline deployed to ADF

10. Finally, the last step is to set up a pipeline in Azure DevOps with a CD trigger. We already have a pipeline, which we created in the *Creating an Azure pipeline for CD* recipe:

Figure 9.59: Setting up a pipeline in Azure DevOps

## How it works...

ADF is integrated with a Git repository in Azure DevOps. When changes are made in **VS Code** and pushed back to the repository, the CD trigger in Azure DevOps automatically starts the CI/CD pipeline. The pipeline then builds and deploys the changes to the ADF instance, ensuring that the production environment is updated with the latest changes from the repository.

# Running Airflow DAGs with ADF

ADF's Managed Airflow service provides a streamlined and effective solution for creating and managing Apache Airflow environments, simplifying the execution of data pipelines at scale. Apache Airflow, an open-source platform, empowers users to programmatically design, schedule, and monitor intricate data workflows. By defining tasks as operators and arranging them into **directed acyclic graphs (DAGs)**, Airflow facilitates the representation of data pipelines. It enables scheduled or event-triggered execution of DAGs, real-time workflow monitoring, and task status visibility, making it a popular choice in data engineering and science for orchestrating data pipelines due to its adaptability, extensibility, and user-friendliness. In this recipe, we will run an existing pipeline with Managed Airflow.

## Getting ready

Before we start, please ensure that you have an Azure subscription, Azure storage account, and ADF pipeline set up.

## How to do it...

1. Set up Managed Apache Airflow. Go to the **Manage** tab in ADF. In the left tab, click on **Apache Airflow** and then click **Create Airflow environment**.

Please note that this feature is currently in public preview and is available in specific locations, including East US, South Central US, West US, UK South, North Europe, West Europe, Southeast Asia, and with upcoming availability in East US2, West US2, Germany West Central, and Australia East.

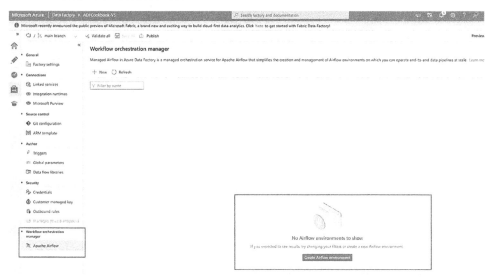

*Figure 9.60: Setting up Managed Airflow*

In the **Airflow environment setup** tab, please ensure that you follow the image below and continue from the previous screen by adding **apache-airflow-providers-microsoft-azure** to the **Airflow requirements** section.

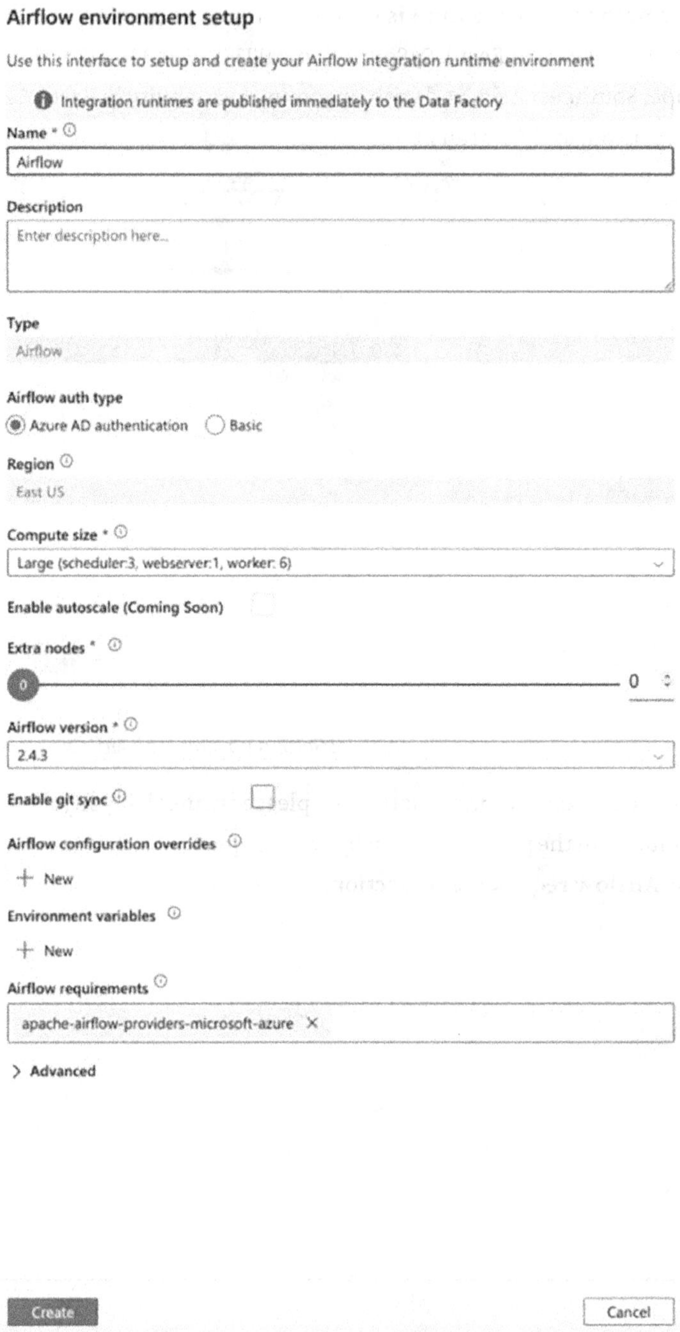

## Airflow environment setup

Use this interface to setup and create your Airflow integration runtime environment

ⓘ Integration runtimes are published immediately to the Data Factory

Name * ⓘ

| Airflow |

Description

| Enter description here... |

Type

| Airflow |

Airflow auth type

◉ Azure AD authentication    ○ Basic

Region ⓘ

| East US |

Compute size * ⓘ

| Large (scheduler:3, webserver:1, worker: 6)                          ⌄ |

Enable autoscale (Coming Soon)

Extra nodes * ⓘ

| ●0 ————————————————————————————————— |                    0  ⇕

Airflow version * ⓘ

| 2.4.3                                                              ⌄ |

Enable git sync ⓘ

Airflow configuration overrides ⓘ

+ New

Environment variables ⓘ

+ New

Airflow requirements ⓘ

| apache-airflow-providers-microsoft-azure  ✕ |

> Advanced

| Create |                                              | Cancel |

*Figure 9.61: Airflow environment setup*

2.  You'll need to create a new service principal or use an existing one and grant it permission to run the pipeline:

    a.  Navigate to Azure Active Directory from the left-hand navigation menu.

    b.  Under **App registrations**, create a new application registration to create a service principal.

    c.  Note down the **Application (client) ID**, as it will be the Client ID of the service principal.

    d.  In the same application registration, go to **Certificates & secrets** and create a new client secret (API key).

    e.  Note down the generated secret value as it will be the client secret (API key) of the Service Principal.

    f.  Once the Service Principal is created, you need to grant it the necessary permissions in ADF. Navigate to the Azure Data Factory where the existing pipelines exist. Go to **Access control (IAM)** from the left hand navigation menu.

    g.  Click on **+ Add** to add a new role assignment. Select the **Contributor** role (or any other required role) from the list of available roles. In the **Select** field, search for and select the name of the Service Principal created in the previous steps.

    h.  Click on **Save** to assign the role to the Service Principal.

    i.  Go to the Airflow UI by clicking **Monitor in Airflow instance. Admin | Connections list | Add new connection**. Fill out all fields. Note the connection ID, as it will be used in the Python DAG file later on.

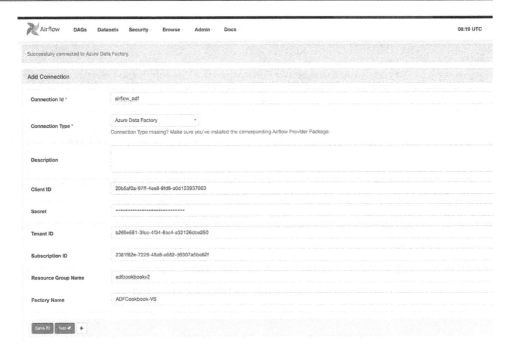

*Figure 9.62: Airflow connection to ADF*

3. We have to define the Airflow DAG, which includes a task to trigger the ADF pipeline. We will create a Python script and use the **AzureDataFactoryRunPipelineOperator** to call the Azure Data Factory REST API and trigger the existing **ADFCopypipeline** (https://github.com/PacktPublishing/Azure-Data-Factory-Cookbook-Second-Edition/blob/main/Chapter09/DAG_adfcopypipeline.py):

```
 ◄ ►    DAG_adfcopypipeline.py  ×
 1   from datetime import datetime, timedelta
 2
 3   from airflow.models import DAG, BaseOperator
 4
 5   try:
 6       from airflow.operators.empty import EmptyOperator
 7   except ModuleNotFoundError:
 8       from airflow.operators.dummy import DummyOperator as EmptyOperator  # type: ignore
 9   from airflow.providers.microsoft.azure.operators.data_factory import AzureDataFactoryRunPipelineOperator
10   from airflow.providers.microsoft.azure.sensors.data_factory import AzureDataFactoryPipelineRunStatusSensor
11   from airflow.utils.edgemodifier import Label
12
13   with DAG(
14       dag_id="example_adf_run_pipeline",
15       start_date=datetime(2022, 5, 14),
16       schedule_interval="@daily",
17       catchup=False,
18       default_args={
19           "retries": 1,
20           "retry_delay": timedelta(minutes=3),
21           "azure_data_factory_conn_id": "airflow_adf",  #This is a connection created on Airflow UI
22           "factory_name": "ADFCookbook-V5",  # This can also be specified in the ADF connection.
23           "resource_group_name": "adfcookbookv2",  # This can also be specified in the ADF connection.
24       },
25       default_view="graph",
26   ) as dag:
27       begin = EmptyOperator(task_id="begin")
28       end = EmptyOperator(task_id="end")
29
30       # [START howto_operator_adf_run_pipeline]
31       run_pipeline1: BaseOperator = AzureDataFactoryRunPipelineOperator(
32           task_id="run_pipeline1",
33           pipeline_name="ADFCopyPipeline",
34           parameters={"myParam": "value"},
35       )
36       # [END howto_operator_adf_run_pipeline]
```

*Figure 9.63: Airflow DAG file*

4. The next task is to store this file in Blob storage. Create a container named `airflow` and create a `dags` folder inside it. Then, simply upload the file into the `dags` folder.

5.   Import the uploaded file to Apache Airflow, as shown in the following screenshot:

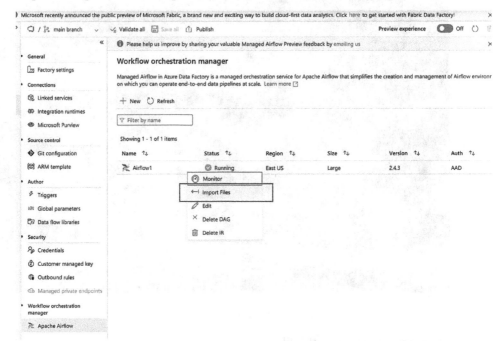

*Figure 9.64: Importing files to Airflow*

6.   Now, when you click on **Monitor** in **Airflow1**, you will open the classic Airflow interface in a web browser. Here, you can view the newly created DAG, access the graph diagram, check logs, and perform various tasks. To trigger the ADF pipeline from your Airflow instance, schedule it, and monitor its execution, follow these additional steps:

   1.   To trigger the ADF pipeline, navigate to the DAG you created and click on the **Trigger DAG** option.

   2.   To schedule the ADF pipeline for regular execution, click on the **Schedule** button and configure the desired schedule interval.

   3.   Monitor the execution of the ADF pipeline by checking the task status, logs, and any related metrics in the Airflow interface.

   4.   You can also set up email alerts or notifications for specific events or failures in your ADF pipeline by configuring the appropriate Airflow features.

*Figure 9.65: Airflow UI*

# How it works...

In Managed Apache Airflow for ADF, DAGs serve as the core mechanism for defining and orchestrating data workflows. DAGs represent a sequence of tasks that need to be executed, with each task encapsulating a specific operation or action in the workflow. While ADF itself provides orchestration capabilities, there are scenarios where opting for orchestrating from Airflow makes sense. Here's why Managed Airflow in conjunction with ADF can be beneficial:

- **Complex workflows**: Managed Airflow is particularly useful when you have complex data workflows that involve multiple dependencies, branching, and conditional execution. It offers a more extensive set of tools for defining and managing these intricate workflows.

- **Task flexibility**: Airflow allows you to define tasks with a wide range of operators, which can include not only ADF pipeline triggers but also custom Python scripts, container orchestrations, and more. This flexibility is valuable when your workflow requires diverse task types beyond what ADF natively provides.

- **Monitoring and error handling**: Airflow provides robust monitoring and error-handling capabilities. You can set up alerts, notifications, and retries for tasks, making it easier to ensure the reliability and resilience of your data pipelines.

- **Scheduling and coordination**: Airflow's scheduling capabilities are well-established, allowing you to define precise execution times and intervals for your workflows. It also provides features like dynamic scheduling and prioritization of tasks.

- **Third-party integrations**: Airflow has extensive third-party integrations, making it easier to connect with various data sources, services, and tools. This can be advantageous when your data ecosystem includes components beyond Azure services.

By integrating Managed Airflow with ADF, you can combine the strengths of both orchestration engines. ADF excels in Azure-specific data integration and transformation, while Managed Airflow enhances orchestration with features tailored for complex workflows, scheduling, and monitoring. This integration empowers users to efficiently manage and automate even the most intricate data pipelines in Azure while leveraging Airflow's extensive capabilities.

## Join our community on Discord

Join our community's Discord space for discussions with the authors and other readers:

`https://discord.gg/U229qmBmT3`

# 10

# Monitoring and Troubleshooting Data Pipelines

**Azure Data Factory** is an orchestration and integration tool that helps engineers transfer data between multiple data stores, both within and outside of the Microsoft Azure ecosystem. However, data integration is rarely straightforward, and errors can and do occur. In this chapter, we will introduce tools to help you manage and monitor your Azure Data Factory pipelines. You will learn where and how to find more information about what went wrong when a pipeline failed, how to debug a failed run, how to set up alerts that notify you when there is a problem, and how to identify problems with your integration runtimes.

The following is a list of the recipes in this chapter:

- Monitoring pipeline runs and integration runtimes
- Investigating failures – running pipelines in debug mode
- Rerunning activities
- Configuring alerts for your Azure Data Factory runs

## Technical requirements

We will be examining Azure Data Factory tools and working with existing pipelines. Specific instructions on how to create or import the pipelines to work with are provided in the *Getting ready* section of each recipe.

You will need access to an Azure Data Factory instance and a GitHub account to access the files and templates we provide for the recipes. If you do not have a GitHub account, you can sign up for a free one at `https://github.com/`.

# Monitoring pipeline runs and integration runtimes

Data integration can be tricky, and it is helpful to be able to visualize progress or evaluate inputs/ outputs of the pipelines in your Data Factory. This recipe will introduce you to the tools that help you gain an insight into the health and progress of your pipelines.

## Getting ready

In this recipe, we will give you an overview of the features of the **Monitor** tab in the Azure Data Factory **Author** interface. If you have access to a data factory with a few pipelines already configured, you will be able to follow along. Otherwise, create a new data factory instance and design and run two or three pipelines. If you followed the first two or three recipes from *Chapter 2, Orchestration and Control Flow*, you will have sufficient material to understand the capabilities of the **Monitor** interface.

## How to do it...

Without further ado, let's explore the **Monitor** tab interfaces and customize them for our needs:

1. In the ADF Studio, navigate to the **Monitor** tab. You will see that this tab has several sections: **Runs**, **Runtimes & sessions**, and **Notifications**. Let's start with the pipeline runs. In this interface, you can see the history and progress of your pipeline runs. *Figure 10.1* shows a typical **Pipeline runs** interface with several successfully completed pipelines and one pipeline that is still running:

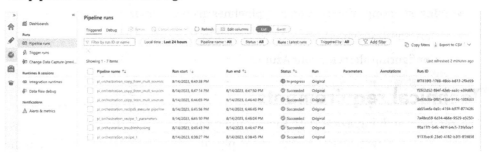

*Figure 10.1: The Monitor tab – Pipeline runs*

Note that you have to manually refresh the view by clicking the **Refresh** button when you want to see updates. As of the current version, auto-refresh is not supported. We are actively working on implementing auto-refresh functionality and plan to enable it in a future update. Stay tuned for further announcements regarding when auto-refresh will be available:

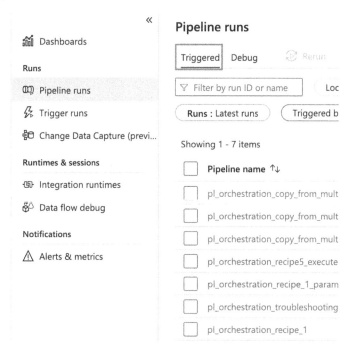

*Figure 10.2: Triggered versus debug mode pipelines*

You can start a pipeline run either in debug mode or by a trigger (scheduled or manual). In the **Monitor** tab, triggered and debug pipelines are placed under their respective tabs.

2. We will customize this view to place **Status** and **Duration** immediately after the pipeline name and remove the **Run ID** column from the view.

NOTE

**Run ID** is a unique identifier of a particular run and can prove very useful in analyzing it. In this recipe, we do not have a practical use for the information provided by the run ID, so we remove that column from the interface.

First, let's edit the columns that we want to display. Click on the **Edit columns** button to bring up the **Edit columns** blade. In the **Edit columns** blade, drag the **Status** field to be immediately after the **Pipeline name** field. Similarly, rearrange the **Status** field to follow **Duration**. Finally, delete the **Run ID** field. Click the **OK** button to save your changes. After this, your interface will look similar to the following:

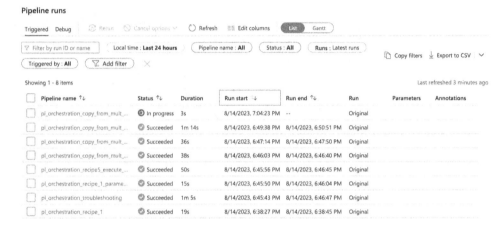

*Figure 10.3: Pipeline runs table with edited columns*

3.  If you hover over any of the pipelines, you will see additional buttons:

| Pipeline name ↑↓ | Status ↑↓ | Duration | Run start ↓ |
|---|---|---|---|
| pl_orchestration_copy_from_mult_sources | In progress 3s | 3s | 8/14/2023, 7:04:23 PM |
| pl_orchestration_copy_from_mult... | Succeeded | 1m 14s | 8/14/2023, 6:49:38 PM |
| pl_orchestration_copy_from_mult_sources | Succeeded | 36s | 8/14/2023, 6:47:14 PM |
| pl_orchestration_copy_from_mult_sources | Succeeded | 38s | 8/14/2023, 6:46:03 PM |
| pl_orchestration_recipe5_execute_pipeline | Succeeded | 50s | 8/14/2023, 6:45:56 PM |

*Figure 10.4: Additional buttons in the pipelines*

The first one, which looks like a play button encircled in arrows, is the rerun button (we will explore the rerun functionality in a later chapter). The second one, which looks like a miniature table, is for the consumption report. Click on it to examine the units consumed during the run:

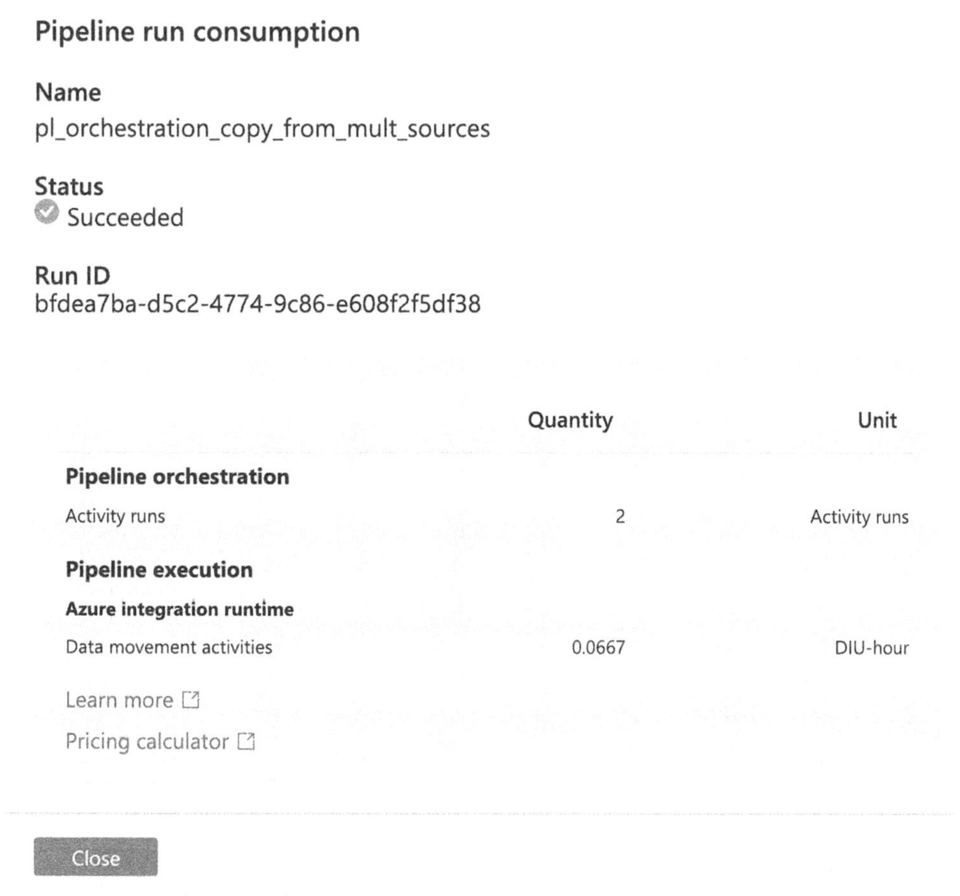

## Pipeline run consumption

### Name
pl_orchestration_copy_from_mult_sources

### Status
✅ Succeeded

### Run ID
bfdea7ba-d5c2-4774-9c86-e608f2f5df38

|  | Quantity | Unit |
|---|---|---|
| **Pipeline orchestration** | | |
| Activity runs | 2 | Activity runs |
| **Pipeline execution** | | |
| **Azure integration runtime** | | |
| Data movement activities | 0.0667 | DIU-hour |

Learn more ☑
Pricing calculator ☑

Close

*Figure 10.5: Consumption report*

4.   We can customize the interface to make it more convenient for us. Data Factory allows us to create custom annotations for our pipelines. In this recipe, we shall annotate the pipelines we created in *Chapter 2, Orchestration and Control Flow*, with annotation orchestration.

To annotate a pipeline, go to the **Author** tab and select the pipeline you want to update. Click on the **Properties** symbol, which is located at the top right of the window (it is pointed out by the red arrow in the following screenshot). This will bring up the **Properties** blade. In the **Properties** blade, click on the **New** button under **Annotations**, and type Orchestration in the text field:

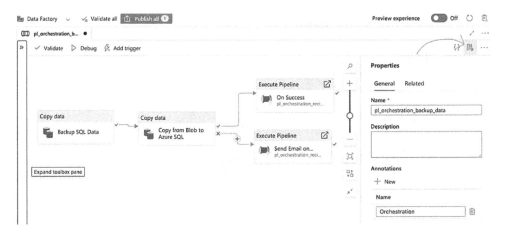

*Figure 10.6: Adding an annotation*

Publish your changes. Next, run the pipeline that you annotated. You will not see the annotations in the **Monitor** tab until the pipeline has been run again.

5.  Go to the **Monitor** tab and look at your pipeline runs again. You should see that the pipelines that you annotated show a little tag icon.

6.  We can now filter our pipelines based on custom annotations. To do this, click on the **Add filter** button and choose **Annotations**. Select **Orchestration** from the list:

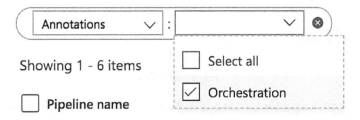

*Figure 10.7: Filtering based on user-defined annotations*

After applying this filter, you will only see the pipelines that have the **Orchestration** tag.

7.  Finally, let's have a look at our integration runtimes. Under **Runtimes & sessions**, select **Integration runtimes**. By default, the interface shows you all of your available integration runtimes, providing an overview of each runtime's key details such as its name, status, and type. You can switch to the **Self-Hosted**, **Azure**, or **Azure-SSIS** tab to filter and view only the integration runtimes of a particular type, allowing you to focus on specific subsets of your runtimes:

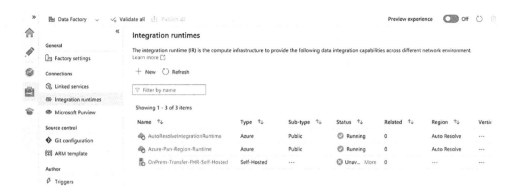

*Figure 10.8: Integration runtimes interface*

If you have a self-hosted integration runtime, you can click on its name in the interface to see the details about the computer nodes on which the integration runtime is installed, the software version, memory consumption, and networking state.

## How it works...

The **Monitor** tab gives us tools to understand the functioning of our data factory, including to examine the progress of our pipeline runs, look into the status and health of the integration runtimes, and investigate which resources the data factory is consuming and how they are being used.

The interface is very useful and flexible without any modification, but customizing it gives you even more power. For instance, in *steps 2 through 5*, we changed the order of the columns and filtered displayed runs based on status. This simple customization allowed us to focus specifically on the attributes of the pipelines that were of most interest to us, making the monitoring process more efficient and tailored to our needs. Additionally, custom annotations, which we created in *step 6*, provide us with even more advanced filtering options. You can use custom annotations to apply your own business logic for filtering your list and further enhancing your interface, ensuring that you get precisely the insights you require.

The consumption reports (such as the example we gave in *Figure 10.5*) are especially convenient when you need to control costs. In the context of this chapter's screenshots, the pipelines we used were relatively small in scale, handling only a moderate volume of data, and therefore, they should not incur significant costs. However, in a real production environment, where tera- and petabytes of data are frequently moved, cost considerations become paramount. For instance, when dealing with such massive data volumes, every resource and activity becomes a potential cost factor. The consumption report will help you identify the most expensive resources and activities, providing insights into where your expenditures lie and allowing you to strategically apply your optimization efforts for maximum impact.

If you work with pipelines that access on-premises servers/SSIS, it is necessary to configure self-hosted integration runtimes. When such a pipeline has issues, it is not unusual to discover that a corrupted or unavailable node in the self-hosted integration runtime is the culprit:

*Figure 10.9: Self-hosted integration runtime overview*

The integration runtime overview interface, which we encountered in *step 7*, is very helpful in investigating these problems. For example, the preceding screenshot shows an integration runtime where both nodes are unavailable and will therefore cause problems if a pipeline is using those integration runtimes to access on-premises data stores.

# Investigating failures — running pipelines in debug mode

When your Azure Data Factory pipeline does not work as expected, it is useful to have tools to examine what went wrong. The debug mode allows us to run a pipeline receiving immediate feedback about its execution.

In this section, we'll explore how to investigate a pipeline failure using debug mode capabilities. We will cover how to identify errors, understand error messages, and troubleshoot activities to resolve a failed pipeline.

## Getting ready

In order to prepare your environment for this recipe, follow these steps:

1. Set up an Azure SQL server and create `Airline`, `Country`, and `PipelineLog` tables and an `InsertLogRecord` stored procedure. Use the `CreateAirlineTable.sql`, `CreateCountryTable.sql`, and `CreateActivityLogsTable.sql` scripts to create these objects. These were also required for *Chapter 2, Orchestration and Control Flow*. If you followed the recipes in that chapter, you should have the database and table stored procedures already set up.

2. Create a new data factory from a template. You can download the template from https:// github.com/PacktPublishing/Azure-Data-Factory-Cookbook-Second-Edition/ blob/main/Chapter10/adf-template.json, then navigate to https://portal.azure. com/#create/Microsoft.Template and select **Build your own template** in the editor option. Copy the contents of the template file into the space provided and click **Save**. You should see a form similar to the one in *Figure 10.10*:

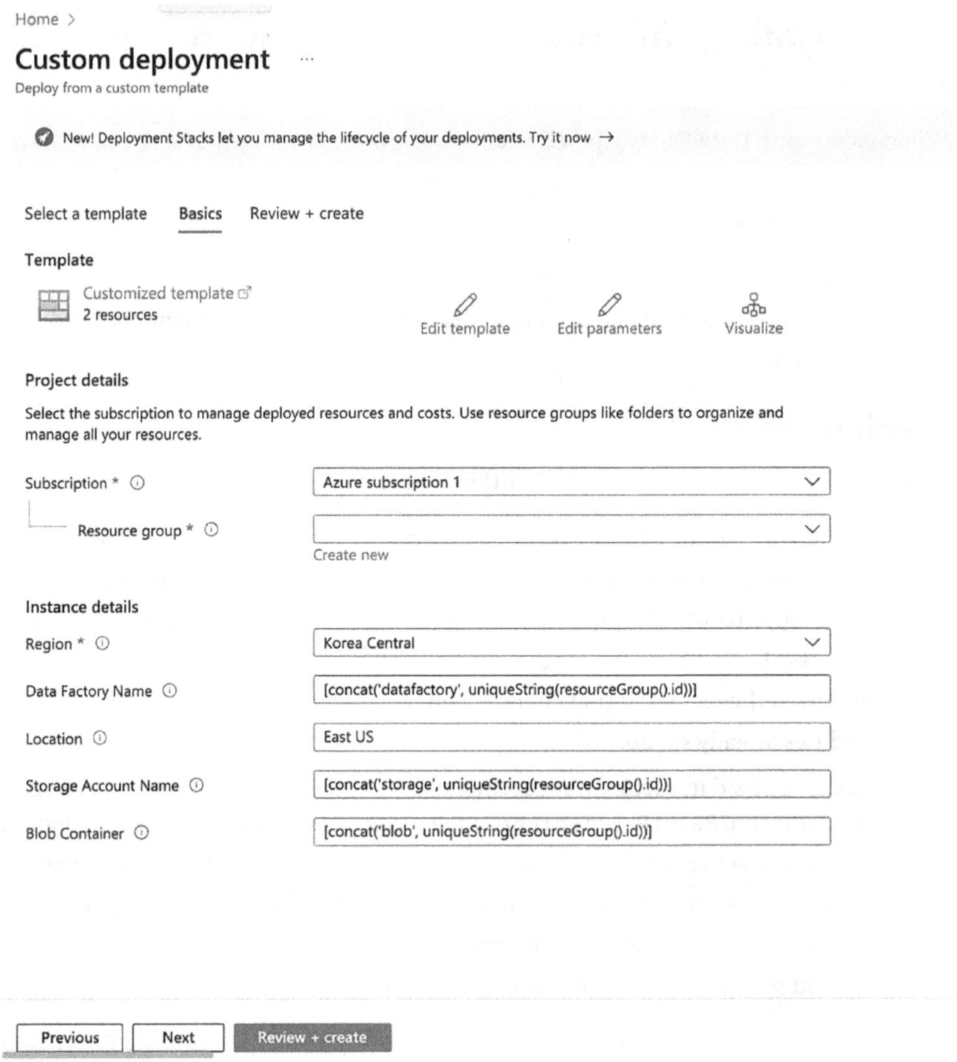

Home >

## Custom deployment  ···

Deploy from a custom template

🛡 New! Deployment Stacks let you manage the lifecycle of your deployments. Try it now →

Select a template     **Basics**     Review + create

**Template**

⊞  Customized template ⌐'
    2 resources

        ✎                    ✎                   ⬡
    Edit template      Edit parameters      Visualize

**Project details**

Select the subscription to manage deployed resources and costs. Use resource groups like folders to organize and manage all your resources.

| | |
|---|---|
| Subscription * ⓘ | Azure subscription 1 ⌄ |
| └─ Resource group * ⓘ | ⌄ |
| | Create new |

**Instance details**

| | |
|---|---|
| Region * ⓘ | Korea Central ⌄ |
| Data Factory Name ⓘ | [concat('datafactory', uniqueString(resourceGroup().id))] |
| Location ⓘ | East US |
| Storage Account Name ⓘ | [concat('storage', uniqueString(resourceGroup().id))] |
| Blob Container ⓘ | [concat('blob', uniqueString(resourceGroup().id))] |

[ Previous ]  [ Next ]  [ Review + create ]

*Figure 10.10: Deploying a data factory from a template*

Choose a resource group where you want your data factory to be created, and click on **Review + create**. On the next screen, wait until validation is done, and hit **Create**. Wait until your factory is created.

3.  Create an *AzureSQLDatabase linked service* in this new data factory. The steps to do so are described in detail in *Chapter 2, Orchestration and Control Flow*, in the *The power of dynamic pipelines* recipe.

4.  Create a pipeline from the template. First, download the pl_troubleshooting_pipeline.
    zip file from https://github.com/PacktPublishing/Azure-Data-Factory-Cookbook-
    Second-Edition/blob/main/Chapter10/pl_troubleshooting_pipeline.zip.

    Next, go to the data factory you created in *step 2* and launch the Azure Data Factory Studio.
    In the **Author** tab, click on the **plus sign** next to the filter text box to add a new resource:

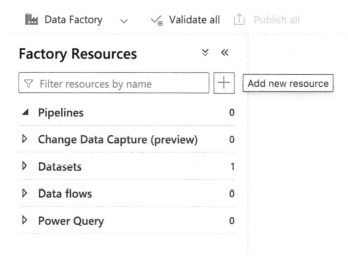

*Figure 10.11: Add new resource*

From the menu, choose **Pipeline**, then **Import from pipeline template**. Select the pl_
troubleshooting_pipeline.zip file that you downloaded earlier.

5.  After you have selected the template, you will see the **Preview** interface, similar to the
    following:

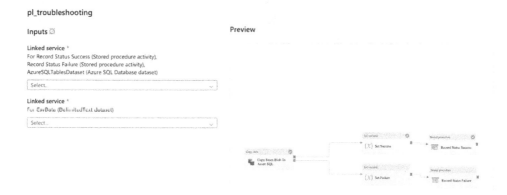

*Figure 10.12: Creating a pipeline from a template*

This pipeline first backs up the files in a storage account, then copies the contents of the files into a table in Azure SQL Database. If the copy activity succeeds, we set the **Status** pipeline variable to **Success**; otherwise, the value is set to **Failure**. Finally, the last activity records the status and some other metadata about this run into the `PipelineLog` Azure SQL table.

6. Fill in the user inputs from the dropdowns by selecting the drop-down options as shown in *Figure 10.13*. Click on **Use this template** to create the pipeline.

7. Publish to save your changes.

NOTE

Even though we execute the pipeline in debug mode, the data is still being moved! Be sure not to run any pipelines in debug mode in your production environment. Rather, create test-linked services and datasets, and only debug on a small set of data to save on costs. Once your pipeline is fine-tuned, you can use connectors that point to the real data sources and sinks.

## How to do it...

In this recipe, we will run a failing pipeline, look for the root cause of the failure, fix the error, and rerun the pipeline to ensure that our fix worked:

1. Start by running the pipeline in debug mode. Open the factory that you created in the *Getting ready* section and open the **ADF Studio**. In the **Author** tab, open the **pl_trouble-shooting_pipeline** pipeline.

2. Click on the **Debug** button at the top of the authoring canvas to run your `pl_troubleshooting_pipeline` in debug mode. This pipeline is designed to demonstrate troubleshooting techniques and may exhibit different behaviors than the rerun pipeline you encountered earlier, as it serves a different purpose:

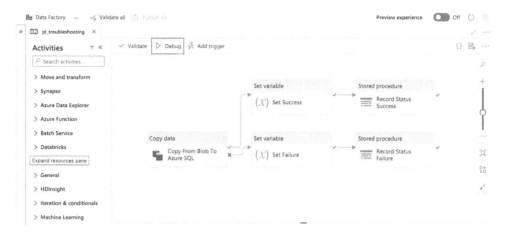

*Figure 10.13: Debug button*

This will start your pipeline run. Note that after you have started the pipeline, the **Debug** button is replaced with a **Cancel options** button. You can use this if you need to stop/cancel your pipeline run:

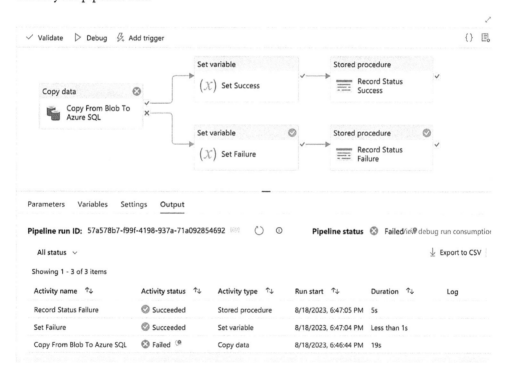

*Figure 10.14: Pipeline running in debug mode*

3.  Uh-oh! The pipeline failed! Click anywhere on the canvas to bring up information about the activities in the **Output** pane at the bottom. In the **Output** pane, hover with your cursor over the row representing the **Copy from Blob to Azure SQL** activity. You will see additional icons appearing between the **Activity name** and **Activity type** columns:

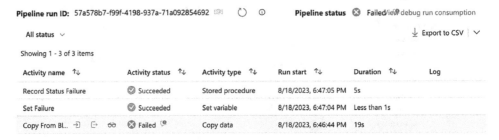

*Figure 10.15: Examining input, output, and error messages*

The additional icons are buttons that will help us to gather even more information about what went wrong:

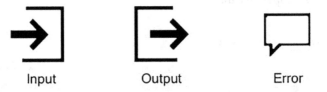

*Figure 10.16: Activity input, activity output, and error message (detail)*

Click on the error message button and enlarge the window. You should see an error message similar to the following:

*Figure 10.17: Error message*

**NOTE**

At the top of the error message, in the **Error Code** field, there is a link to the Microsoft documentation. This really comes in handy when you are investigating activity failures!

4.  Read the error message. The message says **The required Blob is missing**, and gives further details about the missing file: the container is the storage account that we created in the *Getting ready* section, and the file is `airlines.csv`.

    Examine the **Copy from Blob to Azure SQL** activity. Click on it and then go to the **Source** tab at the bottom. You will see that the activity uses the `CsvData` dataset. `CsvData` requires a filename as a parameter, and the current configuration specifies `airlines.csv` as the filename. The `CsvData` dataset represents the Azure Blob storage account we created in the *Getting ready* section. We did not create any containers in that Blob storage account, nor did we upload any files!

5.  To fix this error, open another tab in your browser to the Azure portal (`https://portal.azure.com`), go to the storage account you created in the *Getting ready* section, and create a container called data. Next, download the file called `airlines.csv` from `https://github.com/PacktPublishing/Azure-Data-Factory-Cookbook-Second-Edition/blob/main/Chapter10/data/airlines.csv` and upload it to the data container.

6.  Rerun your pipeline in debug mode. It should succeed this time: we have found and fixed the error.

## How it works...

If your pipeline does not behave as expected – or fails – you need to spend some time understanding what went wrong. The **Debug** functionality helps you do that. As we illustrated in this recipe, you can perform test runs before finalizing your design, and use the **Output** pane to view the execution results as your pipeline progresses from activity to activity.

In the **Output** pane, each row represents an activity and shows you the activity name, status, when it started, how long it has been running for, which integration runtime it is using, and the run ID.

In *step 3*, when we examined the **Output** pane, we saw that the first activity, **Backup SQL Data**, succeeded, but the second activity in our pipeline, **Copy from Blob to Azure SQL**, failed. Following that, subsequent activities succeeded, which means that the state of the run was captured by the stored procedure.

This gave us a clue that the problem occurred in the **Copy from Blob to Azure SQL** activity. With the help of the **Output** pane, we identified the root cause by examining the error message. Finally, we were able to correct the error by providing the required data to the data source and uploading the airlines.csv file, and verified that we indeed fixed the error by running in debug mode again and seeing that the run succeeded.

## There's more...

After going through the preceding steps, your pipeline is configured correctly and can copy data from source to destination. Open the pipeline and click anywhere on the canvas to display the pipeline run information in the **Output** pane. Hover over the **Copy From Blob to Azure SQL** activity (similar to what we did in *step 3* of the *Monitoring pipeline runs and integration runtimes* recipe. Click on the spectacles icon to view the report:

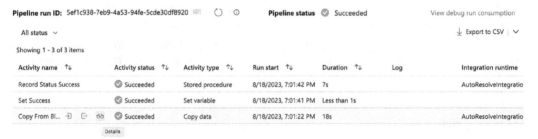

*Figure 10.18: Copy activity details*

You will see the **Copy Activity Details** report, which contains lots of useful information about the copy activity data transfer. The following screenshot shows the report:

*Figure 10.19: Copy activity performance report*

Use this report when you are designing and refining data transfers containing the copy activity. You can view it while the data movement is in progress, too, and you will gain insight into the process: the number of rows read versus the number of rows written to the sink connector, the number of open connections, the degree of parallelism, and so on. This report is very helpful when you need to identify data transfer bottlenecks between connectors.

## See also

Microsoft maintains an extensive collection of troubleshooting guides, which will be of great help to you if and when you encounter errors. Here are links to some of the guides that can serve as starting points:

- Troubleshooting activities: `https://docs.microsoft.com/azure/data-factory/data-factory-troubleshoot-guide`

- Troubleshooting connectors: `https://docs.microsoft.com/azure/data-factory/connector-troubleshoot-guide`

- Troubleshooting integration runtimes:

  - Troubleshooting self-hosted integration runtimes: `https://docs.microsoft.com/azure/data-factory/self-hosted-integration-runtime-troubleshoot-guide`

  - Troubleshooting SSIS integration runtime management in Azure Data Factory: `https://docs.microsoft.com/azure/data-factory/ssis-integration-runtime-management-troubleshoot`

  - Using the diagnose connectivity feature in the SSIS integration runtime: `https://docs.microsoft.com/azure/data-factory/ssis-integration-runtime-diagnose-connectivity-faq`

## Rerunning activities

When our data transfers fail for one reason or another, we frequently need to rerun affected pipelines. This ensures that appropriate data movement is performed, albeit delayed. If our design is complex, or if the pipeline is moving large volumes of data, it is useful to be able to repeat the run from the point of failure, to minimize the time lost in the failed pipeline.

In this section, we will look at two features of Azure Data Factory that help us to troubleshoot our pipelines and rerun them with maximum efficiency. The first feature is breakpoints, which allow us to execute a pipeline up to an activity of our choice. The second feature is rerunning from the point of failure, which helps to minimize the time lost due to a failed execution.

## Getting ready

Preparing your environment for this recipe is identical to the preparation required for the previous recipe in this chapter, *Investigating failures – running pipelines in debug mode*. We will be using the same **Azure Data Factory** template, but a different **pipeline** template.

The template for this recipe is `pl_rerunning_pipeline.zip`. It can be found at `https://github.com/PacktPublishing/Azure-Data-Factory-Cookbook-Second-Edition/blob/main/Chapter10/pl_rerunning_pipeline.zip`. Detailed instructions on how to import a pipeline from an existing template are provided in the previous recipe.

> Note that if you have completed the previous recipe already, you will not need to create Azure Data Factory from the template again; however, it is necessary to reverse the 'fix' that we applied after debugging a failing pipeline in order to set the environment back to its original state. To provide more context, the 'fix' was applied to address a specific issue for debugging purposes. Now, as we move on to this recipe, it's important to reset the environment to its initial configuration to ensure that the subsequent steps align with the expected state of the system. To reverse the 'fix,' go to the storage account that was established as you created the data factory in the previous recipe, and remove the data container and its contents. (If you skipped the previous recipe, then this step is not required.)

## How to do it...

In the following steps, we shall again deal with a failed pipeline and learn how to set a breakpoint to pipeline execution, and then rerun the pipeline from any point of our choosing:

1. Go to the data factory you set up in the *Getting ready* section and launch the ADF Studio. In the **Author** tab, run the pipeline that you imported in debug mode. Wait until it completes (it will fail).

2.  We see that it is the **Copy From Blob to Azure SQL** activity that fails. Let's run the pipeline
    again, but stop execution after this failing activity. To do this, click on it – you will see a
    hollow red circle above it:

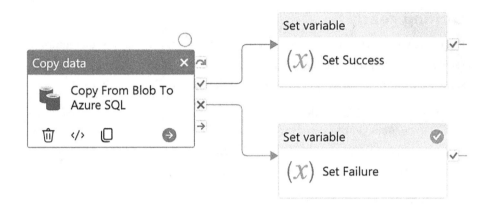

*Figure 10.20: Selected activity in the Author interface*

Click inside this circle. It will fill in red, and subsequent activities become faded, as shown
in the following screenshot. This indicates a breakpoint in your pipeline:

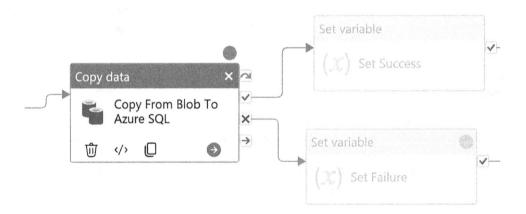

*Figure 10.21: Setting up a breakpoint*

Now, run your pipeline in debug mode (refer to the *Investigating failures – running pipelines in debug mode* recipe in this chapter if you are unsure of how to do that). You will see that the execution only continues up to the breakpoint. This behavior is intentional and allows you to isolate and investigate the specific portion of your pipeline where the issue occurs. As a result, neither the **Set Success/Failure** activities nor the **Record Status** activities are executed beyond the breakpoint, helping you to focus on troubleshooting the relevant components.

3.  Let's now rerun this pipeline from the point of failure. After all, we know that the **Backup SQL Data** activity succeeded, and we do not need to rerun it again.

    Before you can rerun your pipeline, you need to publish and trigger it. Publish your pipeline, and, once it is published, trigger it to start a run. Do not use the **Debug** mode this time.

    Once your pipeline has run, go to the **Monitor** tab. There, under the **Pipeline Runs** section, you will see a list of rows, each row representing a run of this pipeline. Make sure you are looking under the **Triggered** tab (we went over the structure of the **Pipeline runs** section in the *Monitoring pipeline runs and integration runtimes* recipe). When you hover over a row, you will see the rerun, consumption report, and error icons:

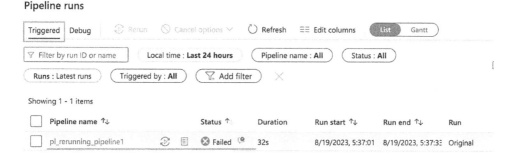

*Figure 10.22: Rerun and consumption buttons*

4.  If we click on **Rerun** here, the data pipeline will rerun starting from the very first activity. Instead, click on the pipeline name; this will open the pipeline run details interface:

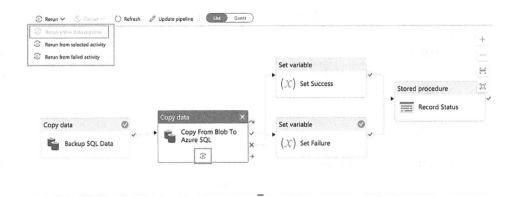

*Figure 10.23: The pipeline run details interface*

Here, you can see the rerun options: we can rerun from the selected activity or we can rerun from the failed activity (in our case, this is the same activity, since we selected the activity that failed). Click on any of these buttons (in our case, they all will rerun the pipeline from the **Copy from Blob to Azure SQL** activity).

After your rerun is completed, the graphical representation of your pipeline looks like this:

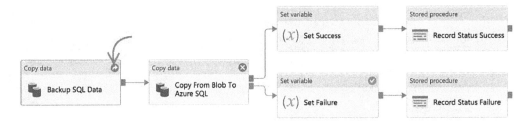

*Figure 10.24: Pipeline after rerun from failed activity*

Note the grayed-out arrow in the **Backup SQL Data** activity. This indicates that this activity was not executed; we rerun from the point of failure, bypassing the first activity.

# How it works...

In this recipe, we tried out two very intuitive but powerful features of Azure Data Factory. If your pipeline failed, setting a breakpoint as we did in *step 2* allows you to execute only the problematic portion of your pipeline – the activities that failed, or the ones that require your scrutiny. There is no need to waste time waiting for the whole pipeline to finish if you know that the activities beyond the breakpoint function perfectly.

After you have performed an investigation and fixed your pipeline, you can rerun it from the point of failure or from any activity within the pipeline. It's important to note that when you choose to rerun from any activity within the pipeline, it will involve executing all preceding activities up to the selected point. This feature is very useful when your pipeline takes some time to complete. For example, many pipelines move data to a staging area and then perform data transformation. If the transformation activity (or activities) failed for some reason, but export to the staging area was successful, rerunning the pipeline from the beginning will be both lengthy and costly, and, ultimately, unnecessary. You can avoid both the wait and the extra expense by rerunning from the point of failure and skipping successful steps.

# Configuring alerts for your Azure Data Factory runs

When a failure in data processing happens, we have to react as fast as possible to avoid impacting downstream processes. Azure Data Factory gives us tools to automate monitoring by setting up alerts to inform the engineers when there is a problem. We already introduced a custom email alert in the *Branching and chaining* recipe in *Chapter 2, Orchestration and Control Flow*. It sent a notification if that particular pipeline failed. In this chapter, we shall create an alert that will notify on-call engineers via email or a phone call whenever any of the pipelines in our data factory have a problem.

# Getting ready

In order to follow this recipe and configure the alerts, we first need to register with the Insights resource provider:

1. In the Azure portal, go to your subscription, and from the menu on the left, select **Resource providers**.

2. Use the **Filter by name...** text field to search for the `microsoft.insights` resource provider.

3.  If the **Status** column does not say **Registered**, click on the **Register** button:

*Figure 10.25: Registering microsoft.insights resource provider*

4.  Wait until the registration is complete.

After we go through the recipe and configure the alert, we will test it on a failed pipeline. We shall use the pipeline that we designed in *Chapter 2*, *Orchestration and Control Flow*, in the *Using parameters and variables in a pipeline* recipe. If you did not complete that recipe, do so now so that you have a simple pipeline handy. Alternatively, if you already have a simple pipeline you know well and can make fail, you can use it for this recipe.

## How to do it...

In this recipe, we shall configure an alert that notifies on-call engineers when any of the pipelines in our data factory have a failure:

1.  Go to your data factory instance and launch the ADF Studio. Navigate to the **Monitor** tab.

2.  In the **Monitor** tab, select **Alerts & metrics** in the **Notifications** section, as shown in the following screenshot. Then, click on **New alert rule** in the interface:

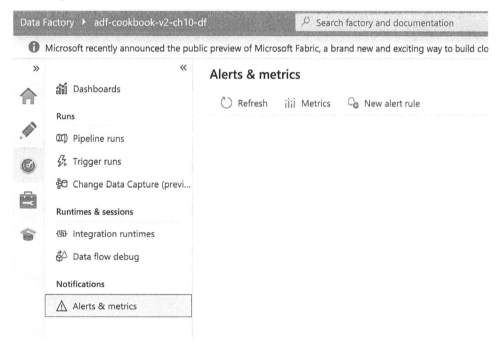

*Figure 10.26: Alerts & metrics interface*

3.  In the **New alert rule** blade, configure your new alert. Name your alert `Pipeline Failures Detected`. From the **Severity** drop-down option, choose **Sev2**.

4.  Next, we shall configure the target criteria. Click on **Add criteria** under the **Target criteria** section. You will see a long list of metrics that you can utilize in order to configure your alerts. Select **Failed activity runs metrics**; this will give us the most general failure metrics:

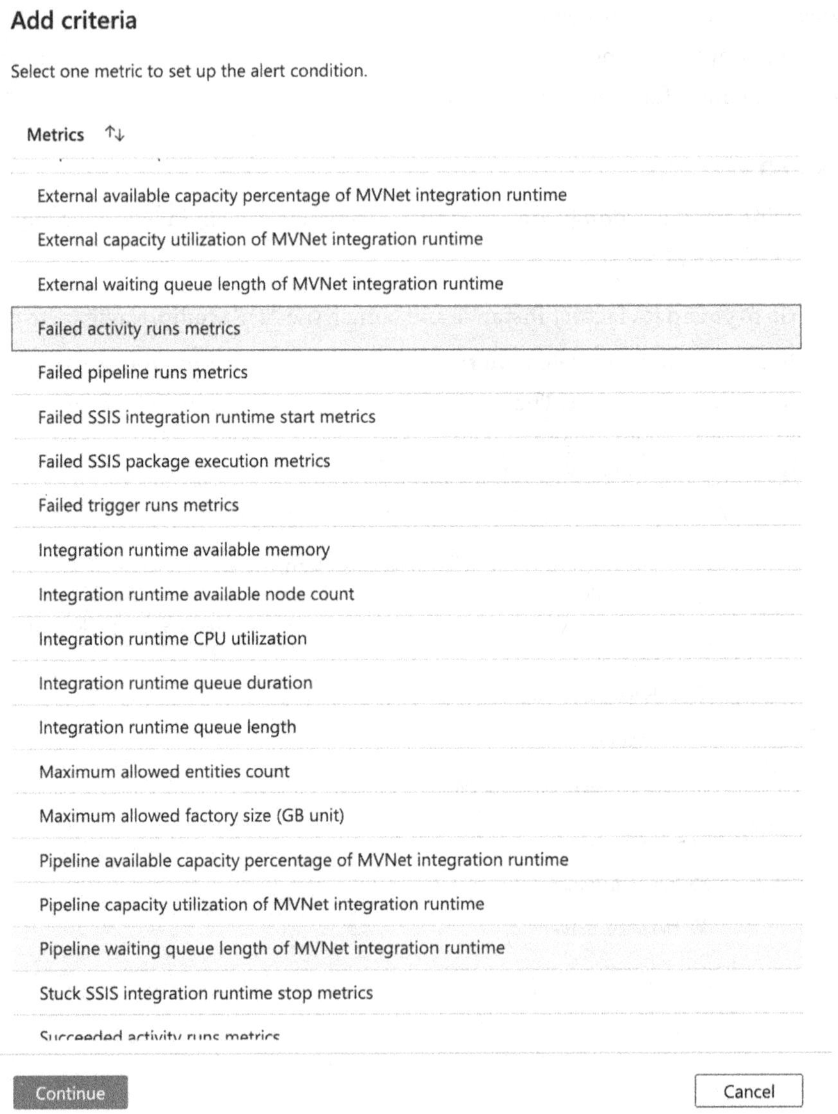

## Add criteria

Select one metric to set up the alert condition.

Metrics ↑↓

| |
|---|
| External available capacity percentage of MVNet integration runtime |
| External capacity utilization of MVNet integration runtime |
| External waiting queue length of MVNet integration runtime |
| Failed activity runs metrics |
| Failed pipeline runs metrics |
| Failed SSIS integration runtime start metrics |
| Failed SSIS package execution metrics |
| Failed trigger runs metrics |
| Integration runtime available memory |
| Integration runtime available node count |
| Integration runtime CPU utilization |
| Integration runtime queue duration |
| Integration runtime queue length |
| Maximum allowed entities count |
| Maximum allowed factory size (GB unit) |
| Pipeline available capacity percentage of MVNet integration runtime |
| Pipeline capacity utilization of MVNet integration runtime |
| Pipeline waiting queue length of MVNet integration runtime |
| Stuck SSIS integration runtime stop metrics |
| Succeeded activity runs metrics |

Continue                                                          Cancel

*Figure 10.27: Add alert criteria*

5.   Hit **Continue**. This will take you to the blade where you can set up additional alert logic. At this time, we shall leave all the values at their defaults to make sure that we receive a notification whenever there is any type of failure in any of the activities. Click the **Add criteria** button to finalize the target criteria and return to the alert configuration:

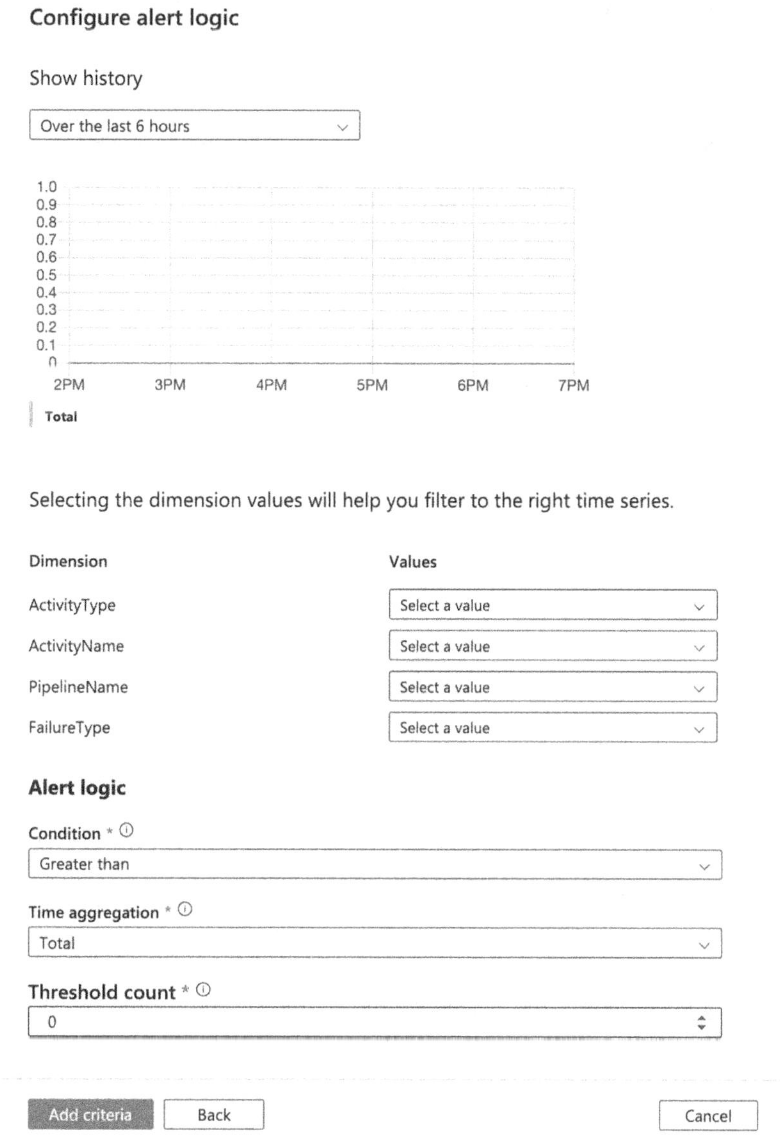

Configure alert logic

Show history

Over the last 6 hours

```
1.0
0.9
0.8
0.7
0.6
0.5
0.4
0.3
0.2
0.1
  0
    2PM      3PM      4PM      5PM      6PM      7PM
```
Total

Selecting the dimension values will help you filter to the right time series.

| Dimension | Values |
| --- | --- |
| ActivityType | Select a value |
| ActivityName | Select a value |
| PipelineName | Select a value |
| FailureType | Select a value |

**Alert logic**

Condition *

Greater than

Time aggregation *

Total

Threshold count *

0

Add criteria     Back                                    Cancel

*Figure 10.28: The Configure alert logic blade*

6.   Next, specify the notification method. Click on **Configure notification**. We shall create a new action group to send our notifications to. Enter `On-call Engineers` as your action group name for this recipe, and `On-call` for **Short name**. Next, click on the **Add Notifications** button.

7.   You will see the **Add notification** blade. Here, you can set up how you want to receive your alert. In this recipe, we shall send alerts via email and SMS so that the engineers know as soon as possible if there is a problem.

Fill in the fields in the **Add notification** blade, as shown in the following screenshot (fill in the appropriate contact email and phone number):

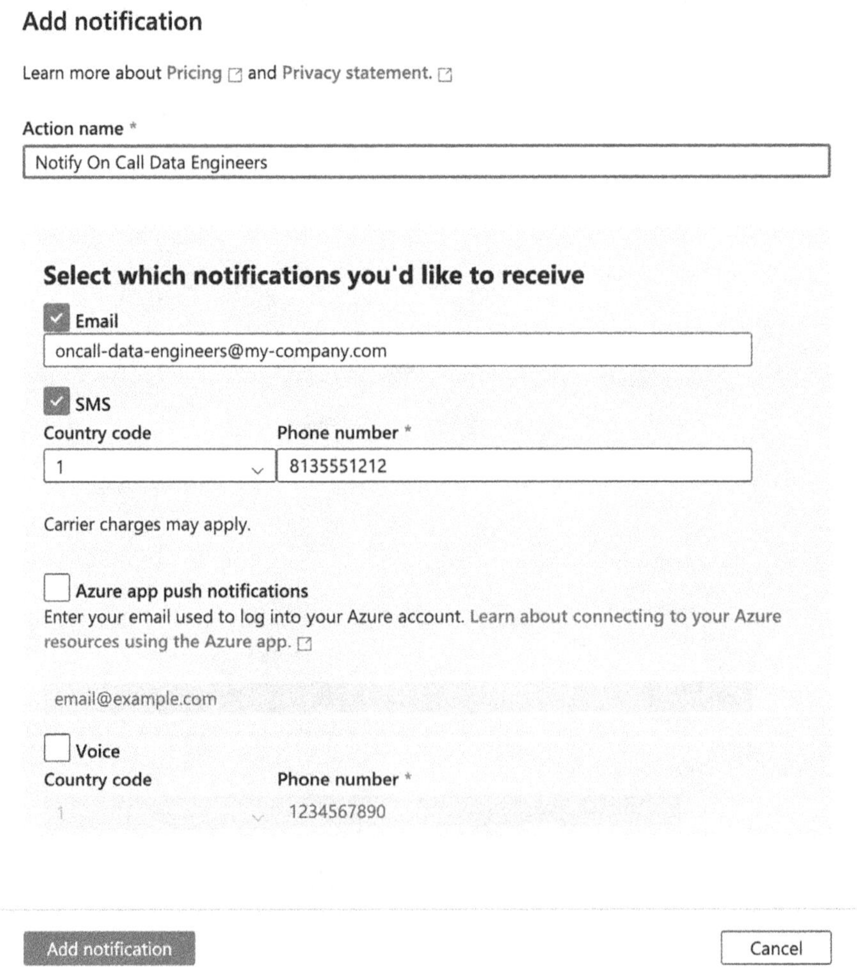

## Add notification

Learn more about Pricing ☐ and Privacy statement. ☐

Action name *

Notify On Call Data Engineers

### Select which notifications you'd like to receive

☑ Email

oncall-data-engineers@my-company.com

☑ SMS

Country code                    Phone number *

1                         ⌄      8135551212

Carrier charges may apply.

☐ Azure app push notifications
Enter your email used to log into your Azure account. Learn about connecting to your Azure resources using the Azure app. ☐

email@example.com

☐ Voice
Country code                    Phone number *

1                         ⌄      1234567890

Add notification                                              Cancel

*Figure 10.29: Add notification configuration*

Click on the **Add notification** button to return to the **Configure notification** blade.

8.  We have specified an action group and notification method for our notifications. Click on the **Add action group** button to finalize this action group and return to the **New alert rule** blade. Review your alert rule configuration; it should look similar to the following:

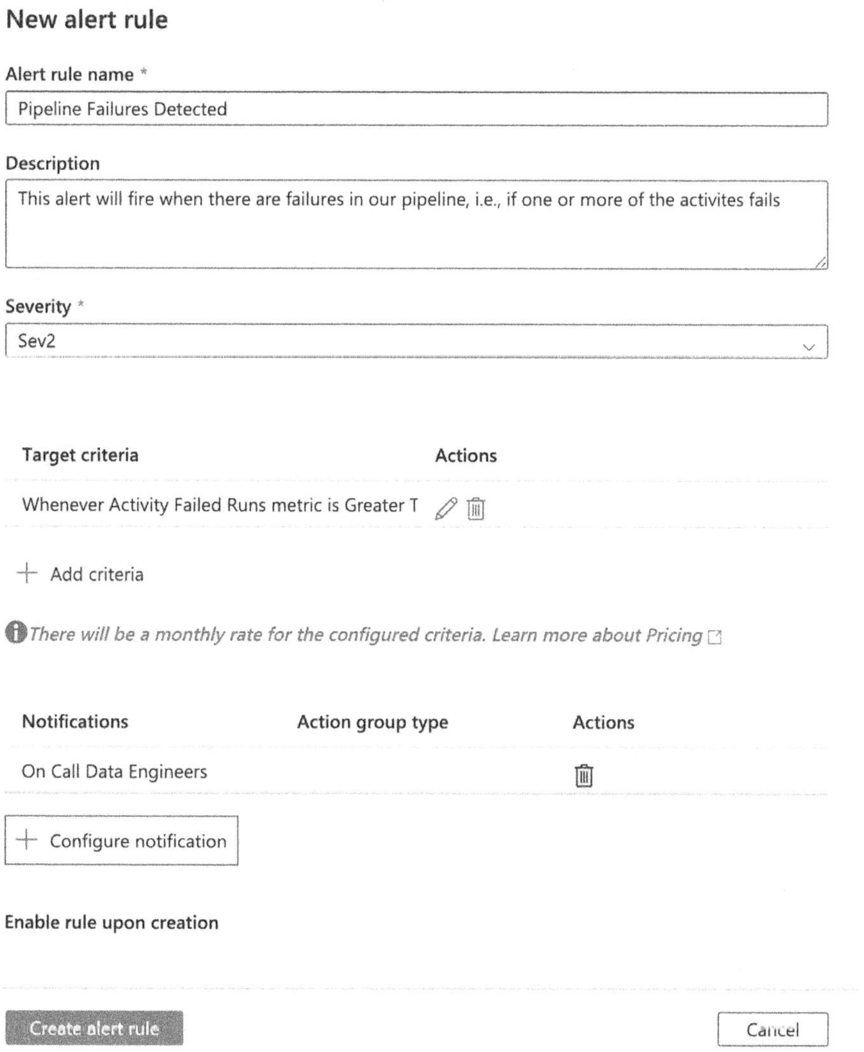

## New alert rule

**Alert rule name** *

Pipeline Failures Detected

**Description**

This alert will fire when there are failures in our pipeline, i.e., if one or more of the activites fails

**Severity** *

Sev2

| Target criteria | Actions |
| --- | --- |
| Whenever Activity Failed Runs metric is Greater T | 🖉 🗑 |

+ Add criteria

*There will be a monthly rate for the configured criteria. Learn more about Pricing*

| Notifications | Action group type | Actions |
| --- | --- | --- |
| On Call Data Engineers | | 🗑 |

+ Configure notification

**Enable rule upon creation**

[ Create alert rule ]     [ Cancel ]

*Figure 10.30: Configured alert rule*

9.  Click on **Create alert rule** to finalize your new rule and create an alert. You should see this
    alert in the **Alerts & metrics** interface:

*Figure 10.31: Alert rule in the Alerts & metrics interface*

Your action group has been created, and members of that group will receive an email and
an SMS informing them they have been added to the group. This is what you will see after
the group is created:

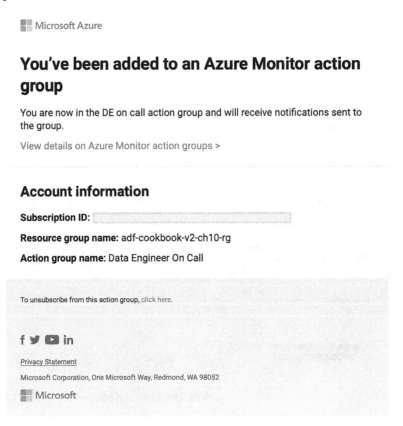

*Figure 10.32: Informational email*

10. Let's test this alert. Take a simple pipeline we designed in *Chapter 2, Orchestration and Control Flow*, in the *Using parameters and variables in a pipeline* recipe, and make it fail. All we need to do is to change the tableName parameter in **Source dataset** for the **Backup SQL Data** activity. Do not forget to publish your changes!

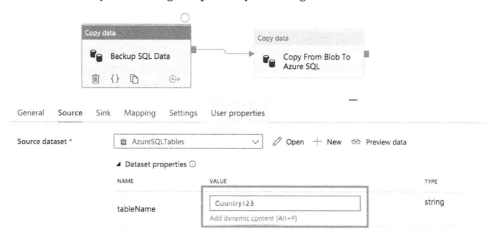

*Figure 10.33: Entering an incorrect tableName value to cause pipeline failure*

After publishing, trigger the pipeline. It will fail, because it won't be able to find the Country123 table. After it fails, the alert will send an email and an SMS to the addresses/phone numbers you specified in *step 7*.

A sample email alert looks like this:

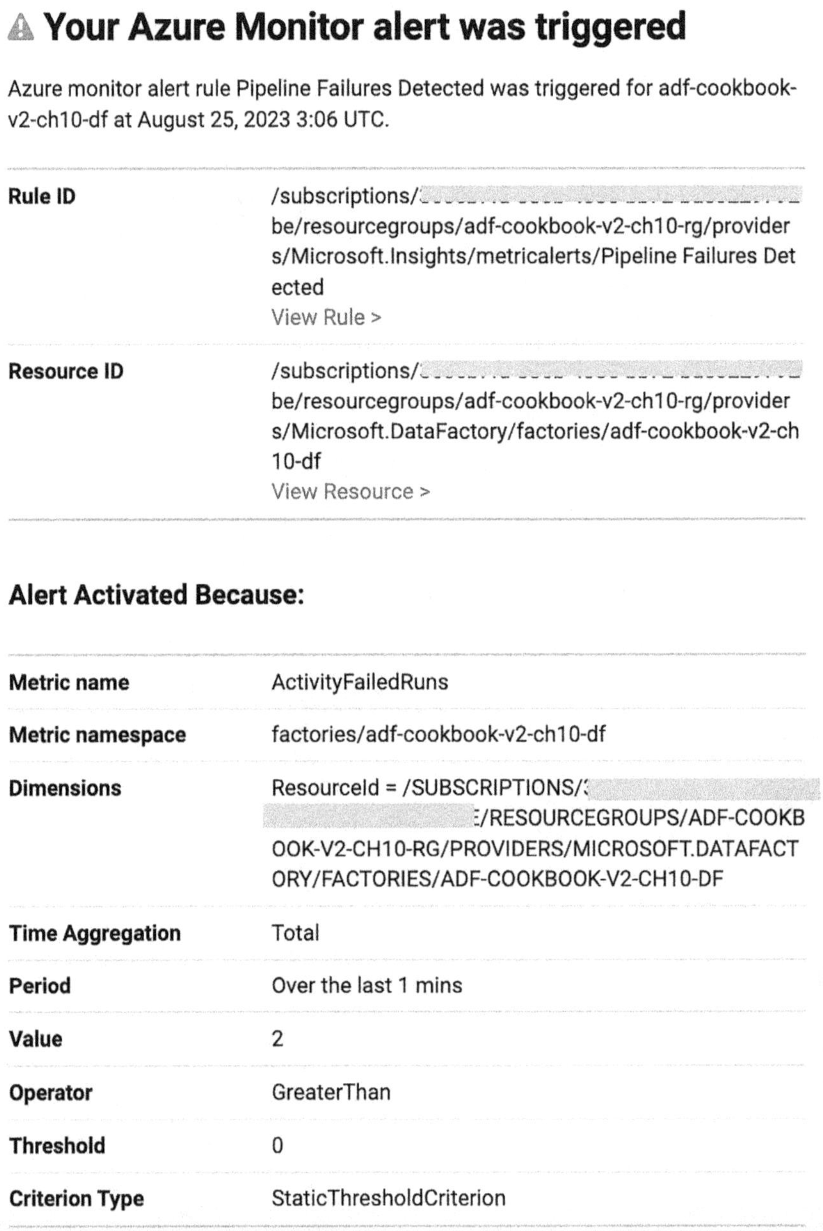

## ⚠ Your Azure Monitor alert was triggered

Azure monitor alert rule Pipeline Failures Detected was triggered for adf-cookbook-v2-ch10-df at August 25, 2023 3:06 UTC.

| | |
|---|---|
| **Rule ID** | /subscriptions/[redacted]be/resourcegroups/adf-cookbook-v2-ch10-rg/providers/Microsoft.Insights/metricalerts/Pipeline Failures Detected<br>View Rule > |
| **Resource ID** | /subscriptions/[redacted]be/resourcegroups/adf-cookbook-v2-ch10-rg/providers/Microsoft.DataFactory/factories/adf-cookbook-v2-ch10-df<br>View Resource > |

## Alert Activated Because:

| | |
|---|---|
| **Metric name** | ActivityFailedRuns |
| **Metric namespace** | factories/adf-cookbook-v2-ch10-df |
| **Dimensions** | ResourceId = /SUBSCRIPTIONS/[redacted]/RESOURCEGROUPS/ADF-COOKBOOK-V2-CH10-RG/PROVIDERS/MICROSOFT.DATAFACTORY/FACTORIES/ADF-COOKBOOK-V2-CH10-DF |
| **Time Aggregation** | Total |
| **Period** | Over the last 1 mins |
| **Value** | 2 |
| **Operator** | GreaterThan |
| **Threshold** | 0 |
| **Criterion Type** | StaticThresholdCriterion |

*Figure 10.34: Sample email notification*

Examine the email that you received. Click on the **View Resource** link in the email; it will take you right to the data factory where the failure occurred, and you can start debugging immediately.

## How it works...

Azure Data Factory provides a sophisticated interface to offer fine-grained control over your alert logic. In *steps 4* and *5*, we configured a general alert to demonstrate how to receive a notification when any problem occurs. However, for more specific business and engineering requirements, you can leverage the same interface to refine the criteria for your alerts and specify various parameters. This includes specifying which pipelines or activities to monitor, defining the types of failures you are interested in, and setting how frequently the data factory should be polled to detect issues.

In *steps 6* to *8*, we configured the information about our responders by entering their email and SMS details to be notified in case of pipeline failures. This interface offers remarkable flexibility in setting up notifications; you can choose any combination of email, SMS, voice, or Azure app push notifications. Additionally, it's worth noting that you can configure multiple notifications per alert using the same interface. For instance, in the event of a problem, you might want to send both an email and an SMS to on-call engineers and simply an informational email to the rest of your engineering team.

Moreover, for even more advanced alerting and customization options, you can explore Azure Logic App and web activity to send custom failure emails with detailed error messages. These tools can be particularly useful when you need to provide specific context and information to your responders when an issue occurs.

## There's more...

It is always useful to have the ability to notify the user (or an on-call engineer) if a failure occurs. In this book, we have shown a way to notify the user if a failure occurs in a certain activity within one pipeline (refer to *Chapter 2*, *Orchestration and Control Flow*, the *Branching and chaining activities* recipe), and how to set up an alert if one or more pipelines fail in a certain data factory. What if we want to be notified whenever a failure occurs in any of our data factories?

One way is to configure separate alerts in all the data factories we need to monitor. There is another way, which offers much more sophisticated control over the metrics you want to monitor: you can use the Azure Monitor service. Azure Monitor lets you configure the export of the logs to several platforms, including Azure Log Analytics. Once you export your logs to Log Analytics, you can use this robust platform to gain insight into your pipeline runs or configure alerts based on data gathered across resources.

## See also

If you are interested in exploring the Azure Monitor or Log Analytics service for your data factory alerts, there is no better place to start than the following link: `https://docs.microsoft.com/azure/data-factory/monitor-using-azure-monitor`


## Join our community on Discord

Join our community's Discord space for discussions with the authors and other readers:

`https://discord.gg/U229qmBmT3`

# 11

# Working with Azure Data Explorer

In this chapter, we delve into two key services within the Azure Data platform: **Azure Data Factory (ADF)** and **Azure Data Explorer (ADX)**. ADX is a fast and highly scalable data exploration service for log and telemetry data offered by Microsoft Azure. It provides real-time analysis capabilities, helping organizations to rapidly ingest, store, analyze, and visualize vast amounts of data. The use cases for ADX span across a range of sectors and applications, from IoT solutions to user behavior analytics and application monitoring, all with the goal of turning raw data into actionable insights.

In the context of ADX, ADF can be used to automate the process of data ingestion from various sources into ADX, perform the necessary transformations, and manage data workflows.

We will cover the following recipes:

- An introduction to ADX, its architecture, and key features
- Overview of common use cases for ADX and ADF
- Setting up a data ingestion pipeline from Azure Data Factory to ADX – a step-by-step guide to ingest JSON data from Azure Storage
- Transforming data in ADX with the Azure Data Factory Copy activity

By the end of this chapter, we will understand how to utilize Azure Data Factory for data ingestion and management in ADX. Whether you're dealing with large streams of real-time data or analyzing historical data for patterns, this chapter will equip you with the necessary knowledge to leverage Azure's powerful data exploration and integration tools.

# Introduction to ADX

ADX is one of the many managed services (SaaS) offered by Azure. It represents a highly effective, fully managed platform for big data analytics, empowering users with the ability to analyze extensive data volumes in close-to-real-time scenarios. Equipped with a comprehensive suite of tools, ADX facilitates end-to-end solutions for data ingestion, querying, visualization, and management.

Since ADX is a cloud product, we don't need to spend much time deep-diving into the ADX architecture. The following diagram shows the high-level architecture of the product:

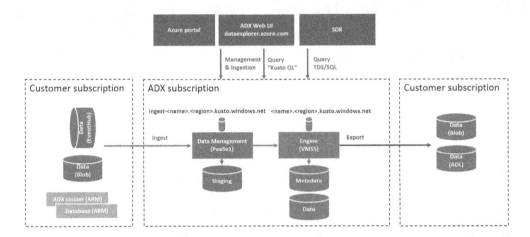

*Figure 11.1: ADX solution architecture*

The ADX platform simplifies the process of extracting critical insights, identifying patterns and trends, and building forecasting models by analyzing structured, semi-structured, and unstructured data across time series and using machine learning. As a secure, scalable, robust, and ready-for-enterprise service, ADX is well suited for log analytics, time-series analytics, IoT, and general-purpose exploratory analytics.

Several other services extend ADX's capabilities, leveraging its query language – **Kusto Query Language (KQL)**. These include Azure Monitor Logs, Application Insights, Time Series Insights, and Microsoft Defender for Endpoint.

ADX has many use cases. It works great for streaming use cases and can be integrated with various data sources. Moreover, it is often used for traditional analytics use cases and serves as a data warehouse or data platform where we can consolidate all data and analyze it with KQL, build visualizations, or apply machine learning functions. The following is an example of an Azure solution architecture with ADX in the middle:

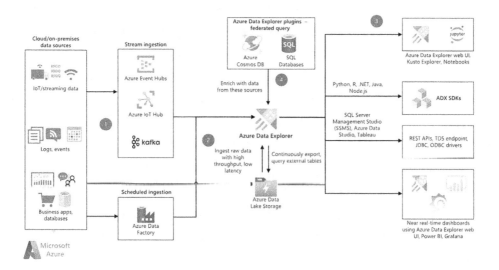

*Figure 11.2: ADX solution architecture*

Another interesting fact about ADX is that it reached out to GigaOm to perform an independent benchmark of ADX against some of Azure's most common competitors when it comes to Log Analytics (i.e., Google BigQuery and Snowflake). Overall, the test results were insightful and revealed the query execution performance of the three platforms tested. The highlights included the following:

- ADX outperformed Google BigQuery and Snowflake on all 19 test queries with a single user and 18 of 19 queries with 50 concurrent users.

- ADX completed all 19 queries in under 1 second with a single user, while the average execution time on BigQuery and Snowflake was 15 and 13 seconds per query, respectively.

- ADX completed all 19 queries in under 10 seconds with 50 concurrent users.

- BigQuery and Snowflake both had 8 queries (different ones) that did not complete within the 2-minute timeout.

They found the cost of data ingestion and query execution on ADX to be significantly lower than on Google BigQuery, Snowflake, and Elasticsearch/OpenSearch. You can learn more about this benchmark test in this article: `https://research.gigaom.com/report/log-data-analytics-testing/`.

## See also

You can learn more about ADX by reading the whitepaper that was published in September 2018: `https://azure.microsoft.com/en-us/resources/azure-data-explorer/`. It includes an ADX architecture overview, query planning and execution, performance observations, and an examination of the underlying storage technology.

# Creating an ADX cluster and ingesting data

In this recipe, we will create an ADX instance in the Azure portal and ingest the sample Storm Events data using the ADX UI.

## Getting ready

In this recipe, we will create an ADX cluster; we will be using these in future recipes for Data Factory pipelines.

## How to do it...

1.  Go to the Azure portal at `https://ms.portal.azure.com/`.
2.  Find **Azure Data Explorer Clusters**.
3.  Click **Create**.
4.  In the first tab, we need to fill in the **Subscription**, **Resource group**, **Cluster name**, **Region**, and **Workload** fields:

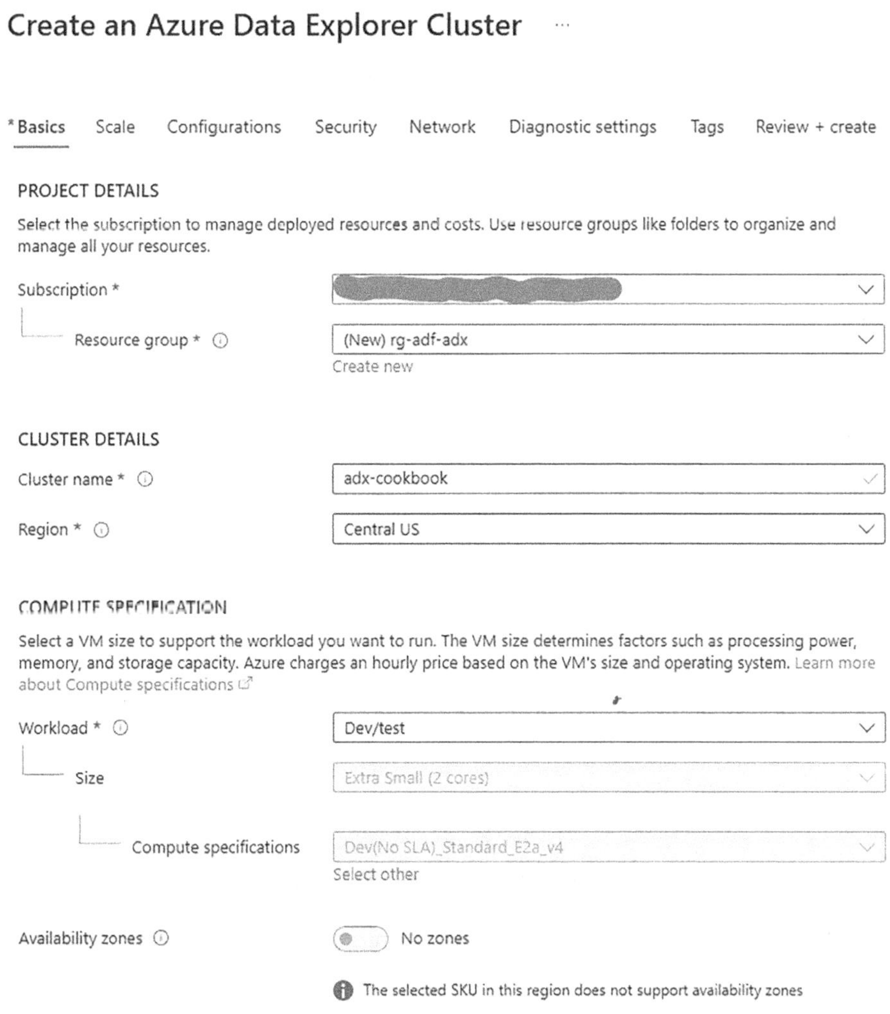

# Create an Azure Data Explorer Cluster   ...

*Figure 11.3: Creating an ADX cluster*

Microsoft provides us a cheap workload option for testing and prototyping – **Dev/test**. Running production workloads in ADX is expensive and will easily burn all your free credits.

5.  Next, click on **Review + create** and, after some quick validation, we can click **Create**.

6.  When the creation is complete, click on **Go to Resource** and it will open the ADX UI.

# How it works...

Azure will execute an ARM template with the given parameters and, after some time, you will be able to access the ADX workspace:

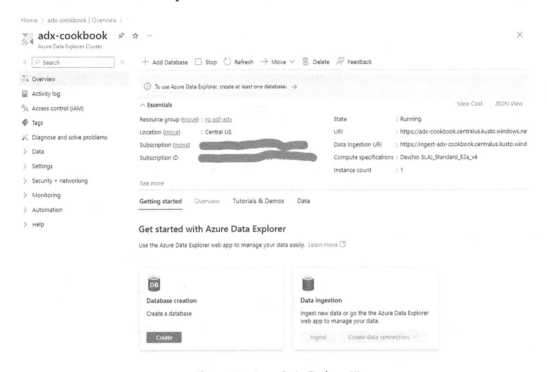

*Figure 11.4: Azure Data Explorer UI*

Using the Azure UI, we can create a new database, initialize data ingestion, query the data, and even build a dashboard.

There are several options for working with ADX. We can use the Azure portal UI, the Azure CLI and PowerShell, or we can use the desktop client.

While we are in the menu, we can quickly create a new database as our destination for the data pipelines:

1.  In the **Database creation** tile, click on **Create**.

2.  Enter cookbook for the database name and click **Create**. The cluster will create a new database.

3.  Next, we can ingest the data into ADX using the Storm Events data. In the Chapter 11 directory in the book's GitHub repo, there is a file called StormEvents.zip. Let's download the file, unpack it, and use it for ingestion into ADX.

4. In the ADX workspace, click on **Ingest**. You can find this in the **Data ingestion** tile. It will open the ADX portal where you can provide the information for ingestion:

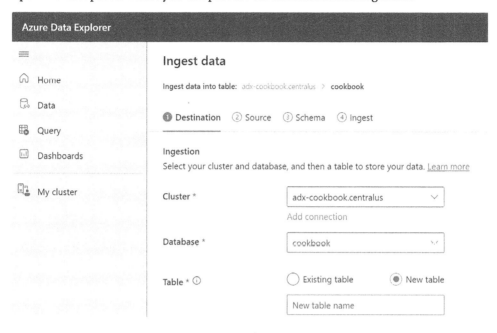

*Figure 11.5: ADX data ingestion UI*

5. We will provide StormEvents as the table name and click **Next: Source**.

6. Leave the **Source Type** set to **File**, then upload the StormEvents.csv file and click **Next: Schema**.

7. ADX is smart enough to recognize the schema and nested JSON inside the CSV, which would be hard for a traditional ETL tool to do. Click **Next: Start ingestion**.

8. It will take some time to ingest, but afterward, we will see a data review showing the sample table output. Moreover, ADX gives us a **Quick Queries** option, or we can use KQL and query the data ourselves.

## How it works...

We just ingested the CSV file into ADX. ADX is a managed cloud service that can parse, ingest, and store the data. We can observe the ADX metrics and overall performance of the ADX cluster in Azure Metrics. For example, in the following screenshot, note the spike in **Ingestion result** after we ingested the file.

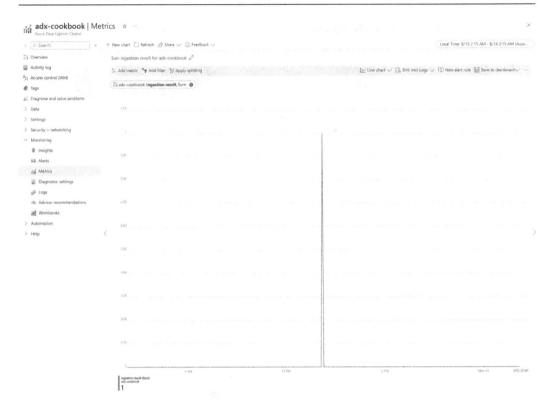

*Figure 11.6: ADX Ingestion result metric overview*

More information about various ADX metrics can be found in the Microsoft documentation at `https://learn.microsoft.com/en-us/azure/data-explorer/using-metrics`. Usage metrics are the most useful information for monitoring the health and performance of the ADX cluster.

## See also

ADX in production should be deployed using private endpoints or with virtual network injection. You can learn more about this in the Microsoft documentation: `https://learn.microsoft.com/en-us/azure/data-explorer/security-network-overview`.

If you want to work with the desktop client, you can download *Kusto.Explorer*: `https://learn.microsoft.com/en-us/azure/data-explorer/kusto/tools/kusto-explorer`.

Finally, if KQL feels unfamiliar to you, you can find lots of resources on this powerful query language on Microsoft Learn at `https://learn.microsoft.com/en-us/azure/data-explorer/kusto/query/kql-quick-reference`.

# Orchestrating ADX data with Azure Data Factory

In the recipe, we highlight the orchestration capabilities of ADF in conjunction with ADX. The focus is on the **ADX Command** activity within ADF, which facilitates the direct execution of ADX commands.

We will begin by querying the Storm Events table in ADX to extract specific records where direct deaths exceed 5 and place them into the new table, DeadlyStorms. Following this extraction, the recipe outlines the steps to ingest this dataset into a new table within ADX using ADF.

By the end of this recipe, you will have a clear understanding of how to orchestrate data processes and manage data movement within ADX using Azure Data Factory, enhancing your capability to perform intricate data operations within Azure.

## Getting ready

We will continue to use our existing ADX cluster and will need to use the service principal that we created in *Chapter 1, Getting Started with ADF* – or you can use any other service principal. We need the service principal to grant access to ADF to access the **cookbook** ADX database and perform certain actions.

## How to do it...

Let's get back to our data factory:

1.  If you have closed the **Data Factory** console, you should open it again. Search for Data factories and click **Enter**.

2.  Go to **Author** and create a new pipeline.

3.  From among the available activities, find the ADX **Command** and drop it on the canvas.

4.  Before we connect to ADX, we should make sure that ADF can access the ADX cluster and the cookbook ADX database. Using our **service principal**, we should grant access to the database. In the ADX cluster workspace, go to **Data-> Databases** and click on the **cookbook** database.

5.  Choose **Permissions** and click **Add**. Find your service principal and attach it as **Admin**.

6.  Moreover, we should make sure that both ADF and ADX access control (IAM) have the service principal set as a **Contributor**.

7.  Next, we should modify the **Connection** tab by adding an ADX linked service. Click **New**. Fill in the information about your ADX cluster and use the service principal as an authentication method or any other method. You can also leverage Azure Key Vault to store the secrets and reference your vault from ADF.

*Figure 11.7: Adding an ADX linked service in ADF*

8.  We can now test the connection; it should be successful. Click **Create**.

9.  Next, let's add the command to execute. This command is shown in the following screenshot and is available in the Chapter 11 directory on the book's GitHub repo.

*Figure 11.8: ADX command for (re)creating a new table*

10. We can validate the pipeline by clicking on **Debug** and reviewing the output of the activity as well as finding the new DeadlyStorms table in ADX:

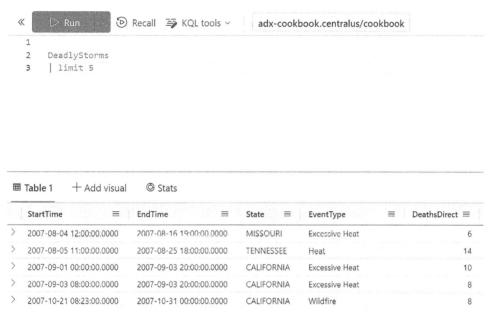

*Figure 11.9: Query result of the new table in the ADX console*

## How it works...

Within the ADF UI, we initiated a new pipeline to orchestrate the data processing between ADX and other sources. Our primary tool for this operation was the ADX **Command** activity, a functionality in ADF that allows the direct execution of commands specific to ADX.

Our initial step was to target the **StormEvents** table in ADX. We crafted a query to filter out records where direct deaths exceeded 5, and then proceeded to sort these records based on the **StartTime** in descending order. The query, executed via the **Command** activity, fetched the precise dataset we were interested in.

Once the data was retrieved, the next step in the pipeline involved ingesting this data into a new table within ADX. To ensure the seamless transfer and correct mapping of data, we defined both the source and destination datasets in ADF. The source dataset represented the output of our query, while the destination dataset signified the new table structure in ADX.

Upon successful execution of the pipeline, the data was ingested into the new table. The entire operation can be monitored and verified within the **Monitor** section of ADF, where detailed logs of the job run are maintained.

## There's more...

There are other ADF activities available for use with ADX, including **Copy, Lookup, Mapping Data Flows**, and so on. You can read more about them and their pros and cons at https://learn.microsoft.com/en-us/azure/data-explorer/data-factory-integration.

## See also

You can find more information about the ADX ingest queries in the Microsoft documentation at https://learn.microsoft.com/en-us/azure/data-explorer/kusto/management/data-ingestion/ingest-from-query.

Finally, you can expand your knowledge by studying a specific use case – *Copy in bulk from a database to Azure Data Explorer by using the Azure Data Factory template*. It allows you to copy big volumes of data from the relational database into ADX. You can read about this specific use case in the official Microsoft documentation at https://learn.microsoft.com/en-us/azure/data-explorer/data-factory-template.

# Ingesting data from Azure Blob storage to ADX in Azure Data Factory using the Copy activity

In this recipe, we explore the versatility of ADF in its interactions with ADX. Azure Data Factory can both extract data from and ingest data into ADX, serving the dual roles of source and sink. This flexibility ensures that data flow and transformation between various Azure services are seamless and efficient.

While there are multiple ways to work with data in this context, our focus in this recipe will be on the **Copy** command within ADF. Utilizing this command, we'll guide you through the process of ingesting data from Azure Blob storage directly into ADX. This method simplifies the data migration process, ensuring that your information is rapidly available in ADX for analysis and exploration.

## Getting ready

For this recipe, we need an existing Azure Storage account and an ADX cluster. We will add one more file to the storage account and use it as a source file that we will load into an ADX table.

# How to do it...

We created the ADF job with the UI. Let's review the CDT:

1.  We will create a new pipeline in ADF. Add a new pipeline.

2.  Our pipeline will consist of two activities. First, we will create the table in ADX and then we will copy the data from the storage account into this table.

3.  Drag and drop the **Azure Data Explorer Command** activity on the canvas.

4.  Open the **Connection** and choose the already-existing **Azure Data Explorer linked service** that we created in the previous recipe – **AzureDataExplorer1**.

5.  Move to the **Command** tab and paste in the script for table creation. You can find the script in the GitHub repo and in the following screenshot:

*Figure 11.10: Script for creating a table in ADX*

6.  Next, we will add the **Copy** activity. Drag and drop the **Copy data** activity onto the canvas and connect it to **Azure Data Explorer Command**:

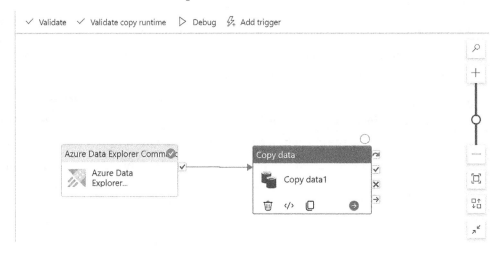

*Figure 11.11: Copy data on success of ADX Command*

7.  Now, we can configure the **Source** and **Sink** settings of the **Copy data** activity. In the Chapter 11 folder in the book's GitHub repo, you can find the sample.json file. This needs to be uploaded to the Azure Storage account that was used in *Chapter 1*.

8.  For **Source**, we will create a new **Sink dataset**. Click on **New** and choose **Azure Blob Storage**. For the format, choose **JSON**, and click **Continue**.

9.  From the drop-down menu, we can see the available linked service that was created earlier – **AzureBlobStorage1**.

10. For **File path**, click on the little folder icon and choose the path where we upload the JSON file.

11. We can preview the dataset by clicking on **Preview data** in the **Source** tab.

ope                                                                                                                    ↗ ✕

### Preview data

Linked service: AzureBlobStorage1

Object:          sample.json

```
[
  {
    "name": "Adeel Solangi",
    "language": "Sindhi",
    "id": "V59OF92YF627HFY0",
    "bio": "Donec lobortis eleifend condimentum. Cras dictum dolor lacinia lectus vehicula rutrum. Maec
    "version": 6.1
  },
  {
    "name": "Afzal Ghaffar",
    "language": "Sindhi",
    "id": "ENTOCR13RSCLZ6KU",
    "bio": "Aliquam sollicitudin ante ligula, eget malesuada nibh efficitur et. Pellentesque massa sem,
    "version": 1.88
  },
  {
    "name": "Aamir Solangi",
    "language": "Sindhi",
    "id": "IAKPO3R4761JDRVG",
    "bio": "Vestibulum pharetra libero et velit gravida euismod. Quisque mauris ligula, efficitur portt
    "version": 7.27
  },
  {
    "name": "Abla Dilmurat",
    "language": "Uyghur",
    "id": "5ZVOEPMJUI4MB4EN",
    "bio": "Donec lobortis eleifend condimentum. Morbi ac tellus erat."
```

*Figure 11.12: Preview JSON data*

12. Our next step is to specify the **Sink** option. For the Sink dataset, we need to create a new ADX dataset and specify the new table. Click **New** and choose the available ADX linked service that we created in the previous recipe. Give the table a name. You need to mark the **Edit** in order to provide the table name that doesn't exist in the cookbook database:

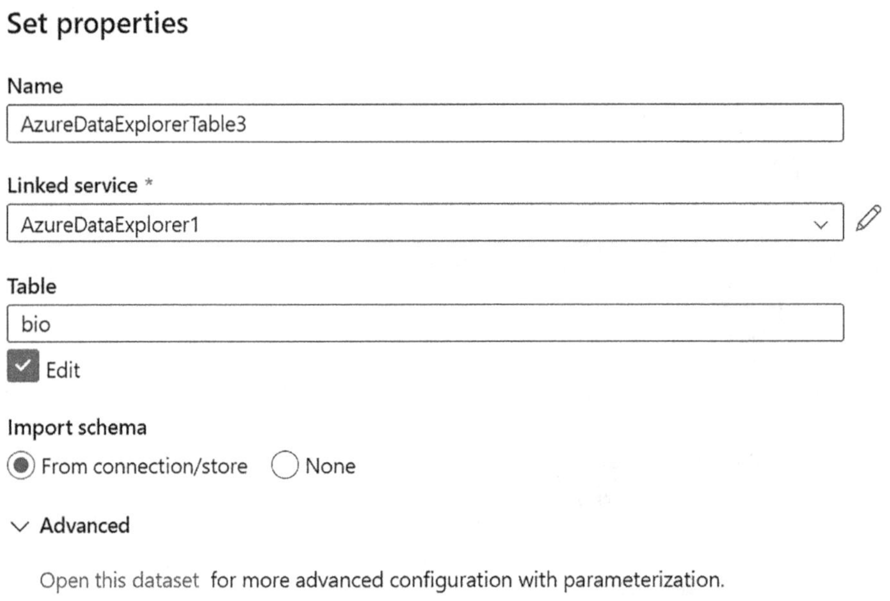

## Set properties

**Name**

    AzureDataExplorerTable3

**Linked service** *

    AzureDataExplorer1

**Table**

    bio

☑ Edit

**Import schema**

◉ From connection/store     ◯ None

∨ **Advanced**

    Open this dataset  for more advanced configuration with parameterization.

*Figure 11.13: Specifying the target table name*

13. We can test the whole pipeline by clicking **Debug**. The pipeline should succeed:

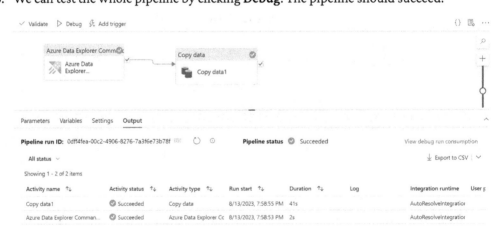

*Figure 11.14: Pipeline succeeded with both activities*

We just created a new ADF pipeline that creates an ADX table and ingests data into it.

## How it works...

In this recipe, we leverage an ADX command to create the target table and predefine the schema, and then push the data into ADX using the ADF **Copy** command.

## There's more...

Knowledge of ADX and KQL gives you the ability to leverage another popular Azure product – Log Analytics, which allows you to query the KQL telemetry of your services, including Azure Data Factory. You can learn more about this at https://learn.microsoft.com/en-us/azure/data-factory/monitor-using-azure-monitor.

## Leave a review!

Enjoyed this book? Help readers like you by leaving an Amazon review. Scan the QR code below for a 20% discount code.

# 12

# The Best Practices of Working with ADF

Welcome to the final chapter of *Azure Data Factory Cookbook*, where we delve into the best practices for working with **Azure Data Factory** (**ADF**) and Azure Synapse. Throughout this cookbook, we've explored a multitude of recipes and techniques to help you harness the power of ADF for your data integration and transformation needs. In this closing chapter, we'll guide you through essential considerations, strategies, and practical recipes that will elevate your ADF projects to new heights of efficiency, security, and scalability.

We will cover the following list of recipes in this chapter:

- Setting up roles and permissions with access levels for working with ADF
- Setting up Meta ETL with ADF
- Scaling your ADF project
- Using ADF disaster recovery built-in features
- Change data capture
- Managing data factory costs with FinOps

## Technical requirements

For this chapter, you will need the following:

- **ADF instance**: You need to have access to Microsoft Azure with an ADF instance created. An Azure free account is sufficient for all recipes in this chapter. To create an account, use the following link: https://azure.microsoft.com/free/. To create an ADF instance, please refer to *Chapter 1*.

- **GitHub repository**: You will need access to the files and templates provided for the recipes: https://github.com/PacktPublishing/Azure-Data-Factory-Cookbook-Second-Edition/tree/main/Chapter12.

# Setting up roles and permissions with access levels in ADF

ADF is built on principles of collaboration, and to work effectively you will need to grant access privileges to other users and teams. By its very nature, ADF relies on integration with other services, therefore entities such as users, service principles, and managed identities will require access to resources within your ADF instance. User access management is a pivotal feature of ADF.

Similar to many Azure services, ADF relies on **Role-Based Access Control (RBAC)**. RBAC enables fine-grained definitions of roles that can be granted, or assigned, to users, groups, service principals, or managed identities. These role assignments determine who can perform specific actions, such as viewing or making changes to pipelines, datasets, linked services, and other components, and ultimately govern access to your data workflows.

Imagine a scenario where a company is using ADF to orchestrate their data pipelines, which involves sensitive customer data. Without proper access management, any user within the organization could potentially view or modify these pipelines, leading to data breaches or unauthorized changes. By implementing RBAC, the company can restrict access to specific roles, such as data engineers having permission to create or edit pipelines, while business analysts can only view them. This ensures that only authorized personnel can interact with the data workflows, maintaining data security and integrity.

In this recipe, we shall introduce the core concepts of ADF RBAC and walk you through creating a role assignment for a user.

## Getting ready

To follow this recipe, you need access to an instance of an ADF, and you need to have an Owner or a User Access Administrator role – those roles will allow you to assign roles to other users. One way to ensure that you have an appropriate role is to create your own data factory – creators are assigned an Owner role automatically.

## How to do it...

In this recipe, we shall use the **Identity and Access Management** interface to assign a built-in Data Factory role to one or more users.

1. Open the Azure portal and navigate to your ADF instance.

2. From the menu on the left, select **Access Control (IAM)**. Click on the **+ Add**, and then on **Add role aAssignment**:

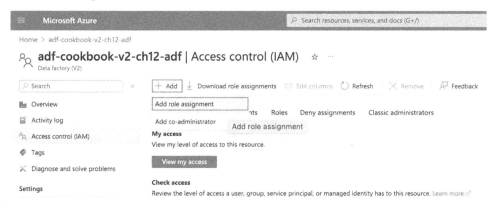

*Figure 12.1: Add role assignment*

3. You will see a **Role Assignment** interface, similar to the following snapshot.

*Figure 12.2: Role assignment interface*

This page has a lot of information about the roles that you can assign to users, service principals, or a managed identity such as a service. There are two tabs: **Job function roles** (less privileged roles, geared towards specific work functions), and **Privileged administrator roles** (general administrator roles – you should carefully consider who can be granted those roles!).

*Figure 12.3: Privileged administrator roles tab*

In the table, you see the role name, brief description, type (all roles shown are built-in roles), and category. In the **Details** column,**View** is a link: click on it to show a blade with more information about the role you are interested in, including an exhaustive list of all permissions that comprise the role, the role's *json* representation, and all existing assignments:

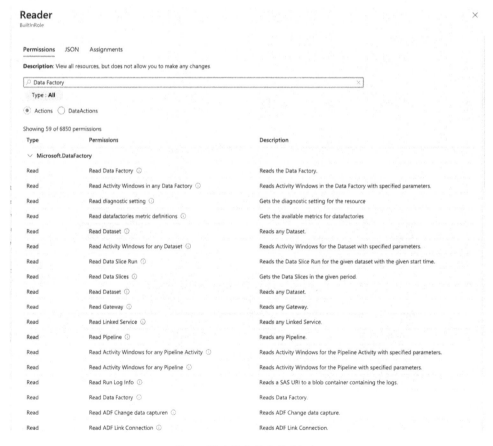

*Figure 12.4: Role Details blade*

4.  From the list of **Job function roles** list, select **Reader** and click **Next**.

5.  On the next screen, leave the radio button on **User, Group, or Service Principal**, and click on **+Select members**. In the **Select members** blade, choose one or more users who will have the Reader role assignment, and click **Select**.

*Figure 12.5: Select members*

Then click **Next** to navigate to the **Review + Assign** screen.

6.  On the **Review and Assign** screen, review the role (**Reader**), the scope of the assignment (it will be your Data Factory resource ID), and the list of users to whom you are granting the role. Click on the **Review + assign** button again to create the role assignment.

After a few seconds, the role assignments will be created and users will be granted access to your Data Factory instance.

## How it works...

In this recipe, we used the **Azure Identity and Access Management (IAM)** interface to assign a built-in **Reader** role to several users within our tenant. A **role** (sometimes called a **Role definition** ) consists of multiple permissions that describe actions that may be performed on a resource, such as read, write, and delete.

As we saw, ADF specifies many built-in, ready-to-use roles, which cover various aspects of working with Data Factory: viewing, creating, updating, and deleting Data Factory instances, linked services, and pipelines, working with logs and monitoring, assigning roles to other users, and so on.

Here are some of the most frequently used ADF roles:

- **Owner:** Owners have full control over the ADF instance. They can manage and configure all aspects of the Data Factory instances, including access control, resource creation, and deletion. The creator of a Data Factory instances is assigned the Owner role immediately upon creation of the instance.

- **Contributor:** Contributors have the authority to create, edit, and delete resources within the Data Factory instances. They can create and manage pipelines, datasets, linked services, and other components, but they cannot manage access control for the Data Factory instances itself.

- **Reader:** Readers have read-only access to the Data Factory instances. They can view the configuration, monitor pipelines, and access metadata, but they cannot make any changes to the resources or configurations.

- **Data Factory Contributor:** This role grants the user the ability to manage all aspects of the Data Factory instances but doesn't provide access to other Azure resources outside the Data Factory instances.

- **Monitoring Contributor:** This role allows users to view monitoring data, diagnose issues, and access logs related to the Data Factory instances operation. They don't have control over the configuration or resources.

NOTE

Every role assignment has a **scope**: a resource, or a group of resources, in which this role assignment is valid. For example, in our recipe, the scope of the role assignment is our instance of the ADF. We granted a **Reader** role with the scope of one ADF instance; these users won't have the same privilege on a different ADF instance.

What if we need to widen our scope: for example, what if we want to grant several users permissions to all Data Factory instances within a certain resource group? We can do this easily: scopes are hierarchical. We just need to assign users to required roles on the resource group level, and these roles will be inherited by every Data Factory instance within that role group. Instead of individually assigning roles to each Data Factory instances, we can assign roles at the resource group level. In a similar fashion, if we assign roles on a subscription or a management group level, this assignment will be valid for all subscriptions within a management group, all resource groups within a subscription, and all resources within a resource group. This hierarchical approach simplifies access management, ensuring consistent permissions across related resources.

By assigning a role to a user or a group of users, you are granting specific levels of access to your Data Factory instances and its resources, which may include confidential data. Always ensure that the level of access aligns with your organization's security and access control policies. As a rule of thumb, users and services should always be granted the minimum level of access or permissions required to perform their tasks, and no more (this rule is called the principle of least privilege).

## There is more...

In this recipe, we walked through assigning a built-in Reader role to several users. What if we need more granular access control, and none of the built-in roles satisfy our requirements?

In this case, we can define a custom role, restricting or granting access to certain resources as needed. For example, we can define a custom role for users who have access similar to **Data Factory Contributor**, but cannot delete a data factory:

1. Log in to the Azure portal, open the resource group or a subscription that contains your Data Factory instances, and select the **Access Control (IAM)** tab.

2. Click on **+Add**, then **Add custom role**. Choose a name for your new role, fill in the description, and choose the **Clone a role** radio button. Select **Data Factory Contributor** as the role to clone.

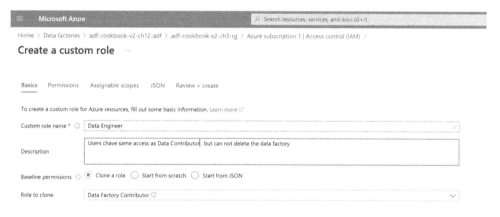

*Figure 12.6: Clone a role*

Click **Next**.

3. On the next screen, click on **+ Exclude permissions**. In the **Exclude permissions** blade, search for the **Microsoft Data Factory** tile, and then click on it. Make sure the **Not Actions** radio button is selected.

4.  Check **Delete : Delete Data Factory**, then click on **Add**.

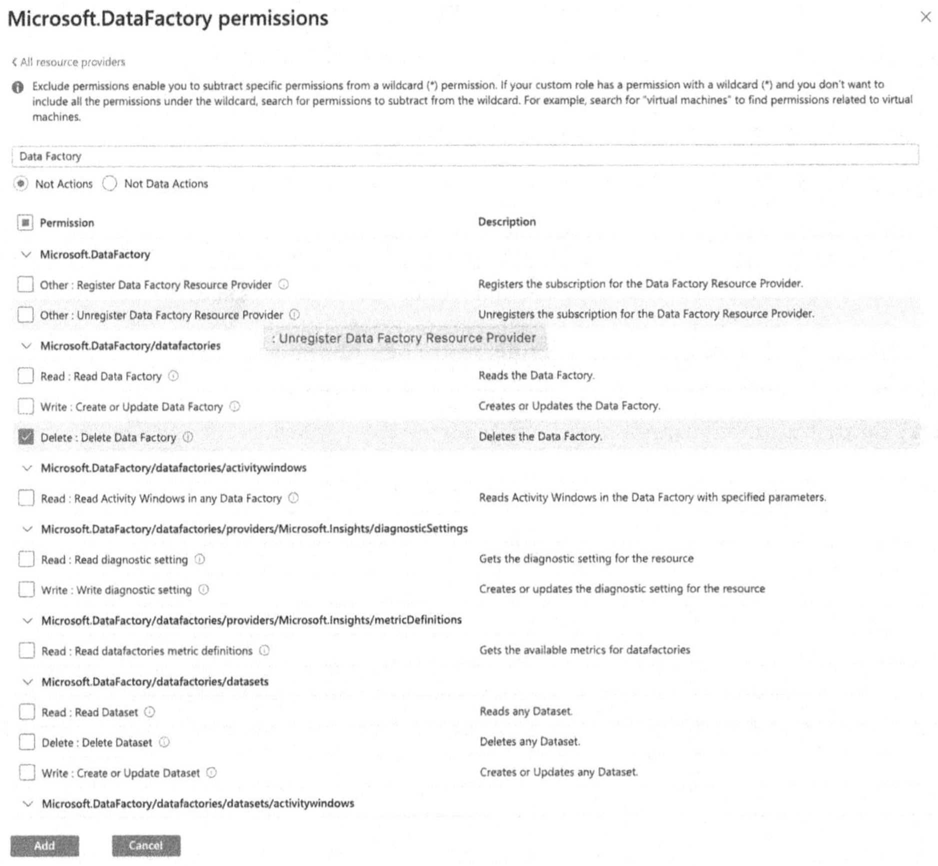

*Figure 12.7: Exclude Delete : Delete Data Factory permission*

You will see a list of granted and excluded permissions. Click **Next**.

5.  On the next screen, you can add or remove scopes for your new role.

6.  Finally, click **Review + create**. After your custom role is validated, click on **Create** and in a few seconds your role will be created.

You can use your custom-defined roles in the same way that you use built-in ones.

# See also

For references on Azure user access administration, it is best to consult documentation prepared and maintained by Microsoft:

- Understanding Azure RBAC: `https://learn.microsoft.com/en-us/azure/role-based-access-control/role-definitions`

- Roles and Permissions for ADF: `https://learn.microsoft.com/en-us/azure/data-factory/concepts-roles-permissions`

- Azure Built-In Role Definitions: `https://learn.microsoft.com/en-us/azure/role-based-access-control/built-in-roles`

# Setting up Meta ETL with ADF

When faced with the task of copying vast amounts of objects, such as thousands of tables, or loading data from a diverse range of sources, an effective approach is to leverage a control table that contains a list of object names along with their required copy behaviors. By employing parameterized pipelines, these object names and behaviors can be read from the control table and applied to the jobs accordingly. "Copy behaviors" refer to the specific actions or configurations associated with copying each object. These behaviors can include parameters such as source and destination locations, data transformation requirements, scheduling preferences, error-handling strategies, and any other settings relevant to the copying process.

Unlike traditional methods that require redeploying pipelines whenever the objects list needs modification (e.g., adding or removing objects), utilizing a control table allows for swift and straightforward updates. Simply updating the object names in the control table is all it takes to reflect the changes, eliminating the need for pipeline redeployment.

Moreover, this method provides a centralized location for monitoring the data copy process. One can easily ascertain which objects have been copied by which pipelines or triggers, along with their defined copy behaviors, all from this single location.

For example, consider a scenario where you need to copy tables from an on-premises SQL Server database to Azure Data Lake Storage. The control table could include columns for the table names, source database connection details, destination storage location, file format preferences, and any required data transformations. Each row in the control table represents a table to be copied, along with its associated copy behaviors. To facilitate this metadata-driven data copy process, ADF's copy data tool offers a seamless and intuitive wizard-based experience. After effortlessly navigating through the flow, the tool generates parameterized pipelines and SQL scripts tailored to create the necessary external control tables. Executing these generated scripts in your SQL database establishes the control table, and your pipelines will automatically read the metadata from it, efficiently applying the specified copy behaviors to the copy jobs.

With ADF's metadata-driven approach, copying data becomes a breeze, allowing you to focus on harnessing the insights derived from your data rather than wrestling with the complexities of data movement.

Experience the ease and efficiency of metadata-driven data copy pipelines with ADF today!

## Getting ready

Before getting started with the recipe, log in to your Microsoft Azure account.

We assume you have a pre-configured resource group and storage account with Azure Data Lake Gen2, ADF, and **Azure SQL Database**:

- In **Azure SQL Database**, you will need to have MovieLens CSV files to be loaded to the dbo schema with the following table names: dbo.movielens_links, dbo.movielens_movies, dbo.movielens_ratings, and dbo.movielens_tags. You can refer to *Chapter 4*, and the *Integrate Azure Data Lake and run Spark Pool jobs* recipe for additional details.

- In Azure Data Lake Gen2, you will need a curated container created under your storage account.

- In ADF, you will need to configure LS_SQL_IngestionConfiguration – linked service to your Azure SQL Database, and LS_ADLS_Ingest – linked service to your Azure Data Lake Gen2.

## How to do it...

We will go through the process of creating metadata ETL using the Azure portal and its web interface. Follow these instructions:

1. Go to the **Home** screen of Azure Data Factory, and click **Ingest.**

2. In the opened window, select **Metadata-driven copy task** for **Task type.**

3. In **Control table data store**, select the **LS_SQL_IngestionConfiguration** linked service, created earlier.

4. Now click **Create new table** and choose the name for your control table – dbo. MainControlTable. For **Task cadence** or task schedule, select **Run once now.** You will see the following **picture.** Then click **Next.**

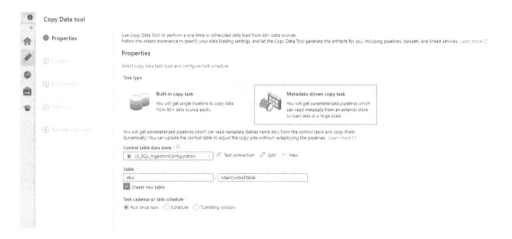

*Figure 12.8: Configure metadata-driven copy task*

5.  Select **Azure SQL Database** for **Source type**. Choose the previously created **LS_SQL_IngestionConfiguration** linked service in **Connection**. In **Select tables from which to copy the data**, select the **movielens tables** in **dbo schema: dbo.movielens_links, dbo.movielens_movies, dbo.movielens_ratings**, and **dbo.movielens_tags**. You will see the following:

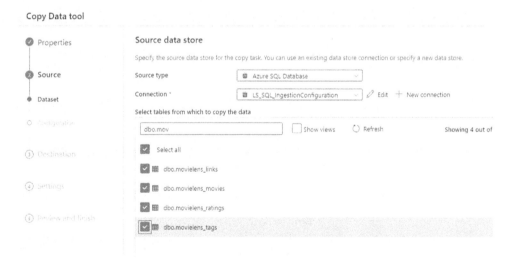

*Figure 12.9: Configure source dataset*

6.  Click **Next**. For **Choose loading behavior**, select **Full load all tables**.

7.  Click **Next**. In **Destination data store**, choose **Destination type** as **Azure Data Lake Storage Gen2,** and choose the previously created **LS_ADLS_Ingest** linked service for **Connection.** Choose the **.CSV** file name suffix. Your screen should look like the following:

*Figure 12.10: Configure destination dataset*

8.  Click **Next**. In **File format settings,** set **File format** as **DelimitedText, Column delimiter** as **Comma, Row delimiter** as **Default,** and select **First row as header**. Your screen should look like the following:

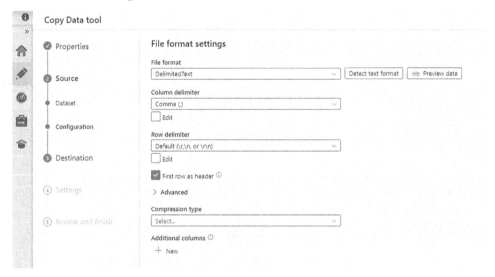

*Figure 12.11: Configure file format settings*

9.  Click **Next**. In **Settings,** set the prefix for your pipelines and datasets in Azure Data Factory as **Metadata_.** Your screen should look like the following:

## Copy Data tool

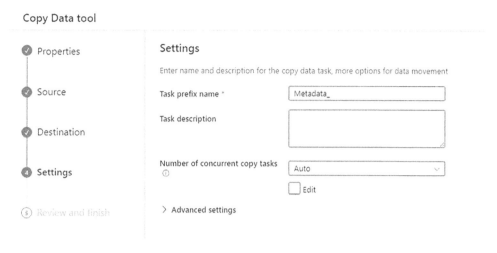

*Figure 12.12: Configure copy data tool settings*

10. Click **Next**. You will see the following **picture** with the **create table** script generated for **MainControlTable**. Copy the script and paste it into **SQL Server Management Studio**, and execute it. The script will create a **dbo.MainControlTable** table in your Azure SQL database and insert all settings information.

*Figure 12.13: Copy the generated SQL script*

11. Now, go to your Data Factory instance. You can see that there are three new datasets and three new pipelines created with the **Metadata_** prefix, as follows:

*Figure 12.14: Find TopLevel pipeline*

12. Debug the **TopLevel** metadata pipeline. Once it succeeds, go to your storage account under the **curated/movielens** folder and check that data from SQL tables has been copied to CSV files in this folder.

*Figure 12.15: Contents of the target folder*

## How it works...

Metadata ETL is designed to make data ingestion flexible, scalable, and easy to maintain:

- The main control table serves as the cornerstone of this metadata-driven approach. It's essentially a central repository for storing crucial metadata about the data copy operation. This table is often hosted in a database, and it plays a pivotal role in orchestrating the data movement process:

*Figure 12.16: Contents of main control table*

- **Source and target metadata**: The main control table contains information about the source (**Azure SQL Database**) and the target (**Azure Data Lake Storage Gen2**). This includes table names, schema definitions, and details about the destination path for CSV files.

- **Mapping instructions**: It holds mapping instructions, describing how data from the source database should be transformed and mapped to the structure of the target CSV files. These mappings specify how each column from the source should be represented in the CSV files.

- **Schedule and trigger information**: The control table may also include scheduling or triggering instructions. This enables you to automate and schedule the data copy pipeline, ensuring data is regularly synchronized according to your requirements.

- There are three pipelines created by the copy data tool:

  - **Metadata_xxx_TopLevel**: In this pipeline, the objective is to determine the total count of objects (such as tables, etc.) that need to be copied during the current run. Subsequently, it calculates the number of sequential batches based on the maximum concurrent copy task limit. After this computation, it initiates the execution of another pipeline responsible for copying these batches sequentially.

  - **Metadata_xxx_ MiddleLevel**: This particular pipeline is designed for the task of copying a single batch of objects. The objects within this batch will be processed concurrently, allowing for efficient and parallel copying.

- **Metadata_xxx_ BottomLevel**: This pipeline is dedicated to copying objects from a specific group. Within this group, the objects will be copied concurrently, ensuring an efficient parallel copy process.

- There are three datasets created by the copy data tool:

  - **Metadata_xxx_ControlDS**: This is a dataset related to data in the main control table (**dbo.MainControlTable** from **Azure SQL Database**).

  - **Metadata_xxx_DestinationDS**: This is a dataset related to data in **Sink** of the copy activity; in our case, it is a CSV file in **Azure Data Lake Storage Gen2**.

  - **Metadata_xxx_SourceDS**: This is a dataset related to data in **Source** of the copy activity; in our case, it is a table in **Azure SQL Database**.

In summary, the metadata-driven approach in the **copy data tool** of **Azure Data Factory** is a powerful method for efficiently copying data from **Azure SQL Database** to **Azure Data Lake Storage Gen2**. It revolves around the central control table, which houses metadata, and utilizes pipelines and datasets to execute the data copy tasks while maintaining flexibility, automation, and data accuracy.

## There's more...

Microsoft documentation on *Builing large-scale data copy pipelines with a metadata-driven approach with the copy data tool*: https://learn.microsoft.com/en-us/azure/data-factory/copy-data-tool-metadata-driven

# Leveraging ADF scalability: Performance tuning of an ADF pipeline

Due to its serverless architecture, ADF is inherently scalable, dynamically adjusting its resource allocation to meet workload demands without the need for users to manage physical servers. This flexible architecture offers users various techniques to enhance the performance of their data pipelines.

One approach for improving performance involves harnessing the power of parallelism, such as incorporating a **ForEach** activity into your pipelines. The ForEach activity allows for the parallel processing of data by iterating over a collection of items, executing a specified set of activities for each item in parallel. This can significantly reduce overall execution time, especially when dealing with large datasets or when multiple independent tasks can be processed concurrently.

For example, suppose you have a pipeline that needs to process data from multiple files stored in Azure Blob Storage. By using a ForEach activity to iterate over each file and performing data processing tasks in parallel, you can achieve faster processing times compared to processing each file sequentially. This parallel execution maximizes resource utilization and minimizes idle time, ultimately improving pipeline performance.

In this recipe, we'll demonstrate an approach to improve pipeline performance by optimizing source and sink data stores and scaling up compute resources, while also highlighting the benefits of incorporating a ForEach activity for parallel processing.

## Getting ready

To work on this recipe, we will need an instance of a Microsoft SQL server and two databases: a source database, populated with sample data, and a target, or sink, database, where we'll store the results.

Follow the steps below to create the necessary infrastructure:

1. Log in to the Azure portal, navigate to `https://portal.azure.com/#create/Microsoft.SQLDatabase`, and create an instance of an Azure SQL database. You may need to create an SQL server to host your database as well if you do not have one already. Make sure to enable SQL authentication on your SQL server, and take note of the admin username and password that you select: we shall need this information later.

2. When you create your source database, populate it with sample data: when filling out parameters such as name, region, and so on, in the **Additional settings** tab, under **Use existing data**, select **Sample** as shown in the following screenshot:

*Figure 12.17: Populate a new database with Sample data*

3.  Create another database on the same database server. Do not populate it with any data. This is our archive database.

4.  Open your archive MS SQL database in the Azure portal, and navigate to **Query editor** on the left. You will need to log in with your SQL authentication admin username and password, which was saved in *step 1*.

*Figure 12.18: Log in to Query Editor*

In Query Editor, create an archive schema and a product table by running the following script:

```
CREATE SCHEMA [Archive];

GO

CREATE TABLE [Archive].[Product](
    [ProductID] [int] IDENTITY(1,1) NOT NULL,
    [Name] [nvarchar](37) NOT NULL,
    [ModelName] [nvarchar](100) NOT NULL,
    [Culture] [nchar](6) NOT NULL,
    [Description] [nvarchar](400) NOT NULL,
     CONSTRAINT [PK_Product_ProductID] PRIMARY KEY CLUSTERED
    (
        [ProductID] ASC
    )WITH (PAD_INDEX = OFF, STATISTICS_NORECOMPUTE = OFF, IGNORE_
DUP_KEY = OFF, ALLOW_ROW_LOCKS - ON, ALLOW_PAGE_LOCKS = ON,
OPTIMIZE_FOR_SEQUENTIAL_KEY - OFF) ON [PRIMARY],
    CONSTRAINT [AK_Product_Name] UNIQUE NONCLUSTERED
    (
        [Name] ASC
    )WITH (PAD_INDEX = OFF, STATISTICS_NORECOMPUTE = OFF, IGNORE_
DUP_KEY = OFF, ALLOW_ROW_LOCKS = ON, ALLOW_PAGE_LOCKS = ON,
OPTIMIZE_FOR_SEQUENTIAL_KEY = OFF) ON [PRIMARY],
    CONSTRAINT [AK_Product_ModelNumber] UNIQUE NONCLUSTERED
    (
        [ModelName] ASC
    )WITH (PAD_INDEX = OFF, STATISTICS_NORECOMPUTE = OFF, IGNORE_
DUP_KEY = OFF, ALLOW_ROW_LOCKS = ON, ALLOW_PAGE_LOCKS = ON,
OPTIMIZE_FOR_SEQUENTIAL_KEY = OFF) ON [PRIMARY],
    CONSTRAINT [AK_Product_Description] UNIQUE NONCLUSTERED
    (
        [Description] ASC
    )WITH (PAD_INDEX = OFF, STATISTICS_NORECOMPUTE = OFF, IGNORE_
DUP_KEY = OFF, ALLOW_ROW_LOCKS = ON, ALLOW_PAGE_LOCKS = ON,
OPTIMIZE_FOR_SEQUENTIAL_KEY = OFF) ON [PRIMARY]
    ) ON [PRIMARY]
    GO

    SET IDENTITY_INSERT [Archive].[Product] ON;
```

You can download the script at `https://github.com/PacktPublishing/Azure-Data-Factory-Cookbook-Second-Edition/blob/main/Chapter12/scripts create_archive_table.sql`.

5.  Download the `ArchiveProductAndDescription` file from `https://github.com/PacktPublishing/Azure-Data-Factory-Cookbook-Second-Edition/blob/main/Chapter12/templates/ArchiveProductAndDescription.zip`.

## How to do it...

In this recipe, we shall create a pipeline to transform and archive sales data utilizing a mapping data flow. The pipeline ingests data from several tables, performs several joins and projects necessary fields, and finally writes results into the destination table in the "archive database." We shall first run this pipeline with default settings and then apply changes to the source, compute, and sink components of the pipeline to improve its efficiency:

1.  Open your instance of **Azure Data Factory Studio** and go to the **Author** tab. Under **Factory Resources**, click on the plus sign (**+**) to add a resource, select **Pipeline**, and then choose **Import from pipeline template**:

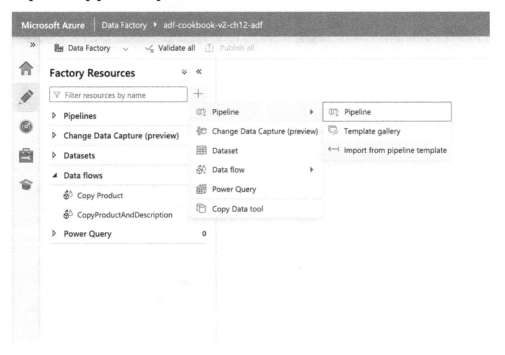

*Figure 12.19: Create a pipeline from the template*

Select the `ArchiveProductAndDescription.zip` file, which you downloaded from GitHub (see the *Getting Ready* section, *step 5*). Create the two linked services (one for the source database, and another one for the database that will store the archived data) to fill in the inputs, then click on the **Use this template** button. This will create the data flow with all required transformations as well as the pipeline using this data flow.

2. Publish your changes and run your pipeline several times. After the run is completed, navigate to the **Monitor** tab and take note of the average duration of the pipeline:

*Figure 12.20: Pipeline runs status*

Here, you can see that the pipeline took about 3 minutes and 30 seconds to complete (your time might differ; this will depend on many factors).

3. Go back to the **Author** tab and open your pipeline. In the **Settings** tab of the **Configuration** panel, change **Compute size** to **Large**.

4. Next, open your data flow, and select the first source transformation, **AdventureWorksProduct**. In the **Source options** tab of the **Configuration panel**, select **Read uncommitted**. Do this for all four sources.

5. Finally, select the **sink** transformation **Archive**. In the **Settings** tab, add a **Pre SQL Script** (note that one **Pre SQL Script is** already present – do not delete it!), and enter the following text:

```
ALTER INDEX ALL ON [Archive].[Product] DISABLE
```

6. Next, add a **Post SQL Script**, and enter the following code:

```
ALTER INDEX ALL ON [Archive].[Product] REBUILD
```

Your **Settings** tab should look similar to the following screenshot:

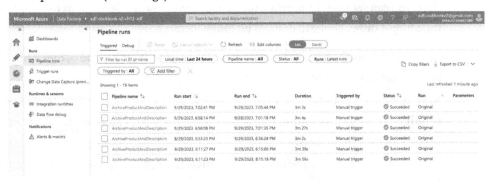

*Figure 12.21: Pre-and Post-SQL scripts*

7.  Publish your changes, trigger the pipeline again, and run it several times. You should see an improvement (on average) of 15-30 seconds.

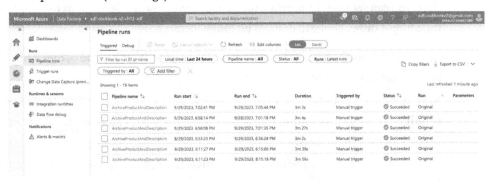

*Figure 12.22: Optimized runs*

## How it works...

In this recipe, we worked with a pipeline that used a mapping data flow to load data from four tables (**Product, ProductModel, ProductModelProductDescription**, and **ProductDescription**), perform several joins, and write the resulting dataset into the table in the "archive" database (the sink transformation we named **Archive**).

When we ran the pipeline, we used default settings, which use generic, non-optimized values. We started to optimize by updating the settings on the source transformations: we changed the isolation level on every source table from **Read committed** to **Read uncommitted**. In other words, we allowed ADF to perform "dirty" reads: reads on rows written by other transactions but not committed yet. By doing this, we optimize read performance on the source tables and avoid database locks.

Next, we updated the **Compute** layer of the pipeline by updating **Compute size** of the Spark cluster on which the pipeline is running. By default, the pipeline was configured to run on **Small** compute: a general-purpose Spark cluster with four cores. We changed the setting to run the pipeline on a **Large** cluster – this is a **memory-optimized** Spark cluster with 16 CPU cores. By doing this, we not only increased processing power but also minimized out-of-memory exceptions that might occur when data is being processed.

Finally, we optimized the **sink** performance (the archive database) by temporarily disabling indexes on the destination table.

NOTE

While indexes are disabled, database queries will experience degradation of performance or might fail completely. If you use this optimization, make sure that your pipelines run when tables with disabled indexes are not used by other applications.

## There is more...

There are many ways to optimize performance, and your approach will depend on the kind of pipeline you are running, what activities you use, what data stores you have for sources and sinks, and so on. The possibilities are endless; however, there are always four main components of optimization:

- Cluster startup time
- Ingestion (source layer)
- Compute layer
- Write (sink layer)

When you are faced with the task of improving the performance of a pipeline, start by creating a baseline load – a pipeline that mimics the most common use case for a data store, data partitioning, size, and type of data.

Once you run this baseline pipeline, you can examine the execution and performance report for your pipeline's activities to determine the bottlenecks (as described in *Chapter 10*, *Monitoring and Troubleshooting Data Pipelines*, in the *Investigating failures – running in debug mode* recipe). This investigation will help you to focus your optimization on the components where faster processing will benefit the most.

Optimization efforts need to find a balance between optimizing for time and cost: it is easy to incur additional charges by increasing DIUs and compute size. Costs add up quickly, and the optimal balance is ultimately determined by business needs.

## See also

Every pipeline is different and will require its own analysis and approach to performance optimization. Refer to the following guides for general guides to performance improvement:

- https://learn.microsoft.com/en-us/azure/data-factory/copy-activity-performance
- https://learn.microsoft.com/en-us/azure/data-factory/concepts-data-flow-performance

# Using ADF disaster recovery built-in features

ADF provides organizations with the tools they need to effortlessly create, schedule, and oversee data pipelines, facilitating the seamless movement and transformation of data. Maintaining data availability and keeping downtime to a minimum are pivotal aspects of preserving business operations. In this recipe, we'll guide you through the process of designing a disaster recovery solution for your ADF as the ETL/ELT engine for data movement and transformation.

## Getting ready

Before we start, please ensure that you have an Azure subscription and are familiar with the basics of Azure resources such as the Azure portal, creating and deleting Azure resources, and creating pipelines in ADF.

## How to do it...

Before diving into disaster recovery planning, it's crucial to understand that ADF is a **Platform-as-a-Service (PaaS)** offering by Azure. Azure PaaS provides a ready-to-develop and deploy infrastructure, including systems, storage, networks, and development tools, fully managed by Microsoft Azure. Users don't need to worry about system maintenance or upgrades.

Azure provides **Business Continuity and Disaster Recovery (BCDR)** guidelines for ADF, defining **Recovery Point Objective (RPO)** and **Recovery Time Objective (RTO)**. RPO is the amount of potentially acceptable data loss, while RTO is the time it takes to recover from a disaster.

Azure's RPO & RTO for ADF are available 24/7 and guaranteed at least 99.9% availability, backed by a financial SLA.

Manual failover is necessary when the default ADF settings do not meet your organization's **ADF instance**. It gives you control over the failover process to meet your specific requirements. To initiate the manual failover, follow these steps:

1. To ensure that the ETL metadata is up to date in source control, it is essential to follow the required process. If this has not been completed yet, you can refer to the instructions provided in the first recipe, *Setting up Azure DevOps*, located in *Chapter 9*.

2. To get started, let's provision a new ADF instance in the target region. Begin by navigating to the Azure portal and creating a new ADF instance in the nearest available region to your data. For enhanced disaster recovery capabilities, it's advisable to select the paired region. You can find the list of available regions by following this link: `https://learn.microsoft.com/en-us/azure/reliability/cross-region-replication-azure#azure-cross-region-replication-pairings-for-all-geographies`

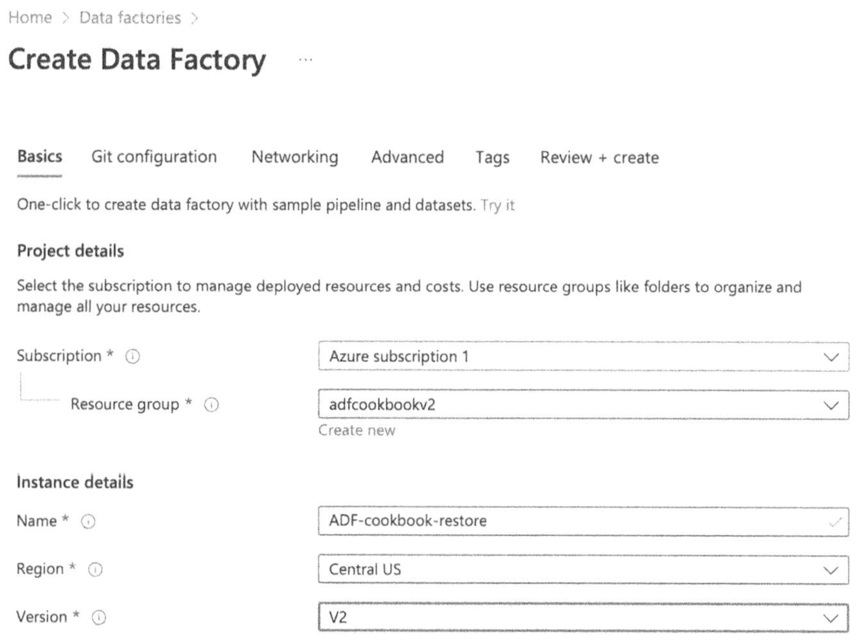

Home > Data factories >

## Create Data Factory  ...

| Basics | Git configuration | Networking | Advanced | Tags | Review + create |

One-click to create data factory with sample pipeline and datasets. Try it

**Project details**

Select the subscription to manage deployed resources and costs. Use resource groups like folders to organize and manage all your resources.

Subscription *  ⓘ      Azure subscription 1

Resource group *  ⓘ      adfcookbookv2
       Create new

**Instance details**

Name *  ⓘ      ADF-cookbook-restore

Region *  ⓘ      Central US

Version *  ⓘ      V2

*Figure 12.23: Creating a new data factory in the paring region*

3.  Next, we'll proceed with restoring ADF data from source control. In order to replicate your ADF configurations and retrieve the ETL metadata along with monitoring data, which includes pipeline, trigger, and activity runs, you have to access ADF Studio and set up a connection to your existing repository within DevOps Git. This will allow you to seamlessly access and restore your ADF.

## Configure a repository

⌖  Default Directory (b269e661-3fcc-4f34-8ac4-a32126dce250)

Specify the settings that you want to use when connecting to your repository.

◉ Select repository    ○ Use repository link

**Azure DevOps organization name** * ⓘ

| adfcookbook2ed | ⌄ |
|---|---|

**Project name** * ⓘ

| ADF DevOps | ⌄ |
|---|---|

**Repository name** * ⓘ

| ADF DevOps | ⌄ |
|---|---|

**Collaboration branch** * ⓘ

| master | ⌄ |
|---|---|

**Publish branch** * ⓘ

| adf_publish | ⌄ |
|---|---|

**Root folder** * ⓘ

| / |
|---|

**Custom comment**
☑ Use custom comment

**Import existing resources**
☐ Import existing resources to repository

[ Apply ]  [ Back ]  [ Cancel ]

*Figure 12.24: Setting up connections to an existing DevOps Git repository*

4.  The next step is to address **Integration Runtimes (IRs)** so that IRs that are not set to auto-resolve manually update to paired regions to ensure data movement and transformation capabilities are maintained.

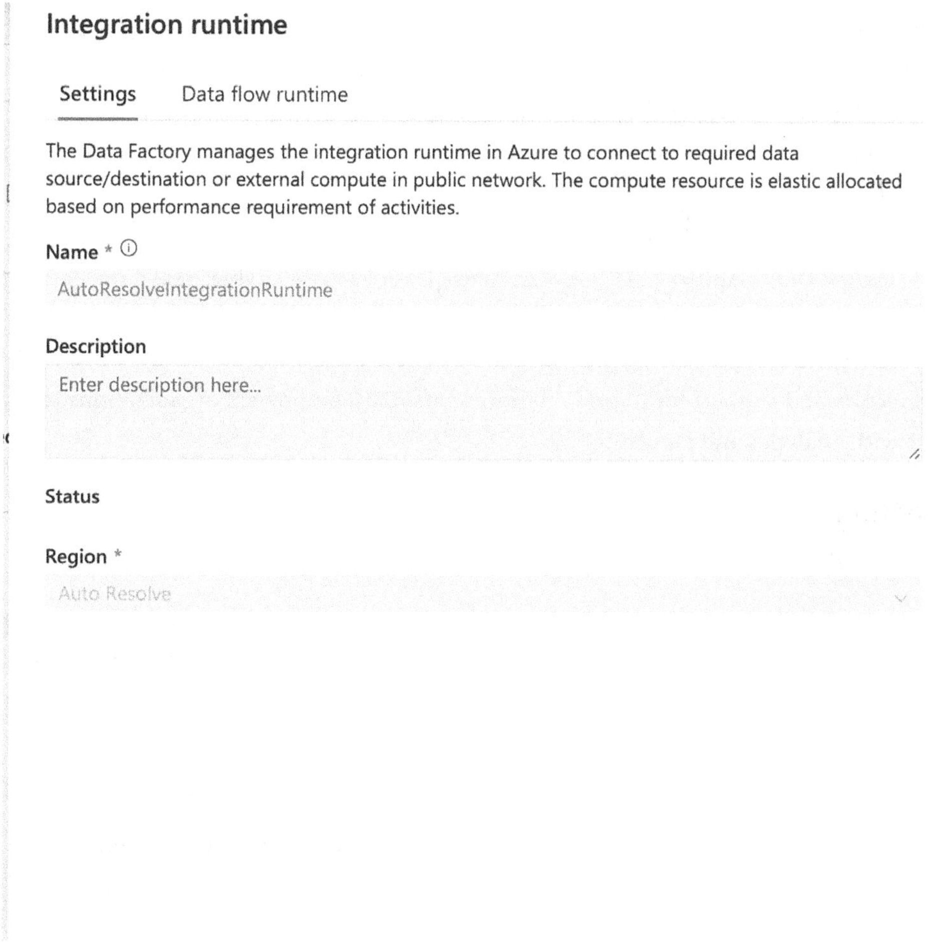

## Integration runtime

**Settings**     Data flow runtime

The Data Factory manages the integration runtime in Azure to connect to required data source/destination or external compute in public network. The compute resource is elastic allocated based on performance requirement of activities.

**Name** * ⓘ

AutoResolveIntegrationRuntime

**Description**

Enter description here...

**Status**

**Region** *

Auto Resolve

*Figure 12.25: Integration runtime*

5.  During the failover process, be vigilant and consider the following:

    - ETL pipeline schedules might not initiate immediately or could experience delays and interruptions.

    - After completing the user-initiated manual failover, restart ETL scheduled triggers.

    - Ensure your ETL designs account for adequate restart ability and data loss prevention. ETL pipelines should resume from the last successful run that occurred before the disaster recovery failover.

## How it works...

Manual failover in ADF allows you to take control of the disaster recovery process. By provisioning a new ADF instance in a suitable region and automating this process, you minimize downtime and speed up the recovery. Keeping ETL metadata in source control ensures that your configurations are readily available while restoring data from source control replicates your ADF setup. Addressing IRs and monitoring the failover process helps ensure a seamless transition. This approach helps maintain business continuity and minimize data loss during unexpected incidents.

# Change Data Capture

The **Change Data Capture (CDC)** tool in **Azure Data Factory** enables real-time data synchronization by efficiently tracking and capturing only the changed data. It optimizes data integration workflows, reduces processing time, and ensures data consistency across systems. With built-in connectors and support for hybrid environments, **CDC** empowers organizations to stay up to date with analytics and reporting.

## Getting ready

Before getting started with the recipe, log in to your Microsoft Azure account.

We assume you have a pre-configured resource group and storage account with **Azure Data Lake Gen2**, **Azure Data Factory**, and **Azure SQL Database**. To set these up, please refer to *Chapter 1, Getting Started with ADF*, and the *Creating and executing our first job in ADF* recipe.

- In **Azure SQL Database**, you will need to have movielens CSV files to be loaded to the **dbo** schema with the following table name: `dbo.movielens_ratings`.

- In **Azure Data Lake Gen2**, you will need a **curated** container created under your storage account.

- In **Azure Data Factory**, you will need to configure **LS_SQL_IngestionConfiguration** – linked service to **Azure SQL Database,** and **LS_ADLS_Ingest** – linked service to Azure Data Lake Gen2.

- You will need to have **SQL Server Management Studio** installed and connected to **Azure SQL Database.**

- As the Incremental column in **CDC** should be in DATETIME format, please add a new column to your dbo.movielens_ratings table with the following SQL script from **SQL Server Management Studio:**

```
ALTER TABLE dbo.movielens_ratings
ADD ConvertedDate DATETIME;

UPDATE dbo.movielens_ratings
SET ConvertedDate = DATEADD(SECOND, CAST(unix_timestamp AS INT),
'19700101');
```

## How to do it...

1.  Open **Azure Data Factory**, go to **Author**, choose **Change Data Capture**, and select **New CDC**.

2.  Name the CDC tool **adfcdc1**. Set **Source type** as **Azure SQL Database**, and **Source linked service** as **LS_SQL_IngestionConfiguration**. Search for the **dbo.movielens_ratings** table, select the table, and in **Incremental column**, choose **ConvertedDate**. You will see the **picture** as follows.

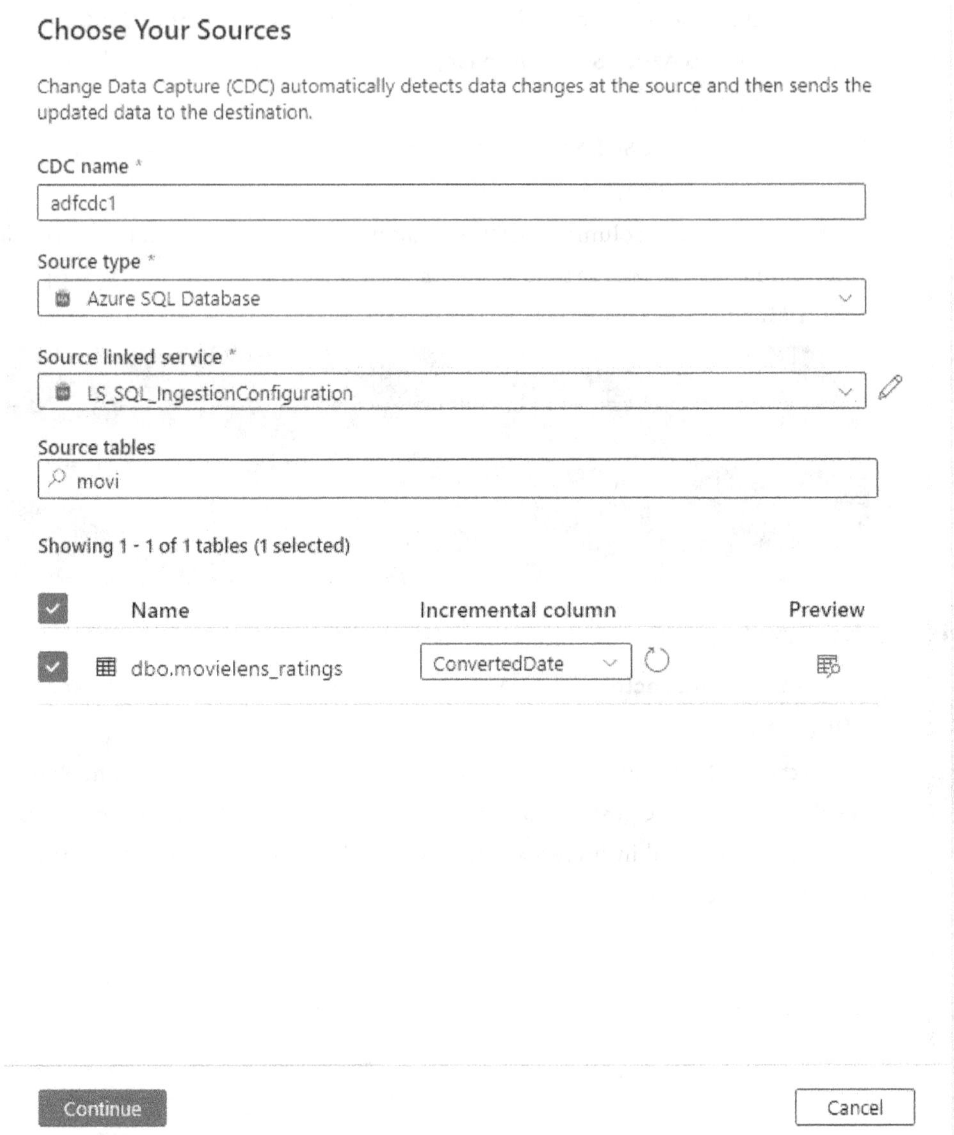

## Choose Your Sources

Change Data Capture (CDC) automatically detects data changes at the source and then sends the updated data to the destination.

CDC name *

adfcdc1

Source type *

🖬 Azure SQL Database                                              ⌄

Source linked service *

🖬 LS_SQL_IngestionConfiguration                                  ⌄    ✎

Source tables

🔍 movi

Showing 1 - 1 of 1 tables (1 selected)

| ✓ | Name | Incremental column | Preview |
|---|------|--------------------|---------|
| ✓ | ⊞ dbo.movielens_ratings | ConvertedDate ⌄ ↻ | ⧉ |

Continue                                                           Cancel

*Figure 12.26: Configure Change Data Capture source*

3.  Click **Continue**, and in the next window, set **Target type** as **Delta** and **Target linked service** as **LS_ADLS_Ingest**. In **Target base path**, choose **curated**, and specify curated/ cdc/dbo.movielens_ratings as in the following figure:

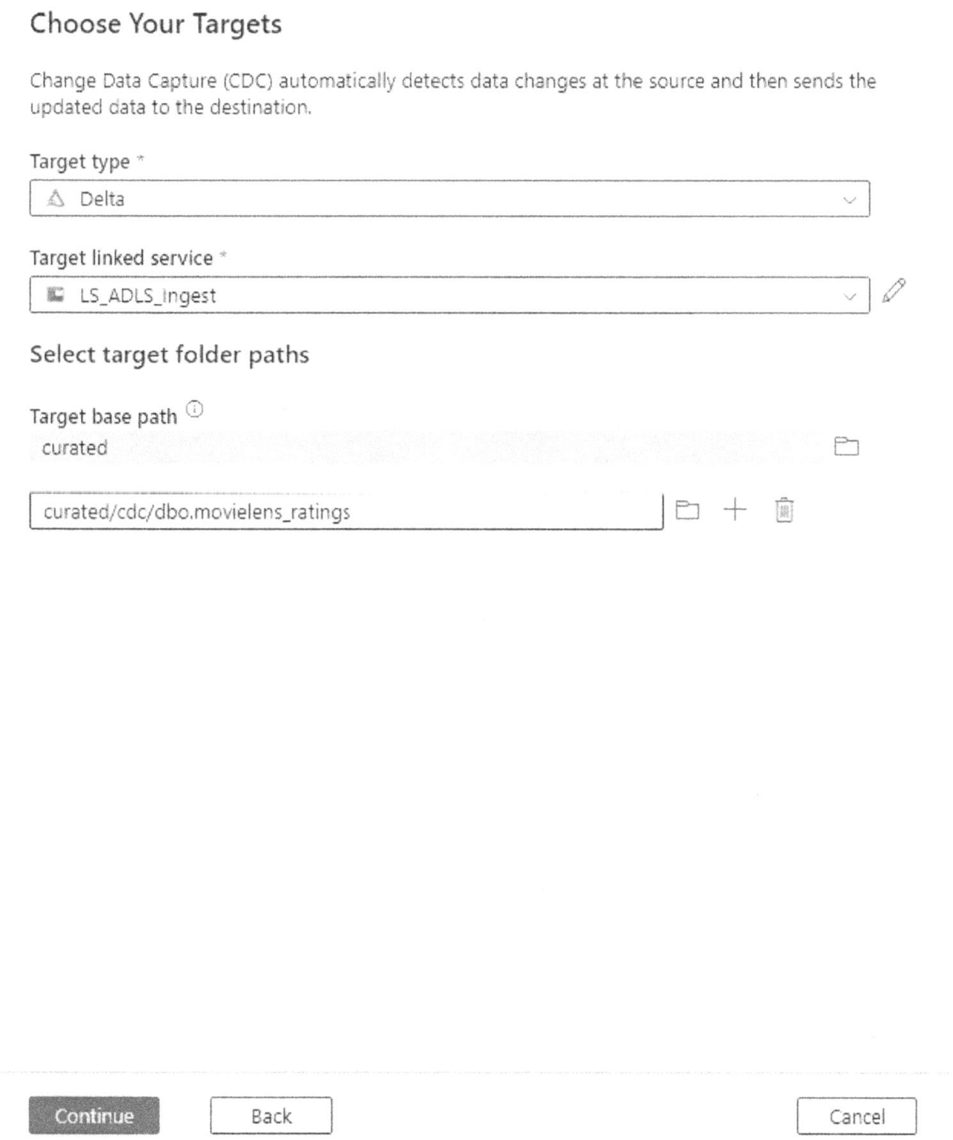

## Choose Your Targets

Change Data Capture (CDC) automatically detects data changes at the source and then sends the updated data to the destination.

Target type *

△ Delta

Target linked service *

▣ LS_ADLS_ingest

### Select target folder paths

Target base path ⓘ

curated

curated/cdc/dbo.movielens_ratings

Continue    Back    Cancel

*Figure 12.27: Configure Change Data Capture target*

4. Click **Continue**. A new window with the source and target will be opened. Choose the **Auto-map** option. Click on **Set Latency** and choose **Real-time** as in the following figure.

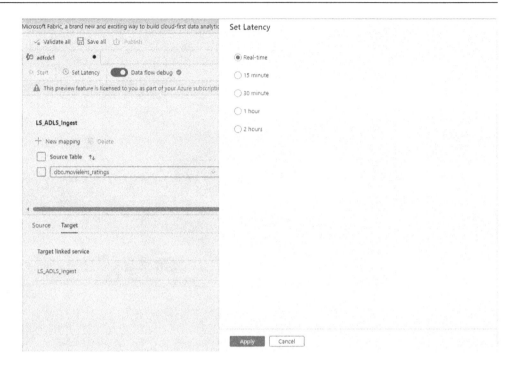

*Figure 12.28: Setting latency of Change Data Capture*

5.  Click **Apply** and then **Publish all**. Click **Start** to start the Change Data Capture. It will constantly update the target from the source in real time.

6.  Now, you can monitor how the changes are being captured. Let's go to **SQL Server Management Studio**, connect to your database, and update and insert new records in dbo. movielens_ratings with the following SQL script:

```sql
UPDATE [dbo].[movielens_ratings]
SET ConvertedDate = GETDATE()
WHERE movieId = 2

INSERT INTO [dbo].[movielens_ratings] (userId, movieId, rating,
timestamp, ConvertedDate)
VALUES
(1, 2, 4.0, 964982703, GETDATE()),
(12, 4, 4.0, 964981247, GETDATE()),
(1, 5, 4.0, 964982224, GETDATE()),
(13, 67, 5.0, 964983815, GETDATE()),
(1, 12, 5.0, 964982931, GETDATE()),
(1, 34, 3.0, 964982400, GETDATE())
```

7. Go to the **Monitor** page of **Azure Data Factory**, select **Change Data Capture**, then click on **adfcdc1**. You will see the graph showing changes read from the source and written to the target as follows.

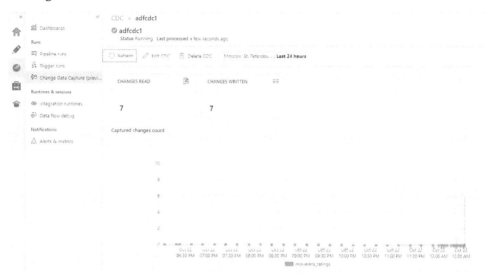

*Figure 12.29: Monitor Change Data Capture*

8. Navigate to your storage account and select a curated container and the **cdc/dbo.movielens_ratings** folder. You will see the delta files with two partitions: one for update, and one for insert as follows.

*Figure 12.30: Checking the ADLS Gen2 folder*

# How it works...

The innovative **Change Data Capture** resource in **Azure Data Factory** introduces a robust solution for capturing data changes with precision and efficiency. This resource operates seamlessly, providing near real-time **CDC** capabilities through an intuitive configuration process.

As you leverage **CDCs** in your data workflows, the billing model is transparent and straightforward, with charges associated with the utilization of four v-cores within the general-purpose data flows.

One of the standout features of this **CDC** resource is its real-time latency, which constantly monitors your source data, swiftly detecting changes in intervals of less than a minute. This ensures that your data changes are promptly identified and processed, allowing for timely and informed decision-making.

Additionally, for scenarios where a different latency threshold is preferred, such as a 15-minute interval, the CDC resource remains adaptable. In such cases, it efficiently processes your source data and captures any modifications that have occurred since the last processing cycle, accommodating various data synchronization requirements. This adaptability ensures that your **CDC** process aligns precisely with your specific needs and time constraints, all within the **Azure Data Factory** environment.

## There is more...

- Microsoft documentation on *Change data capture in Azure Data Factory and Azure Synapse Analytics*: `https://learn.microsoft.com/en-us/azure/data-factory/concepts-change-data-capture`.
- Microsoft documentation on *Capture changed data from Azure Data Lake Storage Gen2 to Azure SQL Database by using a change data capture resource*: `https://learn.microsoft.com/en-us/azure/data-factory/how-to-change-data-capture-resource`.

# Managing Data Factory costs with FinOps

Data Factory is a crucial service for data processing in Azure, but managing its costs effectively is essential to avoid unexpected expenses.

FinOps is a set of practices and principles that help organizations manage their cloud costs efficiently. It involves collaboration between finance, IT, and business teams to optimize cloud spending, allocate costs accurately, and drive accountability. The goal of FinOps is to strike a balance between cost optimization and enabling cloud innovation.

Examples of applying FinOps principles to ADF include:

- **Resource Right-sizing:**: Analyze the compute resources used by your Data Factory pipelines and adjust them based on actual workload requirements. For instance, if certain pipelines consistently underutilize resources, consider downsizing the compute instances to save costs.

- **Schedule Optimization**: Leverage Data Factory's scheduling capabilities to run pipelines during off-peak hours or when compute resources are less expensive. This ensures efficient use of resources and reduces costs associated with running pipelines during peak times.

- **Monitoring and Alerting**: Set up monitoring and alerting mechanisms to track Data Factory usage and costs in real time. This allows you to identify any unexpected spikes in usage or costs and take proactive measures to address them.

- **Cost Allocation**: Implement tagging and cost allocation strategies to accurately attribute Data Factory costs to specific projects or departments. This helps in identifying areas of overspending and optimizing resource usage accordingly.

- **Reserved Capacity**: Consider purchasing reserved capacity for Data Factory compute resources if you have predictable workload patterns. This can lead to significant cost savings compared to pay-as-you-go pricing models.

By incorporating these practices into your ADF management strategy, you can effectively optimize costs while ensuring the smooth operation of your data workflows.

This recipe will guide you through the process of using **FinOps (Financial Operations)** principles to manage and optimize your ADF costs with practical examples.

By implementing these best practices, you can maintain control over your expenses while ensuring your data workflows run smoothly.

## Getting ready

Before we start, please ensure that you have an Azure subscription and are familiar with the basics of Azure resources such as the Azure portal, creating and deleting Azure resources, and creating pipelines in ADF.

## How to do it...

In this recipe, we will explore how to apply FinOps principles to effectively manage costs within ADF:

1. Before you begin using ADF, it's advisable to calculate the estimated costs. You can do this by utilizing the ADF pricing calculator: `https://azure.microsoft.com/en-us/pricing/calculator/?service=data-factory`.

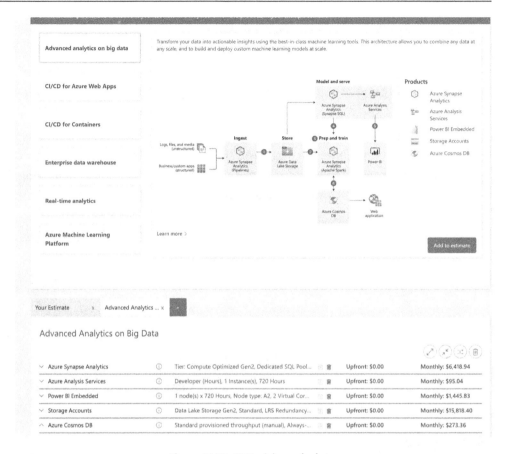

*Figure 12.31: ADF pricing calculator*

2.  Before you can manage your actual Data Factory costs, you need to understand where the costs are coming from. Use Azure Cost Management and Billing to analyze your consumption. Follow these steps:

    1.  Log in to the Azure portal.

    2.  Navigate to **Cost Management + Billing**.

3. Review your cost data to identify which resources are consuming the most resources and incurring the highest costs.

*Figure 12.32: Cost Management + Billing dashboard*

3. Sometimes, you might require a more detailed breakdown of operational costs within your ADF instance. It can provide a precise breakdown of billing charges for each individual pipeline. To activate the per-pipeline detailed billing feature, follow these steps:

- Navigate to the Azure portal.
- In the **Manage** tab, locate **Factory settings** within the **General** section.
- Select **Show billing report by pipeline**.
- Publish the changes to enable per-pipeline detailed billing for your factory.

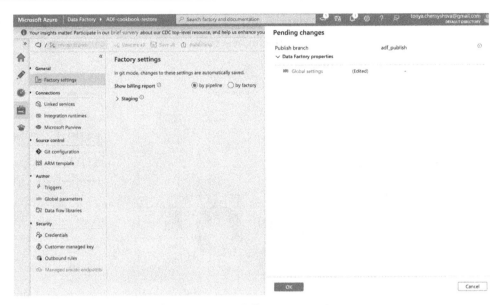

*Figure 12.33: ADF billing report settings*

After activating this feature, your billing report will provide distinct entries for each pipe-line. This detailed breakdown displays the precise cost associated with each pipeline during the selected time frame. It empowers you to track spending patterns and quickly identify any instances of overspending, should they arise.

4.   You can set up cost tracking for services and enable cost tracking specifically for your Data Factory resources. You can use tags to help identify different projects, teams, or environ-ments within your Data Factory instance. This allows for more granular cost tracking and allocation.

  •   Go to your Data Factory resource in the Azure portal.

  •   Navigate to the **Tags** section and add relevant tags to your Data Factory resources.

  •   Tags might include project names, environments, or department codes.

*Figure 12.34: Add tags to ADF*

5.  Setting up a budget is a fundamental step in FinOps. It helps you establish a spending limit and ensures you're not exceeding your allocated budget:

    *   In **Azure Cost Management + Billing**, go to **Budgets**.

    *   Create a budget for your Data Factory resources, setting limits and defining alert thresholds.

    *   Consider using a monthly or quarterly budget, aligning it with your billing cycle.

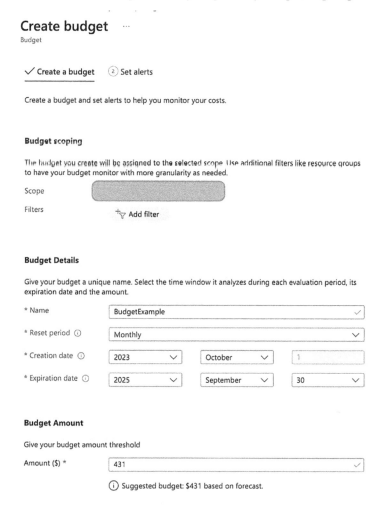

*Figure 12.35: Creating a budget*

6.  To receive timely notifications when you approach or exceed your budget thresholds, set up alerts.

7. In the same **Budgets** section, configure email alerts.

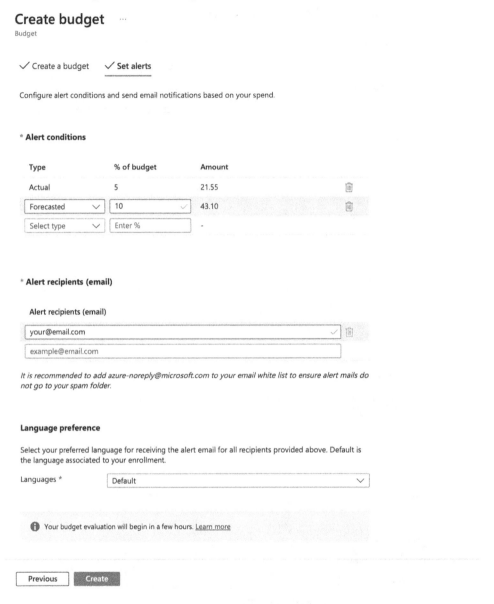

*Figure 12.36: Setting up alerts*

8. Regularly review your Data Factory pipelines and activities to identify opportunities for optimization:

   - Analyze pipeline execution history to spot inefficient or redundant processes.

- Optimize data movement by choosing the right copy activity settings, such as compression and partitioning.

- Schedule pipelines during off-peak hours to take advantage of lower data transfer costs.

- Utilize Azure Monitor to track the performance and resource utilization of your Data Factory pipelines.

## How it works...

FinOps is an ongoing process. Continuously monitor your Data Factory costs and adjust your budget, alerts, and optimization strategies as needed.

By applying FinOps principles to your ADF instance, you can effectively manage and optimize costs while ensuring efficient data workflows. FinOps promotes collaboration between teams, cost transparency, and accountability, making it an essential approach for managing cloud costs in a structured and efficient manner.

## Join our community on Discord

Join our community's Discord space for discussions with the authors and other readers:

https://discord.gg/U229qmBmT3

# Other Books You May Enjoy

If you enjoyed this book, you may be interested in these other books by Packt:

**Azure Data Engineer Associate Certification Guide**

Newton Alex

ISBN: 9781801816069

- Gain intermediate-level knowledge of Azure the data infrastructure
- Design and implement data lake solutions with batch and stream pipelines
- Identify the partition strategies available in Azure storage technologies
- Implement different table geometries in Azure Synapse Analytics
- Use the transformations available in T-SQL, Spark, and Azure Data Factory
- Use Azure Databricks or Synapse Spark to process data using Notebooks
- Design security using RBAC, ACL, encryption, data masking, and more
- Monitor and optimize data pipelines with debugging tips

**Data Engineering with AWS – Second Edition**

Gareth Eagar

ISBN: 9781804614426

- Seamlessly ingest streaming data with Amazon Kinesis Data Firehose
- Optimize, denormalize, and join datasets with AWS Glue Studio
- Use Amazon S3 events to trigger a Lambda process to transform a file
- Load data into a Redshift data warehouse and run queries with ease
- Visualize and explore data using Amazon QuickSight
- Extract sentiment data from a dataset using Amazon Comprehend
- Build transactional data lakes using Apache Iceberg with Amazon Athena
- Learn how a data mesh approach can be implemented on AWS

# Packt is searching for authors like you

If you're interested in becoming an author for Packt, please visit authors.packtpub.com and apply today. We have worked with thousands of developers and tech professionals, just like you, to help them share their insight with the global tech community. You can make a general application, apply for a specific hot topic that we are recruiting an author for, or submit your own idea.

# Share your thoughts

Now you've finished *Azure Data Factory Cookbook*, we'd love to hear your thoughts! Scan the QR code below to go straight to the Amazon review page for this book and share your feedback or leave a review on the site that you purchased it from.

https://packt.link/r/1803246596

Your review is important to us and the tech community and will help us make sure we're delivering excellent quality content.

# Index

# Download a free PDF copy of this book

Thanks for purchasing this book!

Do you like to read on the go but are unable to carry your print books everywhere?

Is your eBook purchase not compatible with the device of your choice?

Don't worry, now with every Packt book you get a DRM-free PDF version of that book at no cost.

Read anywhere, any place, on any device. Search, copy, and paste code from your favorite technical books directly into your application.

The perks don't stop there, you can get exclusive access to discounts, newsletters, and great free content in your inbox daily

Follow these simple steps to get the benefits:

1.  Scan the QR code or visit the link below

https://packt.link/free-ebook/9781803246598

2.  Submit your proof of purchase
3.  That's it! We'll send your free PDF and other benefits to your email directly

www.ingramcontent.com/pod-product-compliance
Lightning Source LLC
Chambersburg PA
CBHW060639060326
40690CB00020B/4451